THE SHROPSHIRE & MONTGOMERYSHIRE LIGHT RAILWAY

S & M Rly

THE SHROPSHIRE & MONTGOMERYSHIRE LIGHT RAILWAY

THE RISE AND FALL OF A RURAL BYWAY

PETER JOHNSON

PEN & SWORD
TRANSPORT
AN IMPRINT OF PEN & SWORD BOOKS LTD.
YORKSHIRE – PHILADELPHIA

Title page: Ex-London & South Western Railway 0-6-0 *Hesperus* with a train of stock obtained from the Midland Railway, all freshly painted ready for the line's opening in April 1911. (John Scott Morgan Collection)

Back of Title: Hawthorne, Leslie 0-6-2T *Pyramus*, delivered to the Shropshire & Montgomeryshire Light Railway in 1911, sold to the War Department circa 1916.

Front Cover: One of the Ward Department's 0-6-0STs in action on the Light Railway.

Rear Jacket, upper: Hudswell, Clarke 0-602T *Pyramus*, one of two locomotives supplied new to the Light Railway.

Rear Jacket, lower: The only known photograph of a Potteries, Shrewsbury & North Wales Railway train, seen at Shrewsbury.

First published in Great Britain in 2024 by
Pen and Sword Transport
An imprint of
Pen & Sword Books Ltd.
Yorkshire - Philadelphia

ISBN 978 1 52677 617 4

A CIP catalogue record for this book is available from the British Library.

Typeset in Palatino 11/13 by SJmagic DESIGN SERVICES, India.

Printed and bound by Printworks Global Ltd, London/Hong Kong.

Pen & Sword Books Ltd incorporates the imprints of Pen & Sword Books Archaeology, Atlas, Aviation, Battleground, Discovery, Family History, History, Maritime, Military, Naval, Politics, Railways, Select, Transport, True Crime, Fiction, Frontline Books, Leo Cooper, Praetorian Press, Seaforth Publishing, Wharncliffe and White Owl.

For a complete list of Pen & Sword titles please contact

PEN & SWORD BOOKS LIMITED
George House, Units 12 & 13, Beevor Street, Off Pontefract Road,
Barnsley, South Yorkshire, S71 1HN, England
E-mail: enquiries@pen-and-sword.co.uk
Website: www.pen-and-sword.co.uk

or

PEN AND SWORD BOOKS
1950 Lawrence Rd, Havertown, PA 19083, USA
E-mail: uspen-and-sword@casematepublishers.com
Website: www.penandswordbooks.com

CONTENTS

Nantmawr
tk in situ
Llynclys
(Cambrian Heritage Rly)
A5
Blodwell Jct
Shropshire Union Canal
Montgomery Branch
River Mordu
Nantmawr Branch
closed
closed
Llanymynech
Maesbrook
Wern Las
SML
Kinnerley Junction
Afon Vyrnwy
Edgerley
SML - Criggion Branch
Chapel
Lane
Cambrian Railways
Offa's Dyke
Melverley
Llandrinio
Road
Crew
Green
Criggion
closed
Shropshire Union Canal - Montgomery Branch
Great Western & London and North Western Railways
Shrewsbury - Welshpool
Westbury

THE SHROPSHIRE & MONTGOMERYSHIRE LIGHT RAILWAY

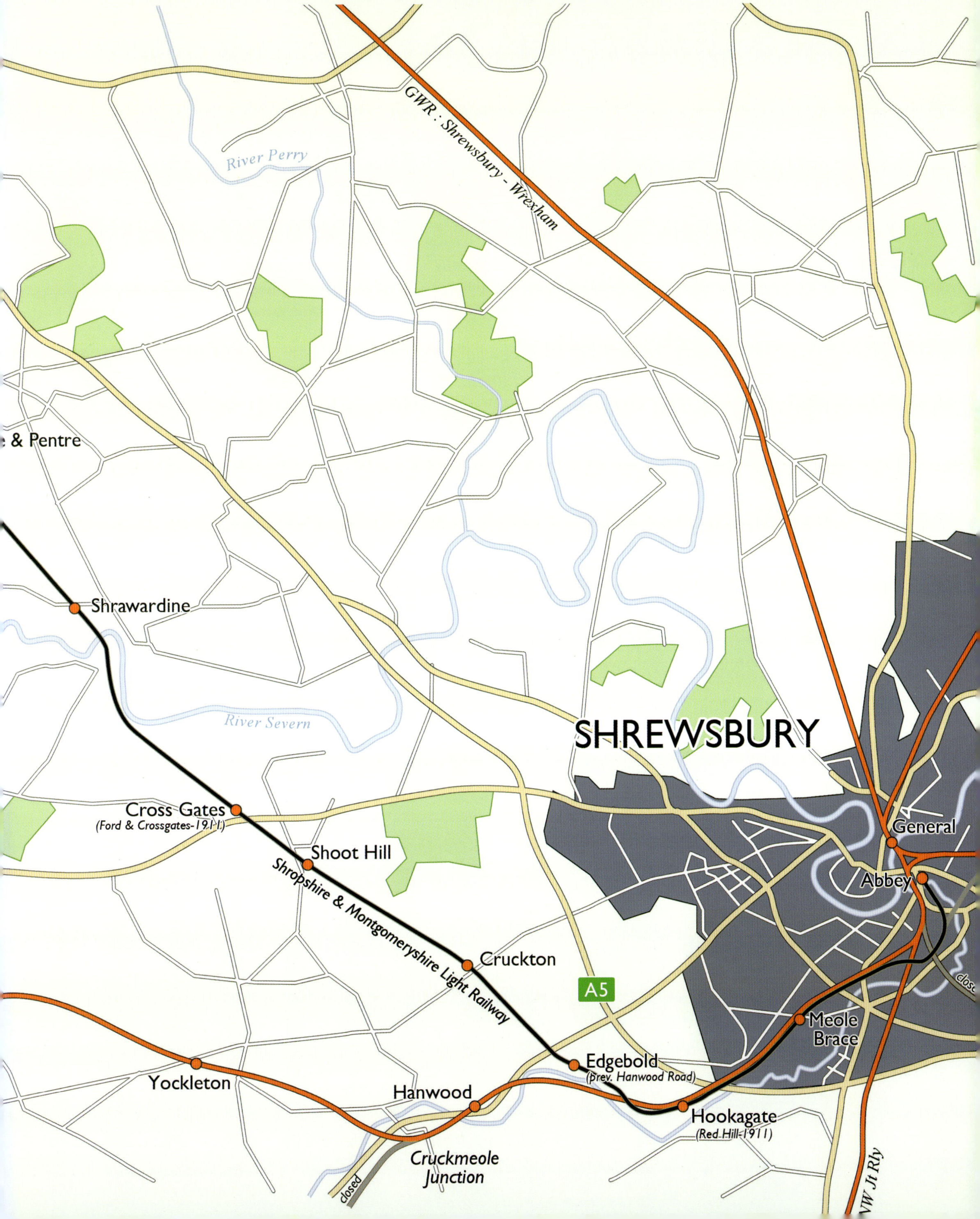

INTRODUCTION

The Shropshire & Montgomeryshire Light Railway had its origins in the 1860s railway mania, a period when many railways were being promoted with the intention of selling them to an existing railway company for profit. It is not clear if that was the intention of the promoters in this case, and there appears to have been no attempt to sell the Potteries, Shrewsbury & North Wales Railway, the railway that became the Shropshire & Montgomeryshire Light Railway, when it was first opened in 1866.

Running between Shrewsbury and Llanymynech, the Potteries Railway set off a chain of events that made it as memorable in the annals of British railway history as any main-line railway and led the way to the Light Railway, which made its own mark on railway history.

Starting as the West Shropshire Mineral Railway, it already had a convoluted back story and opened with a reputation as the most expensive non-metropolitan railway then built, with authorised capital close to £2 million, £213 million in 2022, and noted for the nine Acts of Parliament obtained. Despite its opening, the authorised railway remained incomplete, and some parts were never built.

The railway, a main line and branches totalling 30 miles, served an area on the Welsh border to the west of Shrewsbury, which was predominantly agricultural with two stone-quarrying centres, a small population, and surrounded by existing railways, notably the Great Western and the London & North Western, which connived to prevent the newcomer from reaching its full potential.

The start of operations did not signify the end of the railway's problems, for by the end of the year the company was in receivership and its services suspended. Reopened two years later, it lasted only until 1880, when a dissatisfied passenger's letter of complaint to the Board of Trade led to the directors deciding that the capital required to make it safe and to operate it in accordance with the Board's requirements could not be raised.

An abandoned railway with £2 million capital, albeit not worth that, attracted much interest and in 1890 the Shropshire Railways Company was formed to take it over, rebuild it and resume operations. Reconstruction was started but a dispute between the company and its financiers caused it to be abandoned once again.

During the first decade of the twentieth century the indefatigable light railway engineer and entrepreneur Colonel Holman Fred Stephens took an interest in the derelict line. Known for the light railways that he ran and the eclectic collections of locomotives and rolling stock with which he equipped them, he was convinced that it could be revived and made to pay.

With an order obtained under the 1896 Light Railways Act and renamed the Shropshire & Montgomeryshire Light Railway, it was reopened in 1911. Where the Shropshire Railways had failed, H. F. Stephens apparently succeeded but the railway he created was something of a sham, its veneer of success, payment of dividends and debenture interest dependent on capital expenditure made from revenue not being depreciated, and on creditors not pursuing payment. Without the war the railway would have been closed as soon as any of the creditors refused further credit. The likelihood is that the railway would have been abandoned once again, for want of sufficient assets to justify receivership and liquidation.

The War Office turned out to be the railway's saviour, in 1941 deciding that it was ideally located to supply ammunition depots that it wished to develop in the area. As a result, most of the railway was re-laid and continued in use until 1960, giving it nearly twenty years of worthwhile existence.

So, the railway that had first been opened in 1866 justified its survival for barely two decades. Except for the extremities at Nantmawr and Shrewsbury Abbey, which remained in use for a few years longer, the track was being lifted scarcely 100 years after the venture started.

In the final analysis the railway should not have been built, and it was more by luck than judgement that it lasted as long as it did. In the first instance a proper examination of traffic prospects should have produced just short branches to serve the stone quarries. As it was, the ambition to develop a network resulted in a railway with little potential traffic and the wastage of vast sums of money.

Remarkably, a small part of the original railway still lies abandoned, with rails in place barely visible in the undergrowth, and the subject of a scheme to revive it. The Nantmawr branch was the only consistent success, part of it remaining in use for its original purpose, the transport of stone, until 1971. Nowadays, only the cognoscenti knows where the Shropshire & Montgomeryshire Light Railway used to pass but it is not forgotten. Its complex and chequered history, together with Stephens' involvement and its operation by the Royal Engineers, combine to keep its memory alive where other similar lines have long been forgotten. The railway was the triumph of enthusiasm over reason, with a marginal existence and precarious finances until the War Department took it over and extended its life.

- The attempts to make a railway to serve the Tanat Valley, including those of the Potteries Railway and the Shropshire Railways, are included in a forthcoming history of the Tanat Valley Light Railway, also by Peter Johnson.

Welsh place names

Historically, the areas on the Welsh borders west of Shrewsbury were not inflicted with invasions of English visitors corrupting the spelling of local, Welsh, place names but those who did visit insisted on spelling Blodwel and Llanyblodwel as Blodwell and Llanyblodwell. The correct versions are used here, as are Welsh names of places further away that are occasionally mentioned or quoted, such as Dolgellau or Porthmadog. Historically, Nesscliff was spelled thus although the locality is now known as Nesscliffe.

No 118 Abbey Foregate Shrewsbury, the on the right of this photograph, was occupied by Alfred Judd, the Potteries, Shrewsbury & North Wales Railway's general manager from 1873 until 1880. To the left of the house's neighbour is the Shrewsbury & Potteries Junction Railway's cutting, now the road named Bage Way. The Abbey Station is less than half a mile away.

ACKNOWLEDGEMENTS AND SOURCES

In 1971 I acquired a copy of the late Eric Tonks' slim self-published book on the Shropshire & Montgomeryshire Light Railway as reissued by the Industrial Railway Society, which eventually led to the publication of my own book, *An Illustrated History of the Shropshire & Montgomeryshire Light Railway* (Oxford Publishing Co., 2008).

Before Tonks, the first to write about these lines, with articles published in *The Railway Magazine*, was Thomas Richard Perkins (1872–1952), a pharmacist from Wolverley, Worcestershire. With his brother George Mitchelson Perkins (1875–1952), also a pharmacist, and their friends Frank Ernald Fox Davies (1881–1941), a grocer in Llanymynech, and Edward Lloyd Morton (1870–1910), a Kinnerley resident who also took a few photographs of the derelict railway, they explored the derelict Potteries, Shrewsbury & North Wales Railway, Fox Davies taking the lead in photographing the scenes of dereliction that they saw. Without their efforts the photographic record of the abandoned railway would be considerably poorer. They maintained their interest with the

The only known 'railtour' of the Shropshire Railways. One fine day in 1903 T. R. Perkins and friends made an extensive tour of the railway, traction being provided by former Potteries guard Richard Reeves, seen here in shirtsleeves with G. M. Perkins standing alongside him, and his trolley. Seated, from left, are F. E. Fox Davies, T. R. Perkins and E. L. Morton. (F. E. Fox Davies)

railway's revival as a light railway, Perkins and Fox Davies seeing or travelling on the first train on 13 April 1911 and Perkins having a free 'all stations' first-class pass valid for ten years, until 31 March 1921, signed by H. F. Stephens.

After his death, Perkins' collection was acquired by W. E. Hayward and is now available to view, with much other material, as a part of the WEH-LYN Collection at the National Archives at Kew.

The present book includes material from my 2008 book, together with new research and information obtained from the digitised newspapers at the British Newspaper Archive (www.britishnewspaperarchive.co.uk).

The *London Gazette*, also available online, was of use in determining the progress of legislation and the military career of Colonel Stephens. Most of the Board of Trade returns were studied at the University of Leicester Library.

I examined records created by the Board of Trade, the Ministry of Transport, the British Transport Commission, the War Office, Companies House, the Treasury, and the Cambrian, the Great Western and London & North Western railways at the National Archives. Records deposited there by the former British Railways Records Office include minute books and stock and transfer registers. Plans deposited in connection with the various Acts of Parliament were seen at the Parliamentary Archives, in the House of Lords. The availability of these organisations' catalogues online has been a great help.

Biographical information was extracted from www.ancestry.co.uk, the General Register Office's online indices and digitised newspapers. The Bank of England's online Inflation Calculator was used to obtain updates on the value of money.

Hugh Ballantyne, Vic Bradley, Alan Donaldson, John Keylock and Vic Mitchell, all now deceased, and Tim Edmonds, Tony Jervis, John Milner, John Scott Morgan, Robert Phipps, Mike Shaw, Andrew Smith, Richard Ward (Parliamentary Archives) and Jonathan Williams-Ellis were a great help in providing assistance, support and/or the loan of material or information. Special thanks are due to Gordon Rushton for providing the plan on pages 6/7 and redrawing the track layouts in Appendix 15.

Myself, I have had a fascinating journey trawling through over 150 years of documents and newspapers to uncover the railway's story.

For the last seven of my books published by Pen & Sword Transport I had the benefit of the support and advice of my editor, Barnaby Blacker. Sadly, he died in March 2022, aged only 61. His successor will have a hard act to follow.

Except where indicated, illustrations are from my collection or taken by me. A few of them included for historical interest may not be technically perfect. It remains for me to say that I accept responsibility for any errors.

Peter Johnson
Leicester
July 2023

Abbreviations

The use of abbreviations has been limited as much as possible. Those that survived are listed below. In places the terms 'Potteries Railway' and 'Potteries Junction Railway' have been used as shorthand for the Potteries, Shrewsbury & North Wales Railway and the Potteries Junction & North Wales Railway respectively. The term 'the Light Railway' refers to the Shropshire & Montgomeryshire Light Railway.

BTC	British Transport Commission
GWR	Great Western Railway
LNWR	London & North Western Railway
LSWR	London & South Western Railway
WD	War Department

CHAPTER 1

SETTING THE SCENE – THE MANIA AND THE RAILWAY'S ORIGINS

Briedden looking generally eastwards towards Shrewsbury. Criggion, the source of much stone and some railway traffic, is out of sight on the left of the range. (Photochrom)

The area to the west of Shrewsbury reaching to the Welsh border is largely lush agricultural land that benefits from being a floodplain of the River Severn and its tributaries. Within this area is a triangle of land bordered by three roads: along its eastern side is Telford's Holyhead road, the A5, which reaches an apex with the Oswestry to Newtown road, the A483, near the former, and is completed by the Welshpool to Shrewsbury road, the A458. To the west of the triangle are outcrops of limestone that reach 700ft above sea level at Llanymynech and Nantmawr, and 900ft at Criggion. The earliest signs of quarrying, for copper, lead and zinc at Llanymynech, have been dated to 200BC. Nantmawr produced aggregates, its stone considered to be of high quality, but is now classified as dormant. In the past Criggion produced cobbles and roadstone but now, the only active quarry of the three, it produces aggregates that are transported by road. Used for both grazing and arable farming in the nineteenth century, much of the property was tenanted, being in the estates of either the Earls of Bradford or Powis.

Farm Hall mill, Kinnerley. The railway was behind the photographer. In the 20th Century Light Railway employee E. N. Fardoe lived here (Page 141). (Frith)

Habitation consists of hamlets and small villages, the largest communities being established at Kinnerley and Llanymynech, with around 1,000 residents each, the latter set astride the English–Welsh border. Shrewsbury itself, located strategically on the Severn, is a substantial market town that has trebled in size from the 31,280 residents recorded in the 1801 census.

Prior to the development of the railways the most significant transport links in the area were Telford's road, running north-west from Shrewsbury, and to the west, the Montgomery Canal, a route that was

North Road, Llanymynech, the present A483, dominated by the lime rocks. F. E. Fox Davies, whose family's store is on the left, photographed the while it was derelict. The building still, at the time of writing, exists, looking rather battered. (F. E. Fox Davies)

Nineteenth-century Shrewsbury residents would still recognise this scene in Wyle Cop, although the pedal cycles may date this photograph to the first years of the twentieth century.

particularly advantageous for the stone quarries, and later a part of the Shropshire Union system.

By 1865 the area was surrounded by railways: the Shrewsbury & Chester Railway from 1848, running north–south to the east; the Oswestry & Newtown Railway along the western flank from 1860, and part of the Cambrian Railways from 1864, and the Shrewsbury & Welshpool Railway from east to west, which was to the south, and opened in 1862. A branch of the Oswestry line from Llynclys served quarries at Porthywaen, close to Nantmawr. The lines that radiated out from Shrewsbury were all controlled by the Great Western Railway or the London & North Western Railway, either separately or jointly, these companies having agreed in 1862 that neither would undertake any expansion in the area without the support of the other.

The first proposal to cross the area was made in 1845, when a Bill was deposited for a line from a junction with the proposed Shrewsbury, Oswestry & Chester Junction Railway at Leaton, 4 miles north of Shrewsbury, to a junction with the proposed Worcester & Porth Dynllaen Railway at Llanwddyn, a village

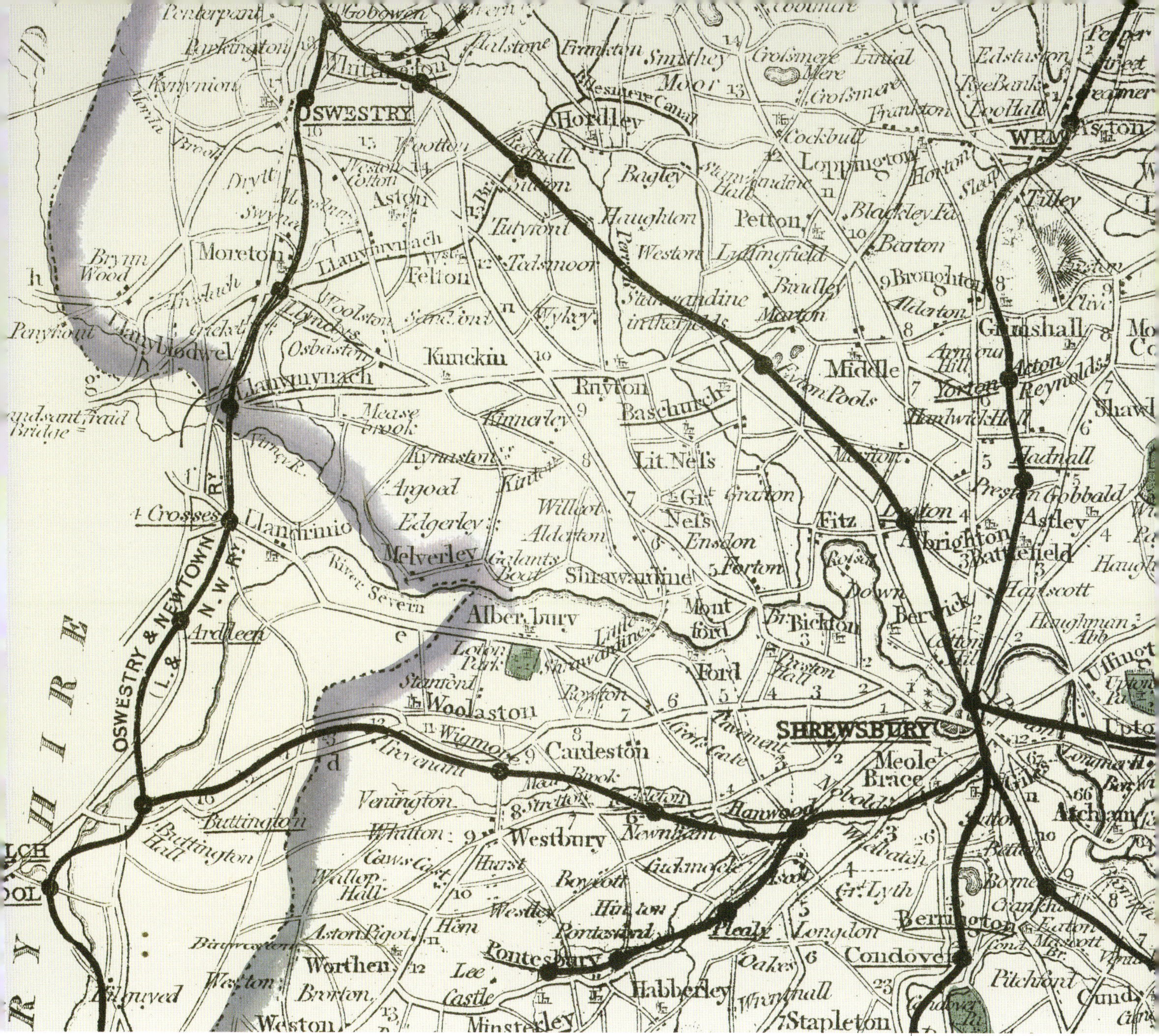

Railways in west Shropshire in the early 1860s, showing the area across which the Potteries Railway was built. (G. F. Cruchley)

submerged following the construction of Liverpool Corporation's Vyrnwy reservoir. Both proposals failed.

Two more proposals to cross the triangle by rail were submitted to Parliament in 1860/1. That of the West Midland, Shrewsbury & Coast of Wales Railway was intended to be a trunk route for traffic to and from Ireland, the route from a junction with the Shrewsbury & Welshpool Railway being via Ford, Shrawardine, Nesscliff, Kinnerley, Knockin, Porthywaen, Llanfyllin, Llanrhaeadr, Llangynog, Bala, Dolgellau and Harlech before reaching Porthmadog, where it would connect to a proposed railway to Porthdinlleyn. A tunnel a mile and a half long would have taken the 90-mile route through the Berwyns near Llangynog.

At a meeting held in Criccieth in support of the Porthdinlleyn line on 24 September 1860, Richard Samuel France explained that while working for the West Midland Railway it had taken a 999-year lease on the Severn Valley Railway, which made it better to start any extension into Wales at Shrewsbury, rather than Worcester. Deputed to investigate the options, he saw the possibilities offered by the 'rich plain' to the west of Shrewsbury and the lime rocks near Porthywaen, which led to the Tanat valley's inclusion in the Coast of Wales Railway's route (*Eddowes's Journal*, 26 September).

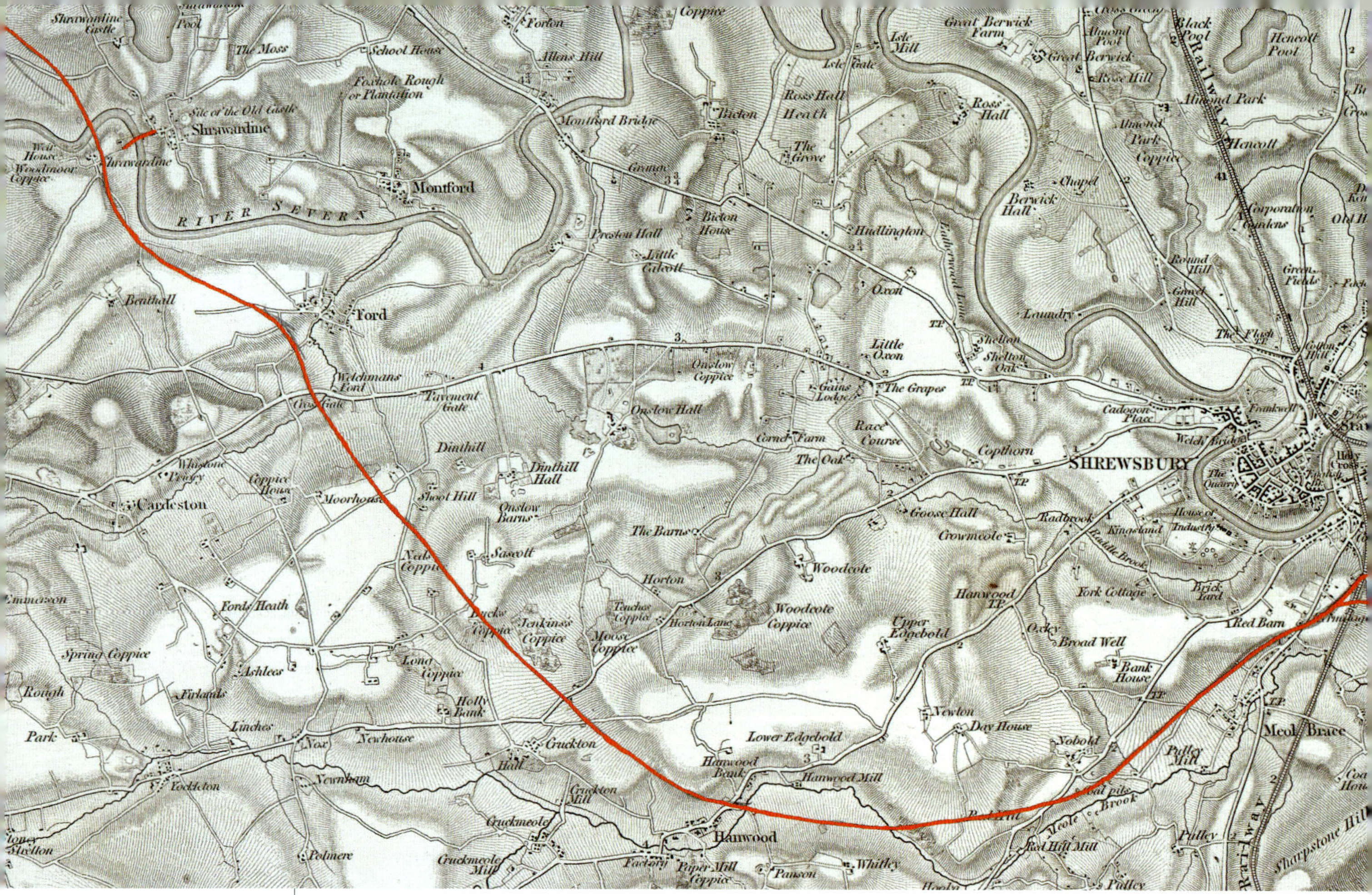

The eastern section of the West Midland, Shrewsbury & Coast of Wales Railway's 1861 proposed route to Porthmadog. The detached section indicates the location of a road and bridge to have been built across the Severn at Shrawardine by the railway company. (Parliamentary Archives)

The West Midland, Shrewsbury & Coast of Wales Railway's route westwards from Kinnerley to the Welsh border, with branches to the Shropshire Union Canal at Llanymynech and to Porthywaen. (Parliamentary Archives)

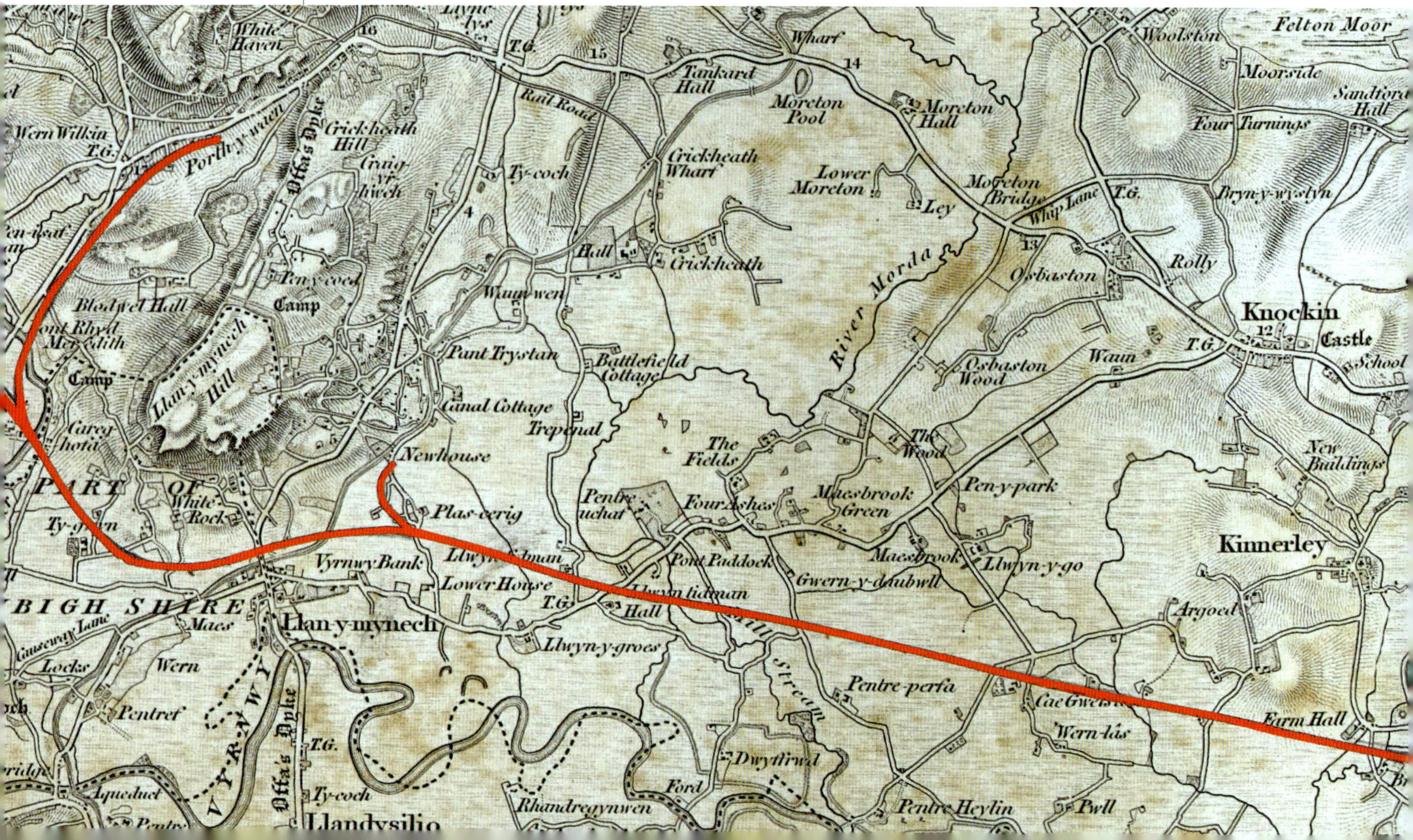

The railway's engineer was Edward Wilson (1842–1907), engineer of the West Midland Railway and other undertakings. The West Midland had agreed to work it for 52½% of its revenue (*Birmingham Journal*, 8 September 1860 / *The Welshman*, 22 February 1861) but in January 1861 the Parliamentary process was adjourned while the plans were referred to an engineer to adjudicate on alleged inaccuracies in levels (*Morning Herald*, 31 January) and the Bill failed to pass standing orders (*Eddowes's Journal*, 24 February 1864).

R. S. France was the son of a Plealey, Shropshire, landowner. In 1851 he had been a farmer but was taking an interest in railways by 1853, when he attended a meeting to discuss the Shropshire & Montgomeryshire Railway proposal (*Shrewsbury Chronicle*, 7 October), and becoming secretary of the Shrewsbury & Welshpool Railway by 1856 and the Mid Wales Railway by 1860. These must have been part-time positions that fitted in with his work for the West Midland Railway and as a contractor, for he also secured the contracts for the Shrewsbury & Welshpool Railway, opened in 1862, the Mineral Railway (*Morning Herald*, 2 September 1862) and the Mold & Denbigh Junction Railway, opened in 1869. He also leased quarries at Llanymynech, Nantmawr and Criggion and a coal mine near Oswestry.

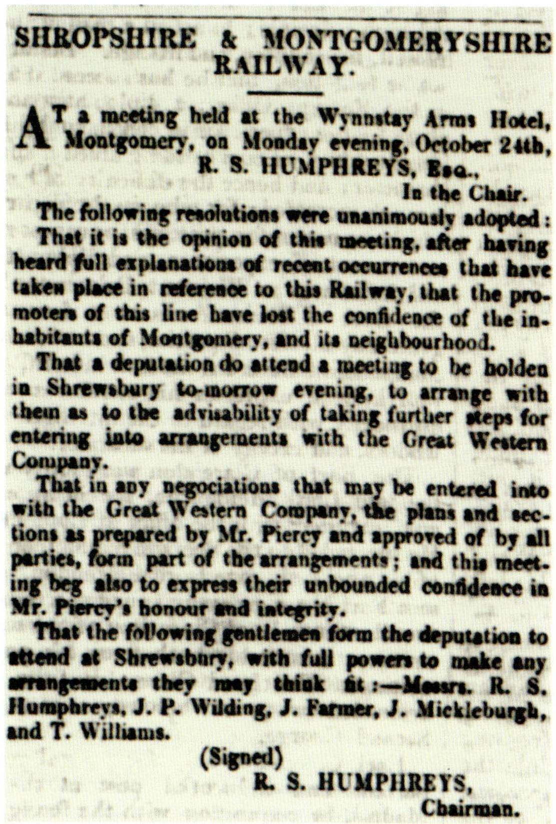

SHROPSHIRE & MONTGOMERYSHIRE RAILWAY.

AT a meeting held at the Wynnstay Arms Hotel, Montgomery, on Monday evening, October 24th, R. S. HUMPHREYS, Esq., In the Chair.

The following resolutions were unanimously adopted:

That it is the opinion of this meeting, after having heard full explanations of recent occurrences that have taken place in reference to this Railway, that the promoters of this line have lost the confidence of the inhabitants of Montgomery, and its neighbourhood.

That a deputation do attend a meeting to be holden in Shrewsbury to-morrow evening, to arrange with them as to the advisability of taking further steps for entering into arrangements with the Great Western Company.

That in any negociations that may be entered into with the Great Western Company, the plans and sections as prepared by Mr. Piercy and approved of by all parties, form part of the arrangements; and this meeting beg also to express their unbounded confidence in Mr. Piercy's honour and integrity.

That the following gentlemen form the deputation to attend at Shrewsbury, with full powers to make any arrangements they may think fit:—Messrs. R. S. Humphreys, J. P. Wilding, J. Farmer, J. Mickleburgh, and T. Williams.

(Signed) R. S. HUMPHREYS, Chairman.

An advertisement regarding the first Shropshire & Montgomeryshire Railway, published in the *Shrewsbury Chronicle* on 28 October 1853.

Apparently convinced that the route across Shropshire and into Wales could be worthwhile, later in 1861 he promoted the cause of the West Shropshire Mineral Railway, which started at a junction with the Oswestry & Newtown Railway at Llanymynech and, running via the Shrewsbury & Welshpool Railway at

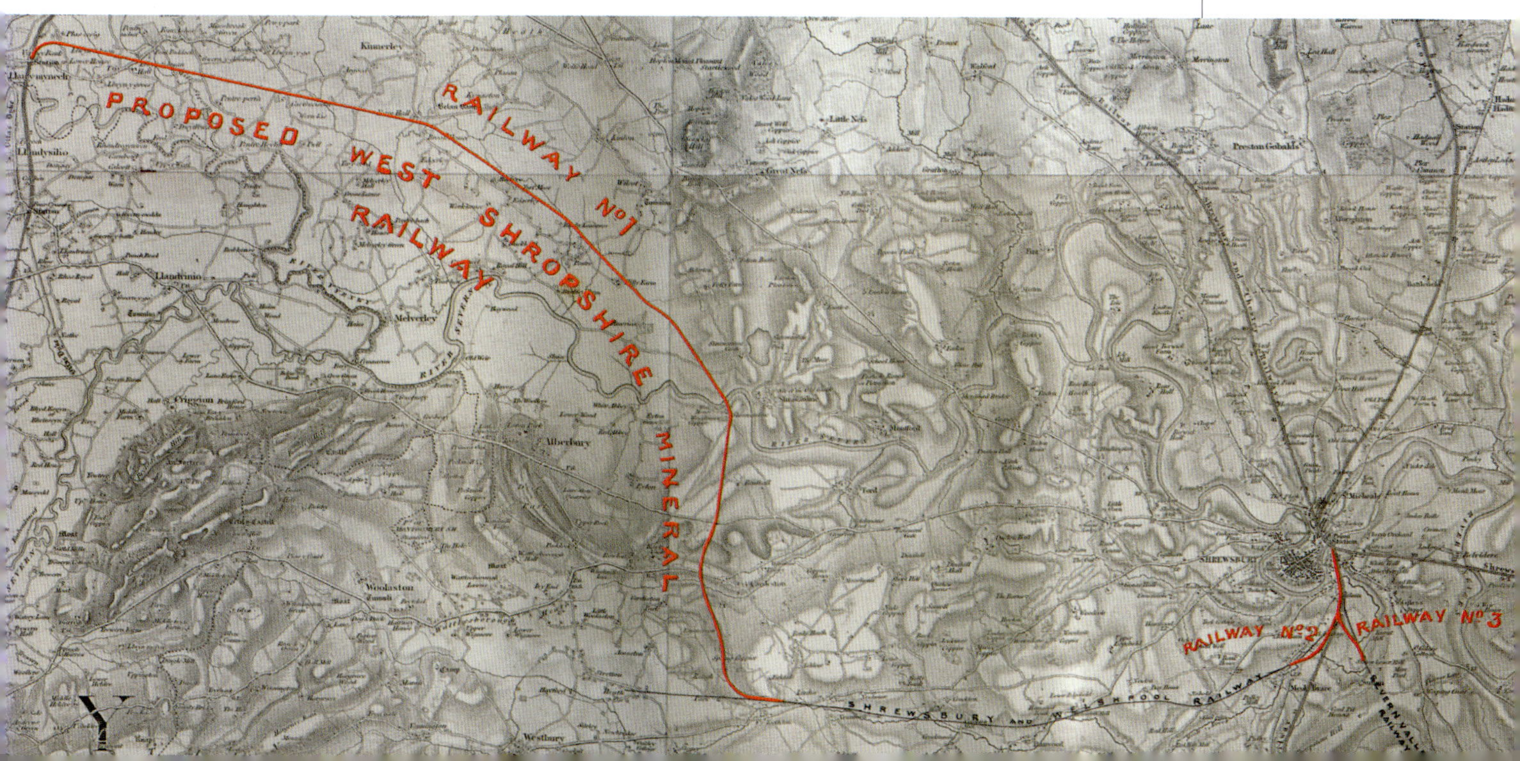

A section from the West Shropshire Mineral Railway's deposited plan from 1862. (Parliamentary Archives)

The West Shropshire Mineral Railway's seal.

Yockleton, terminated at a junction with the Severn Valley Railway on the south bank of the Severn at Shrewsbury.

At a meeting held in Llanrhaeadr in 1864 to promote the then proposed extension to Llangynog, France said that the Mineral Railway was the first instalment of a direct route to Wales (*Eddowes's Journal*, 24 February).

The West Shropshire Mineral Railway Act gained royal assent on 29 July 1862, naming William Walter Cargill (1814–94), Richard Augustus Bethell (1830–75), Arthur Pittar Lattey (1816–84), Elias Mocatta (1798–1881) and Charles Pool Froom (1830–78), as the promoters and the first

The West Shropshire Mineral Railway's 1863 plan, showing the Moat Hill and Nantmawr tramways and the Llangynog branch. (Parliamentary Archives)

directors. The company seal featured a primitive illustration of an early 2-2-2, but no locomotives were acquired.

Despite not being named as a promoter in the Act, France was identified as such in an agreement made with the LNWR on 12 June 1862, where its objection was withdrawn on receiving his undertaking that the railway would not build proposed branches to Shrewsbury General station, withdraw its application for running powers over the Shrewsbury & Welshpool, grant the LNWR running powers, and not compete with the LNWR or the Shrewsbury & Welshpool.

The 1862 Act authorised the railway to raise share capital of £90,000 and to borrow up to £30,000. Level crossings were permitted at Kinnerley and Shrawardine. Alongside rates for the carriage of goods were, notwithstanding the railway's title, those for the carriage of three classes of passengers. Perhaps the company was not intending to work all trains itself, or indeed any, as it was empowered to charge for 'the use of engines for propelling carriages'. The use of the word 'carriages' in this context was a portmanteau word to refer to any vehicle used on the railway. The Oswestry & Newtown was allowed to make use of the railway with its own 'engines, carriages and wagons'; the Act contained no reference to the LNWR.

Before France and the Mineral Railway could find a solution to their wish to have direct access to Shrewsbury, a group of Tanat valley residents held a meeting that resolved to ask for the railway to be extended to Llangynog (*Shrewsbury Chronicle*, 24 October 1862), which led to the West Shropshire Mineral Railway (Extension and Deviation) Bill being deposited.

Primarily, this sought powers to abandon the authorised railway between Pentre and Yockleton and to replace it with a deviation to the Shrewsbury & Welshpool Railway at Red Hill, some 7 miles closer to Shrewsbury, where the present A5 Shrewsbury bypass is crossed by the Shrewsbury & Welshpool Railway, but it also sought powers for a north-facing junction with the Oswestry & Newtown Railway, extensions to Llanyblodwel and Llangynog and tramways from Llanyblodwel to Nantmawr and from Red Hill to Moat Hall.

Receiving the royal assent on 14 July 1863, the Act approved the deviation and the Moat Hall Tramway along with an additional £60,000 share capital and £20,000 mortgage borrowing. Traffic agreements were permitted to be made with the LNWR, the GWR, the West Midland Railway, the Shrewsbury & Welshpool Railway and the Oswestry & Newtown Railway, and the conditions for connecting with the Shrewsbury & Welshpool Railway at Red Hill were specified.

Had it been built, the Moat Hall line would have given access to the Shropshire coalfield, less than 2 miles from France's family home at Plealey. If the company had chosen to use horses, haulage could have been charged for at the same rate as if locomotives had been used.

In the meantime, another 1862 Act had a significant effect on future events relating to the Mineral Railway and its development. The Limited Liability Act was the third of a series intended to encourage enterprise whilst limiting the personal liability of company members. This was not applicable to railway companies created by statute but it did create a boom in promotions of all sorts and by 1866 more than 3,000 companies had been registered. A consequence of this was that some of the new companies were lending money to ventures that were ill-conceived.

Two more Bills were deposited on 10 November 1863, one for branches and alterations, the other for new lines. The first sought power to make branches to Breidden and Nesscliff, to make lateral and vertical deviations to the authorised route and to change the company's corporate name. The second revived the Llangynog proposal as well as adding branches to Nantmawr, Porthywaen and making connections to the Llanfyllin branch at Carreghofa and to the Shropshire Union Canal at Llanymynech.

The resulting Acts received the royal assent on 30 June 1864. The West Shropshire Mineral Railway (New Lines) Act not only authorised the works described in the Bill but permitted the use of the Oswestry & Newtown Railway's Llanymynech station and gave the Oswestry & Newtown Railway rights to use the Llanfyllin branch connection and the line to Porthywaen. £200,000 capital was also authorised.

The Shrewsbury & North Wales Railway Act bore the company's new name, as well as authorising the construction of the proposed branches and deviations. The deviation descriptions sound as though the original route had been examined and found not to be as practical as it might have been. The LNWR was permitted to make use of the railway and the Oswestry & Newtown's powers to use it were extended to include the deviations. The Act added another £100,000 to the company's capital.

While this Parliamentary activity was under way France had started work, the directors reporting on 27 February 1863 that a considerable quantity of the land required had been purchased and

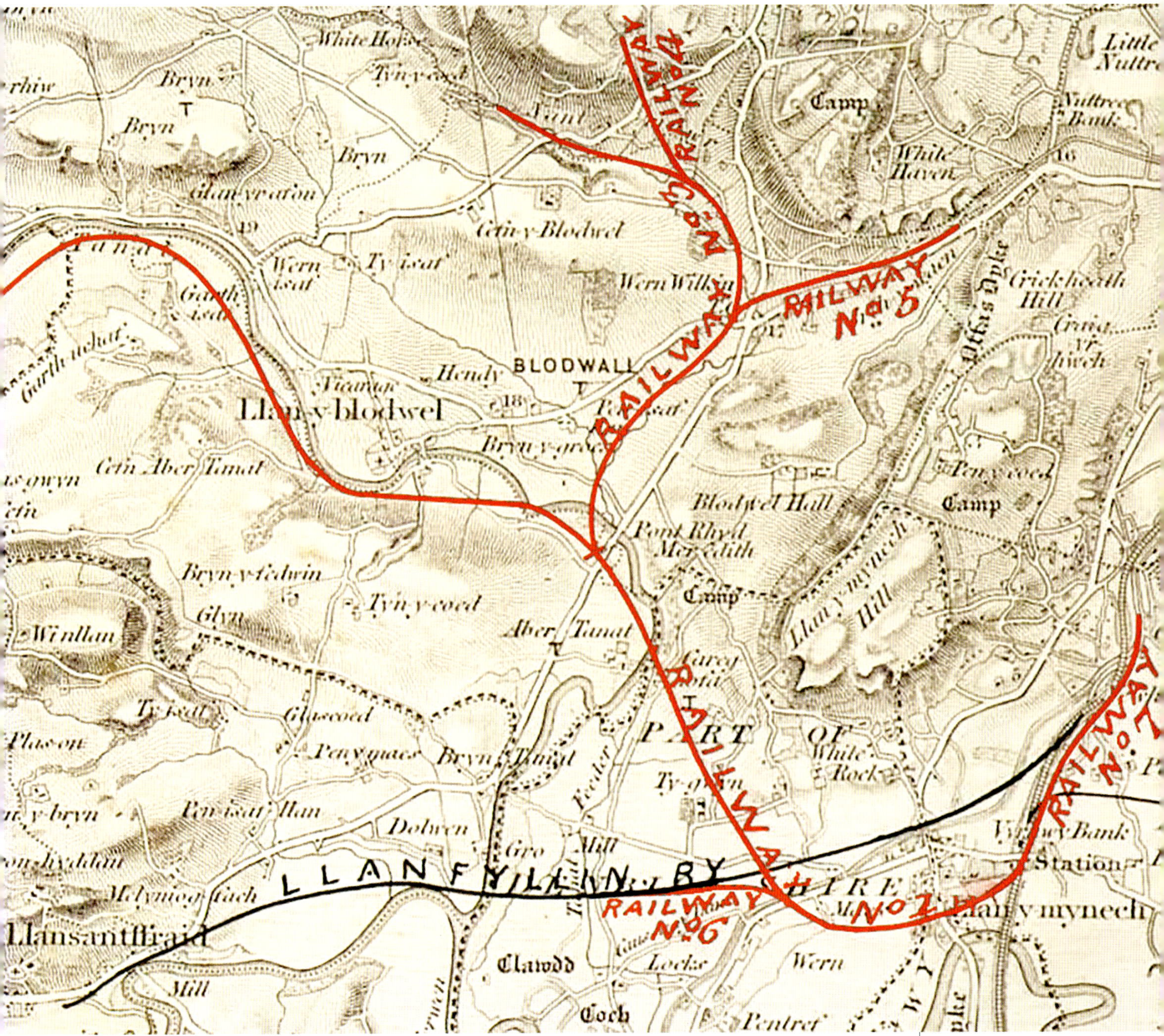

fenced. Work between Shrawardine and Shrewsbury had been suspended as a better route, shorter and with more favourable gradients, had been found, requiring fresh powers to be obtained (*Shrewsbury Chronicle*, 6 March). In fact, its main function was to reduce the length of the Shrewsbury & Welshpool Railway that required running powers. The company had spent £129,537 15s 1d and had £1,862 4s 11d in hand.

The *Shrewsbury Chronicle* (24 April), reporting that France had employed a Mr Taylor of Llanymynech, who had been a sub-contractor on the Oswestry & Newtown Railway's Llanfyllin branch, said that several gangs of navvies were active between Llanymynech and Kinnerley and forecast that several miles would soon be ready for a ballast engine. France had, said the paper, established a timber yard with steam

A West Shropshire Mineral Railway 1864 plan showing several branches and a connection to the Oswestry & Newtown Railway's Llanfyllin branch. (Parliamentary Archives)

The West Shropshire Mineral Railway's second 1864 plan, showing changes to the earlier proposals and branches to Breidden and Nesscliff. (Parliamentary Archives)

Road to be Diverted
Road to be Diverted
Road to be Diverted
Deviation of Canal
Line of 1863
Public Road
Canal
Road
SHREWSBURY
Baschurch
Baschurch Station
Boreatton Hall
Birch Park
Marton Pool
Middle Castle
Newton on the Hill
Yarton
Merrington
Preston Gobalds
Little Nefs
Great Nefs
Fitz
Grafton
Leaton Station
WOOLASCOT
Albrighton
Battlefield
HARLECOTT
Mytton
Forton
Shrawardine
Montford
Montford Bridge
RIVER SEVERN
Ford
Bicton
Isle Park
Leaton Knolls
LITTLE BERWICK AND NEWTON
Great Berwick Farm
Berwick Hall
Ross Hall
COTTON
SHELTON AND OXEN
Onslow Hall
Copthorn
Race Course
Cardeston
Woodcote
MEOLE
Meole Brace
Sutton
St Julians
Locomotive Department
HOLY CROSS
St Micheals
Station
HANWOOD
Hanwood
PULLEY
BETTON
Sharpstone Hill
Shrewsbury & Welshpool Branch Railway
Shrewsbury and Chester Railway
Chester and Shrewsbury Railway
Yockleton
Station

The Shrewsbury & North Wales Railway's company seal.

sawing machine, smith's forge, stabling, cottages and workshops at Llanymynech and a workshop at Kinnerley was building wagons and barrows. France's 'man on the ground' throughout the contract was his brother, William Hanmer France (1839–1909), although he was not mentioned in reports until after the railway had been opened (*Oswestry Advertiser*, 15 August 1866).

Work was proceeding on the Shrawardine-Red Hill deviation at Edgebold on 30 December 1863 when Robert Thomas, aged 44, fell under a wagon and was killed (*Birmingham Daily Post*, 4 January 1864). Another fatality occurred on 15 February, when Edward Jones, aged 49, died from injuries received when 'a large quantity of earth' fell on him. The inquest jury called for the men employed on the railway to employ more caution. Neither the report in the *Shrewsbury Chronicle* (26 February) nor the death register entry gave the accident's location.

The directors' report to shareholders published for the shareholders' meeting held on 29 February 1864 had stated: 'the contractor has used great energy in the construction of the line, which is now in a very advanced state. The whole of the land is in the possession of the contractor. Notwithstanding that some of the work has been of a more severe character than was anticipated, the directors have every confidence … that the line will be open during the ensuing summer.'

In the same document, engineer John Ashdown (1830–78) reported that the earthworks between Red Hill and Shrawardine were well advanced despite one of the cuttings taking more effort than anticipated. The piers and cylinders of the Shrawardine river crossing were complete and most of the girders delivered and were in course of erection. Ashdown was also the Potteries Junction Railway's engineer.

Two men claim to have been the railway's resident engineer. A retirement notice for James Richard Bell (1842–1913) states that after completing his articles he had held the post (*Mid Sussex Times*, 3 November 1896), while an obituary for William Henry Bickerton states that he had been engaged on the railway's construction 'as engineer under Mr France' (*Shrewsbury Chronicle*, 13 September 1907); it is possible that one of them was employed on the Mineral Railway and the other on the Potteries Junction line.

Local courts were called upon to assess the merits of two cases that involved the railway during 1864. In March Arthur Jones, a contractor, sued sub-contractor

William Henry Bickerton, who claimed that he worked for R. S. France on the construction of the Potteries Railway, was buried with other family members in the churchyard of St Peter's in Myddle, to the north of Shrewsbury.

Taylor for £19 5s, for work and labour done. After some examination on the way the work was measured, the records having been destroyed, the jury found in Jones' favour (*Shrewsbury Chronicle*, 18 March).

On 28 May the case of John Owen (alias Brendrick), a former militiaman, charged with stealing 11s 6d from a hut occupied by labourers working on what was already being called the Shrewsbury & North Wales Railway, was remitted to the quarter sessions (*Shrewsbury Chronicle*, 3 June). No report of the second hearing has been found. In 1879 Brendrick was sentenced to two months' hard labour for his part in the theft of cigars in Bury St Edmunds, Suffolk (*Bury Free Press*, 13 September).

The incline to the Shrewsbury station site was the location of three accidents during 1864. On 24 June William Evans survived when he sustained head injuries when run down by wagons, but four days later Francis Allen, aged 40, was killed by the earth that fell on him near the LNWR sheds; his death certificate recorded that he died at the Infirmary, the inquest jury returning a verdict of 'accidental death'. In the same incident Thomas Bowdler appears to have survived a broken spine (*Shrewsbury Chronicle*, 1 July / *Bridgnorth Chronicle*, 2 July).

On 12 October an unnamed man was using a horse to move some wagons at Shrewsbury and was run down when they ran away and collided with some that were stationary (*Shrewsbury Chronicle*, 14 October).

A sign that construction was nearing completion came with the opening of Llanymynech's new presbyterian chapel on 26/27 October, when France ran trains enabling Shrewsbury residents to attend the ceremony, making no charge for the service.

The railway was complete enough to be opened for goods and mineral traffic between Llanymynech and Red Hill Junction on 1 December 1864, an announcement to that effect published in the *Shrewsbury Chronicle* on 25 November being signed by George Jones Holt (1832–1905), France's agent, who for a period in 1863 had been a traffic manager with the GWR.

Notice of intention to obtain further powers was advertised in the *London Gazette* on 29 November 1864. Once again it was necessary for a deviation to be made from a railway recently approved, in this case part of the lines authorised in the 1863 West Shropshire Mineral Railway Act and the 1864 (New Lines) Act.

The works were authorised by the Shrewsbury & North Wales Railway Act of 1865 on 26 May. The £100,000 capital required to fund them was also authorised, and the company was permitted to issue shares divided into half shares, one being designated preferred, the other as deferred. Whenever there were insufficient profits to pay a 5% dividend on the total, priority would be given to the preference shares; any deficiency was not allowed to be carried forward. Subject to approval at a general meeting, holders of existing shares could apply to have them divided.

Receiving Parliamentary attention at the same time as this Act, and an integral part of this story, was a Bill for the Shrewsbury & Potteries Junction Railway, which received the royal assent on 5 July 1865. This railway was intended to connect Shrewsbury with Stoke-on-Trent via a junction at Market Drayton. Its promoters were Michael Daintry Hollins (1816–98), William Matthews,

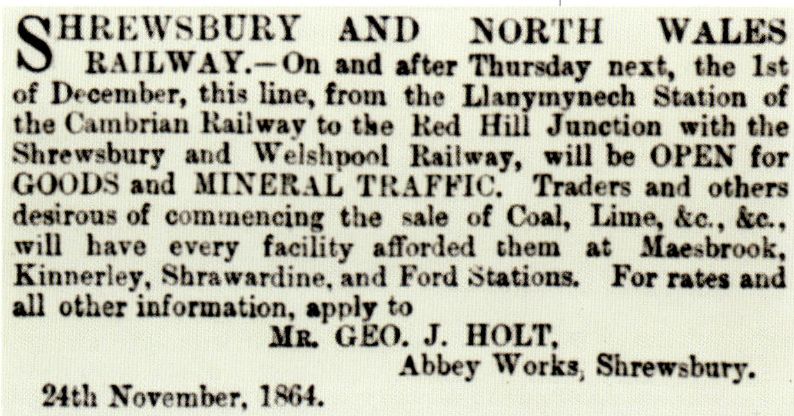

SHREWSBURY AND NORTH WALES RAILWAY.—On and after Thursday next, the 1st of December, this line, from the Llanymynech Station of the Cambrian Railway to the Red Hill Junction with the Shrewsbury and Welshpool Railway, will be OPEN for GOODS and MINERAL TRAFFIC. Traders and others desirous of commencing the sale of Coal, Lime, &c., &c., will have every facility afforded them at Maesbrook, Kinnerley, Shrawardine, and Ford Stations. For rates and all other information, apply to

MR. GEO. J. HOLT,
Abbey Works, Shrewsbury.

24th November, 1864.

Notice for the opening of the Shrewsbury & North Wales Railway published in the *Shrewsbury Chronicle* on 25 November 1864.

A market scene in Market Drayton, the target for several proposed railways from Shrewsbury. (The colourisation is contemporary with the postcard's publication in the early years of the twentieth century.)

Richard Thomas Rowley (1807–87), Major-General Henry Pelham Burn (1807–82), W. W. Cargill and A. P. Lattey. They were already Mineral Railway directors and Burn was to become chairman of the Potteries Railway.

Among its several rail connections at Shrewsbury, the Potteries Junction Railway was empowered to make an independent line from a junction with the GWR/LNWR joint line from Shrewsbury to Wellington to Red Hill and to make junctions there with the Shrewsbury & North Wales and the Shrewsbury & Welshpool railways. It was also authorised to make a branch from this line into Shrewsbury, terminating 'by a junction with the Shrewsbury & Hereford Railway near the south end of the viaduct of that railway adjoining the Abbey pool'.

On 24 March 1865, an extraordinary meeting of the Shrewsbury & North Wales Railway had approved a contract with France for doubling the railway between Llanymynech and Red Hill Junction. No explanation was offered for undertaking this extra work when the railway had only been opened for a few weeks and the traffic on offer could not have justified it.

As contractor, France's efforts had been transferred to the Llanyblodwel branch, where a double fatality occurred during the construction of the Carreghofa cutting, Peter Robinson, aged 38, and Samuel Jones, 37, being buried in several tons of earth on 22 June 1865. At the inquest, witnesses, their co-workers, tended to ascribe the blame to the victims, for having loosened fresh earth, which fell on them, instead of loading earth loosened previously. A verdict of accidental death was recorded (*Shrewsbury Chronicle*, 30 June 1865).

The Shrewsbury & North Wales Railway's 1865 plan. (Parliamentary Archive)

On 18 December Pryce Williams (aged 19) was also killed when the track was being ballasted at the same place. He tried to jump on a rake of moving ballast wagons to save a short walk but slipped and was run over, dying on arrival at Salop Infirmary. His death certificate recorded the cause of his death merely as 'accident'.

Reverting to Potteries Junction Railway administration, a contract with France to build the twenty-four-mile-long line had been approved at a special meeting on 30 August 1865. He was to take land for a double track and was expected to complete it by 1 July 1866.

Notices of intention to deposit four more Bills were published in the *London Gazette* on 28 November 1865 but only three of them passed into law. The one that failed was the Shrewsbury & Potteries Junction Railway (Extension) Bill, seeking powers for branches to Minsterley and Bishop's Castle; it passed its first reading but went no further, probably the result of LNWR and GWR objections. There is no plan of the proposed routes in the Parliamentary Archives.

The primary reason for the Shrewsbury & North Wales Railway (Meifod Valley Extension &c.) Bill was to make a railway from Carreghofa to Llanfair Caereinion but it was also intended to alter the Tanat Valley route at Llanyblodwel, the Shropshire Union Canal branch at Llanymynech and the Moat Hall Tramway, and to make other lesser works. The Meifod line being rejected in

The Shrewsbury & North Wales Railway's 1866 proposal for a branch from the later Wern Junction to Llanfair Caereinion. (Parliamentary Archives)

S & P. J. RY
AUTHORISED SHREWSBURY & NORTH WALES RY
RAILWAY No 2
RAILWAY No 1
Shrewsbury and Birmingham Railway
Shrewsbury and Chester Railway
Crewe Branch Railway
WEM
Station
Whixall
Prees
Cockshut
Loppington
Weston
Clive
Baschurch
Shawbury
Preston Gobalds
Harlescott
WOOLASCOT
POYNTON
HOUGHTON
RODEN
COTTON
SHREWSBURY
MEOLE
HANWOOD
BERWICK
Little Ness
Montford
Upton Magna
Withington

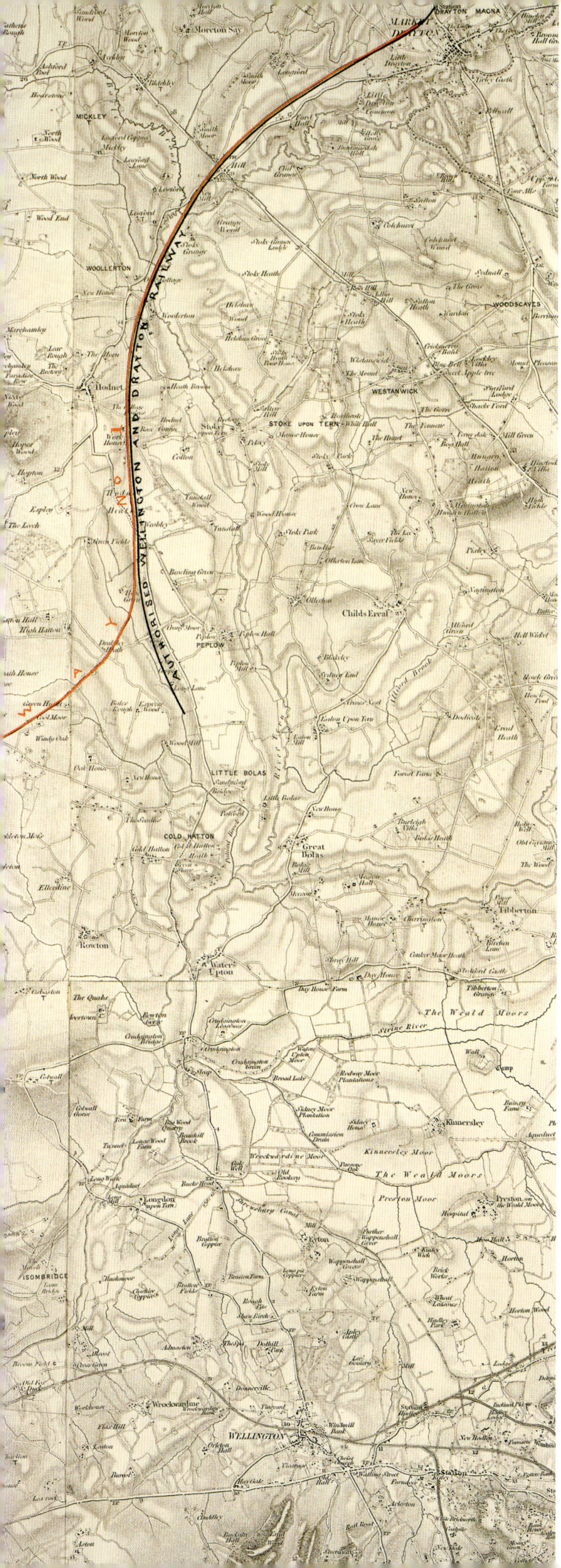

The Shrewsbury & Potteries Junction Railway's 1866 proposals for junctions at Shrewsbury and a line to Market Drayton. (Parliamentary Archives)

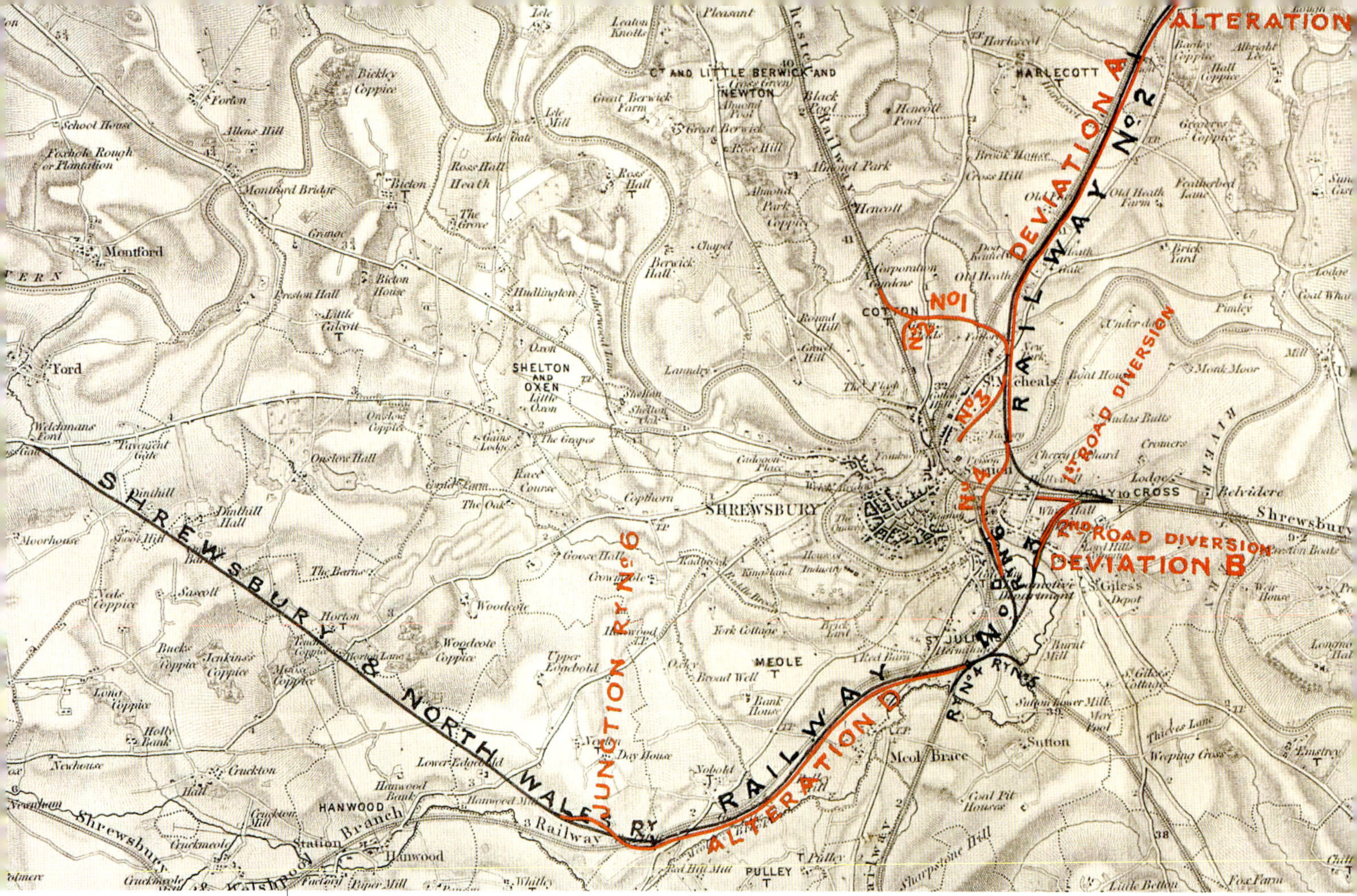

More changes at Shrewsbury in 1866. The 1866 proposals are notable for introducing the parallel route into Shrewsbury. (Parliamentary Archives)

the House of Lords, the remainder were authorised by the Shrewsbury & North Wales Railway (Deviations &c) Act.

The Shrewsbury & Potteries Junction Railway Bill sought to make several changes to parts of the route in the Shrewsbury area approved in the 1865 Act, including the independent line from Red Hill to the Shrewsbury & Wellington Railway, the branch to what became the Abbey station site and junctions with the Severn Valley and the Shrewsbury & Hereford railways.

Seal for the Potteries, Shrewsbury & North Wales Railway.

Finally, the Shrewsbury & North Wales and Potteries Junction (Amalgamation) Bill dissolved the companies and created the Potteries, Shrewsbury & North Wales Railway Company, deemed to be an amalgamation as defined by the Railway Clauses Act, 1863. The first directors were those of the original companies. The phoenix in the combined undertaking's seal was obviously meant to symbolise the union but it was not born out of fire but of debt. The capital of the combined undertakings is shown in the table.

The preference shares had priority for 5% interest but no deficiency could be carried forward. The Shrewsbury & North Wales £5 preferred shares had priority over the remainder. A total of 18,975 of the Potteries Junction 1865 shares had been paid at

	Mortgages	Preference Shares	Ordinary Shares	Total
1862 West Shropshire Mineral Railway	£30,000		£90,000	£120,000
1863 West Shropshire Mineral Railway	£19,990		£60,000	£79,990
1864 West Shropshire Mineral Railway (New Lines)	£66,000		£200,000	£266,000
1864 Shrewsbury & North Wales Railway	£33,000		£100,000	£133,000
1865 Shrewsbury & North Wales Railway	£33,000	£100,000		£133,000
1865 Shrewsbury & Potteries Junction Railway	£133,000		£248,200	£381,200
	£314,990	£100,000	£698,200	£1,113,190
Unissued, or issued but not paid up				
1863 West Shropshire Mineral Railway	£10			£10
1865 Shrewsbury & Potteries Junction Railway	£300		£151,800	£152,100
1866 Shrewsbury & North Wales Railway (Deviations &c.)	£26,000		£80,000	£106,000
1866 Shrewsbury & Potteries Junction Railway (Deviations)	£26,600		£80,000	£106,600

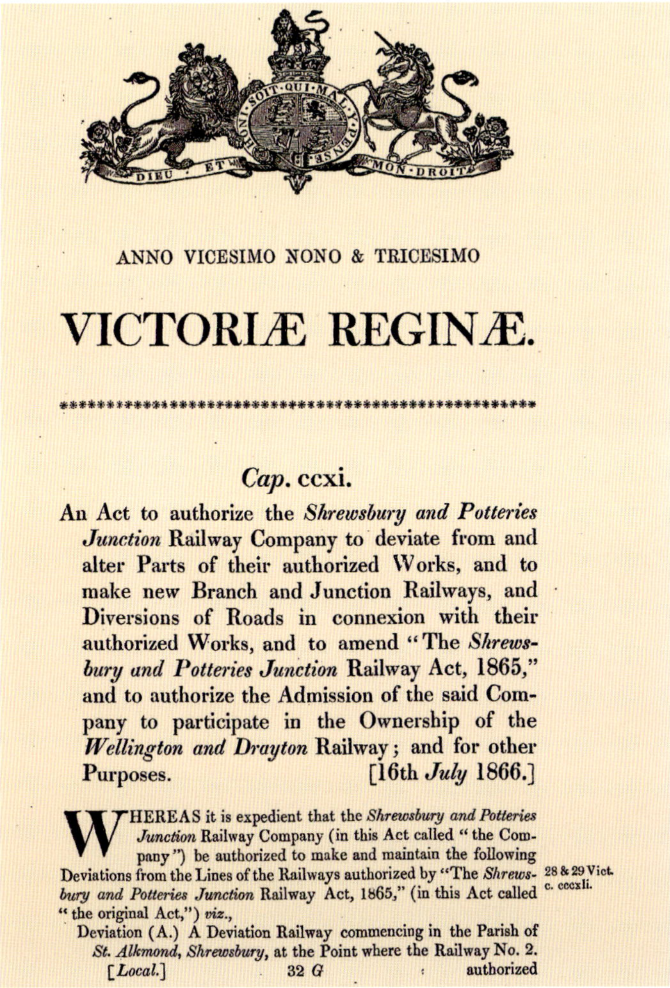

ANNO VICESIMO NONO & TRICESIMO

VICTORIÆ REGINÆ.

Cap. ccxi.

An Act to authorize the *Shrewsbury and Potteries Junction* Railway Company to deviate from and alter Parts of their authorized Works, and to make new Branch and Junction Railways, and Diversions of Roads in connexion with their authorized Works, and to amend "The *Shrewsbury and Potteries Junction* Railway Act, 1865," and to authorize the Admission of the said Company to participate in the Ownership of the *Wellington and Drayton* Railway; and for other Purposes. [16th *July* 1866.]

WHEREAS it is expedient that the *Shrewsbury and Potteries Junction* Railway Company (in this Act called "the Company") be authorized to make and maintain the following Deviations from the Lines of the Railways authorized by "The *Shrewsbury and Potteries Junction* Railway Act, 1865," (in this Act called "the original Act,") *viz.*, 28 & 29 Vict. c. cccxli.

Deviation (A.) A Deviation Railway commencing in the Parish of *St. Alkmond, Shrewsbury*, at the Point where the Railway No. 2. [*Local.*] 32 *G* authorized

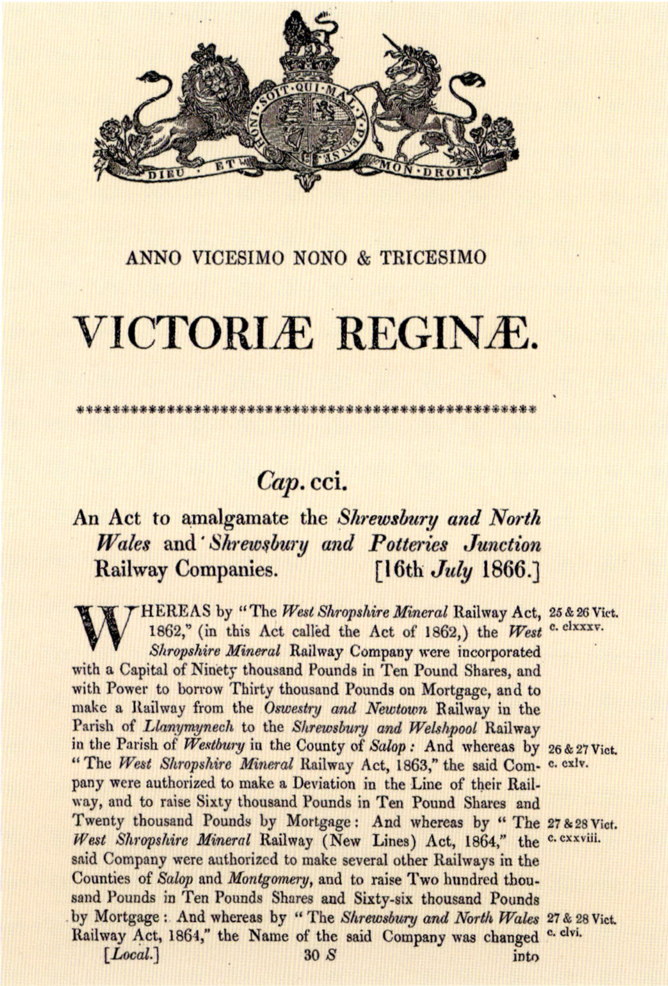

ANNO VICESIMO NONO & TRICESIMO

VICTORIÆ REGINÆ.

Cap. cci.

An Act to amalgamate the *Shrewsbury and North Wales* and *Shrewsbury and Potteries Junction* Railway Companies. [16th *July* 1866.]

WHEREAS by "The *West Shropshire Mineral* Railway Act, 1862," (in this Act called the Act of 1862,) the *West Shropshire Mineral* Railway Company were incorporated with a Capital of Ninety thousand Pounds in Ten Pound Shares, and with Power to borrow Thirty thousand Pounds on Mortgage, and to make a Railway from the *Oswestry and Newtown* Railway in the Parish of *Llanymynech* to the *Shrewsbury and Welshpool* Railway in the Parish of *Westbury* in the County of *Salop*: And whereas by "The *West Shropshire Mineral* Railway Act, 1863," the said Company were authorized to make a Deviation in the Line of their Railway, and to raise Sixty thousand Pounds in Ten Pound Shares and Twenty thousand Pounds by Mortgage: And whereas by "The *West Shropshire Mineral* Railway (New Lines) Act, 1864," the said Company were authorized to make several other Railways in the Counties of *Salop* and *Montgomery*, and to raise Two hundred thousand Pounds in Ten Pounds Shares and Sixty-six thousand Pounds by Mortgage: And whereas by "The *Shrewsbury and North Wales* Railway Act, 1864," the Name of the said Company was changed into 25 & 26 Vict. c. clxxxv. 26 & 27 Vict. c. cxlv. 27 & 28 Vict. c. cxxviii. 27 & 28 Vict. c. clvi.

[*Local.*] 30 *S*

Above left: Shrewsbury & Potteries Junction Railway Act 1866.

Above right: Shrewsbury & North Wales Railway and Shrewsbury & Potteries Junction Railway Amalgamation Act 1866.

A Shrewsbury & North Wales Railway ticket.

£2 each as their holders had been unable to pay the full amount.

With amendments imposed or agreed during the Parliamentary process, the three Bills were enacted on 16 July 1866.

Reviewing the Parliamentary activity, of nine Acts in four years, there does not appear to have been much in the way of strategic thinking, with amendments to routes being proposed within months of approval being given to them. The extensions and branches being thrown off in all directions must be symptomatic of the difficulty experienced in selling shares; add new destinations and people who might use the services might invest in them. In 1888 it was said that shares and debentures had been sold at a discount, although lists of stocks issued do not show any discrepancy with the capital available to the company. Another example of the lack of strategy is demonstrated by the existence of unused Shrewsbury & North Wales Railway tickets.

A total of £200,000 of capital obtained from the London Finance Association was repayable over 50 years, the length of R. S. France's Nantmawr leases. In 1865, Brown, Shipley & Co., described as 'general merchants in the city', had loaned £100,000 to France against the security of £66,500 in debentures and £69,070 in shares in what became the Potteries Railway, £14,000 of Lloyds' bonds held by the Mold & Denbigh Railway and £108,000 of Mold & Denbigh shares. The lender expected to receive interest from France plus any dividend or interest payable on the various stocks.

The promotional costs must have been considerable, with every Bill opposed by both the LNWR and the GWR. When the junction was made at Red Hill the LNWR refused to permit its use and gave the Cambrian a rebate on traffic routed via the Shrewsbury & Welshpool to discourage it from making use of the Potteries line.

Earlier, on the Shrewsbury & North Wales Railway, work was still under way in the cutting at Edgebold on 15 January 1866 when the cutting face had collapsed, killing Thomas Cheshire, aged 32. The face had been undermined three days previously, but bad weather had delayed pulling it down; no lookouts had been posted when work resumed, and Cheshire was unable to escape when it fell. Returning a verdict of accidental death, the inquest jury blamed the ganger for putting the men to work when the earth was unstable (*Shrewsbury Free Press*, 20 January).

A few weeks later several men were injured in another earthfall, near Red Hill on 5 March, but only Richard Fox and Richard Preece sufficiently to warrant being taken to the infirmary, where Fox was treated for a dislocated knee and Preece for a broken leg (*Eddowes's Journal*, 7 March).

A few months later, the 'near completion of the Shrewsbury and North Wales Railway' was responsible for the publication of an advertisement promoting the auction of thirty cart horses to be held on 26 June, 'by order of Mr R. S. France' (*Eddowes's Shrewsbury Journal*, 20 June).

Brief reports relating to Potteries Junction Railway construction included one in *The Times* (7 July 1866) that had more to say about the discovery of human remains on the Shrewsbury station site. Known as the 'Abbey site' despite being detached from it since Thomas Telford had built the Holyhead road through the town earlier in the nineteenth century, thirty or forty skeletons of unknown origin had been found about 3ft below the surface. Bought from a Mr Scott (*Wellington Journal*, 23 July 1892), the railway site was adjacent to land

France had bought in 1863 (*Shrewsbury Chronicle*, 25 November 1864) to use as a base for his contracting business. The independent station was required because the LNWR and GWR had made it clear that his railways would not be given access to Shrewsbury's general station.

On 18 June 1866 company secretary, and solicitor, Charles Chandler (1821–87) informed the Board of Trade that the first part of the Shrewsbury & North Wales Railway, from the Shrewsbury & Welshpool Railway junction at Red Hill to Llanymynech, would be ready for inspection on 26 June. On the same date John Wade (1833–1909), the Potteries Junction Railway's secretary, wrote in similar terms regarding that line's works in Shrewsbury. Born in Shrewsbury, Wade had been the Mid Wales and the Shrewsbury & Welshpool Railways' secretary, was an officer of the London Finance Association and became the Potteries Railway's secretary in 1872.

In sending the plans of both undertakings to the Board of Trade on 21 June, incidentally, Ashdown, the engineer, noted that the 'Abbey yard branch' was to be used 'only temporarily as a passenger line pending the construction of other portions of the railways ...'

Colonel Frederick Henry Rich (1824–1904) started his inspection on 3 July, taking two days and submitting

One of the eleven overbridges, this one at Edgebold, seen in 1937. (John Scott Morgan Collection)

his report on 8 July. Of the Shrewsbury & North Wales, he said that the line was 16 miles 24 chains long, with double track, 70lb double-head rail laid in 28lb chairs spiked to transverse sleepers; it was 'well ballasted' with gravel. There were stations at Llanymynech, Maesbrook, Kinnerley, Nesscliff, Shrawardine, Ford and Hanwood. Turntables had been installed at Llanymynech and Shrewsbury. Of the nine overbridges, four had brick arches, three had wooden decks on masonry abutments and two had cast iron sides. There were eleven underbridges, two of brick, six with timber decks, and three with wrought iron sides on masonry abutments: the greatest span was 32ft. He said that there were seven viaducts with a total of twenty-four openings, all quite small except that at Shrawardine, which had two 60ft spans, two of 41ft 9in and two of 40ft 9in. It consisted of wrought iron girders supported on cast iron columns and masonry abutments. The other viaducts had both masonry columns and abutments. Some of these structures would have been flood relief channels in the vicinity of watercourses subject to flooding. He found that the works 'appeared to be substantially constructed and of sufficient strength'. An accommodation arch at 14m 9ch required pointing and watching.

There were no station buildings but platforms, signals and small timber booking offices had been provided. Ashdown undertook to complete some small works immediately: stops to all level crossing gates, to prevent them from being opened outwards; lamps placed on the gates; a hand rail on the parapet of the underbridge at Hanwood to prevent passengers stepping out on to the parapet; chains of the signal lamps to be marked so that the porter in charge could tell when they were home and the Breidden (Criggion) branch to be guarded by a pair of facing points set for the main line. Clocks were to be installed at the stations and the junction.

Rich also called for a pair of gates to close across the railway and road to be erected at 'the public level crossing at 1m 50ch in the parish of Kinnerley and the lodge which is now building to be completed without delay'. He added: 'These works can be done in a few days and the line may be opened for passenger traffic if their lordships are satisfied as to the public level crossings …' He had found seven crossings over public roads, one of which, near Ford, had not been specified in the legislation. He thought that the plans showed a bridge at the location, saying that the company should either prove that it was a private crossing or be required to provide gates and a lodge and then to undertake to submit a bill to Parliament 'next session' for approval. If approval was denied then the company should build a bridge within three months. Cae Gwynsyn crossing, between Maesbrook and Kinnerley, had only a small hut for the keeper, and he thought that the company should be required to undertake to build a lodge within three months.

Despite his earlier remark about the railway being fit for passenger traffic, Rich concluded that it 'cannot be opened for passenger traffic without danger to the public using the same by reason of the … the proper gatekeepers' lodge … and by reason of the unauthorised public level crossing …'

On 12 July 1866 solicitor Chandler sent the Board of Trade a sealed undertaking, signed by the chairman, Elias Mocatta, and himself, to construct the lodge at Cae Gwynsyn within three months. He also submitted a certificate from the warden of Ford parish declaring that the road with the unauthorised crossing was only used as a public bridle road. The Board of Trade replied that the line could be opened as soon as the works required by Rich had been carried out.

Of the Potteries Junction line between Red Hill and the Shrewsbury–Wellington line, sometimes known as the loop line, which he inspected at the same time, Rich said that it was 3m 25ch long with a 35ch branch to Shrewsbury Abbey yard station. The gradient on the branch was

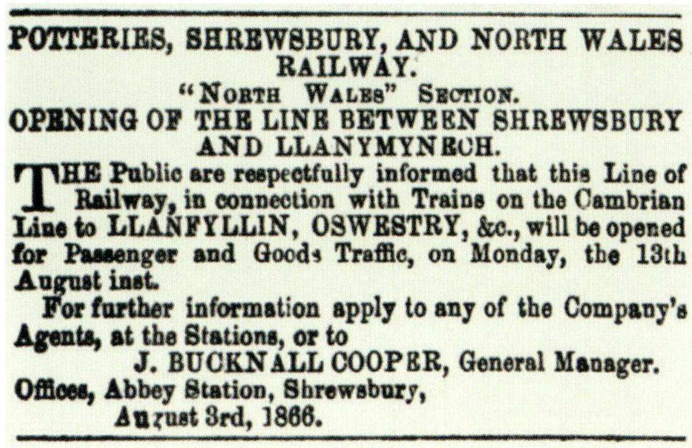

POTTERIES, SHREWSBURY, AND NORTH WALES RAILWAY.

"NORTH WALES" SECTION.

OPENING OF THE LINE BETWEEN SHREWSBURY AND LLANYMYNECH.

THE Public are respectfully informed that this Line of Railway, in connection with Trains on the Cambrian Line to LLANFYLLIN, OSWESTRY, &c., will be opened for Passenger and Goods Traffic, on Monday, the 13th August inst.

For further information apply to any of the Company's Agents, at the Stations, or to

J. BUCKNALL COOPER, General Manager.

Offices, Abbey Station, Shrewsbury,
August 3rd, 1866.

Cooper's 11 August advertisement informing Shrewsbury residents of the railway's forthcoming opening.

John Bucknall Cooper, the first general manager of the Potteries, Shrewsbury & North Wales Railway.

1 in 47, all trains were to be brought to a stand at the junction with the Potteries Junction 'main line', and worked at very low speed into the station. There were two overbridges with stone abutments and cast iron sides and five underbridges with stone abutments and wrought iron girders. The largest span was 48ft. Once again, the works appeared to be substantially constructed and of sufficient strength.

Ashdown had undertaken to install spring buffers on the arrival platform and to take out a set of facing points by the junction at the top of the incline. With only these requirements, Rich recommended that it could be opened to passenger traffic. Formal approval was given to the company on 14 July, although it was 6 August before John Bucknall Cooper (1838–1910), the general manager, gave notice of the intention to open for passenger traffic on 13 August and placed an advertisement to that effect in the *Shrewsbury Free Press* on 11 August.

Born in Liverpool, Cooper had worked for the LNWR at Rugby and took the Shrewsbury position while also working as the manager of the Stafford & Uttoxeter Railway, residing in Shrewsbury.

Making the railway double track between Llanymynech and Potteries Junction, otherwise Red Hill, was in anticipation of trains running through to Market Drayton and beyond and explains the easing of curves and gradients. A yard with five sidings was established for the exchange of traffic at Potteries Junction, and wagon repairs were also carried out there. Coleham Junction was the name given to the divergence between the Abbey branch and the loop line.

The Breidden and Llanyblodwel branches, which took the railway into Montgomeryshire, although the latter quickly returned to Shropshire, had probably been opened for goods during 1865, with a service operated by France. The Breidden line terminated at the foot of Breidden Hill (1,204ft/367m), close to the Criggion quarry. A 'tramway' extended the Llanyblodwel branch to serve France's quarry at Nantmawr, although it had the same physical characteristics as the branch line that served it.

In addition to the terminals there were stations at Red Hill, Hanwood Road, Ford, Shrawardine, Nesscliff (sometimes spelled Nesscliffe), Kinnerley, and Maesbrook. Whether the stations that were later established on the branches for passengers

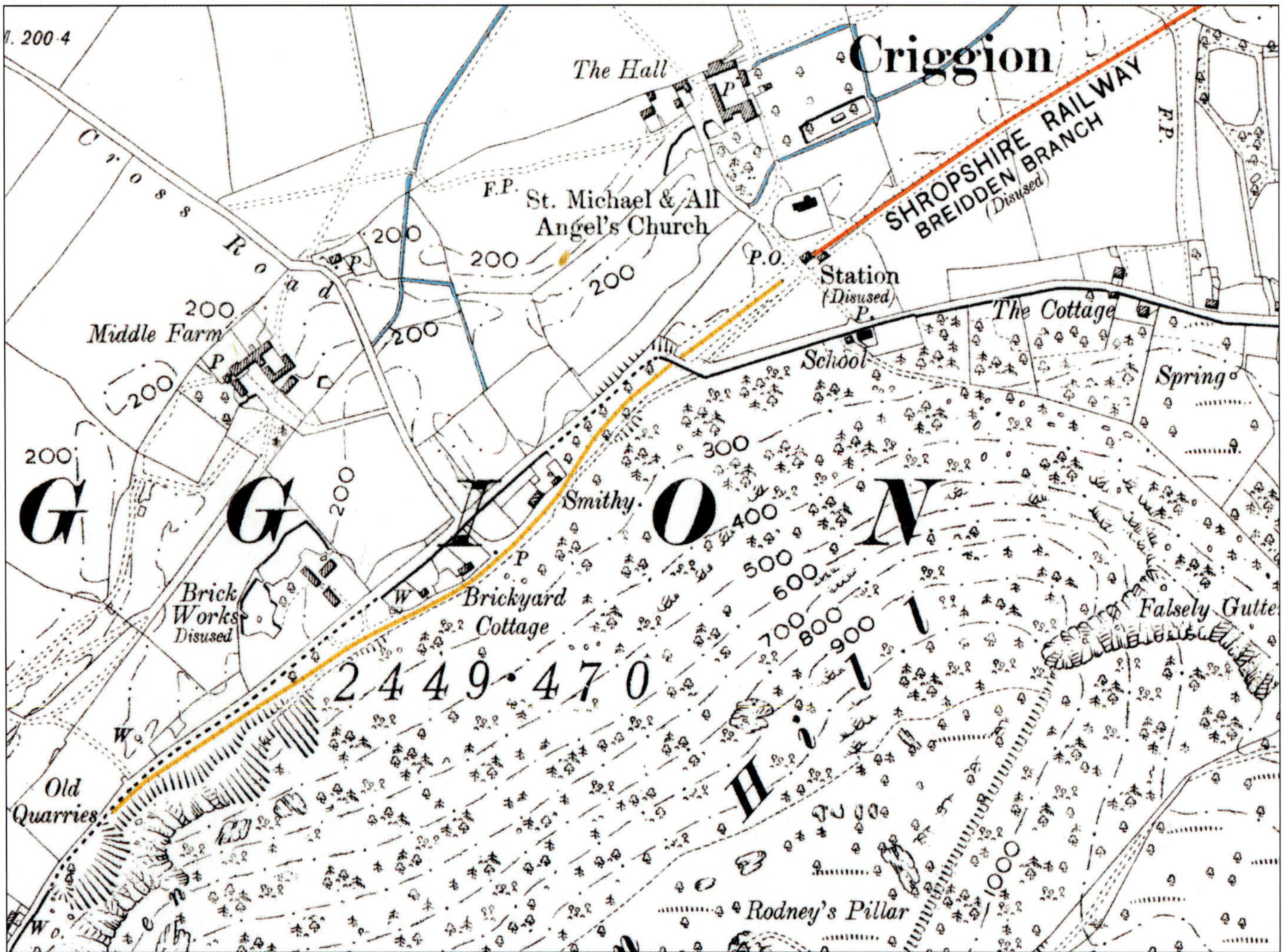

Map showing Briedden branch terminus and quarry connection. (Ordnance Survey)

had existed previously for goods traffic has not been established. As was so often the case in rural areas, none of the stations was particularly close to the places they purported to serve. Minimal facilities were provided for passengers, although the houses constructed for the crossing keepers were quite substantial. There were crossings of the Severn, at Shrawardine on the main line, and at Melverley on the Breidden (Criggion) branch. The railway's mileage was 28, 18 of which were used by passenger trains. The Nantmawr quarry incline was not, incidentally, a part of the statutory railway, although both France and the company considered it to be so; with no direct connection to the railway, it was 1,640ft long on a gradient of 1 in 7.

France had had a busy year, for in addition to bringing the Potteries Railway to fruition and supporting its Parliamentary activities, he had been injured in a railway collision at Wellington (*Oswestry Advertiser*, 28 March 1866) and was also engaged on the construction of the Mold & Denbigh Railway and said to have been the contractor of the Mawddwy Railway, which opened on 30 September 1867.

Many obstacles had been overcome to get the railway ready for opening but its future faced many more. The year 1866 was not a good one in which to be opening a railway. The discount house Overend & Gurney & Co. and the English Joint Stock Bank, both heavily invested in railway shares, had collapsed in May, pulling the rug from under any railway that was due to be opened but which still needed capital for its rolling stock and stations.

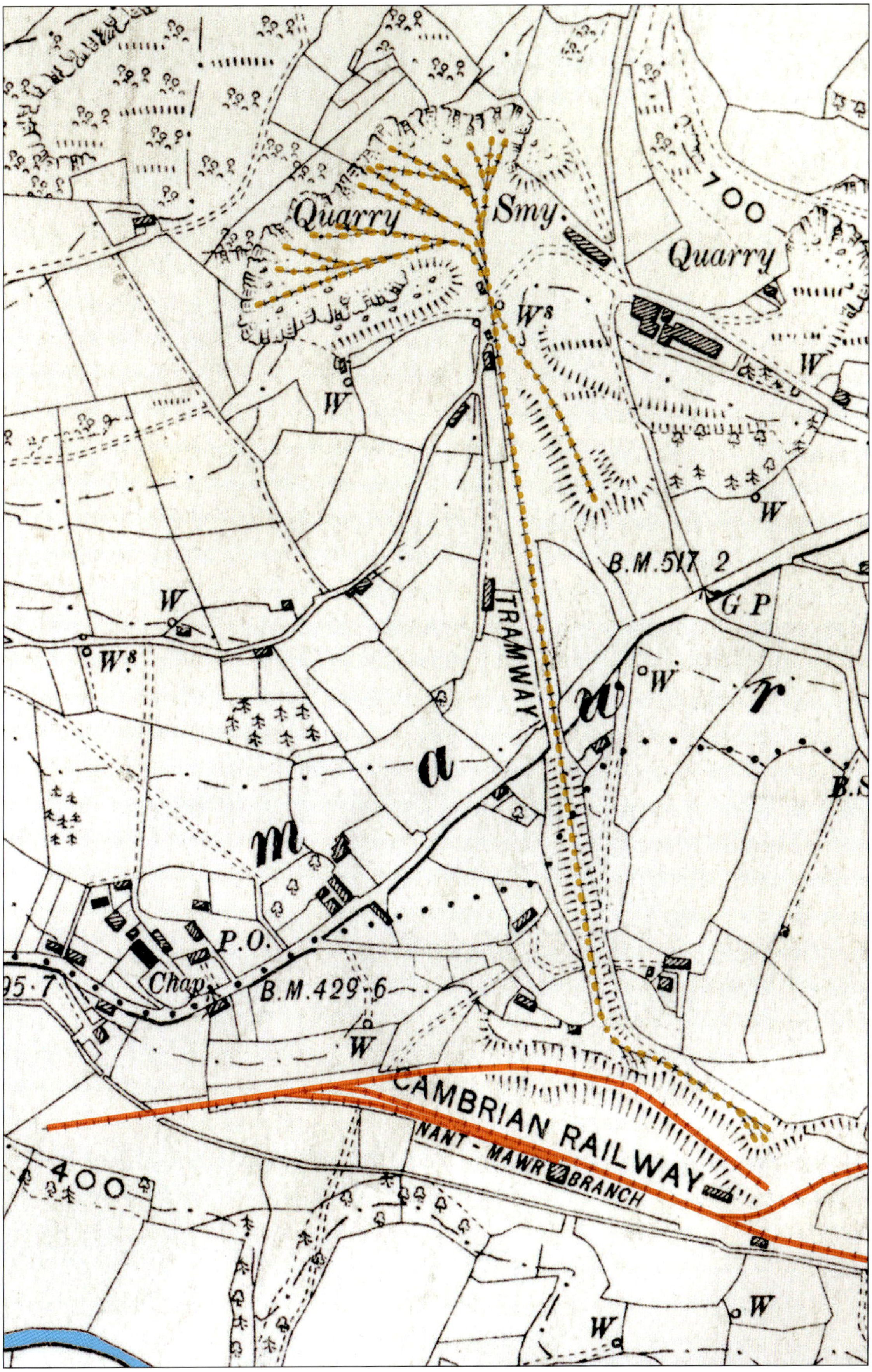

Nantmawr terminus and quarry lines. (Ordnance Survey)

CHAPTER 2

THE POTTERIES, SHREWSBURY & NORTH WALES RAILWAY

A well-known photograph that continues to be the only one known of a Potteries, Shrewsbury & North Wales Railway train, at the Abbey station. Obtained from the LNWR in May 1872, the locomotive had been built in 1847.

Services were started on 13 August 1866 without ceremony, the *Oswestry Advertiser* (15 August) saying that traffic was expected to be heavy because it was Shrewsbury carnival week. The *Birmingham Daily Gazette* (14 August) said that 'heavy trains ran backwards and forwards' over the line and that the 'Potteries section' was in course of construction. The company's advertisements were sub-headed 'North Wales Section'. For four days from 15 August it offered excursion fares (2s 1st class, 1s covered carriages) on three trains each day, the first leaving Shrewsbury at 6.35am (*Eddowes's Journal*, 15 August).

The earliest known public timetable, published in the *Wellington Journal* on 8 September, showed five trains in each direction on weekdays, which included Saturdays, and two return workings on Sundays; a notice in the *Shrewsbury Free Press* on the same date advised that the times had been altered. After an interval of four hours, the last return working left Shrewsbury at 7.30pm. The Sunday

afternoon working to Llanymynech, surely an excursion as it was over three hours before it returned, took an hour, while the fastest working only stopped at Kinnerley and took thirty-five minutes. Two train sets were needed to work the five-train service, so even if there was an unadvertised goods train service the railway was not making good use of its double track.

No change of carriage was required for the market day excursions, fare 2s 8d, offered between Shrewsbury and Oswestry in the *Shrewsbury Free Press* (8 September) but of course the advertisement did not indicate if there was any change of locomotive. In the same issue day trip and three-day trips to Aberystwyth and Borth via Llanymynech were also offered. The three-day trips ran on alternate Saturdays from the same date, the day trips on alternate Mondays from 10 September, the use of through carriages being noted. The return train carried both groups.

There were rates for three classes of passengers until second class was abolished in 1875. The shareholders' reports show that only around 300 second-class tickets had been issued annually, 'compensated' by an increase in first-class issues. In 1902–30 T. R. Perkins (Bibliography) found a poster announcing the change in the abandoned Ford & Crossgates station; first-class tickets were issued at the rate of 2d per mile and third class for half that amount.

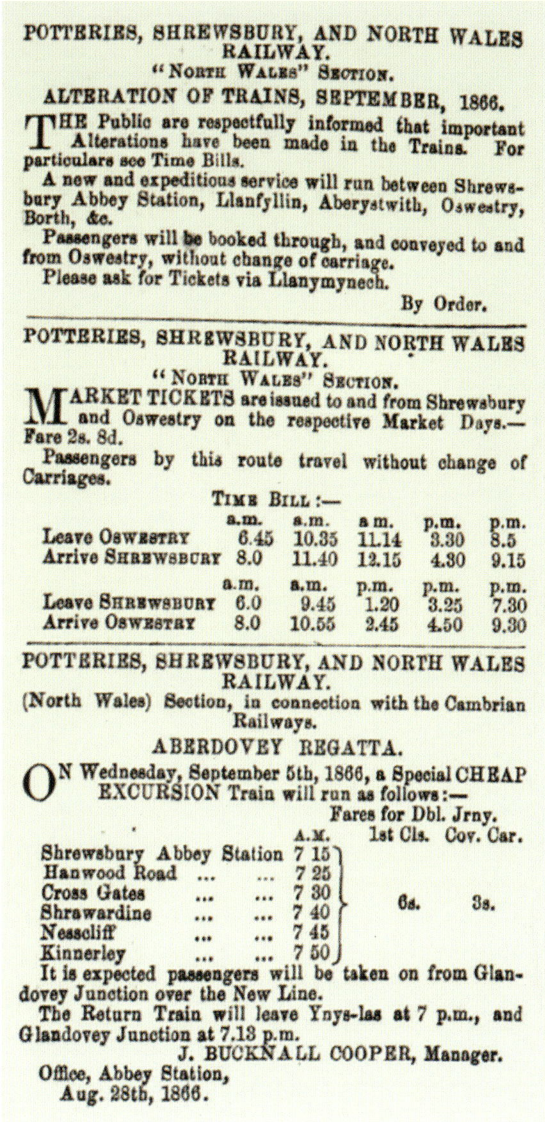

POTTERIES, SHREWSBURY, AND NORTH WALES RAILWAY.
"NORTH WALES" SECTION.
ALTERATION OF TRAINS, SEPTEMBER, 1866.

THE Public are respectfully informed that important Alterations have been made in the Trains. For particulars see Time Bills.

A new and expeditious service will run between Shrewsbury Abbey Station, Llanfyllin, Aberystwith, Oswestry, Borth, &c.

Passengers will be booked through, and conveyed to and from Oswestry, without change of carriage.

Please ask for Tickets via Llanymynech.

By Order.

POTTERIES, SHREWSBURY, AND NORTH WALES RAILWAY.
"NORTH WALES" SECTION.

MARKET TICKETS are issued to and from Shrewsbury and Oswestry on the respective Market Days.—Fare 2s. 8d.

Passengers by this route travel without change of Carriages.

TIME BILL:—

	a.m.	a.m.	a.m.	p.m.	p.m.
Leave OSWESTRY	6.45	10.35	11.14	3.30	8.5
Arrive SHREWSBURY	8.0	11.40	12.15	4.30	9.15
	a.m.	a.m.	p.m.	p.m.	p.m.
Leave SHREWSBURY	6.0	9.45	1.20	3.25	7.30
Arrive OSWESTRY	8.0	10.55	2.45	4.50	9.30

POTTERIES, SHREWSBURY, AND NORTH WALES RAILWAY.
(North Wales) Section, in connection with the Cambrian Railways.
ABERDOVEY REGATTA.

ON Wednesday, September 5th, 1866, a Special CHEAP EXCURSION Train will run as follows:—

	A.M.	1st Cls.	Cov. Car.
		Fares for Dbl. Jrny.	
Shrewsbury Abbey Station	7 15	6s.	3s.
Hanwood Road	7 25		
Cross Gates	7 30		
Shrawardine	7 40		
Nesscliff	7 45		
Kinnerley	7 50		

It is expected passengers will be taken on from Glandovey Junction over the New Line.

The Return Train will leave Ynys-las at 7 p.m., and Glandovey Junction at 7.13 p.m.

J. BUCKNALL COOPER, Manager.

Office, Abbey Station,
Aug. 28th, 1866.

An advertisement for services and excursions published in the *Shrewsbury Free Press* on 1 September 1866. The 2s 8d market day fare to Oswestry would cost about £13 in 2022.

The lack of capital for finishing touches meant that the railway had to depend on R. S. France's fleet of locomotives and wagons for rolling stock, which was not intended to be used on operational railways, and which was, in any event, in poor condition. These were supplemented by four-wheeled carriages and additional locomotives bought second hand. The latter included a Bury, Curtis & Kennedy 0-4-2 No 1859 obtained from the LNWR in 1872 and disposed of quite quickly, but not before it was photographed with a train of four-wheeled carriages.

France had been given £134,018 of shares and debentures in payment for work done and materials supplied but had stopped working on the Potteries Junction section in July 1866, the company then undertaking some capital works with the benefit of a £3,600 fund contributed by shareholders and creditors (*Bradshaw's Guide, Manual and Shareholders' Directory*, 1870).

The new company's first general meeting was held on 6 August, when John Ashdown, the engineer, reported that the branches were nearly complete and that the line around Shrewsbury, which would connect with the Shropshire Union Railway and the Shrewsbury & Hereford Railway, was 'in a forward state' (*The Times*, 7 August). Saying that there were 'vast' lime deposits in the district, Herapath's *Railway Journal*

The surviving Edgebold bridge abutment, seen in 2006, was obviously altered when the decision was taken to make the railway double track.

(11 August) forecast that when the Breidden and Nantmawr branches were complete the Staffordshire market for it would be sufficient to pay a fair return on the railway's capital.

Mary Ann Briscoe was an early passenger, but she had an unfortunate experience when she travelled from Shrewsbury to Ford in a third-class carriage on 29 October. The carriage had four compartments with half-height partitions; there were no other passengers in it when Stephen Kinsey, a 35-year-old butcher from Llanymynech, who had been drinking, was put in one of the other compartments. After the train left, he climbed over to her compartment and assaulted her, ignoring her requests to desist. Her attempts to call the station master as the train passed through Red Hill and for the guard were unsuccessful and she fell when Kinsey grabbed her as she left the train at Ford. At Shrewsbury magistrates' court on 5 November, where Kinsey was described as being married with seven children, the magistrates sent him for trial at the quarter sessions, bailing him for £50 and two sureties of £25 (*Shrewsbury Free Press*, 10 November 1866). Within a month of the hearing, however, he had sold his property in Llanymynech and fled to America, taking his family with him and apparently settling in Canada.

With the railway open for traffic there were a number of problems, some of which would pursue it for the rest of its existence. At £60,000 per mile to construct, it was claimed to be the most expensive railway in a non-metropolitan area in England. To service the capital and the debt at 5% would require some £60,000 profit per annum, an unlikely outcome for an agricultural line.

Whether France was profligate in the railway's construction can only be judged by analysing the construction costs, where known, or capital of other similar railways built at the same time. It was certainly not alone in being built with a double-track formation but it was unusual in laying down a second track when the traffic did not warrant it; the surviving bridge abutment at Edgebold, which was built in two segments, shows that at least part of

the railway was built as single track and then altered, which would have increased costs. Possibly railway funds were used to build the Nantmawr quarry incline, too.

The passage of time shows that France's stone and brick overbridges were quite sound, and most of them survive. Three of his iron beam bridges survive on the Nantmawr branch, one carrying modern traffic apparently unmodified, one requiring support to do so, while the third is an underbridge that now carries only light pedestrian traffic. Of his river bridges, that at Shrawardine lasted nearly 100 years before being rebuilt, only to be demolished shortly afterwards, and that on the Breidden branch obviously suffered by being built on the cheap, lasting only until *c*.1910, when it was renewed, again cheaply. His timber structures did not last long but they received no maintenance either, so that can be no surprise.

The company had no working capital and quickly attracted £40,000 of court judgements against it. The landowners upon whose property the line had been built remained unpaid. The most likely fruitful source of traffic, the Nantmawr quarry, was not obliged to use the line in its entirety and could bypass it at the whim of the quarry's proprietor, as proved to be the case.

France was responsible for maintenance until 1869. During 1866 'locomotives engaged in construction work' hauled 6,067 tons. The figure was 2,000 tons fewer in 1867.

After the finance house Overend & Gurney collapsed in May 1866 it was not long before France's own financial problems were manifest on the railway. Engaged on constructing the Mold & Denbigh Junction Railway as well as the erstwhile Potteries Junction Railway east of Shrewsbury, where work was stopped during July, a notice that three inspectors of his affairs in bankruptcy had been appointed was published in the *London Gazette* on 14 August.

Then, after a debenture holder obtained a judgment against the company for arrears of interest, bailiffs took possession of Shrewsbury station just before the 1.40pm

The Nantmawr quarry and incline played a significant role in the history of the Potteries Railway. The author knows of no contemporary illustrations of the incline and in its present overgrown condition its true impact is lost. In places rails are exposed where the tarmac has deteriorated.

The Nantmawr incline road bridge was built with the same style of stonework as the bridges built by France for the Potteries Railway. The same design, with the casting mark of William F. Sim & Co. of Liverpool on the beams and all dated 1865, was used at Porthywaen. William Fisher Sim (1823–88), a Whitehaven man resident in Birkenhead, always identified himself as an iron merchant and the company was identified as metal brokers. As neither appear to have operated a foundry, it would be reasonable to assume that the company acted as an intermediary for obtaining the beams.

was due to leave on 27 November. It being a fair day in Shrewsbury, the railway was busy with passengers holding return tickets. Manager J. B. Cooper persuaded under-sheriff Joshua John Peele (1805-73), a solicitor, to allow the train to run with a bailiff on board, holding a free pass, to ensure that the train returned. Later, Peele agreed to the operation of a train at 6.15pm (*Daily News*, 28 November / *Wellington Journal*, 1 December).

On 28 November *Eddowes's Journal* advertised an auction for the sale of a steam locomotive, carriages, vans, weighing machines, furniture and other effects belonging to the railway to take

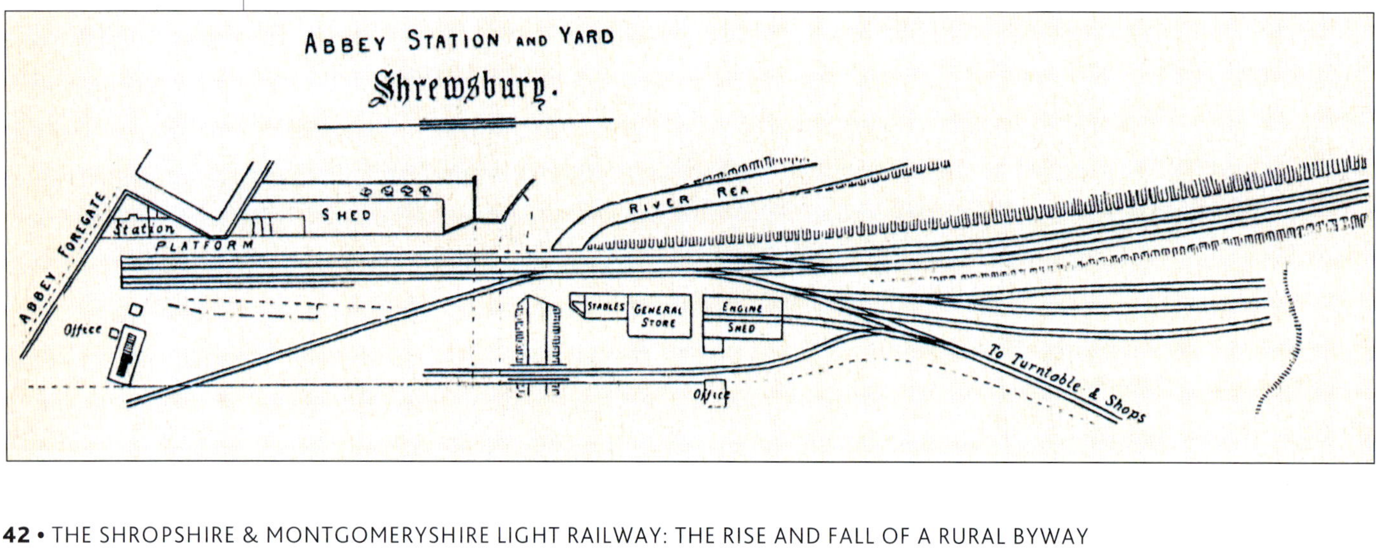

A sketch of the original track layout at Shrewsbury. (T. R. Perkins)

place on 4 December but an item in the *Wellington Journal* (1 December) cast doubt on the ability of the creditors to sell the rolling stock.

The debenture holder's action was not really to his benefit, as stopping the trains from running reduced the funding available to debenture holders or any other creditors. As will be seen, the government was prompted to prevent creditors from seizing a railway's assets in a manner that prevented it from operating. This was not the only local railway to be in financial difficulty, for the Bishop's Castle Railway, which had opened on 1 February 1866, was also seized by bailiffs in December, its assets being sold on 23 January 1867.

Normal services resumed on 3 December 1866, still with a bailiff on board (*Manchester Courier*, 4 December). There is a story often told, that may be apocryphal, that on one occasion the train stopped at Kinnerley for shunting purposes and when the bailiff looked out of the window to seek the reason for the delay, he found that his carriage had been detached from the train that was now disappearing into the distance and that the station was locked up. Allegedly he walked back to Shrewsbury in the dark, a hazardous experience for the unprepared in the days before light pollution was heard of. It was said that on subsequent days he avoided travelling in the last carriage.

Notwithstanding, trains continued running with a bailiff, who remained with it overnight (*Shrewsbury Free Press*, 8 December). The proposed auction had been postponed at the last minute, the paper said, confirming that the *Wellington Journal* had been right to be doubtful about it. However, without notice, William Quilter (1809–88) was appointed receiver on 11 December and the railway was closed on 21 December 1866, although no news reports have been found relating to this.

The under-sheriff advertised the sale of five locomotives, coal trucks, wagons, weighing machines, stores and other property by private treaty in *Eddowes's Journal* on 19 December 1866, giving ten

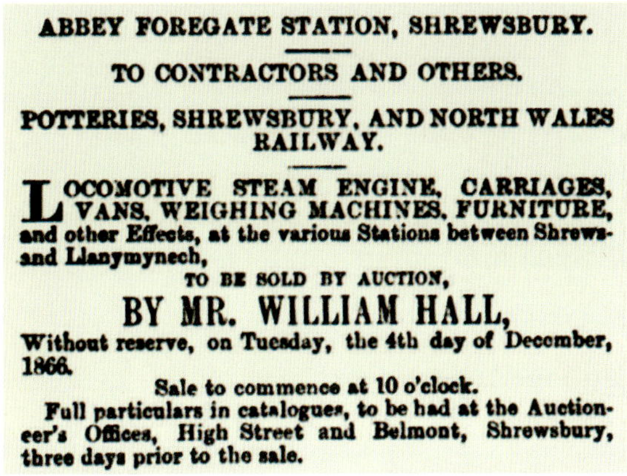

ABBEY FOREGATE STATION, SHREWSBURY.

TO CONTRACTORS AND OTHERS.

POTTERIES, SHREWSBURY, AND NORTH WALES RAILWAY.

LOCOMOTIVE STEAM ENGINE, CARRIAGES, VANS, WEIGHING MACHINES, FURNITURE, and other Effects, at the various Stations between Shrewsbury and Llanymynech,

TO BE SOLD BY AUCTION,

BY MR. WILLIAM HALL,

Without reserve, on Tuesday, the 4th day of December, 1866.

Sale to commence at 10 o'clock.

Full particulars in catalogues, to be had at the Auctioneer's Offices, High Street and Belmont, Shrewsbury, three days prior to the sale.

The first advertisement for sale of locomotives and other equipment, published in *Eddowes's Shrewsbury Journal* on 28 November 1866.

days for the submission of tenders. The Industrial Railway Society records that only three locomotives, of unknown identity, were sold in December 1866 so maybe the others did not attract adequate bids.

An appeal court hearing in February 1867, Powys v the Shrewsbury & Potteries Junction Railway, over the purchase of land, also produced a ruling relevant to the situation in Shrewsbury; that debentures contained no power of foreclosure, or right to interfere with a railway, or to attach any of its capital or property, they only gave a charge on tolls, and that directors could only mortgage future calls on shares, and surplus land, but not anything necessary to work the traffic (*Eddowes's Journal*, 6 February). The ruling overturned previous judgments and was introduced into law.

The previous situation meant that a disgruntled debenture holder could overturn the will of Parliament, which

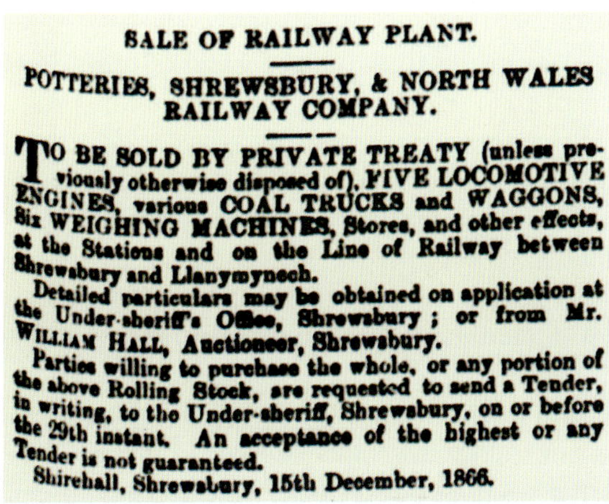

SALE OF RAILWAY PLANT.

POTTERIES, SHREWSBURY, & NORTH WALES RAILWAY COMPANY.

TO BE SOLD BY PRIVATE TREATY (unless previously otherwise disposed of), FIVE LOCOMOTIVE ENGINES, various COAL TRUCKS and WAGGONS, Six WEIGHING MACHINES, Stores, and other effects, at the Stations and on the Line of Railway between Shrewsbury and Llanymynech.

Detailed particulars may be obtained on application at the Under-sheriff's Office, Shrewsbury; or from Mr. WILLIAM HALL, Auctioneer, Shrewsbury.

Parties willing to purchase the whole, or any portion of the above Rolling Stock, are requested to send a Tender, in writing, to the Under-sheriff, Shrewsbury, on or before the 29th instant. An acceptance of the highest or any Tender is not guaranteed.

Shirehall, Shrewsbury, 15th December, 1866.

The second advertisement, placed by the under-sheriff in *Eddowes's Shrewsbury Journal* on 26 December 1866.

was that there should be a railway and that it was in the public interest. Whether the ruling had any influence on the sale advertised earlier is not known. As the Powys estate had brought its claim against a company that no longer existed it was not allowed to continue until it had added the Potteries Railway as a defendant to its suit.

Of services in 1867, the *Wellington Journal* continued to publish timetables showing four trains daily and two on Sundays, until 23 February, which might have been an oversight on the paper's part. From 2 March it published a blank grid. By the end of the year the railway had made the news just twice.

According to the *Shrewsbury Chronicle* (12 April 1867), the prosecution of Lydia Hughes, Robert Hughes and Thomas Williams at Llanymynech was for the theft of timber and other goods belonging to France from the 'Potteries … Extension Railway', presumably from the Llanyblodwel branch. The Hughes were mother and son and both pleaded guilty. Explaining that one of her children had died recently and another had diphtheria, her solicitor, supported by Chandler, representing France, asked for leniency and the case against her was dismissed. Her son, however, was sentenced to 21 days' hard labour in Montgomery gaol to set an example, but the evidence against Williams was inconclusive and the charge against him was also dismissed. Robert Hughes must have surely felt that the outcome would have been different if the case against Williams had been heard first.

On 9 November 1867 the *Cambrian News* had reported that a 'large gang of men' was employed on repairing the railway but that no date for reopening had been announced. The directors did not offer any explanation for this activity at their half-yearly meetings.

There was a train at Nantmawr on 19 December 1867, when guard Richard Dodgson, aged 29, fell off the brake van while trying to uncouple it while the train was moving and was killed. No reports have been found in local newspapers (*Morning Herald*, 23 December). The report did not say if the train was collecting stone for commercial purposes or for use on railway maintenance. The verdict was 'accidental death'.

The notice published of intention to apply for further powers on 13 November (*London Gazette*, 29 November 1867) did explain that there was activity on the line to Market Drayton near Underdale Lane in Shrewsbury, where the route to Abbey Foregate was intended to be altered. Ashdown had signed an estimate for a double-track 'substituted railway' 4f 6.30ch long, partly in cutting and partly on embankment that would have required four bridges. This replaced railway No 4 that had been authorised by the Potteries Junction Railway's (Deviations) Act in 1866 and part of railway No 3 that had been authorised by that railway's 1865 Act. There were no objections, so the Act received the royal assent on 25 June 1868.

In addition to the changes required, the Act defined the route by which the Potteries Railway should cross the 'Shrewsbury and Birmingham railway of the London & North Western and Great Western Railways Companies' using a single-span girder bridge of not less than 45ft width 'measured on the square', with a clear headway of not less than 15ft. Despite the lack of objection, the railway did not obtain the permission sought to extend the line in the time available to exercise compulsory purchase powers granted in the West Shropshire Mineral Railway's (New Lines) Act in 1864 in respect of two properties in Llanyblodwel.

The year 1868 was mostly one of legal matters, mainly those required to reach a settlement with creditors. To achieve this the company took advantage of the Railway Companies Act, 1867, where article 6 provided for railways unable to 'meet their engagements' with creditors to make a 'scheme of arrangement' with them that defined the rights of shareholders and the terms for raising any further capital that might be required. The Potteries scheme was published on 28 January,

Potteries, Shrewsbury & North Wales Railway 1868 proposals. (Parliamentary Archives)

confirmed on 9 May and enrolled on 13 July.

It made provisions for 'raising a sum of money not exceeding £70,000 by debenture stock, for the completion of certain portions of the company's undertaking and the payment of certain liabilities of the company, for converting the mortgage debt … into debenture stock, and for the issue of £60,000 in ordinary shares and of £19,800 in debenture stock, in satisfaction of certain other liabilities of the company, for the issue of a further sum in debenture stock in satisfaction of other liabilities of the company and for raising £200,000 ... for the construction and completion of other portions of the company's undertaking.' The existing debentures, totalling £314,990, were classified 'B'; the £70,000 of new debentures were classified 'A', and the £200,000 of new debentures were classified 'C', £135,000 of which were issued. A total of £151,800 ordinary shares authorised by the Potteries Junction Railway's 1865 act remained unissued, and were cancelled.

Schemes for the Mid Wales and Mold & Denbigh Junction Railway, both of which had France as their contractor, were processed on the same dates. The Potteries Railway was chosen by *Railway News* (23 May) to be the first in a series called 'Railways in Difficulties' with most of the feature taken by extracts of the agreement. The third in the series was the Mid Wales Railway.

After the scheme had been published two suits had been started by unpaid landowners. In the first, on 27 February, the railway had taken possession in 1865 but the owner, a Mr Clark, had only recently attempted to eject it, which prompted the judge to say that he had been guilty of great folly in allowing it to be taken before it had been paid for. The railway succeeded in protecting its position with a declaration of the defendant's interest recorded. In the second case the railway was ordered to pay a Mr Marston £895 15s within twenty-eight days (*Morning Advertiser*, 28 February / *London Evening Standard*, 29 February); presumably it was settled after a plot of land in Shrewsbury was sold on 25 September (*Eddowes's Journal*, 12 August), the sale's outcome not being recorded.

In another court hearing on 1 May two bankers sued for £1,193 4s 7d due to them from engineer John Ashdown since 1866 and had sought to obtain it from £1,500 owed to him by the railway. Making no progress under that heading, their barrister argued that surplus land should be identified and sold. The judge agreed with the railway's barrister, who observed that the Land Clauses Act gave ten years to decide if land was surplus and to sell it, when the proceeds would be applied to the railway's general funds (*London Evening Standard*, 2 May).

There could be no doubt that the need to contain costs led to the review of the double-track main line. On 18 September 1868, Chandler informed the Board of Trade that the company intended 'to work a portion of the railway as a single line only' and asked if it needed to be re-inspected as a consequence. On 25 September he was informed that 'the responsibility of working the railway as a single line must rest with the company and that the Board of Trade cannot re-inspect it as their doing so might be held to imply that they approved the conversion of the double line into a single line'.

It would have been thought that the Board would have been interested in the operating procedures to be adopted following the singling at the very least, but in the event the line was altered between Ford and Llanymynech without its involvement.

The line was reopened without a fuss on 14 November 1868, the *Shrewsbury Chronicle* (20 November) referring to it as 'Mr France's Railway' and the 'Shrewsbury and North Wales Railway', and adding that it would be a boon to farmers attending Shrewsbury and Oswestry markets. Cooper, the manager, published a timetable with the same date in the same issue, showing four trains daily and one on Sundays. The connection to the Wellington line was also opened, but not that at Red Hill.

A quantity of railway grease, oil, cotton waste and other materials that might be expected to be required in connection with locomotive operating were sold at auction on 15 December, presumably a fund-raising exercise (*Shrewsbury Chronicle*, 11 December 1868) but the disposal of such materials would not be expected when trains were running.

Two reports from February 1869 refer to the train service though. The *Shropshire Chronicle* published a note complaining about the operation of trains on Sundays on 5 February and on 20 February the *Shrewsbury Chronicle* published a report about the appearance of Henry Taylor at the magistrates' court charged with 'feloniously and maliciously' placing a pair of trolley wheels on the track with intent to derail a train. Evidence was given that the padlock that had secured the wheels had been broken. At the assizes on

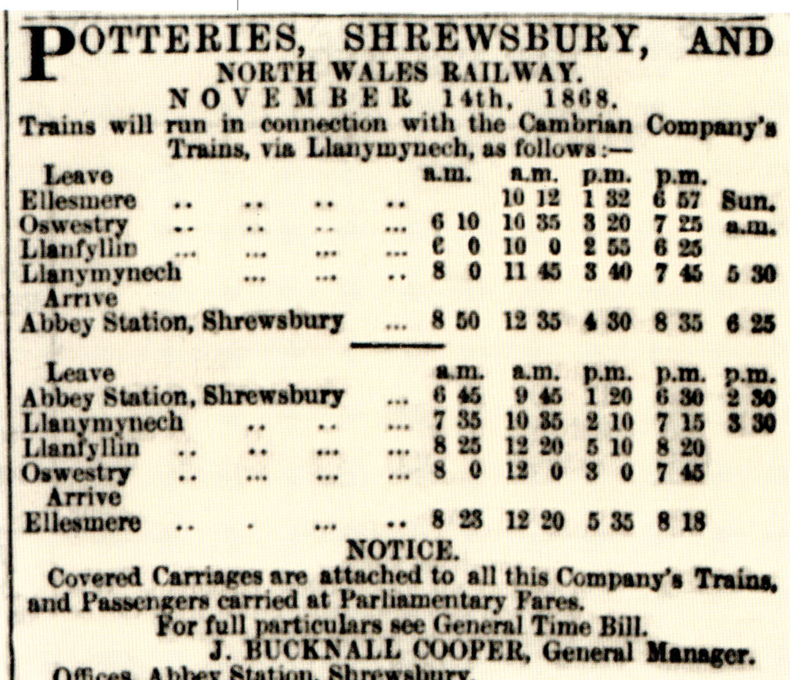
POTTERIES, SHREWSBURY, AND NORTH WALES RAILWAY.
NOVEMBER 14th, 1868.
Trains will run in connection with the Cambrian Company's Trains, via Llanymynech, as follows:—

Leave	a.m.	a.m.	p.m.	p.m.	Sun. a.m.
Ellesmere		10 12	1 32	6 57	
Oswestry	6 10	10 35	3 20	7 25	
Llanfyllin	6 0	10 0	2 55	6 25	
Llanymynech	8 0	11 45	3 40	7 45	5 30
Arrive					
Abbey Station, Shrewsbury ...	8 50	12 35	4 30	8 35	6 25

Leave	a.m.	a.m.	p.m.	p.m.	p.m.
Abbey Station, Shrewsbury ...	6 45	9 45	1 20	6 30	2 30
Llanymynech	7 35	10 35	2 10	7 15	3 30
Llanfyllin	8 25	12 20	5 10	8 20	
Oswestry	8 0	12 0	3 0	7 45	
Arrive					
Ellesmere	8 23	12 20	5 35	8 18	

NOTICE.
Covered Carriages are attached to all this Company's Trains, and Passengers carried at Parliamentary Fares.
For full particulars see General Time Bill.
J. BUCKNALL COOPER, General Manager.
Offices, Abbey Station, Shrewsbury.

Timetable for the resumption of services on 14 November 1868, *Shrewsbury Chronicle*, 20 November.

Llanymynech looking towards Welshpool in 1931, and showing, joining from the left the line from Shrewsbury, and diverging to the right, the line to Llanyblodwel and Nantmawr. (John Scott Morgan Collection)

17 March Taylor said that another boy had told him to put the wheels on the track. His mother, who had previously taken her son to the station to apologise to Cooper, said that he was 12–13 years old; she had seven children alive and had buried six. He was acquitted (*Wellington Journal*, 20 March).

On 25 March it was the railway's turn for a court appearance, charged with non-payment of poor rates amounting to £3 11s 2½d. The company not being represented, the magistrates gave judgment against it (*Liverpool Mercury*, 27 March).

An error of judgement by cowman William Hughes, aged 64, resulted in his death when he was run down by the train from Llanymynech at Llwyntidmon on 3 July 1869. He had been taking a herd of cows across the line when he saw the train, so he closed the first gate, dividing the herd, and crossed the line safely. But when the gate swung open, he was run down when he started to cross back to close it again. At the inquest questions were asked about the liability for maintaining gates. The railway had installed them but was it responsible for their maintenance? The train crew could not answer, and Cooper was not there to answer for the company.

The driver, Samuel Povey (1827–90), said he did not see his engine hit Hughes because his view was obstructed by its tank. After the train had stopped he went with the guard to the point of impact, saying 'I believe we have killed a man.' The jury returned a verdict of accidental death (*Wellington Journal*, 10 July). The death certificate merely said that he had been accidentally killed, without mentioning the circumstances.

At the general meeting on 10 August the chairman, H. P. Burn, congratulated the shareholders on the line being reopened and expressed a wish, forlorn throughout the railway's existence, that the traffic would increase sufficiently to enable the payment of debenture interest.

The company's legal problems were not completely resolved by the scheme of arrangement. On 10 December Philip Minor (1839–87), a local debenture holder, complained to the Chancery Court that while some creditors had been paid, he had not received the debenture interest to which he was entitled. After two days of legal discussion, it was ruled that although he might have had judgment against the

A director from 1862 and chairman from 1865, Major General H. P. Burn was buried in Edinburgh's Greyfriars Kirkyard. His personal estate was valued at £3,860, £368,222 in 2022.

company for the amount of his debenture, the interest, and costs, he was still a debenture holder and could only share in the proceeds of the company with other debenture holders, so he had wasted his money in going to court (Aris's *Birmingham Gazette*, 11 December / *Shrewsbury Chronicle*, 24 December / *Railway News*, 25 December 1869).

Services at the end of 1869 were interrupted when the line was damaged between Shrawardine and Nesscliff by flooding following sustained heavy rain. The Abbey station was also flooded and the passengers of a train that had left for Llanymynech but could go no further than Shrawardine were disembarked in the cutting where the Potteries Junction line passed under the Abbey Foregate, becoming possibly the only passengers to travel on that section of the railway (*Shrewsbury Chronicle / Wellington Journal*, 24 December).

After the hiatus in services, expansion had been triggered on 18 December 1869, Chandler informing the Board of Trade that it was intended to open a further portion of the railway, railways Nos 1 and 3 sanctioned by the West Shropshire Mineral Railway (New Lines) Act in 1864, from Llanymynech to Llanyblodwel, giving notice on 14 March 1870 that the branch would be ready for inspection from 20 March. By this time Julian Horn Tolmé (1836–78), a member of the Institution of Civil Engineers who worked on railways in the UK and in Sweden, had taken over as engineer and he submitted the plans.

Rich reported on 29 March 1870, saying that the lines were single with sidings at each end with land taken for a double track. The two railways were contiguous, from the point where railway No 1 made a junction with the Cambrian Railways about 1,000yd west of Llanymynech station to where railway No 3 ended, for passenger purposes, at Llanyblodwel station. Railway No 3 continued beyond Llanyblodwel for mineral trains only. Railway No 1 was 1m 7ch long and railway No 3 43ch long, the only station being Llanyblodwel.

The track consisted of 70lb double-head rail in 24ft lengths, fishplated and laid in 30lb chairs. The chairs were fixed to transverse sleepers with wrought iron spikes, the half-round sleepers being laid at 3ft intervals. The steepest gradient was 1 in 88 and the sharpest curve, at the Cambrian junction, had a radius of 10ch. The line was well ballasted.

Llanyblodwel station in 1902. The derelict building had been erected under J. H. Tolmé's supervision in 1870. The shed was erected by the Cambrian for the management of the Nantmawr traffic. When the Tanat Valley Light Railway was opened in 1904 the station was renamed Blodwel Junction. (F. E. Fox Davies)

Six overbridges were constructed of brick and stone and a seventh had cast iron girders. The single underbridge had stone piers and a timber deck. There were two timber viaducts that made crossings of the Tanat. The viaduct on railway No 1 had seven 15ft spans and that on railway No 3 had five spans of 20ft. Rich found that the viaduct on railway No 3 was weak in the bearing beams and that there was lateral strain on the piles.

The aqueduct that carried the Montgomeryshire Canal over the railway at Wern consisted of an iron trough carried on wrought iron girders. Its abutments were stone while the centre supports were iron columns. At Llanymynech, the branch made a double junction with the Cambrian, the points and signals being 'arranged on the locking principle'.

Llanyblodwel station, which consisted of a platform and signals was, like the rest of the branch, on a gradient of 1 in 88. The line was double in the station with catch points at the down end leading to a siding. Another trap point beyond the station prevented mineral wagons running through it. The formation beyond the station, to the Nantmawr quarries, was sufficient for just a single track, although Rich did not comment on this feature as it was not intended for passenger use.

Rich required the largest viaduct to be strengthened and Llanyblodwel station to be provided with a booking hut and urinal. The track required 'a little packing and regulating'. He also required undertakings from the company regarding its method of operating the branch and that passenger trains would only be worked by tank engines. He was not yet prepared to sanction its opening for passenger trains.

Tolmé had the viaduct ready for inspection on 7 April. The undertaking that the railway would be worked with tank engines on the 'train staff system' was sealed on 16 April. Following a further inspection, on 23 April the company was notified that the line could be opened for passenger traffic.

The bridge over the Tanat on the Llanyblodwel branch, the photograph showing the additional supports added by Tolmé. (F. E. Fox Davies)

Sometime before 1874, when the 6in Ordnance Survey was made, a siding was laid in to serve the Shropshire Union Canal at Carreghofa. Its installation and use were not recorded in the company's surviving records.

Targeting residents in the Tanat valley, Cooper had already placed advertisements in English and Welsh in the *Oswestry Advertiser* in March, saying that from 1 April there would be through trains to Shrewsbury from Llanyblodwel and reduced return fares available on market days. Connections would also be made with Cambrian trains at Llanymynech.

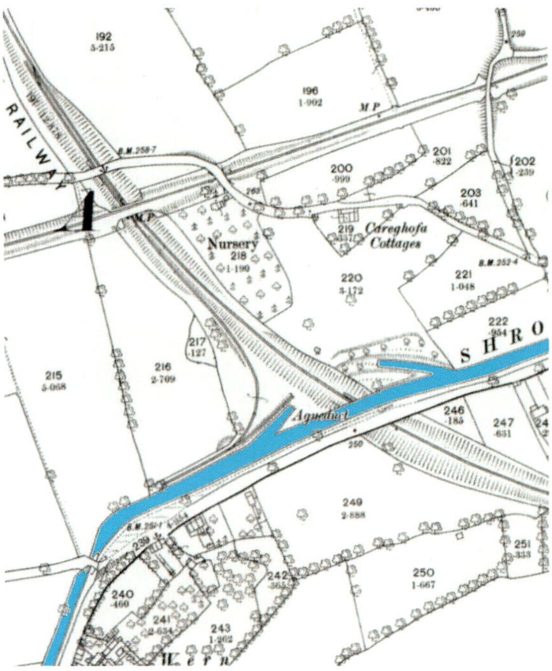

The 25in Ordnance Survey showing the siding, the existence of which is not otherwise recorded, that served the Shropshire Union Canal at Carreghofa. (Ordnance Survey)

POTTERIES, SHREWSBURY, AND NORTH WALES RAILWAY.

NOTICE.

THE Inhabitants of LLANGYNOG, LLANRHAIADR, LLANGEDWYN, and Neighbourhood, are respectfully informed that this Company's Railway is expected to be opened for Passenger, Goods, and Mineral Traffic to LLANYBLODWEL, on April 1st, 1870, when a Through Service of Trains will run to Shrewsbury and in connection with the Cambrian Company's Trains at Llanmynech.

Special Return Tickets will be issued on Market Days, at Cheap Fares.

For full particulars see the published Time Bills, or apply to

J. BUCKNALL COOPER,
General Manager.

Abbey Station, Shrewsbury, March 19th, 1870.

RHEILFFORDD Y POTTERIES, AMWYTHIG, A GOGLEDD CYMRU.

RHYBUDD.

RHODDIR yma hysbysrwydd i Drigolion LLANGYNOG, LLANRHAIADR, LLANGEDWYN, a'r Gymydogaeth, y disgwylir y bydd i Reilffordd y cwmni uchod gael ei hagor i deithwyr, ac i gludo nwyddau a mwnau, i LANYBLODWEL, ar y Dydd Cyntaf o Ebrill, 1870, pan y rhedir trens drwodd i'r Amwythig, ac mewn cysylltiad a threns cwmni y Cambrian yn Llanymynech.

Ceir Tocynau rhad i fyned yn ol a blaen ar Ddyddiau Marchnad.

Am fanylion pellach edrycher y Time Bills, neu ymofyner a

J. BUCKNALL COOPER,
Arolygydd Cyffredinol.

Prif Swyddfa, Abbey Station, Amwythig.

A bilingual notice advertising the opening of the Llanyblodwel branch on 1 April 1870, which was deferred, published in the *Oswestry Advertiser* on 30 March.

POTTERIES, SHREWSBURY AND NORTH WALES RAILWAY.

THE PUBLIC are respectfully informed that this Company's Railway from Llanyblodwel to Llanymynech will be opened for Passenger Traffic on Monday, April 18th, 1870.

Passengers will be carried during the week from Llanyblodwel to Shrewsbury and back for TWO SHILLINGS EACH.

For full particulars see Time Bill.

J. BUCKNALL COOPER.

Office, Shrewsbury, April 14th, 1870.

POTTERIES, SHREWSBURY, AND NORTH WALES RAILWAY.

LLANYBLODWEL BRANCH.

ON and after MONDAY, April 18th, 1870, Trains will run as follows :—

UP TRAINS. — Week Days. — Fares.

	a.m.	a.m.	p.m.	p.m.	1st. s. d.	2nd. s. d.	Gov. s. d.
Leave Llanyblodwel	7 25	10 25	4 5	7 10	—	—	—
Llanymynech ar	7 35	10 35	4 15	7 20	0 5	0 4	0 2½
Oswestry	8 0	12 0	4 28	7 40	1 8	1 4	0 8
Ellesmere	8 23	12 20	5 8	8 8	3 2	2 4	1 3½
Whitchurch	8 50	12 50	5 32	8 32	5 5	3 10	2 2½
Welshpool	—	11 15	5 0	8 8	2 5	2 0	1 0
Maesbrook	8 7	11 2	4 47	7 52	0 10	0 7	0 4½
Kinnerley	8*15	11 10	4 55	8 0	1 3	0 11	0 6½
Nescliff	8 20	11 15	5 0	8 5	1 8	1 2	0 9
Shrawardine	8 25	11 20	5 5	8 10	2 0	1 5	0 11
Cross Gates	8 30	11 25	5 10	8 15	2 5	1 8	1 1
Hanwood-road	8 45	11 35	5 20	8 25	3 1	2 1	1 4
Red Hill	8 50	11 40	5 25	8 30	3 8	2 2	1 5
Shrewsbury	9 0	11 50	5 35	8 40	3 11	2 10	1 8½

DOWN TRAINS.

	a.m.	a.m.	p.m.	p.m.
Leave Shrewsbury (Abbey station)	6 35	9 35	3 20	6 20
Redhill	6 45	9 45	3 30	6 30
Hanwood-road	6*48	9 48	3 33	6 35
Cross Gates	6 55	9 55	3 40	6 40
Shrawardine	7 2	10 2	3 47	6 47
Nescliff	7 10	10 10	3 55	6 55
Kinnerley	7 15	10 15	4 0	7 0
Maesbrook	7 25	10 25	4 5	7 5
Welshpool	7 10	—	3 55	6 55
Whitchurch	—	9 45	1 12	6 30
Ellesmere	—	10 12	1 39	6 57
Oswestry	6 10	10 35	4 15	7 25
Llanymynech	7 50	11 0	4 35	7 45
Arrive Llanyblodwel	8 0	11 10	4 45	7 55

On Fair Days and Market Days Return Tickets will be issued at following Fares :—

	s.	d.
Llanyblodwel to Shrewsbury	2	0
Oswestry	1	1
Welshpool	1	6

* This Train runs between Shrewsbury and Llanymynech on Tuesday (the Salop Fair Day), Wednesdays and Saturdays only.

For full particulars see General Time Bills.

J. BUCKNALL COOPER,

Offices, Shrewsbury. General Manager.

The branch actually opened on 18 April, as advertised in the same paper on 20 April.

MR. WRIGHT

BEGS to inform the Public that a COACH runs every Week-day in connection with the Trains of the Potteries, Shrewsbury, and North Wales Railway Company, at Llanyblodwel, as follows :—

		a.m.	p.m.
Leave	Llanrhaiadr	9 0	6 0
	Llangedwyn	10 0	6 50
Arriving	Llanyblodwel	10 30	7 20
Trains arrive at—			
	Oswestry	12 0	7 40
	Shrewsbury	11 50	8 35
	Welshpool	11 15	8 8
Passengers by Trains—			
Leaving	Shrewsbury (Abbey Station)	9 30	6 15
	Welshpool	7 10	6 55
	Oswestry	...	7 25
Arrive at	Llanyblodwel	10 45	7 30
Coach arrives at—			
	Llangedwyn	11 15	8 0
	Llanrhaiadr	12 0	8 45

FARES:

Llanyblodwel to Llanrhaiadr .... 1s. 6d.

„ Llangedwyn.................... 1s.

Parcels will be carried to and from the Railway Station, and forwarded to all parts of the Kingdom.

The enterprising Mr Wright ran a coach service connecting with the Llanyblodwel train, which he promoted in the *Oswestry Advertiser*, 18 May 1870.

POTTERIES, SHREWSBURY, AND NORTH WALES RAILWAY.

EXCURSION AND PIC-NIC SEASON, 1870.

ON and after Monday, May 9th, 1870, the following arrangements will come into operation :—RETURN DAY TICKETS will be issued at SHREWSBURY, Red Hill, and Hanwood Road, to

	First Class.		Cov. Cars.
Nesscliff	1s. 6d.	......	9d.
Llanymynech .... } Llanyblodwell .... }	2s.	......	1s.

Special arrangements can be made to convey parties to Llangedwyn, or the famous WATERFALL of PISTYL RHAIDR, by Coach, from Llanyblodwell, at exceedingly LOW FARES.

The power of refusing these Tickets is reserved, as it is intended they should be available only to pleasure parties.

☞ Special arrangements can be made for Societies, Institutions, and Schools.

J. BUCKNALL COOPER,

Shrewsbury, May 4th, 1870. General Manager.

POTTERIES, SHREWSBURY, & NORTH WALES RAILWAY.

FOR the convenience of persons attending Markets, special arrangements have been made, and RETURN DAY TICKETS are issued at the LLANYBLODWELL STATION as follows :—

SHREWSBURY MARKET.

(On Wednesdays, Saturdays, and Fair Days).

To Abbey Station & back 2s.

The Company's Waggon meets the Trains, and Baskets containing Butter, Poultry, &c., are delivered into the Market at a small charge.

On Mondays to WELSHPOOL & Back... 1s. 6d.

On Wednesdays to OSWESTRY & Back 1s. 1d.

Goods, Cattle, and Minerals will be received at the Llanyblodwell Station, and can be forwarded to any part of the kingdom.

Residents desiring to have their Goods sent to Llanyblodwell should consign them to Shrewsbury, thence per Potteries, Shrewsbury, and North Wales Railway.

For further particulars apply to the Station Master, or to

J. BUCKNALL COOPER, General Manager.

Offices, Abbey Station, Shrewsbury.

Manager J. B. Cooper saw the Llanyblodwel branch as an opportunity to promote excursions to the Tanat valley and market day services for farmers in *Eddowes's Shrewsbury Journal*, 25 May 1870.

However, as further advertisements were placed from 20 April (*Oswestry Advertiser*) giving 18 April as the first date, it appears that the company had confidence to proceed before receiving the Board of Trade's notice.

Evidently not one to miss an opportunity, over the next few weeks Cooper placed more advertisements, promoting half-fare return tickets for members of the South Shropshire Yeomanry in uniform and picnic excursions for groups (*Oswestry Advertiser*, 11/18 May). A Good Friday excursion to Llanymynech that had required several trains to accommodate all the passengers offering, and Cooper's part in it, had been the subject of a brief complimentary report in *Eddowes's Journal* on 20 April.

During 1870 there were four reported incidents that had affected the railway that were beyond its control. On 3 January 1870 Samuel Hilditch, a former teacher aged 50, and so well known in the area that the *Oswestry Advertiser* (12 January) named him in its headline, had placed a rail chair on the track. Fortunately, it was seen and removed before the train arrived. He said that he had done it because the railway went through a relative's land and had not paid for it. At the assizes Chandler said that he had known Hilditch for twenty years and in his opinion, he was not fit to plead. The judge agreed and Hilditch was ordered to be detained at Her Majesty's pleasure. Removed to the county asylum, he was released nearly seven years later. He died in Holloway's sanatorium in Virginia Water, Surrey, on 2 July 1899, leaving assets valued at £700 11s 3d for his nephew, John Edgerley Hilditch, a barrister, to administer.

Secondly, Henry Williams, 'a lad', was charged with throwing stones at a locomotive passing through the Bell cutting on the Potteries Junction section on 3 September. He failed to attend the magistrates court and was fined 10s with 8s 6d costs (*Shrewsbury Chronicle*, 16 September).

Thirdly, on 4 October William Humphreys, an eccentric-looking individual (*Shrewsbury Chronicle*, 14 October), was seen pasting posters on one of the railway's bridges. Chandler said that had they been posters 'of an ordinary character' then an apology would have sufficed, with no proceedings taken, but these 'reflected on the character of an ordinary person'. Humphreys defended himself with a 'rambling speech, delivered in an impudent tone' that cost him a £3 fine, 6d damages and costs, or two months' imprisonment.

Lastly, James Probert, aged six, lived near Nantmawr sidings and died of his injuries after he had fallen from a wagon being shunted and run over on 1 November 1870. He had been in the habit of playing on the sidings and the shunters had done nothing to stop him climbing on the wagons. His mother said she had not seen him go out. Returning a verdict of accidental death, the jury censured his mother for not sending him to school and the shunters for allowing him to get on the wagon.

In contrast a Harry Evans was fined 13s 4d on each charge of travelling without a ticket and assaulting Ford station master George Horner and Beriah Barrow on 21 October (*Shrewsbury Chronicle*, 4 November), so that became an expensive journey for him.

There was excitement in Shrewsbury on 12 November 1870, when a train of twenty-five loaded wagons lost its grip on ice that coated the rails on the incline to the station, word going round the town that it had gone through the stop blocks and crossed Abbey Foregate. In fact, the stop blocks had done their work, although some carriages were damaged and two wagons forced onto the platform (*Eddowes's Journal*, 16 November).

Compared with the Llanyblodwel branch, opening the Breidden branch for passengers was nowhere near as straightforward. The saga had started on 28 May 1870, when Chandler again informed the Board of Trade that the directors intended to open a further portion of the railway, 'the Breidden branch, described as railway No 1 in the West Shropshire Mineral Railway (Branches etc.) Act 1864'. A second notice on 21 October stated that the line would be ready for inspection from 24 October and Tolmé submitted the plans.

Rich reported from Chester on 29 October. The branch was, he said, 5m 11ch long and single throughout, with sidings. The track was the same as that used elsewhere on the railway, with broken stone used for ballast. The track required lifting and regulating and the ballast was too large.

There were two bridges, one with stone abutments and seven brick arches, the other also with stone abutments but with a timber deck. There were two underbridges, one of timber, the other also with stone abutments and a timber deck.

Rich described three timber viaducts, the largest with seven 38ft spans; the others had two and three spans respectively.

There were four level crossings over public roads, one of which had not been authorised. Local landowners had petitioned for a bridge but Rich thought that as the road crossing 'appears to be of small importance' it should be retained. The keeper lived nearby, and the company would build a lodge if the crossing was approved.

Another crossing that had been authorised did not, in Rich's opinion, cross a public road. The road served only a field and the gates had been locked against it for four or five years without any objection being made. The other crossings were satisfactory, and he noted that they were provided with 'good houses for the gate keepers'.

Stations were located at Melverley, Crew Green, Llandrinio Road and Criggion. 'They are incomplete and require clocks, well-constructed platforms, shelter and booking offices …' The junction at Kinnerley needed an independent platform and signals to control sidings in the vicinity, which needed to be interlocked with the junction signals. The company had told him that it proposed to work the branch with one tank engine in steam. He was concerned about the branch's susceptibility to flooding, and advised the company to plan for such an eventuality to prevent accidents.

Due to the incompleteness of the work, he concluded that the branch could not be opened for passengers. The Board of Trade would not accept the recommendation to accept the unauthorised crossing and required the company to seek Parliamentary approval within twelve months. The opening was therefore postponed for one month.

The company apparently did not attach any urgency to the requirements, for when Rich returned on 29 November, he found that none of the works had been done. On receiving the second notification that the branch could not be opened to passengers Chandler withdrew the application.

He resubmitted the application on 15 May 1871 and Rich returned a week later, finding the platform at Kinnerley too short, the signalling works not done, a check rail still needed for the loading dock siding, a handrail required on an underbridge to prevent passengers from leaving a train there when the platform was extended, and the other platforms and the track and ballast still deficient. Crew Green station required a gate on its access path and a handrail on the underbridge, and a tree that obscured the view of the Llandrinio Road distant signal needed to be cut down. He restated the requirement for the company to make an undertaking concerning the unauthorised level crossing and asked for a formal undertaking concerning the proposed method of working.

Apparently undeterred by this third rejection, on 7 June Chandler requested further copies of the printed form required to request an inspection. The request was made, the inspection undertaken and on 17 June Rich reported that the works had been completed, recommending that the branch be opened for passenger traffic providing the company gave undertakings concerning the crossing, to work passenger trains with a tank engine, not to use the junction at Kinnerley for passenger traffic, and to work it on the train staff principle with only one engine in steam, or two engines coupled together. The undertaking was sealed on 11 July and on 18 July 1871 the Board of Trade gave its approval for the branch to be opened to passenger traffic.

The company did not wait for the paperwork to be completed, for the branch had been opened on 21 June (*Eddowes's Journal*, 21 June). The timetable published in the same newspaper showed four trains daily and an extra one on Wednesdays.

The only explanation that can be offered for the delay in dealing with Rich's requests is that there was something of a hiatus between J. B. Cooper's departure and Elijah Elias' appointment in March 1871 to replace him (*Shrewsbury Chronicle*, 10 March). The former had resigned because his Stafford & Uttoxeter duties had increased; he remained in Shrewsbury until 1875, when he took up the appointment

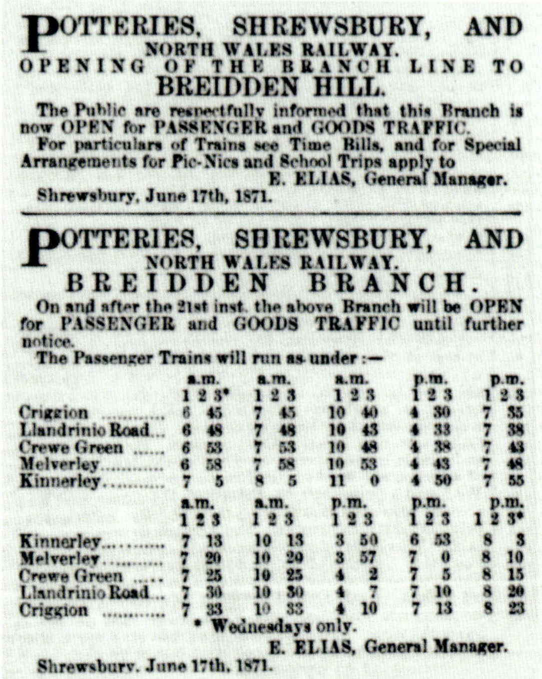

POTTERIES, SHREWSBURY, AND NORTH WALES RAILWAY.

OPENING OF THE BRANCH LINE TO BREIDDEN HILL.

The Public are respectfully informed that this Branch is now OPEN for PASSENGER and GOODS TRAFFIC.

For particulars of Trains see Time Bills, and for Special Arrangements for Pic-Nics and School Trips apply to

E. ELIAS, General Manager.

Shrewsbury, June 17th, 1871.

POTTERIES, SHREWSBURY, AND NORTH WALES RAILWAY.

BREIDDEN BRANCH.

On and after the 21st inst. the above Branch will be OPEN for PASSENGER and GOODS TRAFFIC until further notice.

The Passenger Trains will run as under :—

	a.m. 1 2 3*	a.m. 1 2 3	a.m. 1 2 3	p.m. 1 2 3	p.m. 1 2 3
Criggion	6 45	7 45	10 40	4 30	7 35
Llandrinio Road...	6 48	7 48	10 43	4 33	7 38
Crewe Green	6 53	7 53	10 48	4 38	7 43
Melverley............	6 58	7 58	10 53	4 43	7 48
Kinnerley...........	7 5	8 5	11 0	4 50	7 55

	a.m. 1 2 3	a.m. 1 2 3	p.m. 1 2 3	p.m. 1 2 3	p.m. 1 2 3*
Kinnerley...........	7 13	10 13	3 50	6 53	8 3
Melverley............	7 20	10 20	3 57	7 0	8 10
Crewe Green	7 25	10 25	4 2	7 5	8 15
Llandrinio Road...	7 30	10 30	4 7	7 10	8 20
Criggion	7 33	10 33	4 10	7 13	8 23

* Wednesdays only.

E. ELIAS, General Manager.

Shrewsbury, June 17th, 1871.

An advertisement for the opening of the Briedden branch from the *Shrewsbury Chronicle*, 23 June 1871.

J. B. Cooper retired to Belfast – some of his children had stayed there when he returned to England – and was buried in Carnmoney cemetery. He died intestate. (Robert Phipps)

of manager of the Belfast Central Railway, another double appointment that he held alongside that of consulting manager of the Neath & Brecon Railway. Bankrupt in1892, when he was secretary and manager of the Felixstowe Dock & Railway Company, he attributed his poor financial situation to having a large family, fourteen children, and the loss of £500 on a house that he had had built (*East Anglian Times*, 28 March 1892). He died in Belfast in 1910.

Elias, born in Llanidloes in 1824, had been the Cambrian Railways' traffic manager from 1866 until July 1870, resigning when he had been accused of carrying Thomas Savin's stone traffic at a loss, so this post was a fortunate opportunity for him. The earliest indication of his engagement with the railway is a public notice about train times that he signed on 20 March. In 1873 he signed the directors' half-yearly report to say that the railway's structures and plant, including locomotives, had been maintained in good condition (*Birmingham Daily Post*, 9 August) despite, on the face of it, not being qualified to do so.

The *Shrewsbury Chronicle* (23 June 1871) credited him with bringing the Breidden branch up to passenger-carrying standards. In the half-yearly report, the directors said that they expected the company to benefit from his local knowledge and would soon be paying interest (*Birmingham Daily Gazette*, 9 August). He would, of course, be concentrating his efforts on their railway and not sharing them with another.

At the half-yearly meeting held on 21 February, incidentally, Tolmé had reported that 'station buildings on the main line had been erected where ordered … and opened as completed', which implies that for nearly five years there had been no shelter at all or most of the intermediate stations.

France maintained his connection with the railway despite his financial difficulties, entering into an agreement with it concerning the use of the Nantmawr branch and the quarry incline on 22 January 1872. So long as he leased 'certain quarries called Nantmawr rocks', he was to work the incline. The railway was to supply a weighbridge and additional rails to enable the incline to be widened.

The remainder of the double track, between Shrewsbury and Ford, became an issue in July 1872. Apparently oblivious to the background, on 23 July Elias had visited Rich to seek advice on the procedure to be adopted to single it. The next day, acknowledging a letter from Rich, he asked whether the railway should first submit plans for approval or whether it should have the work done and then request an inspection. Rich's letter was not retained but it seems likely that he had either not been available to see Elias or had refused to see him without an appointment.

Rich, who seems to have forgotten what had happened in 1868, and who did not read the file, sought advice from the Board of Trade's secretary, being advised that as a company could 'shut up a line entirely they can therefore, I imagine, convert a double line to a single one'. Plans were requested.

Chandler, who also seems to have forgotten the correspondence that he had conducted on the same subject in 1868, gave notice of intention to proceed on 6 August 1872, saying that it was intended to work the proposed single line with the 'train staff system' and explaining that changes were intended to be made at Shrewsbury, Red Hill, Hanwood Road and Ford, but not submitting the formal second notice to request an inspection until 30 September 1873. Rich was unavailable so Colonel William Yolland (1810–85) was deputed to make it. He submitted his report from Shrewsbury on 8 October 1873.

Noting that the line beyond Ford 'has long since been converted into, and worked as a single line' he explained that as there were only three passenger trains and two goods trains in each direction each day, 'there is no doubt that all the traffic can be safely worked on a single line'. However, he added: 'But the working of the traffic on a single, instead of on a double line, is attended with increased risk to the public', requiring the company to undertake to work the traffic on the absolute block

J. H. Tolmé was the railway's engineer for a few years from around 1869. His estate worth less than £100, he was buried with other family members in London's Highgate Cemetery.

system combined with the train staff and ticket system.

On the ground, Yolland required a down home signal to be placed on the line from Wellington in advance of the fouling points at Abbey junction and opposite the home signal for the Abbey branch, the said home signal to be fully interlocked with others in the locality. One of the facing point switches was 'in a bad state' and needed to be replaced.

Perceiving that the railway did not intend to keep men stationed at Red Hill and Hanwood Road, he required sidings there that connected to the single line to be interlocked with the up and down signals so that nothing might leave the single line or the sidings except when the signals were at danger.

A passing loop at Ford was about 100yd long; facing points at each end were required to be interlocked by the respective distant signals, and the signals with each other. Declaring that the works were incomplete, Yolland declined to

Verdant Shropshire seen from the site of Nantmawr quarry.

approve the working of the line between Shrewsbury and Ford as a single line.

This left the railway in a quandary. It had converted its line and continued to work its traffic, yet the Board of Trade would not sanction its use by passenger trains. John Wade, on Chandler's behalf, wrote on 14 October to say that he was instructed to state that the company was prepared to give an undertaking to comply with Yolland's requirements 'as expeditiously as possible'. In the meantime, he asked 'whether the company is to discontinue to carry passengers until these works are completed or whether the Board of Trade will be satisfied with the undertaking above mentioned'.

The Board was prepared to be flexible and replied that it was prepared to sanction the working of the single line on receipt of a sealed undertaking and providing that Yolland's requirements were carried out expeditiously and that he be permitted to make another inspection. In the meantime, the company was to take every precaution to prevent accidents.

The railway's London solicitors submitted the undertaking on 31 October and, beyond acknowledging its receipt, the Board, judging by the lack of correspondence in its files, and the railway both appeared to forget about the matter. It does seem rather strange that the Board overlooked the previous correspondence concerning the double track and that Yolland was unaware that it had not been inspected. While it can be no surprise that Elias was ignorant of the earlier change as he had only been recently appointed, Chandler ought to have had access to the previous correspondence, to which he should have referred.

With or without approval, from that time the main line was operated as a single-track line, with passing loops at Ford, Shrawardine, Kinnerley and Llanymynech. The second platform at stations without loops was soon demolished.

Although Rich had not been able to inspect the new single line, he had been in Shrewsbury during the year, investigating an accident that had occurred at Hanwood Road station on 21 May, where the recent track works might have played a part. The mixed train included a Cambrian cattle wagon carrying a litter of pigs. Arriving at Hanwood Road from the Llanymynech direction, the driver overshot before stopping but did not set back because there were no passengers boarding or alighting. Three vehicles derailed when the train restarted, the cattle wagon turning on its side. Rich concluded that the combination of the 1 in 100 gradient and the curvature caused the wagons to become buffer locked when the train had stopped suddenly. He did not comment on the track but perhaps he did not visit the site. The piglets were unhurt (*Wrexham Advertiser*, 24 May 1873).

CHAPTER 3

RECEIVERSHIP AND ABANDONMENT

The London Finance Association, which had put up money for the railway's construction and held debentures as surety, had had it put into receivership on 30 January 1873, presumably because the debenture interest remained unpaid. John Wade was appointed receiver, responsible for day-to-day control of revenue and expenditure, and the line was operated under the direction of the court. The receivership escaped the attention of the press.

It does seem remarkable that the directors did not comment on this loss of control in their reports. At the general meeting held on 20 February shareholders were told that the company was 'expending a large amount on the permanent way and rolling stock', and that the balance would have been greater 'had it not been for the price of coals'. Wade said, incidentally, in his affidavit to Parliament in 1881, that he did not publish reports during the receivership. That for the second half of 1878, the last one produced by the company, bears his printed signature.

Wade's accounts are held in the National Archives and reference is made to certain entries elsewhere; some entries can be mentioned here: payments totalling £66 13s 4d annually to the Mid Wales Railway Co., rental for an office; £20 paid for a (very

Abbey station c.1879. The Abbey pulpit is on the left.

expensive) cow killed on the railway, and, on 11 November, £10 (£842 in 2022) to the Reverend J. Luxmore, a donation for the widow Jeffreys.

Edwin Jeffreys, a quarryman aged 33, had been killed when crossing the line at Nantmawr on 4 October 1873 (*Wrexham Advertiser*, 11 October), the cause of death being registered as 'accidentally killed'. He was buried in the churchyard of St Agatha's in Llanymynech, his grave unmarked. His widow, Mary, was left with four children aged 3 to 11 to care for and was two months pregnant with her fifth child when her husband was killed. She cannot be found in the 1881 or subsequent censuses and the child spent his tenth birthday in Llanfyllin workhouse. His brother, also Edwin, became the keeper of Llanymynech's Sun Inn, adjacent to the shop kept by the Fox Davies family (P15).

The railway's relationship with its creator, R. S. France, was not an easy one. It appears that the construction activities east of Shrewsbury, including a crossing of the Severn, had been started on his own initiative. When he sought further funding from the financiers responsible for most

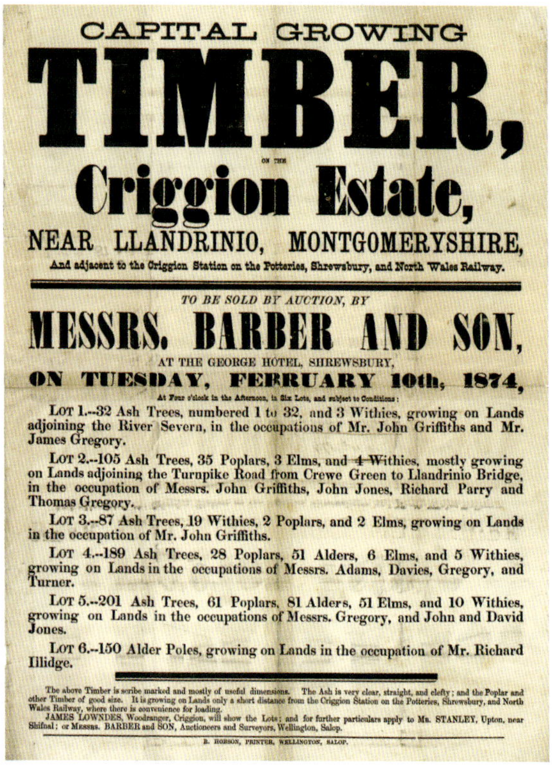

Auctioneers and estate agents often referred to the railway's proximity in their advertising. This 1874 poster is for timber to be felled near Criggion station.

of the railway's capital, they, possibly conscious of the railway's parlous financial position, refused, leading him to threaten to withdraw the Nantmawr stone traffic.

According to J. B. Cooper, speaking in Parliament in 1888, France had carried out his threat in 1872, routing his stone via the Cambrian at Llanymynech, although Cooper said that when he did send his traffic over the railway he did so inconsistently, 1,000 tons one week, nothing the next.

Looking at the traffic returns it is difficult to identify the effect of France's behaviour on the business. Revenue from mineral traffic rose each year until 1874, when it dropped back by some £2,500, peaking at £6,966 in 1875. The peaks and troughs of tonnage carried match those of revenue when it might be expected that if France's traffic was being carried only to Llanymynech the tonnage would remain the same, or similar, but that the revenue would fall.

Only in 1875, when 126,312 tons of stone were carried, did the correlation between volume and revenue alter, which might be accounted for either by some of it being carried a shorter distance, but goods train mileage was increased by 10,000 during the year, or a reduced rate being chargeable because of the increased volume. The latter seems more likely; the railway would have been some £1,500 better off had the 1874 average rate been charged. The directors attributed the 1874 reduction to the 'unsettled state of affairs in south Staffordshire'. During that year the railway carried 34,000 tons of stone less than it had done the year before, but its goods trains operated 2,000 miles more.

However, stone traffic in 1876 was less than half that of the year before and then fell to less than 20,000 tons in 1877, a poor year for all traffic. Whereas the other traffic recovered to near 'normal' levels in 1878–79, the stone did not, achieving less than 25,000 tons in those years. So, if France's activities did affect the railway it was from 1876, not from 1872. The last payment made to him for working the incline was in May 1876.

Meanwhile, on 6 August 1873 the railway had made a funding agreement with the London Finance Association in respect of an extension from Nantmawr to France's colliery between Treflach and Trefonen, on the outskirts of Oswestry, which included a reversing neck and would have crossed the incline in some way. Where the route crossed France's own land, he was to start work in advance of powers being obtained (*Law Times*, 22 March 1884).

A Bill was deposited for the 1874 Parliamentary session and the resulting Act received the royal assent on 21 May. With an estimated cost of £47,406, the extension would have been 3½ miles long. A steep gradient and a reverse would have made it expensive to work. The £50,000 capital required was to be kept separately as the 'Trefonen extension capital' and the operating receipts and expenses were also to be accounted for separately. An unusual article were the

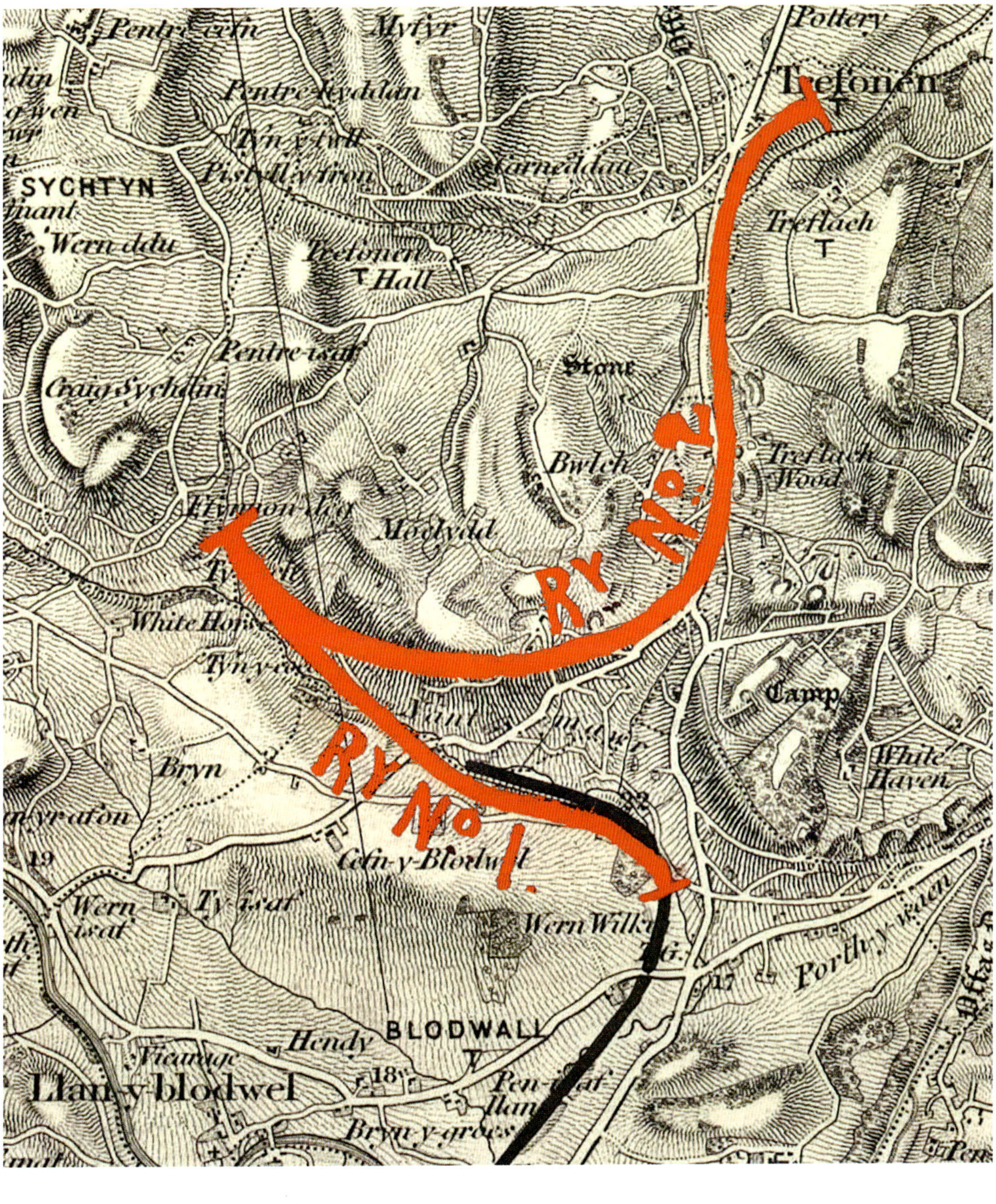

The 1874 plan for an extension to Trefonen. (Parliamentary Archives)

There is no sign of industrial activity in this view of Trefonen, although R. S. France developed a coal mine in the locality.

requirements for the extension to be worked efficiently and for the company to develop the traffic.

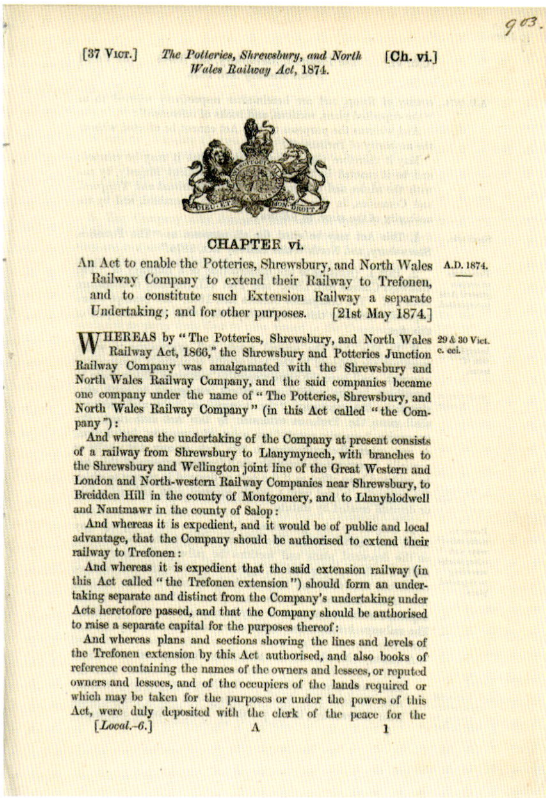

903.

[37 Vict.] *The Potteries, Shrewsbury, and North Wales Railway Act*, 1874. [Ch. vi.]

CHAPTER vi.

An Act to enable the Potteries, Shrewsbury, and North Wales Railway Company to extend their Railway to Trefonen, and to constitute such Extension Railway a separate Undertaking; and for other purposes. [21st May 1874.] A.D. 1874.

WHEREAS by "The Potteries, Shrewsbury, and North Wales Railway Act, 1866," the Shrewsbury and Potteries Junction Railway Company was amalgamated with the Shrewsbury and North Wales Railway Company, and the said companies became one company under the name of "The Potteries, Shrewsbury, and North Wales Railway Company" (in this Act called "the Company"): 29 & 30 Vict. c. cci.

And whereas the undertaking of the Company at present consists of a railway from Shrewsbury to Llanymynech, with branches to the Shrewsbury and Wellington joint line of the Great Western and London and North-western Railway Companies near Shrewsbury, to Breidden Hill in the county of Montgomery, and to Llanyblodwell and Nantmawr in the county of Salop:

And whereas it is expedient, and it would be of public and local advantage, that the Company should be authorised to extend their railway to Trefonen:

And whereas it is expedient that the said extension railway (in this Act called "the Trefonen extension") should form an undertaking separate and distinct from the Company's undertaking under Acts heretofore passed, and that the Company should be authorised to raise a separate capital for the purposes thereof:

And whereas plans and sections showing the lines and levels of the Trefonen extension by this Act authorised, and also books of reference containing the names of the owners and lessees, or reputed owners and lessees, and of the occupiers of the lands required or which may be taken for the purposes or under the powers of this Act, were duly deposited with the clerk of the peace for the

[*Local.-6.*] A 1

The Potteries, Shrewsbury & North Wales Railway Act, 1874, gave legal authority to the Trefonen extension.

France had started to build an embankment and other works, including road diversions, within the extension's limit of deviation on his own land, in the autumn of 1873, the company paying him for the work and having it supervised by its engineer. The work came to an end soon after the Bill became law, but he was not issued with a formal notice to cease work until 1881 (*Law Times*, 22 March 1884).

However, at the committee hearings for the 1881 winding-up Bill, France denied claims that he had done any such work. Saying that the railway had taken no action to exercise its powers under the Act, Wade said that France had altered roads and laid rails without any authority from the company to do so, which contradicts a claim accepted in the 1883 appeal court hearing over the question of compensation for it (*Law Times*, 22 March 1884).

That the railway lacked the resources to maintain its stock properly is implied by a payment of £81 8s 3d to Beyer, Peacock & Co. for 'repairing engines etc.' on 14 July 1873. Payments to the Birmingham Tube Co. for '150 iron tubes', £72 9s, and to T. Turton & Son for 'spring steel for locomotives and wagons', £16 6 9d, give an indication of work that had been carried out. In January and May 1875 the GWR was paid £2 2s 6d for 'repair of locomotive power' and £73 10s for 'engine hire', a regular feature of the accounts. It may not be unconnected that three of the seven locomotives were sold in 1873.

A further indication of poor maintenance is found in the *Wrexham Advertiser* of 21 June, which claimed that a tube burst on one of the engines at Llanymynech on 17 June. As no damage or injuries that would be expected to accompany a burst tube were reported it seems more likely that a fusible plug in the firebox had melted, which could have been caused by poor fitting or allowing the boiler water level to fall too low, and which would have extinguished the fire. Passengers for the 7.32pm departure to Shrewsbury were sent via Buttington.

Elijah Elias' time with the company as manager turned out to be short-lived. No report has been found to explain his leaving, but the *South Wales Daily Telegram* (17 December 1873) announced the appointment of Albert Judd (born 1834) as his successor while regretting his (Judd's) departure from the Monmouthshire Railway, where he had held the post of assistant traffic manager. Elias moved to Birmingham and opened an office as a mineral broker and commission agent (*Star of Gwent*, 23 May 1874), dying in Handsworth on 11 July 1896 (*Wrexham Advertiser*, 11 July).

Before Judd had time to get settled in, one of his passengers expressed his dissatisfaction with two recent journeys on the Breidden branch in *Eddowes's Journal* (7 January 1874). Bound for Criggion, on the first occasion he had arrived at Kinnerley after a journey of 130 miles to be told that the train would only take him as far as Crew Green. A timber crane that had been placed across the line was sufficiently high for the branch engine to pass under it but was too low for the larger locomotive that replaced it when it was out of order. He had to leave his baggage at Kinnerley for later collection and walk, along the track presumably, to his destination.

On the second occasion, he found that the branch train had been abandoned somewhere along the line when the loco had run out of water, so he and the other branch passengers had to wait while the 'big engine' made its way to Llanyblodwel and back, when the Shrewsbury passengers were told that they would have to wait while their train made the return trip to Criggion, the branch passengers reaching their destination at 9.15pm instead of 7.15pm.

The letter writer, who signed himself Sassenach, was also unimpressed with the waiting accommodation provided at Kinnerley, a dark shed with seats round it, no lighting or heating, 'in company with wooden boxes, live geese, humanity in various stages of intoxication, and potato bags'. As Judd had had no time to make his mark on the railway's management, the editor declined to publish another letter complaining about the railway the following week.

Judd had certainly been in post long enough to ensure compliance with foot and mouth disease regulations at Llanymynech on 29 May 1874; fifty infected beasts had been recorded in the Oswestry area. However, the company was fined £5 and 16s 5d costs for carrying cattle in a vehicle that had not been limewashed (*Hour*, 26 June / *Wrexham Advertiser*, 27 June).

The timetable published in *Eddowes's Shrewsbury Journal* on 28 January 1874.

POTTERIES, SHREWSBURY, & NORTH WALES.

WITH THE BREIDDEN BRANCH.

GENERAL STATION: ABBEY FOREGATE, SHREWSBURY.

Mls	STATIONS.	WEEK DAYS.		*				
	Shrewsbury, d.	..	9 30	..	3 10	..	..	6 20
3	Red Hill......	..	9 38	..	3 17	..	..	6 28
4	Hanwood Road	..	9 41	..	3 20	..	..	6 31
7¼	Cross Gates...	..	9 50	..	3 29	..	..	6 40
9¼	Shrawardine..	..	9 58	..	3 36	..	..	6 49
11¼	Nesscliff......	..	10 5	..	3 41	..	We	6 57
13¼	Kinnerley	..	1010	..	3 48	..	only	7 2
	Kinnerley, d	7*18	..	1012	..	3*50	4 55	7*5
	Melverley...	7 25	..	1019	..	3 57	5 2	7 12
	Crewe Green	7 30	..	1024	..	4 2	5 7	7 17
	Llandrinio ..	7 35	..	1029	..	4 7	5 12	7 22
	Criggion, ar.	7 38	..	1032	..	4 10	5 15	7 25
16	Maesbrook ...	..	1015	..	3 53	..	..	7 10
18	Llanymynech, a	..	1020	..	3 58	..	..	7 15
20¼	Llanyblodwil, a	..	1030	..	4 8	..	..	7 24
	Oswestry, ar	..	1155	..	4 24	..	..	9 42

Mls	STATIONS.	WEEK DAYS.			§			SUN
	Oswestry, d.	6 0	..	1030	..	2 48	7 25	..
	Llanyblodwil, d	..	..	1033	..	4‡10	7 28	..
2½	Llanymynech, d	7 50	We	1050	4 5	4 33	7 40	..
4½	Maesbrook ...	7 58	only	1056	4 12	4 40	7 48	‡
	Criggion, de.	7†45	9 45	1040	..	4‡15	7*30	Wed only.
	Llandrinio ..	7 48	9 48	1043	..	4 18	7 33	
	Crewe Green	7 53	9 53	1048	..	4 23	7 38	
	Melverley...	7 58	9 58	1053	..	4 28	7 43	
	Kinnerley, a	8 5	10 5	11 0	..	4 35	7 50	
7	Kinnerley	8 8	..	11 4	4 18	4 46	7 56	
9½	Nesscliff......	8 17	..	1111	4 25	4 53	8 1	..
11	Shrawardine..	8 24	..	1116	4 30	4 58	8 6	..
13¼	Cross Gates...	8 33	..	1124	4 35	5 3	8 11	..
16¼	Hanwood Road	8 46	..	1133	4 45	5 13	8 21	..
17¼	Red Hill......	8 50	..	1136	4 48	5 16	8 25	..
20½	Shrewsbury, ar	9 0	..	1145	4 55	5 23	8 33	..

* Market Trains on Wednesdays and Saturdays only.

† On Saturdays only. ‡ On Wednesdays only. § This train will not run on Wednesdays.

RETURN TICKETS issued at a reduction for the double journey; those of Saturday are available till Monday.

MARKET TICKETS at Cheap Fares to Welshpool on Mondays; Shrewsbury, on Fair Days, Wednesdays, and Saturdays; Oswestry, on Wednesdays; and Llanfyllin on Thursdays.

Criggion quarry terminus, 4 October 1937. (R. K. Cope/John Scott Morgan Collection)

Hecate and its train at Criggion. (John Scott Morgan Collection)

contributed to driver Thomas Hollis, aged 48, being killed when his train was in a collision with three wagons that had run away from Potteries Junction on 16 October 1875. John Ison, the fireman, sustained a broken rib and an injured leg. Inspector F. H. Rich concluded that the accident was caused by 'the want of proper arrangements, such as catch points, at the south end of the Potteries goods yard and neglect of the proper precaution on the part of the second brakeman of the LNWR train for the safety of the wagons' and that, 'The arrangements of the Potteries yard were not subjected to the inspection of a government officer as the yard in question forms a portion of a mineral line which is not used for passenger traffic.'

Although the yard was owned by the Potteries Railway it was also accessible by the GWR and the LNWR, and none of the railways took responsibility for its operation. A supervisor who had been employed by the Potteries Railway in the past had not been replaced after he had left. Tandy, the loco supervisor, gave evidence that the LNWR and GWR effectively controlled the yard, and that their employees became abusive and damaged its wagons if Potteries personnel gave instructions. The inquest jury found that Hollis' death was caused by the reckless conduct of the LNWR employees. Urged to reconsider the use of the word reckless, because it would result in a manslaughter charge, the jury at first declined but was persuaded to substitute the word careless. The inquest had taken seven hours. The cause of death was recorded as 'fracture of skull caused by a collision on the Potteries, Shrewsbury and North Wales Railway'. (*Eddowes's Journal*, 20 October/3 November).

Another accident occurred on 29 December, though fortunately without fatal consequences. A passenger train from Llanymynech to Shrewsbury, left standing opposite Coleham Junction signal box while the cattle trucks it had brought were taken to Potteries Junction, was run into at low speed by a following mineral train that failed to stop, injuring four passengers, all women (*Wellington Journal*, 1 January 1876).

Inspector W. Yolland determined that the collision was the result of the mineral train driver not having brought his train under proper control when approaching the junction. He also established that the distant signal was not working because the signalman had not oiled its mechanism and had also not bothered to light its lamp. The permanent way engineer, though, told him that it was not the custom to use the signal, but admitted that had it been functioning properly the driver might have been prompted to start braking earlier. Commenting that the signalman's hours were too long, Yolland added that it did not appear that the man had any hard work to do. He concluded: 'It is quite useless to recommend that this line should be worked on the block system in addition to the train staff and ticket system. I understand that it does not pay its working expenses and it is evident that the means now provided for working the traffic safely are not made use of.'

Procedural issues mired the Midland Wagon Company's attempt to seize railway assets to recover debt and the railway company's attempt to obtain an injunction to prevent it. The company was already a judgement creditor and should have claimed from the receiver appointed in 1873. For its injunction application, the railway company relied on section 4 of the 1867 Railway Companies Act but the judge ruled that section 5 took precedence in this situation and dismissed the summons, awarding costs to the railway (*Wellington Journal*, 29 April 1876).

Apparently coincidentally, R. S. France's former works, located between the railway's Shrewsbury terminus and the LNWR's Coleham depot, was acquired by the Midland Wagon Company within two months of this hearing. The *Mining Journal* (12 June) reported that the site, which had been empty for some years, was already showing signs of life, with sidings full of wagons, windows and roofs of the buildings repaired and timber and other materials in open storage.

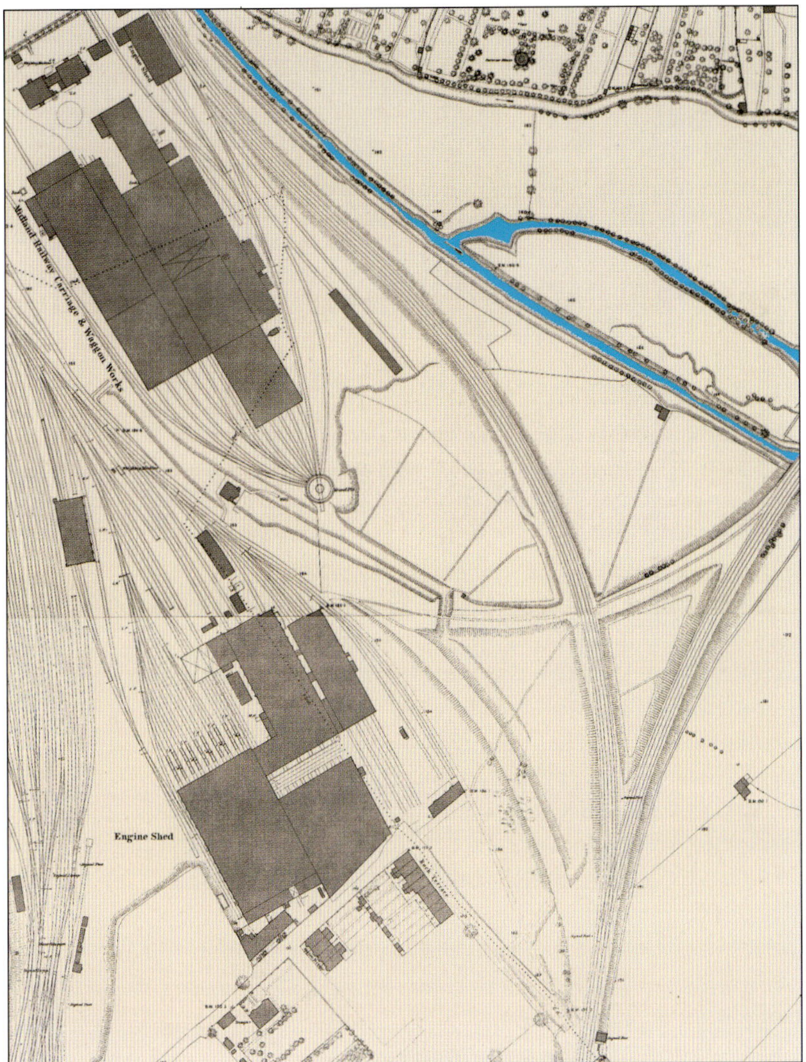

As the years passed, the railway was isolated from its railway neighbours. On 3 June 1876, the GWR and LNWR, which operated the Shrewsbury & Welshpool Railway, running parallel to the railway between Shrewsbury and Red Hill, jointly complained to the Board of Trade about the state of the fence that separated the two railways. Despite its initial opinion that the fence was not its concern, the Board sent Yolland to inspect it. As the line had been opened as recently as 1866, he reported, the fence should still be in good order if it had been sound originally, but the repairs being carried out when he visited would not be cattle-proof, a point he raised with Judd. Later, the GWR and LNWR reported that animals had got onto the Wellington line at Potteries Junction eight times since 1866, seven of them since 1870, and offered to pay for a gated fence to be built, partially on railway land, at Potteries Junction. At some unknown date the Nantmawr branch was also gated near Llanymynech.

Refusing to pay the excess fare for over-riding and assault resulted in three Shropshire militiamen appearing at Oswestry magistrates' court on 26 April 1877. Asked to pay the excess after travelling from Shrewsbury to Maesbrook with Kinnerley tickets, one of them

Above: Extract from the Ordnance Survey 10in map published in 1882, showing the Midland Wagon Works site, previously occupied by R. S. France, and its proximity to the railway, plus the engine shed and turntable.

Right: The wagon works and the spires and towers of Shrewsbury, in the 1950s. (John Scott Morgan Collection)

assaulted William Williams, the station master. He was fined 1s and 8s 9d costs for the fare offence and 5s and 7s 9d for the assault. The others were fined 1s and 8s costs (*Eddowes's Journal*, 2 May).

Farm labourer John Littlehales, aged 75, lost his life walking along the railway at Belle Vue, on the outskirts of Shrewsbury, on 28 August 1879. The driver sounded his whistle but as Littlehales was 'hard of hearing' it had no effect. The inquest jury returned a verdict of 'accidental death' and the cause was recorded as 'accidentally coming into contact with a railway locomotive and train in motion'.

Unhappy at the railway's failure to make a reduction in its indebtedness to them, some of the judgement creditors announced that they intended to call a meeting at which they would reveal how the directors had incurred heavy liabilities despite the appointment of a receiver, appealing for other creditors to make contact. As no report of a meeting has been found, that might imply that there was insufficient support to holding it (*Wellington Journal*, 13 December 1879). The point, it will be seen, is that whatever the creditors thought, the railway did not earn enough to pay its expenses and maintenance.

It must have been apparent to the railway's board and its shareholders from a very early date that the railway was not a viable business. Even in the worst years the majority of its revenue came from stone, yet it did not have the benefit of most mineral railways, a monopoly of the traffic. In the best years the railway was still unable to make a profit, never mind service its considerable debt; by 1875 debenture interest was £168,055 3s 8d in arrears. Of the five locomotives available to the company in 1875, one was hired and three were 'vested in trustees'. Wade recorded monthly payments totalling £14 13s 4d to Brown, Shipley & Co. and £29 6s 8d to the London Finance Association for the hire of the 2-4-0T locomotive *Hope*, which had been new in 1872, the payments ceasing after January 1875.

POTTERIES, SHREWSBURY, AND NORTH WALES RAILWAY.

BREIDDEN, LLANYMYNECH, & NESSCLIFF HILLS.

PARTIES desirous of making EXCURSIONS to these delightful and interesting HILLS can do so by the Trains leaving the Abbey Station at 9·30 a.m. and 3·0 p.m., at the usual Pleasure Party Regulations as to Number and Fares, viz : Six First, or Ten Third-class Passengers.

FARES FOR THE DOUBLE JOURNEY :—

To		1st Class.	CovCars.
BREIDDEN	Available for Wednesdays and Saturdays only.	3s. 0d.	1s. 6d.
LLANYMYNECH		2s. 6d.	1s. 3d.
NESSCLIFF		2s. 0d.	1s. 0d.

A. JUDD, General Manager.

☞ The Scenery of the Breidden is magnificent and beautiful beyond description. There is a very easy ascent from Crewe Green Station to the Belle Isle Inn, situated upon the Plateau between Middletown Hill and Rodney's Pillar, the Proprietor of which will erect a Marquée and provide Refreshments for Visitors at reasonable charges.

Excursion opportunities advertised in the *Wellington Journal* on 24 June 1876. The description of third-class accommodation as 'Cov Cars' is a reference to the earliest days of rail travel and meant that there were no open carriages in the train.

All thirteen carriages and three passenger vans were hired, as were 100 wagons, five covered goods wagons and five cattle trucks, while ten timber trucks, one goods brake van, forty lime wagons and a further 212 wagons were vested in trustees. The purchase lease for carriages, wagons and vans cost £544 6s 8d annually. Wade's accounts show that cattle wagons were hired from the Bishops Castle Railway at an annual cost of £45. The Midland Wagon Co. was paid £374 0s 3d for wagon hire in April 1873, £368 18s 9d on 12 June 1873 and £368 18s 9 on 12 March 1874. As the wagon fleet was not reduced after these payments ceased it may be that ownership was transferred during 1874. In 1879 £2 was paid to the LNWR for the hire of a carriage.

According to the railway's returns to the Board of Trade, a locomotive was disposed of during each of the three years from 1873 and the carriage fleet was reduced by five vehicles in 1877. After the stone traffic collapsed in 1876 trains were run mixed, but the all-round reduction in expenses that followed still did not bring the railway to profit.

On 30 June 1876, the railway withdrew from membership of the Railway Clearing House, leading to the loss of through rates for traffic booked for off railway destinations, as a consequence of the RCH increasing the level of members' surety from £500 to £1,500. France complained about the effect on his rates, probably making him less competitive, but Wade

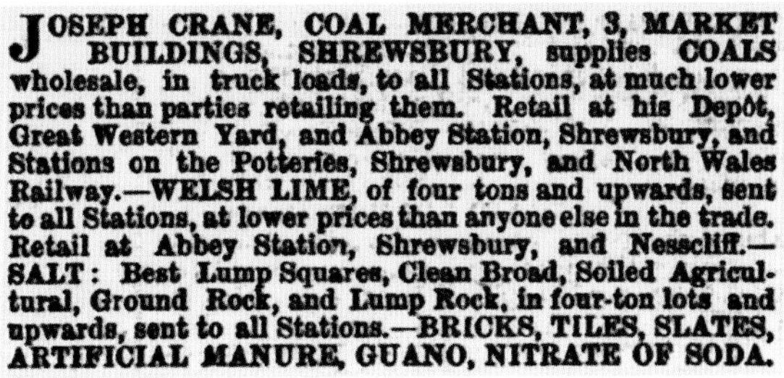

JOSEPH CRANE, COAL MERCHANT, 3, MARKET BUILDINGS, SHREWSBURY, supplies COALS wholesale, in truck loads, to all Stations, at much lower prices than parties retailing them. Retail at his Depôt, Great Western Yard, and Abbey Station, Shrewsbury, and Stations on the Potteries, Shrewsbury, and North Wales Railway.—WELSH LIME, of four tons and upwards, sent to all Stations, at lower prices than anyone else in the trade. Retail at Abbey Station, Shrewsbury, and Nesscliff.—SALT: Best Lump Squares, Clean Broad, Soiled Agricultural, Ground Rock, and Lump Rock, in four-ton lots and upwards, sent to all Stations.—BRICKS, TILES, SLATES, ARTIFICIAL MANURE, GUANO, NITRATE OF SODA.

Advertising his services in the *Wellington Journal* on 14 February 1880, Joseph Crane (1847–1925) was a coal, iron and salt merchant according to his 1881 census return. Ten years later his occupation was simplified to that of mineral merchant.

pointed out that without membership the railway's losses were reduced.

The railway received extra advertising with no charge from February 1880, when coal merchant Joseph Crane (1847–1925) started promoting availability of his wares from its premises (*Eddowes's Shrewsbury Journal*, 14 February). However, his efforts made very little contribution, if any, to securing its future.

Contrary to what might have been expected, it was not impoverished finances that brought about the railway's closure but a complaint from a member of the public concerned about the condition of the river bridge on the Breidden branch.

On 24 April 1880 a doctor from Worcester, Edward Horatio Walker Swete (1827–1912), informed the Board of Trade that he had become concerned about the 'apparently rotten condition' of the bridge when he visited the locality to collect samples of river water in connection with Liverpool Corporation's Vyrnwy reservoir scheme. He had walked over the bridge and found that part of the flooring had fallen into the river. 'To my eye, uneducated in engineering, the whole structure appears frightfully rotten …' The Board copied the letter to Wade, who passed it to Judd, and submitted it to the directors.

They met on 25 May, when Judd submitted a report on the bridge and said that it was safe for traffic. He was ordered to report further on the bridge, whether any further repairs were necessary and to take such steps as he deemed advisable to ensure the safe conduct of traffic, which action Wade reported to the Board. Although, on the face of it, this was a satisfactory response doubts remained.

Melverley bridge, which brought about the railway's closure. (Edward Lloyd Moreton)

It should also be borne in mind that Judd was not an engineer and was not qualified to make engineering judgments. On 27 May, Rich was ordered to inspect the railway at the earliest opportunity.

Rich reported from Shrewsbury on 9 June 1880. The file copy is obviously his draft and was written in haste, lacking sufficient clarity to permit all of it to be quoted verbatim; italics represent Rich's own emphasis.

He had found that the bridge's timber was so badly decayed that part of it had given way and been 'supported in a temporary manner'. The longitudinal timbers that carried the rails were 'quite rotten'. The bridge was not level and about 1ft out of line. Despite branch traffic being worked with 'a small contractors' engine that weighs about 10 tons, *I do not consider this bridge safe for traffic.*' He went on to say that the wooden parts of all the bridges required repair or renewal except some between Kinnerley and Llanymynech that had been renewed. The branch sleepers were decayed and required complete renewal. The fencing was incomplete and signals, level crossing gates and timber station platforms were in need of repair and 'in many cases they should be renewed. The rails are out of line … *I do not consider this branch fit or safe to carry traffic.*'

As regards the main line, the masonry, brickwork and ironwork were all good, although the latter required cleaning and painting. Some settlement in the wing walls of the bridges needed pointing. '… *but the wooden decking, the wooden cross bearers and the longitudinals on the bridges require a thorough repair and in many cases the whole of the hard wood should be renewed.* The sleepers were generally covered with ballast,' he continued, 'but where they are exposed … they are much decayed. Many require renewal.'

'The best and cheapest plan,' he thought, 'would probably be to relay the railway. The fencing, the signals, the points and locking bolts and bars and the wooden platforms at the stations require repairing. *Some of the piles in the first underbridge next to the Abbey station, which consists of five openings of 15ft and some of the wooden piles in a high wooden bridge of some 15ft openings over the River Tanat require repairs and renewal.*'

'Some of the level crossing gates require renewal and others require to be repaired. This railway,' he concluded, 'requires to be thoroughly overhauled and repaired. The rails should be lifted and regulated and the damaged rails should be taken out and renewed. The … line was originally well made. The traffic is small and worked at low speed.'The report was immediately sent to Wade but it was 18 June before he replied with the directors' observations: 'I am desired by the directors … to inform you that they have spent all the moneys received from traffic and other sources after payment of the working expenses and that there are no funds in the hands of the receiver available for carrying out the large and extensive repairs advised by Colonel Rich. Under these circumstances the directors desire to place themselves in your hands and would be glad to know whether you would recommend the whole of the line to be closed or only that portion known as the Breidden branch. I may add that the directors have kept the line open for some years past solely to accommodate the district and they will co-operate with the Board of Trade in any way you can suggest by which the inconvenience caused by the cessation of the goods and passenger traffic may be lessened. May I request the favour of an early reply as the directors do not wish in any way to incur personal responsibility by allowing the trains to run over a line which is not perfectly safe.'

In fact, the branch was closed to passengers the same day, Judd having published a notice to that effect on 14 June. The branch goods service, however, would continue to operate on Wednesdays and Saturdays 'as heretofore'.

The Board's response was immediate. First, a telegram: 'By order of the board and at the request of the Board of Trade you are forthwith to suspend all traffic on the railway. Attend board at 10.30 tomorrow.

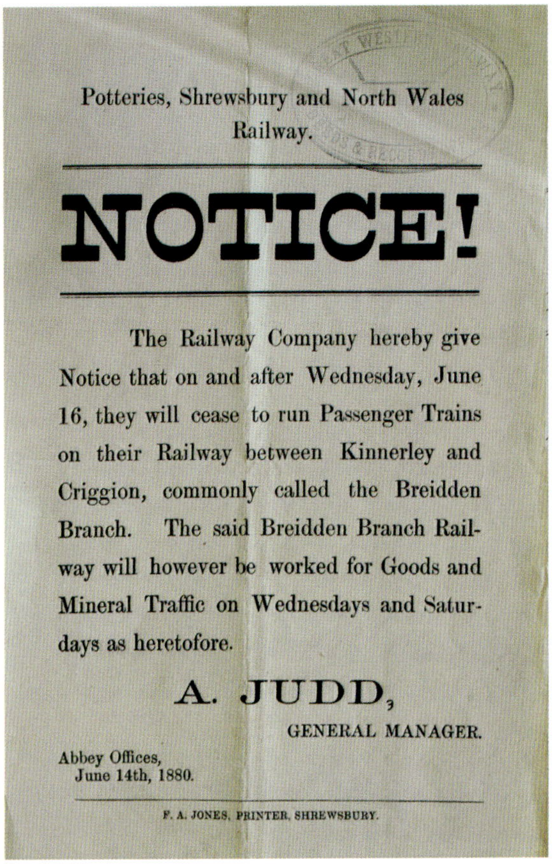
Potteries, Shrewsbury and North Wales Railway.

NOTICE!

The Railway Company hereby give Notice that on and after Wednesday, June 16, they will cease to run Passenger Trains on their Railway between Kinnerley and Criggion, commonly called the Breidden Branch. The said Breidden Branch Railway will however be worked for Goods and Mineral Traffic on Wednesdays and Saturdays as heretofore.

A. JUDD,
GENERAL MANAGER.

Abbey Offices,
June 14th, 1880.

F. A. JONES, PRINTER, SHREWSBURY.

Manager Albert Judd's notice about the Breidden branch's closure.

Telegraph if you have received and carried out above order.' And secondly, a letter: 'I am directed by the Board of Trade to acknowledge receipt of your letter of the 18th inst stating the inability of the Potteries, Shrewsbury & North Wales Railway Company to carry out the works considered necessary by Colonel Rich for putting the railway into a safe condition for public traffic and asking the advice of the Board of Trade in the matter. In reply I am directed by the Board of Trade to inform you as stated in the telegraph forwarded to you this morning that the responsibility of allowing the line to fall into its present condition and the working of it whilst in this condition must remain with the directors but the Board of Trade have no hesitation in saying in reply to your letter that having regard to the public safety the line should be closed at once. The Board of Trade would be glad to learn with the least possible delay what steps have been taken.'

Both were sent on 19 June. Wade replied three days later: 'I am instructed by my directors to acknowledge receipt of your telegram and letter of the 19th inst stating that the Board of Trade had no hesitation in saying that the line should be closed at once and to inform you that in consequence of such telegram and letter my directors gave immediate instructions for closing the line and that all traffic is now stopped.' Shortly afterwards, an agreement was made with the Cambrian whereby that company would work and maintain the Nantmawr branch for a period of two years, paying 3d per ton.

Elsewhere, everything was left just as it had been on 21 June, the last day trains ran (*Wellington Journal*, 26 June). Acting for the receiver, the sheriff took possession on 28 June (*Eddowes's Journal*, 1 December) announcing an auction of four locomotives, 150 wagons and brake vans and all plant, materials, and timber buildings at stations, stating that the sale would be held without reserves (*Eddowes's Journal*, 14 July).

In the local press, the railway's closure was not the stuff of headlines but more a matter of resigned regret. In the absence of any announcement, the *Shrewsbury Chronicle* (25 June) repeated the rumours in circulation, that the line was unfit or there were financial complications. Of course, there had always been financial complications. The involvement of a government officer soon circulated (*Wellington Journal*, 26 June).

IMPORTANT PRELIMINARY ANNOUNCEMENT.

POTTERIES, SHREWSBURY, AND NORTH WALES RAILWAY.

UNRESERVED SALE BY AUCTION OF ROLLING STOCK, 4 LOCOMOTIVE ENGINES, About 150 TRUCKS and BREAK VANS, PLANT, MATERIALS, and WOOD ERECTIONS, &c., at the following Stations :— Abbey-foregate (Shrewsbury), Red Hill, Hanwood Road, Cross Gates, Shrawardine, Nesscliffe, Kinnerley, Melverley, Crewe Green, Llandrinio Road, Criggion, Maesbrook, Llanymynech, and Llanyblodwell.

MESSRS. WILLIAM HALL, WATERIDGE, AND OWEN Have received instructions from the Sheriff of Shropshire to SELL the whole BY AUCTION, on an EARLY DATE.

Further particulars in due course. 6260

Advertisement for the sale of rolling stock and other assets, *Eddowes's Shrewsbury Journal*, 14 July 1880.

The *Shrewsbury Chronicle* (25 June) claimed that the train service had been more punctual of late, and that traffic had been increased, 'thus it must have been enabled to work at a profit'. Of course, the paper had no idea whether services were profitable. All the papers deplored the closure and the inconvenience brought upon those who had used the railway the most, 'virtually excluded from their county town' (*Wellington Journal*, 26 June).

Concurrent with the behind-the-scenes activity that led to the railway's closure, in Parliament a Bill promoted under the name of the Stafford & Uttoxeter Railway by the Midland and Great Northern railways was being processed. Designed to open up an east–west route between Lincolnshire and mid-Wales, it sought running powers over the railway and the Stafford–Wellington–Shrewsbury routes of the LNWR and the GWR. In a piece examining the proposal in some depth, and its benefit to Shrewsbury and the railway in particular, the *Shrewsbury Chronicle* (11 June) admitted that the route via Llanymynech was longer than running directly via the Shrewsbury & Welshpool. By the end of the month the larger railways had succeeded in getting the Bill suspended for the session; it was not resurrected.

Only one resident made the effort to comment on the closure in the local press, 'The Ghost of Humphrey Kynaston' not being convinced that the state of the track was as bad as portrayed. He thought that another rumour had greater validity, that it had been brought about by 'certain great companies' that had done 'their best to prevent the formation of our line' to prevent it from getting into the hands of a formidable competitor. Kynaston had been a member of the local gentry who lived several years as an outlaw, allegedly in the style of Robin Hood, in the fifteenth and sixteenth centuries.

Two parties were sufficiently inconvenienced by the closure to write to the Board of Trade with ideas to circumvent it, the Bradford Estate, at Knockin, and the Midland Railway Carriage & Wagon Co., at Shrewsbury. The former, on seeking permission to work a horse tram between Llanymynech and Kinnerley to transport domestic coal, was told that it was a matter for the company. The latter sought to make use of the section of the railway between its works adjacent to the Abbey station and the junction with the LNWR to transport its goods and materials; the Board had no power, the company was informed.

The Board of Trade's requirements seemed quite unequivocal, the railway must be closed. The railway even went so far as to remove lengths of rail at strategic places to inhibit unauthorised movements. Yet when the Board was approached by France, amongst others, it replied: 'The Board did not order, and had no power to order, the closing of the railway.' Indeed, on 26 June it had written to Wade '… your directors to be so good as to cause the Board of Trade to be informed what steps they propose to take to put the line in question in a proper state of repair'.

Of course, the company had no funds and was unable to do that.

Albert Judd, the manager, incidentally, decided that his future lay in Canada, taking an appointment at the Great Western Railway's Hamilton headquarters and then, in 1882, with the Grand Trunk Railway. In Shrewsbury, his furniture was sold by auction on 20 September (*Shrewsbury Chronicle*, 17 September 1880 / *Hamilton Daily Times*, 23 October 1882).

With the railway closed the Midland Wagon Company made another attempt to recover its debt, applying to the court for the sheriff, acting for the receiver, to relinquish the assets previously seized. The judge ruled that although the legislation envisaged the railway as a going concern, its plant or equipment used for traffic was absolutely protected from seizure and ordered the sheriff to withdraw. As the latter was not allowed to incur any expense, the Wagon Company had to pay his costs (*The Times*, 5 November 1880).

The sheriff having withdrawn, and the intended sale cancelled, the Wagon

Company took possession and on 24 November returned to court with an inventory of seized items to obtain a ruling on the validity of the seizure. Analysing the list of several hundred items, the judge ruled that the only item not protected, necessary for the railway's purposes, was a lady's bonnet box that had been left in the waiting room at Shrewsbury.

Hearing this news, there were those in the locality who thought it would enable the railway to be reopened (*Shrewsbury Chronicle*, 26 November). The paper had heard of a scheme being floated for landowners and farmers served by the railway to pay a 1s per adjacent acre per annum subsidy, which, producing £64 per mile, would be enough to pay for the operation of one train a day. Property values had also been reduced, the paper claimed. Nothing more was heard about the subsidy scheme.

On 20 April 1881, two judgement creditors, William Clemens Abell & Company, wagon builders, owed £255 18s, and the South Wales Colliery Company, £349 12s, brought an action to determine if the railway owned any property that could be sold to settle their debts. As there were no chattels, attention was focused on a plot of land, valued at £700 and purchased in 1870, which could only be sold if the railway had owned it for more than ten years and it was deemed to be unused. The first criterion was obviously met, and the jury decided that the second was also (*Eddowes's Journal*, 27 April).

A few days later R. S. France was the subject of a hearing of a different nature, because on 4 April he had filed a petition for liquidation and a creditors' meeting into his affairs was held at Oswestry's Wynnstay Arms Hotel on 25 April. He had a deficiency of £1,570 9s 10d. This was clearly no ordinary bankruptcy, as France's solicitor claimed that it was not caused by any want of ability, foresight, indiscretion, or extravagance on his client's part but because his stone traffic had been obstructed in an attempt to obtain control of the quarry on behalf of its mortgagee, a Mr Smith, who had also obtained a writ of execution and seized all of France's furniture and loose effects.

The name Smith is unexplainable, as France's property was held by two mortgagees, William Blackmore, who had held part of it since 5 March 1873, and F. E. Lewis, who had held the remainder since 4 April 1881 (*Law Times*, 22 March 1884).

France said that the railway had refused to make any contribution towards the cost of working the incline, which would not be expected as it was not a part of the railway. Excessive rates had prevented him from sending his stone out by rail for five years, and rails had been removed. When the rates were restored, it was of no use to him because the rails were not replaced.

The creditors resolved that his affairs should be liquidated by arrangement and not bankruptcy, that a trustee should be appointed to protect his interests and that he should be discharged immediately. It was unfortunate for France that the layout and levels at Nantmawr prevented him from threatening to cart his stone the short distance to the end of the Cambrian's Porthywaen branch (*Eddowes's Journal*, 27 April / *Wrexham Advertiser, 30 April*). He had more to say on the situation during the Parliamentary hearings for the winding-up Bill, described shortly.

Earlier, during November 1880, the debenture holders had agreed to promote a bill to allow the railway to be sold and to sanction the company's winding up. At a hearing held before a House of Lords select committee over several days in July 1881, objections were presented from 'Humphrey Purnell Blackmore and others', and the 'Imperial Credit Company and another'. Blackmore had been the agent securing £100,000 loaned to France by Brown, Shipley & Co. in 1865. As no other person with this name has been found, it may be said that Blackmore (1835–1929) appears to have been the man who made a name for himself as an archaeologist and founder of the Salisbury and South Wiltshire Museum, and for marrying a woman who was already

married to three other men (*Salisbury & Winchester Journal*, 25 April 1868/ *Western Daily Press*, 5 February 1929). His brother, William, was one of R. S. France's mortgagees.

Francis Alexander Hamilton (1815–1907), the financier's senior partner, explained the background to the loan and said that although France had paid interest on it before his bankruptcy, no dividends or interest had been paid on the securities. He and the other debenture holders were willing to forego 75% of their investment if it meant that the railway could be sold.

In the Commons, Lord Bradford (1819–98, the third Earl), owner of land at Knockin, Nesscliff and Kinnerley, explained that some 30 acres of his land taken by the railway had not been paid for. He thought that the closure was a 'very great injury' to the public.

France was called as an objector. Following the Board of Trade's instruction to close the railway, he had been instructed not to use the incline. His objection was to preserve his rights under the agreement. He did not like the agreement and felt constrained by it but feared its loss, as without it he thought that he could be prevented from exporting his stone via the incline. He had made some repairs to it himself but had not been reimbursed the £210 they had cost him.

He described his quarries and their relationship to the incline in some detail. He went on to say that although he had worked the incline he would prefer not to: 'It is an exceedingly risky business even with all the care we take and we have killed men to do it. We get runaways. We let down at a time 5 ton 10 [cwt] on each wagon. You see the character of these wagons. We cannot use railway wagons there at all.' He paid 3d per ton to use it and considered that the supply of horses and men to move wagons to and from the incline a function of working it.

His wagons were used on the incline, the contents being tipped into the railway's wagons; he had tried to get the drops altered as the existing arrangement had a fall of up to 75ft and converted too much of his stone to chippings.

He was hoping that the Cambrian would take over the responsibility for the incline in addition to the Nantmawr branch; if it would not he would do so for 1d per ton. The Board of Trade's telegram and letter to the railway had been read out earlier, when the chairman ruled that the telegram was unequivocal that the railway was to suspend 'all traffic'.

France attacked the London Finance Association, claiming it was using its influence with the railway in an attempt to take over his quarries by increasing the rates and by discouraging the Cambrian and the GWR from taking over the Nantmawr branch.

The railway's barrister claimed that France had no right to be heard on the subject of the agreement, arguing that as he had mortgaged two of the quarries he was no longer the lessee as defined by it. France got the protective clause he required but he did not get the incline included as part of the railway's undertaking as he had not given notice or produced plans.

The Act received the royal assent on 18 July 1881. The company could be wound up and the liquidator could sell the railway. Of particular interest is article 8, application of purchase money, because it severely restricted the options of both the liquidator and any prospective purchaser. Any monies received had to be dispensed in the following order of priority:

1. Costs of the act and the winding up.
2. Compensation and expenses for completing the purchase of land.
3. 'A' class debenture stock, up to 60% of the holding providing three quarters of holders discharge, in writing, any claim for principal or interest.
4. 'B' class debenture stock, up to 40% of the holding providing ...
5. 'C' class debenture stock, up to 25% of the holding providing ...
6. The company's creditors, up to 20% of the debt, ...

Advertisement for the sale of a locomotive and wagons on behalf of the finance company, *Railway News*, 19 November 1881.

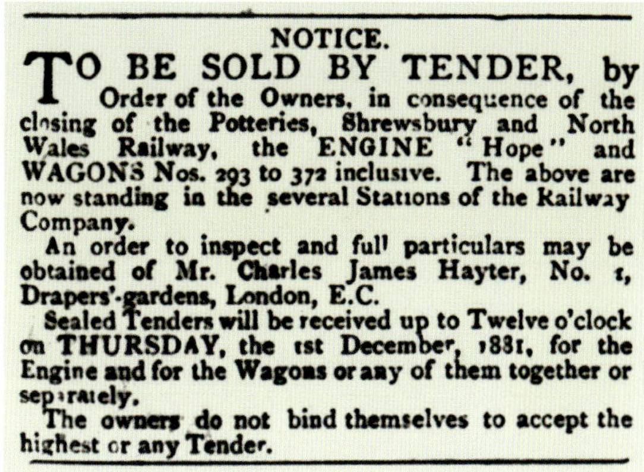

NOTICE.

TO BE SOLD BY TENDER, by Order of the Owners, in consequence of the closing of the Potteries, Shrewsbury and North Wales Railway, the ENGINE "Hope" and WAGONS Nos. 293 to 372 inclusive. The above are now standing in the several Stations of the Railway Company.

An order to inspect and full particulars may be obtained of Mr. Charles James Hayter, No. 1, Drapers'-gardens, London, E.C.

Sealed Tenders will be received up to Twelve o'clock on THURSDAY, the 1st December, 1881, for the Engine and for the Wagons or any of them together or separately.

The owners do not bind themselves to accept the highest or any Tender.

7. Share and stockholders, up to 7% of the holding, subject to majority agreement at a special meeting. If the purchase money was insufficient to pay the percentages then they would be reduced in proportion.
8. Any balance to be distributed to share and stockholders in proportion to their holdings, in addition to any sums due by application of the previous section.

This effectively set a minimum price of around £300,000 and limited the liquidator's scope for negotiation. No one was likely to agree to accept less than the specified percentage and the requirement to pay the landowners in full would always be a sticking point. He was also restricted by article 4, which ruled that the railway could only be sold to another railway, removing the options of either selling part of it or selling it for scrap.

A remarkable feature of the winding-up Act was its description of the railway: 'And whereas for some years the said receiver has been enabled to keep up a small but inefficient service of trains only by devoting the whole of the said tolls and receipts of the company's undertaking to the mere running expenses, and by neglecting the maintenance and repair of the permanent way and bridges, but having no funds to execute certain repairs deemed necessary … the railway was … closed to public traffic … and has since remained so.'

Wade called a meeting for the shareholders to give their approval to the company being wound up (*Morning Post*, 31 March) and a winding-up order was made on 21 April 1882 (*London Gazette*, 2 May). On 8 July Alexander Young, a partner in the chartered accountants Turquand, Young & Co, was appointed liquidator (*London Gazette*, 25 July). Later, Young said that he was appointed because the judge knew him and not the other candidates. His firm became, via several amalgamations, a part of the international accountancy practice Ernst & Young Global Ltd, trading as EY.

Born in Shrewsbury, John Wade was the Shrewsbury & Potteries Junction Railway's secretary before moving to London and becoming a professional railway company secretary, companies he worked for including the Brecon & Llandovery Junction Railway, the Devon & Somerset Railway, which brought him into contact with W. H. Whadcoat, and the Mid Wales Railway as well as the Potteries Railway. He died in London in 1909 and is buried in Shrewsbury's general cemetery. His £16,000 estate would be worth £1.5 million in 2022.

Wade's accounts were completed at the end of 1882. There was sufficient income from rentals to pay for the locomotives to be looked after in the shed at Shrewsbury and to keep the boundary fences under repair. The coaching stock was stored outside, at Shrewsbury, where the elements and vandalism gradually took their toll. The connection with the Shrewsbury–Wellington line to Potteries Junction was lifted, presumably by the LNWR/GWR, and the boundary fenced. At Llanymynech the Cambrian made unofficial use of some of the sidings for stock storage purposes. Elsewhere the railway became overgrown.

Although the railway was disused there was still activity that affected it. The London Finance Association had put the locomotive *Hope* and eighty wagons up for sale by tender, with a closing date of 1 December 1881, (*Railway News*, 19 November) but seems to have abandoned its interest in the loco, offering the wagons only, with a closing date of 31 May 1882 (*Herapath's Railway Journal*, 20 May).

On 21 April, the *Shrewsbury Chronicle* had published a letter that described at some length the reasons for the railway's difficult position. It was in response to a comment made by the 3rd Earl of Powis (1818–91) at a meeting held in Welshpool in opposition to a proposed rivers conservancy Bill that would impose costs on landowners to maintain riverbanks and protect land from flooding, when His Lordship had ridiculed the railway for having located the station on land subject to flooding. Why pick on the Potteries Railway, asked the writer, who signed himself Inquirer, when large parts of Shrewsbury, including the Abbey, had been built on similar land?

There had been little opposition to the railway when it was to be terminated at Red Hill, he continued, but when it was proposed to be extended to Shrewsbury, the LNWR and GWR combined to make it one of the most expensive Parliamentary battles of the session, as well as forcing the railway to incur the expense of its

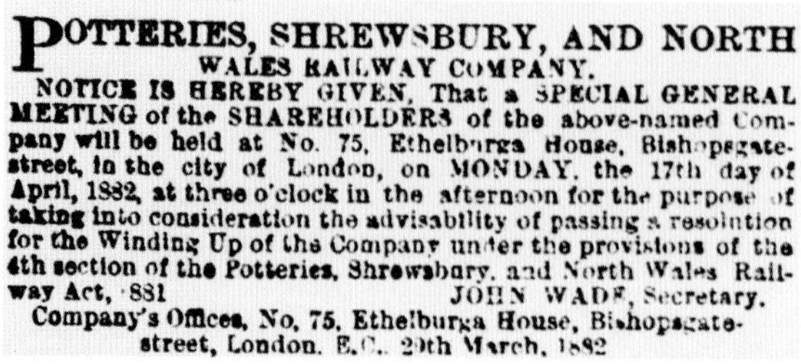
POTTERIES, SHREWSBURY, AND NORTH WALES RAILWAY COMPANY.

NOTICE IS HEREBY GIVEN, That a SPECIAL GENERAL MEETING of the SHAREHOLDERS of the above-named Company will be held at No. 75, Ethelburga House, Bishopsgate-street, in the city of London, on MONDAY, the 17th day of April, 1882, at three o'clock in the afternoon for the purpose of taking into consideration the advisability of passing a resolution for the Winding Up of the Company under the provisions of the 4th section of the Potteries, Shrewsbury, and North Wales Railway Act, 1881

JOHN WADE, Secretary.

Company's Offices, No. 75, Ethelburga House, Bishopsgate-street, London, E.C., 29th March, 1882

The advertisement for the shareholders' winding up meeting, from the *Morning Post*, 31 March 1882.

independent line to Shrewsbury and its own station. As a member of the committee that managed the joint station, his Lordship would have known this, the writer pointed out.

His Lordship had also benefitted from the railway, selling it a small strip of land at Shrawardine for £1,900 and earning some £700 a year in royalties from land at Nantmawr that had previously earned him £30. Writing from London, Inquirer was clearly well informed.

Following the closure there are several reports of incidents involving members of the public using the railway as a footpath but even without trains it could still be dangerous. Charles Sergeant, aged 40, a farm labourer, drowned when he fell through a hole in the bridge crossing the Meole brook on 22 July 1882; ironically, he was found by someone who was also walking along the track. At the inquest, the coroner told the jury that Sergeant was trespassing and that had he been on a public path they could have brought a manslaughter verdict against the owners. As it was, a verdict of accidental death was returned; after prompting, the jury asked for the company to be notified about the state of the bridge (*Eddowes's Journal*, 26 July).

Young responded positively to the coroner's notification, for in March 1883 the Oswestry highway board's surveyor reported that all the bridges in his area had received attention (*Wellington Journal*, 24 March). At the same meeting it was noted that it had been impossible to obtain stone for highway purposes since the railway had been closed and that the price had doubled. The same authority had the previous year received no reply when it had requested permission to make use of

R. S. France was the last to be interred in the family plot at Plealey Methodist church, 7 miles from Shrewsbury. It was a measure of the importance attached to the France family at the church that no other burials took place there. France left property valued at £142, £13,493 in 2022, so he was not well rewarded for his business activities. The chapel has been adapted for residential use.

the railway, and some wagons, to transport stone in its area using horses (*Eddowes's Journal*, 18 January 1882).

R. S. France died in Oswestry on 8 August 1883, aged 55, barely outliving his best-known creation. He died with a mixed reputation, described as eccentric in the way that he ran Nantmawr and its interface with the railway, but as a contractor, and he had built three or four railways, he seems to have been quite competent, finishing the others on time and to budget, to adopt the modern mantra. None of them collapsed in embarrassing circumstances, the Shrewsbury & Welshpool Railway remains a part of the national network, and track remains in situ on the Nantmawr tramway.

Where he did fall down was as a promoter of his own railways, the Potteries and Potteries Junction lines, where his ambitions had been undermined by the collapse of 1866, by the LNWR and GWR conniving to prevent him from having the network access approved by Parliament and the failure of geography to locate his railway in a part of the country where his access could not be blocked. Perhaps the most remarkable thing about him is that he was able to obtain so much support, financially and from City businessmen willing to lend their names to what were ultimately failed ventures.

France might have been dead, but he still featured in a compensation claim heard in the Chancery Division of the High Court on 15 November 1883. His mortgagees and trustee in bankruptcy had claimed in respect of the injury done to his land by the embankment built by France in advance of the 1874 Extensions Act, seeking compensation from the £2,573 13s 6d Parliamentary deposit. The claim had been rejected on 13 February 1882, but at this appeal hearing it was ruled that they had no claim in respect of the embankment's construction but that they did have one in respect of the railway's abandonment (*Law Times*, 22 March 1884).

The Nantmawr quarry lease was acquired by John Parson Smith (1824–1900) in 1885, at which point the quarry and railway had been out of use for some time. On 24 July he agreed to pay the Cambrian £800 to put the Nantmawr branch into good repair to carry the stone traffic, for which purpose the Cambrian had made an agreement with liquidator Young to authorise the use of the railway between Llanymynech and Nantmawr for mineral traffic for seven years from 1 January 1886, making it fit for use and paying a toll of 2d per ton of minerals or quarrying machinery carried.

By now Smith was a successful Shrewsbury businessman, but earlier in his career he had been a railway goods agent, a position that he occupied when he had attended the 1853 Shropshire & Montgomeryshire Railway meeting also attended by France (*Shrewsbury Chronicle*, 7 October).

T. R. Perkins (Bibliography) said that he first visited the railway *c.*1883, finding that the junction with the Wellington line had been removed and a gate placed across the track. Along the line wagons remained as left in 1880 and at Shrewsbury the carriages stood in a siding with doors missing, windows broken, and cushions, parcel racks and other fittings littering the floors, their original colour indeterminable. In the Shrewsbury engine shed were four locomotives. Men appointed by Young, the receiver, patrolled the line by trolley, repairing fences when required. Daylight

could be seen through the floors of bridges, he wrote, and in one case only the rails and girders remained to span the road.

Young had employed Walter Williams (1857–1934) as a watchman in 1883 (*Wellington Journal*, 5 July 1890), although by 1891 he had employment as an engine driver. Richard Reeves (1830–1913), guard of the last train in 1880, was also employed for a time; in the 1901 and 1911 censuses he gave his occupation as railway caretaker and general labourer on the railway respectively but in 1881 and 1891 he gave it as labourer (*Border Counties Advertiser*, 19 April 1911).

Although the physical deterioration had clearly set in before the line had closed, it combined with abandonment to make the railway a target for vandalism and other antics, as instanced by three incidents being reported in the spring of 1887.

On 2 April ten-year-old Thomas Preston was one of a gang of lads pushing a wagon up the gradient at Abbey station and riding back down when he fell, his legs being run over. The accident occurred because two men working nearby determined to put a stop to the high jinks and put a scotch under one of the wheels as the wagon ran past them. Unfortunately, for the boy, the wagon had no floor and the sudden stop dislodged him. One of his legs was amputated immediately and *Eddowes's Journal* (6 April) feared that he might lose the other. By the time of the 1891 census he was working as a tailor but he has not been traced thereafter.

The other two cases involved knocking bricks off a bridge. Samuel Gillam, aged 11, was fined 1s and had to pay 1s damages and costs for an offence committed on 15 May, while William Higginson (aged 16) and Edward Gravener were each fined £1 including costs for offences committed two days later (*Wellington Journal*, 21 May / 28 May). In the first case the prosecuting solicitor said that he did not wish to press the charge but wished to inform the public that the railway did belong to someone who would protect its interests.

Cynicus, Martin Anderson (1854–1932), included the Potteries Railway as one that he targetted for gentle ribaldry and featured in postcards published from 1902, apparently unaware that the railway had been closed since 1880.

CHAPTER 4

THE SHROPSHIRE RAILWAYS

The dissolution of the Shrewsbury, Potteries & North Wales Railway Company was a protracted and complicated affair, not completed until 1 November 1895, with none of the existing companies interested in buying it. Of the most likely and feasible candidates, the GWR and LNWR maintained their monopoly on Shrewsbury traffic as long as it remained closed, and its traffic was of little benefit to them. The Cambrian, which had already secured control of the Nantmawr traffic, was probably not only inhibited by the difficulty it would have had in raising sufficient capital for it but by the knowledge that the larger companies would have objected. The only way out of the impasse would be to form a new company to take over the old.

During 1886, Sir Richard Dansey Green-Price, Baronet, and John Parson Smith decided that they should do just that, making contact with the liquidator, Alexander Young, who introduced them to Captain James Inman.

Green-Price (1838–1909) was a solicitor from Radnorshire who had recently moved to Shrewsbury. He had been a promoter of the Central Wales Railway (Knighton–Llandrindod portion) and a director of the Golden Valley (Pontrilas–Hay) and the Kington & Eardisley Railways (*Wellington Journal*, 29 May 1909). Smith (1824–1900) was a successful Shrewsbury merchant, having been goods manager of the Shropshire Union Canal for fourteen years and lessee of the Nantmawr, the Bellyn Bank

Pontrilas, southern terminus of the Golden Valley Railway, one of the railways with which Sir Richard Dansey Green-Price, instigator of the Shropshire Railways, was associated.

and Criggion quarries since 1885. Inman (1840–1912), formerly in the Royal Marine Light Infantry, lived in Paris at the time and they were told that he was both rich and the owner of property in Wolverhampton. At the time of the select committee hearings in 1888, Green-Price had not met him.

The trio announced their intention to deposit a Bill to revive and extend the railway in December 1887. Under the name of Shropshire Railways, the Bill sought powers to take over the railway, to vary the terms of sale defined in the 1881 winding-up Act, to make new railways, for running powers on the Great Western Railway between Hodnet and Market Drayton on the Wellington and Market Drayton line, which would give access to the North Staffordshire Railway at Silverdale Junction, and all of the North Staffordshire and Cambrian systems, and to maintain the Market Drayton line as a separate undertaking.

The new railways were two short lines in Shrewsbury that raised the existing line above the floodplain, with the benefit of easing the gradient, and making a triangular junction with the Potteries Junction line in order that trains to and from the east could use the station without reversing. Two more lines revived the Potteries Junction Railway target of Market Drayton and Stoke-on-Trent. Railway No 4, between Hodnet and Market Drayton, would run parallel to the existing GWR route between those places but would be dropped if the running powers were granted. A proposal to build a 'direct' route between Oswestry and Kinnerley was dropped before the Bill reached the select committees.

Subject to Parliamentary approval, the promoters made a formal agreement to purchase the railway with Young on 14 March 1888, agreeing to pay £12,300 in cash plus £286,432 3s 4d in stock.

In preparation for the select committee hearings, public meetings were held in Shrewsbury, Nesscliff and Market Drayton, Green-Price putting the case for what he

Eardisley, a station on the Midland Railway line between Hereford and Three Cocks Junction, was the junction with the line to Kington that was intended to be extended to Knighton. The station building on the left has been relocated to Raven Square station on the Welshpool & Llanfair Light Railway.

Above: In 1865, 1887, 1908 and 1918 Market Drayton was the target for proposed railways intending to connect Shrewsbury with Stoke-on-Trent and the Potteries and avoid the LNWR. Needless to say, none of them were constructed.

Right: Hodnet, on the GWR, was proposed to be a junction station in 1865, 1887 and 1918. (James Valentine Ltd)

The Shropshire Railways' 1887 proposed routes in Shrewsbury, put forward in connection with its intended extension to Market Drayton. Railways Nos 1 and 2 were on the alignment of the existing lines but with shallower gradients. (Parliamentary Archives)

called the railway's resuscitation. He also included a potted history of the railway, although as this would have been based on second- and third-hand information it should be treated with a certain amount of caution. It does, however, include the remarkable assertion that France had arranged for the Potteries Railway to give him a rebate on his stone traffic, to the extent that over the years the railway was opened, he had received £25,880, an average of £1,700 a year, which sucked out any profit the railway might have made. A total of £3,500 was raised towards the Bill's expenses at these meetings.

The hearings were held in the House of Lords on 26 and 27 April 1888, and on 23–25 July in the Commons. The promoters' witnesses went first. There was much repetition between them on the merits of the railways, even after the committee chairman had said they had heard enough.

Lord Bradford said that the railway had not paid for land valued at about £10,000 but he wanted it to be resuscitated and was now prepared to take shares valued at £6,000 in the new company in settlement.

The Mayor of Shrewsbury, Vincent Crump (1814–96), said he was 'anxious to see it opened or else I should not have come to London. I have not been here since the exhibition of 1851, and I shall not come again if I can help it.'

Thomas Southam (1818–95), the senior member of Shrewsbury Town Council, said that the railway had failed due to its management: 'It was financed and worked by one man – a Mr France – a very energetic, but a very obstinate man I may say, and he persisted in making the Llanymynech [line] first instead of making the potteries line first.' He claimed that before the line was closed the rolling stock was in a poor state of repair and people refused to travel by it. During one of his four periods in the mayoralty, in around 1866–67, he had been 'memorialised' to petition the Board of Trade about the state of the trains.

Green-Price explained the significance of the Market Drayton line, saying that

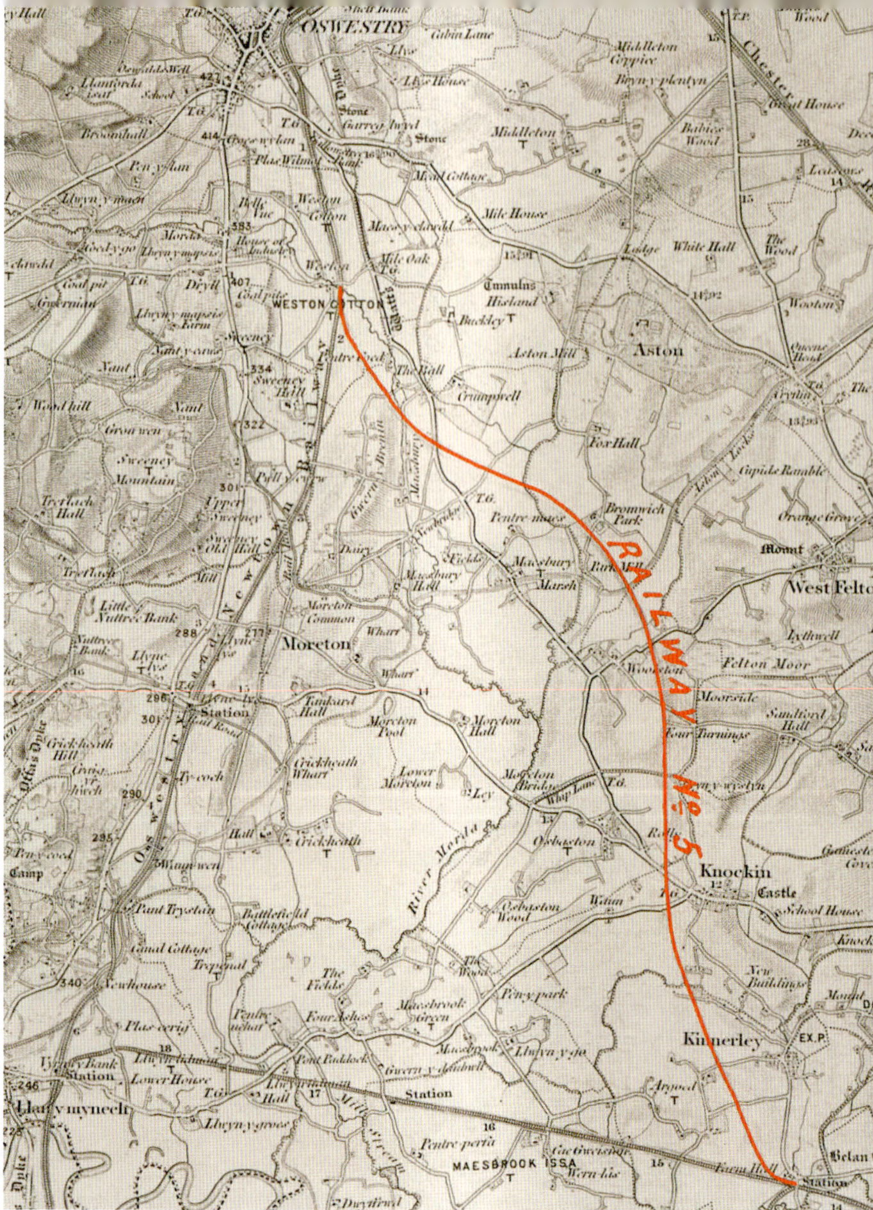

In 1887 the Shropshire Railways also proposed a route between Kinnerley and Weston Cotton, where a junction with the Cambrian Railways would have given it a direct route to Oswestry.

Thomas Southam, four times mayor of Shrewsbury, gave evidence in support of the Shropshire Railways' Bill in the House of Lords in 1888. A member of a distinguished Shrewsbury family, he was buried in Shrewsbury's General Cemetery.

the Nantmawr limestone was of high quality and in demand for fluxing in iron making at works in Hodnet and Hanley; the through route via Market Drayton would be 5 or 6 miles shorter. If the Criggion quarries were developed and their stone available in Staffordshire it would compete well with Clee Hill stone from south Shropshire, saving 2s per ton in transport alone. One of the scheme's supporters was a senior partner in Brown, Shipley & Company, one of the original financiers.

Questioned by the GWR's barrister, Green-Price admitted that the railway would have to earn £35,000 per annum in order to make a 5% return on the proposed £350,000 capital. Previously, the railway's best year had been 1875, when a loss of £2,481 was made on earnings of £13,552.

Green-Price's assertion that the £40,000 needed to fund its restoration would be funded by a first charge on the undertaking, by debentures, was met with a certain incredulity. The £13,056 6s 3d loan that funded the Parliamentary deposit had been provided by the Bank of Scotland.

Young explained that he had received assents to the proposal to issue Shropshire stock as compensation for original shares and debentures to the value of £1,090,000. There had been one dissenter with £217 debenture stock, but it would be impossible to get a 100% response because some holders had died or moved without notifying a change of address. An opposing Q.C. rather laboured the point about a landowner not accepting the terms being offered, despite all of

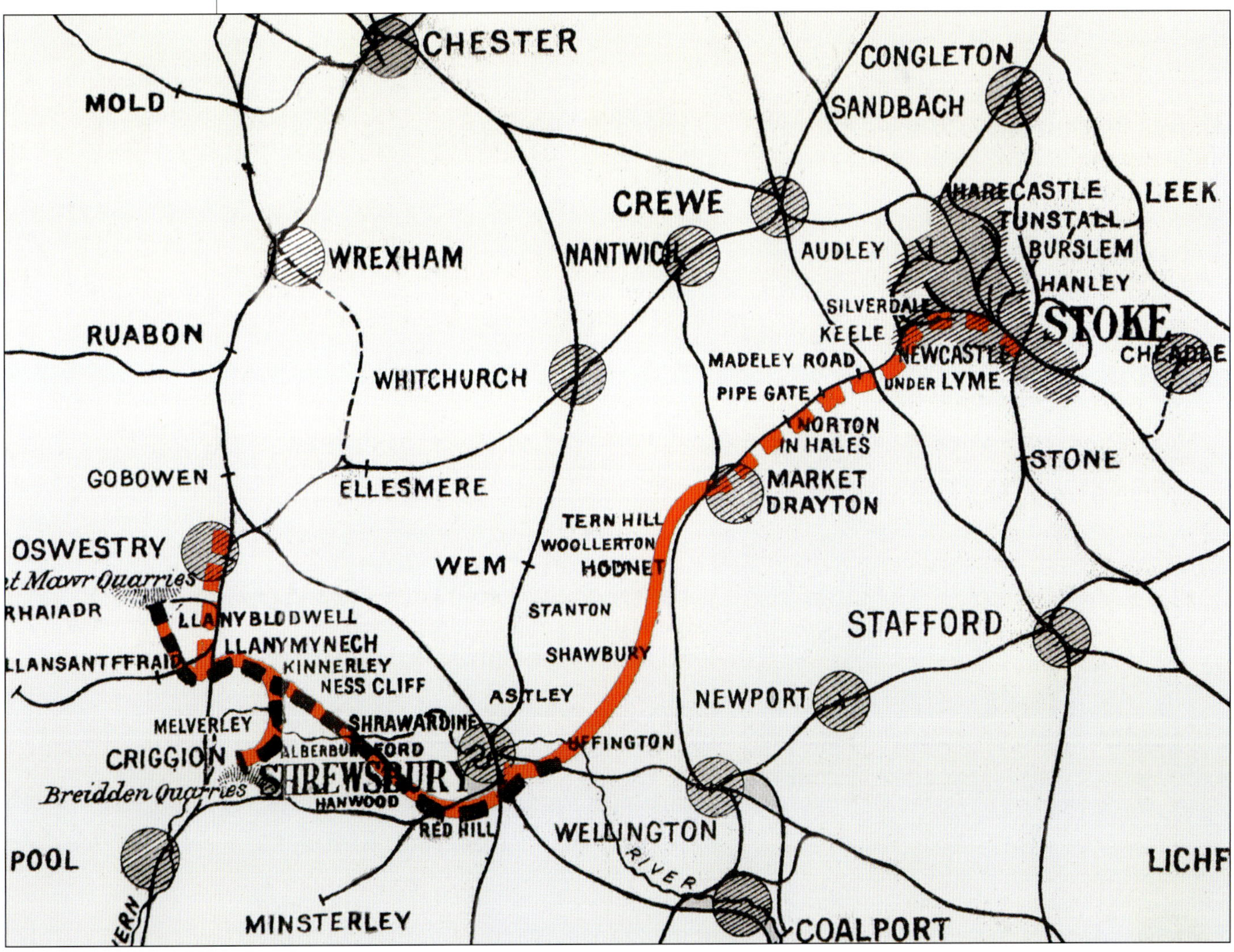

Extract from a map distributed to Shropshire Railways' shareholders.

them accepting, prompting the promoters' Q.C. to make a joke on the point in his questioning of Young and raising a laugh in the committee room.

J.B. Cooper, general manager for the railway's first five years, said that it had never had a fair chance. The track and wagons were very worn. The quarries had been worked intermittently, good traffic some weeks, very little in others. He thought it ought to pay, and what had happened in the past should not be taken as a criterion for the future.

John Russell (1851–1926), the engineer, said that resuscitating the main line would cost £27,000, the Breidden branch £11,000, and the Llanyblodwel branch £3,000. For the new works, the alterations at Shrewsbury were estimated to cost £30,255 and the Market Drayton line £238,702. There was no provision in the estimates for rolling stock.

The only objectors were the GWR and the Shrewsbury & Wellington Railway, known as the joint line, operated as it was by the LNWR and the GWR, so the latter effectively had two bites at the cherry. They did not call witnesses, depending on their cross-examinations and summing up to put their case.

The joint line's QC complained that the Market Drayton line would extract just enough of the traffic to prevent their own line from paying, which is what both of his sponsors had done to the Festiniog Railway with their extensions to Blaenau Ffestiniog. He was convinced that the whole purpose of the scheme was to put pressure on his clients to buy the Potteries line. Both barristers criticised Green-Price for being an outsider and not owning property in Shrewsbury.

Their entreaties were in vain, and the committee took only a few minutes to decide that the Bill's preamble had been proved. It refused, however, to grant running powers over the GWR, thus forcing the promoters to undertake to build its seven-mile-long railway No 4.

In the House of Commons, the same ground was gone over again, with mostly the same witnesses although with the addition of support from the local MPs.

These notes on the select committees are of necessity condensed, as the verbatim record required nearly 300 printed pages. The point is, the case for the Shropshire Railways was, like that for the Potteries Railway before it, extremely ill-founded. Both the vendors and purchasers were blinded by the original £1.3 million expenditure and the settlement requirements of the 1881 Act. The former thought they had an asset with a realisable value, whereas in fact it was, until Green-Price came on the scene, worthless, and the promoters thought they could acquire a substantial asset on the cheap, but it was not cheap enough. Even with the capital written down by 75%, success depended on there being sufficient traffic to service the debt, earning double their predecessor's earnings, and there was no guarantee of that.

The promoters then lumbered themselves with the Market Drayton line, and double track at that, arguing that it was essential if they were to get investors' support for reviving the bankrupt railway. Together, they were touted as an alternative through route, via Llanymynech, from the Midlands to North Wales, which of course was the reason the GWR and the LNWR were so keen to object, although *they* should have known that as Parliament had given essentially the same powers in the past it was unlikely to refuse them this time.

In his criticisms of the Bill, the GWR's Q.C. had commented on the absence of the North Staffordshire Railway from the witness roster, which could also have been said about the Cambrian Railways, especially as their participation was essential to the development of the through route. They would have known that the level of the GWR/LNWR objections and the scheme's underlying weaknesses were likely to lead to the promoters' ambitions being thwarted. Lending support cost nothing.

That the promoters were not prepared to make a public share issue before approaching financiers, or to invest substantial sums of their own money, surely demonstrates the inherent weakness of the scheme. Hindsight is a very precise science.

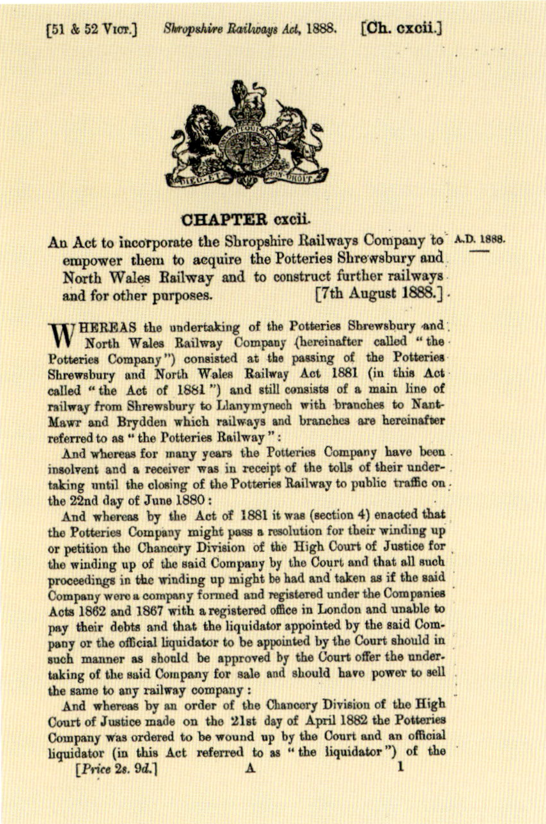

[51 & 52 Vict.] *Shropshire Railways Act*, 1888. [Ch. cxcii.]

CHAPTER cxcii.

An Act to incorporate the Shropshire Railways Company to empower them to acquire the Potteries Shrewsbury and North Wales Railway and to construct further railways and for other purposes. [7th August 1888.]

A.D. 1888.

WHEREAS the undertaking of the Potteries Shrewsbury and North Wales Railway Company (hereinafter called "the Potteries Company") consisted at the passing of the Potteries Shrewsbury and North Wales Railway Act 1881 (in this Act called "the Act of 1881") and still consists of a main line of railway from Shrewsbury to Llanymynech with branches to Nant-Mawr and Brydden which railways and branches are hereinafter referred to as "the Potteries Railway":

And whereas for many years the Potteries Company have been insolvent and a receiver was in receipt of the tolls of their undertaking until the closing of the Potteries Railway to public traffic on the 22nd day of June 1880:

And whereas by the Act of 1881 it was (section 4) enacted that the Potteries Company might pass a resolution for their winding up or petition the Chancery Division of the High Court of Justice for the winding up of the said Company by the Court and that all such proceedings in the winding up might be had and taken as if the said Company were a company formed and registered under the Companies Acts 1862 and 1867 with a registered office in London and unable to pay their debts and that the liquidator appointed by the said Company or the official liquidator to be appointed by the Court should in such manner as should be approved by the Court offer the undertaking of the said Company for sale and should have power to sell the same to any railway company:

And whereas by an order of the Chancery Division of the High Court of Justice made on the 21st day of April 1882 the Potteries Company was ordered to be wound up by the Court and an official liquidator (in this Act referred to as "the liquidator") of the

[*Price 2s. 9d.*] A 1

The Shropshire Railways Act, 1888.

The Act received the royal assent on 7 August 1888, allowing the company to be incorporated and confirming the provisional agreement with Young. The Potteries Railway, together with railways Nos 1 and 2 and a small part of railway No 3, were incorporated into the 'Shrewsbury separate undertaking', with £350,000 capital, the remainder into the 'Market Drayton separate undertaking', with £300,000 capital. Each of the undertakings were permitted £100,000 of borrowings. Article 66 of the Act empowered the Cambrian the use of any part of the railway for any traffic.

The first directors were Green-Price, Inman and Smith together with a Richard Taylor and two others suitably qualified with a holding of £500 of stock in either undertaking. Taylor was probably the Shrewsbury businessman, town councillor and magistrate of that name (1826–1904).

Before the new company got under way, Young ordered the old rolling stock and plant to be sold by auction on 24 August. An advertisement in the *London Evening Standard* (22 August) said there were four locomotives, some 200 wagons of various types, goods brake vans, a travelling crane, a platelayer's trolley and other items to be sold. The *Wellington Journal* (25 August) said that the sale attracted a large crowd and that the Manning, Wardle 0-6-0Ts *Powis* and *Bradford* sold for £210 and £305 respectively, Yorkshire Engine 2-4-0T *Hope* went for £200 and 0-4-2T *Tanat*, a mere £85; wagons fetched between £3 10s and £7 and the crane £54.

The new company's directors met for the first time on 12 October 1888. After Green-Price had been appointed chairman, topics discussed included claims in respect of railway land that had not been paid for. Settling these claims was to be a priority 'with the least possible expenditure of cash'.

William Greer Barcroft (1841–1927), a Mold & Denbigh Railway shareholder who lived in Mold, was appointed a director. He was retired and would, the board was informed, 'be able to devote as much time as might be required'. From County Mayo, he had been a cotton broker.

Young had introduced the original directors to Cutbill, Son & de Lungo, contractors and financiers, who on 30 July agreed to provide the permanent Parliamentary deposit of £13,056 6s 3d in 2¾% Consols (long-term, fixed-rate government stock), allowing the Bank of Scotland's temporary loan to be redeemed; the company was required to make the interest up to 5%. In return for providing the deposit, the financiers had the option of taking cash contracts to build either or both of the Market Drayton or Potteries lines, but if within two years the loan had

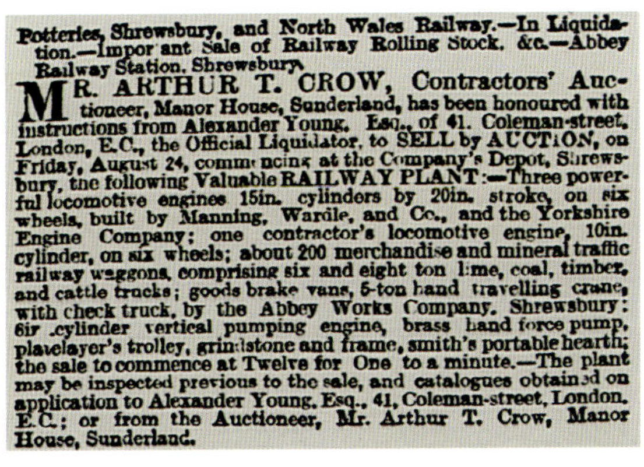

Potteries, Shrewsbury, and North Wales Railway.—In Liquidation.—Important Sale of Railway Rolling Stock, &c.—Abbey Railway Station, Shrewsbury.

MR. ARTHUR T. CROW, Contractors' Auctioneer, Manor House, Sunderland, has been honoured with instructions from Alexander Young, Esq., of 41, Coleman-street, London, E.C., the Official Liquidator, to SELL by AUCTION, on Friday, August 24, commencing at the Company's Depot, Shrewsbury, the following Valuable RAILWAY PLANT:—Three powerful locomotive engines 15in. cylinders by 20in. stroke, on six wheels, built by Manning, Wardle, and Co., and the Yorkshire Engine Company; one contractor's locomotive engine, 10in. cylinder, on six wheels; about 200 merchandise and mineral traffic railway waggons, comprising six and eight ton lime, coal, timber, and cattle trucks; goods brake vans, 5-ton hand travelling crane, with check truck, by the Abbey Works Company, Shrewsbury; 6in. cylinder vertical pumping engine, brass hand force pump, platelayer's trolley, grindstone and frame, smith's portable hearth; the sale to commence at Twelve for One to a minute.—The plant may be inspected previous to the sale, and catalogues obtained on application to Alexander Young, Esq., 41, Coleman-street, London, E.C.; or from the Auctioneer, Mr. Arthur T. Crow, Manor House, Sunderland.

After the liquidation was commenced, a specialist auctioneer was used to sell the railway's stock, advertised in the *London Evening Standard* on 22 August 1888.

not been repaid or the undertakings started then the directors would, at their own expense, apply for an abandonment Bill. On 13 December 1888 the financiers also agreed to advance £5,000 to settle land claims and other preliminary expenses and on 2 August 1889 tendered to reconstruct the Potteries Railway for £70,000, comprising: £16,666 in shares at 60%, £10,000; old rails, £5,800; cash, £54,200, which was accepted.

Walter John Charles Cutbill (1843–1915) was the younger son of Thomas Samuel Cutbill (1805–67), contractor Thomas Brassey's London agent, and had worked on Brassey contracts in India and Mauritius. From 1867 he had been in partnership with Ulysses de Lungo (1841–97), building railways in South America. Since 1 July 1873, when Thomas Brassey & Company was established to undertake contracts after the contractor's death, they were among its partners; the company was dissolved on 8 February 1894 (*London Gazette*, 16 March). In England they were the Bridgwater Railway's contractors (*Wells Journal*, 10 July 1890) and retired in 1894.

In February 1889 the Shropshire directors had asked Young for a further six months to complete the purchase but the court order intended to authorise it, made on 17 July, was unsatisfactory because it only gave possession instead of ownership, which would have left them unable to issue debentures.

By 30 August, however, the order had been amended, and a breakdown of the money needed to reconstruct the railway produced (Appendix 8). The issue of £275,685 0s 9d stock and £5,000 debentures was required to fulfil the requirements of the 1881 Act.

A reminder that a part of the railway was still functioning occurred on 8 September 1889, when a locomotive derailed on points at Llanyblodwel. Edward Jones, the fireman, knocked off and badly injured, was taken to hospital at Oswestry for treatment. It appears that the points had been tampered with. The driver, Henry Wright (1832–1916), said that he had jumped off the loco but later admitted that he had been riding in the van eating his breakfast. The Cambrian had offered a £20 reward for information leading to the identification of the person or persons who tampered with the points but withdrew the

The Cambrian Railways' 0-4-0ST *Prometheus* was involved in the accident at Nantmawr on 8 September 1889. Photographed at Oswestry, the Porthywaen branch brake van is stabled behind it.

offer when Wright admitted his deceit. On 23 October the traffic and works committee dismissed him; by 1891 he had obtained employment driving a forge engine at Plas Power colliery, Wrexham (*Liverpool Mercury*, 9 September / *Oswestry Advertiser*, 11 September).

There appeared to have been some issue with Cutbill's terms, for by March 1890 Green-Price was negotiating with Whadcoat Brothers & Co. Ltd, bankers and contractors of public works. During that month Inman had met Potteries Railway stockholders and had asked *them* if they would buy Shropshire Railway debentures to finance the railway's reconstruction. When it became clear that this was not a fruitful source of inquiry, on 30 April the directors resolved, 'that the chairman be authorised to negotiate an agreement with Messrs Whadcoat Brothers & Co. Ltd for taking the debenture capital and finding money to pay for the reconstruction and reopening of the line between Shrewsbury and Llanymynech and paying out the liquidator and satisfying the landowners and for legal, engineering and directorial expenses …'

An agreement that Whadcoat Brothers would pay £79,500 within fourteen days of the company making a contract with a 'reputable' contractor was accepted on 23 May 1890 and sealed on 3 June. To save money the original iron rails were to be reused rather than being replaced by steel.

The company's first meeting was held in London on 20 June, when Green-Price explained that if something was not done to get the railway working quickly then it would have to be abandoned, losing the money subscribed locally and the effort put into obtaining the Act of Parliament. When the Shrewsbury undertaking had been completed, work would be started on the Market Drayton line. Authority was given to issue debentures for the former and to raise capital for the latter (*Birmingham Daily Post*, 21 June).

On 25 July 1890, the directors resolved to award the contract to Charles Chambers for a price not exceeding £64,000, £44,000 payable in cash, the balance in shares. He was already known to Green-Price through his earlier railway ventures in Herefordshire. He was required to refurbish the line from the Cambrian junction at Llanymynech to the Wellington line junction at Shrewsbury, to construct a new line to the Abbey station on an improved level and to make changes there. The indenture was made on 6 August, enabling the resuscitation contract, which did not include the Breidden branch, to be executed.

Although the land claims were settled straight away – the releases were dated between 28 July and 12 August – Young did not distribute the Shropshire stock to the Potteries stockholders until the autumn; the transfer register was brought into use on 8 October 1890. The landowners accepted shares and subscribers to the Bill, which had cost about £4,000, were paid in 5% debenture stock (*Oswestry Advertiser*, 20 August). The deposit financed by Cutbill remained in place and that company was not reimbursed.

On 19 August Chambers had been authorised to take possession, expecting the work to take fourteen months. The next day he and the directors, along with John Russell, the engineer, rode over the line on 'a couple of trolleys,' stopping for lunch at the Cross Gates Inn, Ford, and returning to Shrewsbury at 7.00pm (*Shrewsbury Chronicle*, 22 August). Travelling on unsprung vehicles over an overgrown railway must have been quite an experience.

Previously, the Midland Wagon Works had been asked to remove its property from railway land at Shrewsbury. The 1888 auction of rolling stock notwithstanding, two locomotives remained, so their sale must have fallen through; £160 was offered for them but on 10 September 1890 the directors required £200. They were still there in October but nothing more was said about them.

Over the next twelve months a good part of the reconstruction was carried out. On 22 November the *Wrexham Advertiser*

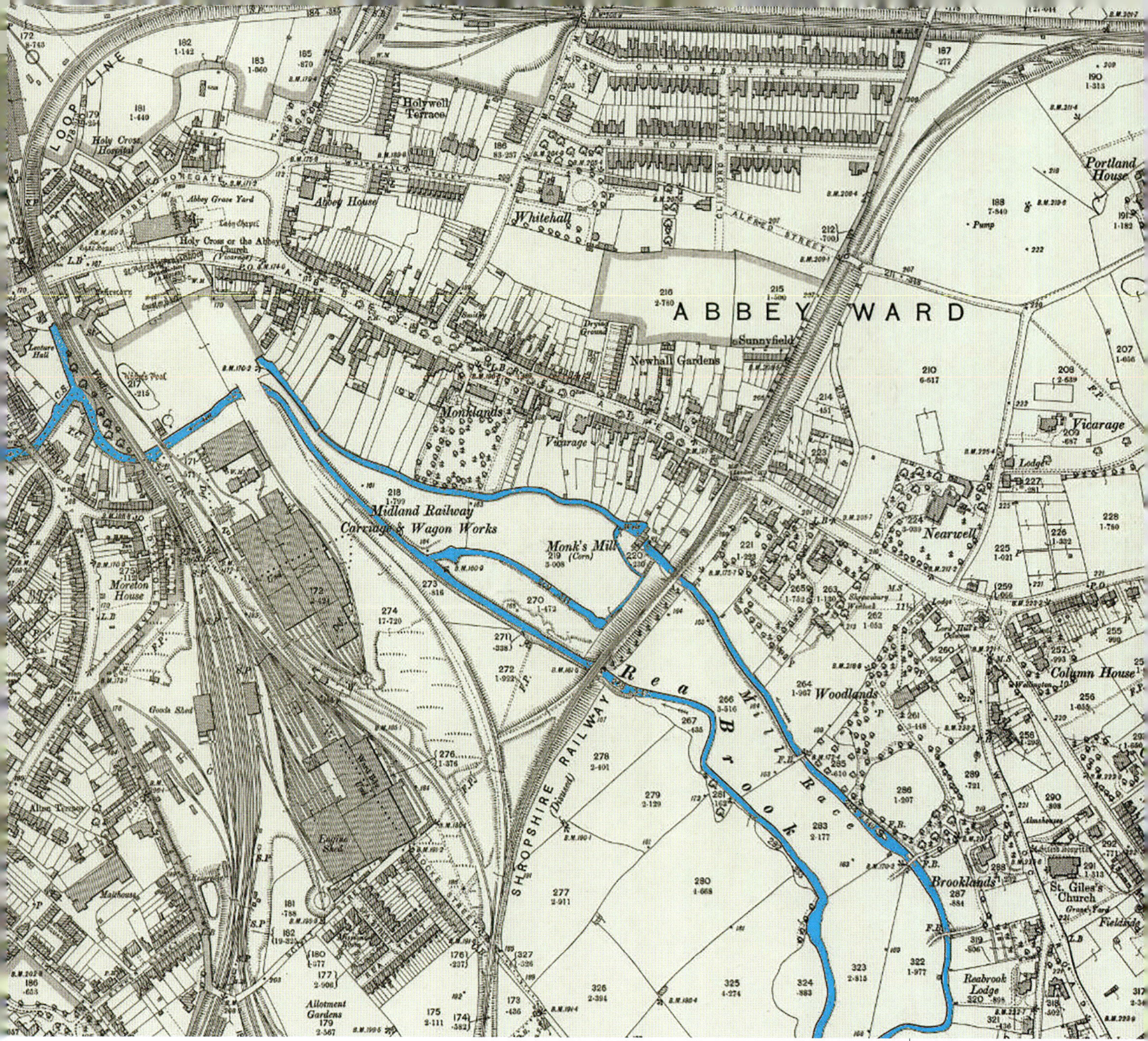

reported that at Shrewsbury the ground was being raised and a new bridge over the Rea was being built. The bridges over the Severn Valley and Welshpool railways had been substantially repaired and work was in hand on bridges that crossed public roads. Between Llanymynech and Kinnerley six timbered bridges and flood openings were being replaced with concrete and brick abutments and girder spans. Three miles of track from Shrewsbury and a greater length from Llanymynech had been re-laid.

Construction works employing navvies were often accompanied by reports of drunkenness. The only one known in this instance is that of Samuel Jones, who was found guilty of being drunk, for which he was fined 10s and costs or seven days' imprisonment, and assaulting a policeman, £1 and costs or fourteen days (*Eddowes's Shrewsbury Journal*, 10 December 1890).

Reporting on 1 April 1891, Russell, the engineer, said that the excavations and embankments were almost completed, twelve bridges were 'practically completed', the abutments built and girders were in place on two others and the arches were turned on another two; the Shrawardine bridge re-decking was nearly complete; three fifths of the 22 miles of railway and sidings had been re-sleepered with new bolts and spikes and had been re-ballasted. About 9,000 sleepers, a large

The 25in Ordnance Survey map from 1902 showing the railway site abandoned.

amount of permanent way and other materials, including new girders for three bridges, were on site ready to be used. Russell had previously reported that 5 miles of new fencing had been erected and 10 miles of hedges laid. He produced a report on the work required at the stations on 21 May, but it is unlikely that much of this, if any, was done.

The relationship with Chambers had got off to a good start but in December 1890 he had been asked to reduce the amount of his monthly certificate. He replied that he could not do this as he had already contracted for the supply of services and materials. At the end of that month £21,300 of work had been certified. When Russell calculated the amount due on certificate No 6, worth £4,100 in March 1891, he reduced the prices payable against the contract; the issue then went to arbitration and the award was made against the company. Chambers issued a writ for £3,000 on 13 May despite the company having said that it accepted the arbitration award, and his solicitor returned the stock certificates due to him on 9 June because they were not accompanied by the money due. When construction stopped in July 1891 Chambers had undertaken work with a certified value of £40,000.

Whadcoat Brothers acted as banker, releasing money on receipt and approval of Russell's certificates and other requests. The company issued mortgage debenture bonds in exchange for the money. When the cheque was received Chambers would be paid. There were further problems during 1890, with Whadcoat Brothers complaining that the company was failing to comply with the terms of the 3 June agreement. Two more agreements were made, on 1 August and 10 December 1890.

The rapport between the company and financier further deteriorated after January 1891, when interest due on debentures was not paid, hardly surprising as the company had no revenue. There was, of course, £5,000 in the budget for interest and Whadcoat Brothers was supposed to give this to the company for the company to pay some of it back to Whadcoat Brothers. The revenue from stocks sold to the public by the company, £3,701 2s by June 1890, was paid to Whadcoat Brothers and an appropriate value of bonds was returned for cancellation.

There was not always unity amongst the directors, with Inman resigning on 13 December 1890. Although a mysterious figure at the time of the Parliamentary hearings, he had attended all the board meetings until 25 October 1890. He had objected to the contract being given to Chambers and his departure had been in the offing for some months, communicating with the board concerning his expenses and other claims via his solicitor while he was still attending meetings. Richard Edmondson (1857–1912), a barrister appointed to the board on 23 May 1890, objected to the change in Chambers' rates while maintaining his directorship. Samuel Clement Southam (1849–1900), another Shrewsbury businessman, replaced Inman on 3 February 1891, but resigned on 24 April.

In February 1891, Green-Price submitted his resignation because he had taken a post with the Local Government Board. However, on submission of an undertaking that the company's meetings would be held in the evening and that he would not let his involvement interfere with his public office the Board sanctioned his continuing with the railway, allowing him to withdraw his resignation on 6 March. On 25 November 1891, when the writing was clearly on the wall, the directors decided to apportion £1,737 10s standing to their credit: Green-Price, Smith and Taylor £347 10s each, Barcroft £322 10s; Inman £276 5s, and Edmondson £96 5s.

Despite the need to focus on raising money and getting the works completed, the directors could not ignore the opportunities to consider expansion. In October 1890, Green-Price and Russell

were to examine, at the request of landowners and residents, the possibility of an extension to serve the Tanat Valley, the board considering that an extension to Llangynog would be in the company's interest. Russell, at the same time, had been asked to assess the works needed to make the Breidden branch fit for goods traffic. His estimate was £9,900, and expenditure on fencing it, £5, was approved in December 1890.

Russell was in constant dialogue with the board over money owed to him. In 1890 he was still due fees and expenses arising from the 1888 Act. By 18 March 1891 he was owed £2,625; at the next meeting he was paid £250 from the Market Drayton account, £50 from the London account and £50 from the Shrewsbury account.

Relationships with the neighbouring railway companies appeared to be good. In November 1890 a draft agreement with the Cambrian covered a connection between the Nantmawr branch and the Cambrian's Llanfyllin line and, within six months of powers being obtained, entering into an agreement 'for the working in perpetuity of your railway … less the Breidden branch'.

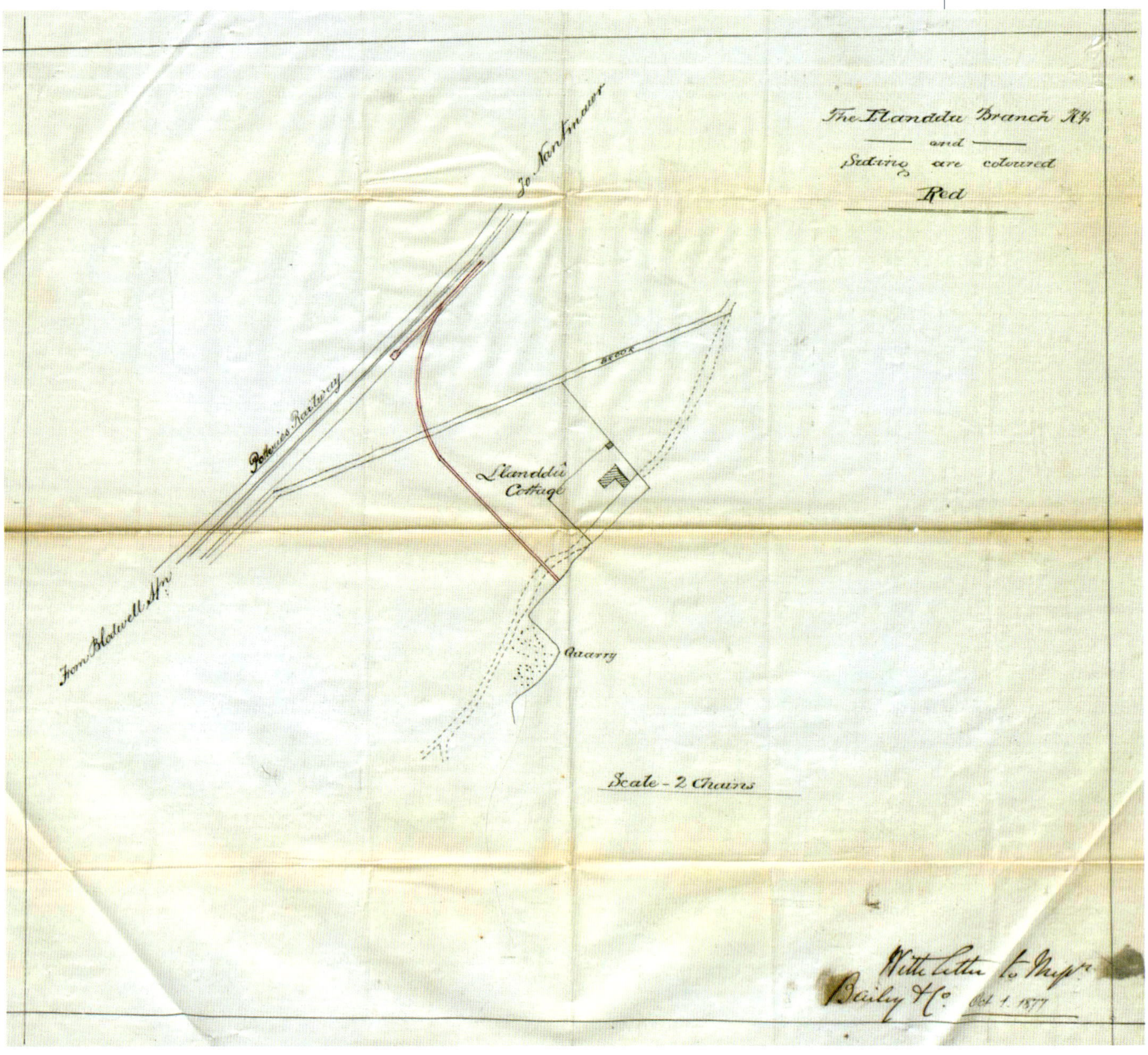

A sketch for the branch proposed to serve Llanddu quarry in 1877. (National Archives)

The company's readiness to have another railway work its services may explain its willingness to dispose of the original locomotives. The Cambrian was also asked to build a siding on the Nantmawr branch for Lord Bradford at Llanddu, the cost to be set against tolls due to the railway. Correspondence with the joint lines over a connection at or near Red Hill was amicable, although not as far as agreeing to give access to the joint station.

Bills applying for powers 'to make new railways, and for other purposes', and to extend the time for the purchase of land and completion of construction and to increase borrowing powers had been deposited in December 1890. The new lines were to modify the Llanyblodwel branch connections with the Cambrian at Llanymynech, which would be largely for the benefit of the Cambrian, and for a branch to Llangynog. The Bills were the cause of complaints by Whadcoat Brothers, who should have been consulted under the terms of their agreement with the company. The British Linen Bank agreed to fund the temporary deposit on payment of 200 guineas commission.

Green-Price had been vigorously promoting the Tanat Valley scheme, raising nearly £1,000 to support its promotion. The shareholders gave their approval at a meeting in Shrewsbury on 8 January 1891 (*Shrewsbury Chronicle*, 9 January).

To appease Whadcoat Brothers after the January 1891 debenture interest went unpaid, the company had given them a lien on all money or stock due to the company from the liquidator as security for the interest, and the interest on that. Prospectuses for '5% perpetual first debenture stock' were issued on 19 January and 6 April 1891. This stock, the would-be applicants were informed, was a first charge on the Shrewsbury Separate Undertaking and the interest was payable in priority to dividends on the ordinary stock.

Whadcoat Brothers agreed to support the prospectuses on what appeared to be their standard terms: any advance was to be repaid within six months together with 10% interest and 5% commission. The January prospectus raised only £11,400. It, unless there was more than one issued on that date, was headed 'special prospectus for the proprietors of the London & North Western, Great Western, North Stafford and Cambrian Railways companies' in red. Whether targeting stockholders of the railway's neighbours in that way was a ruse to try to persuade them that those companies supported the issue is a matter of conjecture.

Meanwhile, in Shrewsbury the town's antiquarians kept a wary eye on the Abbey pulpit, which had fallen into the railway's ownership by an accident of history, uncertainty about the railway's position causing its discussion at the Shropshire Archaeological Society's 1891 AGM. The railway company had wanted to remove

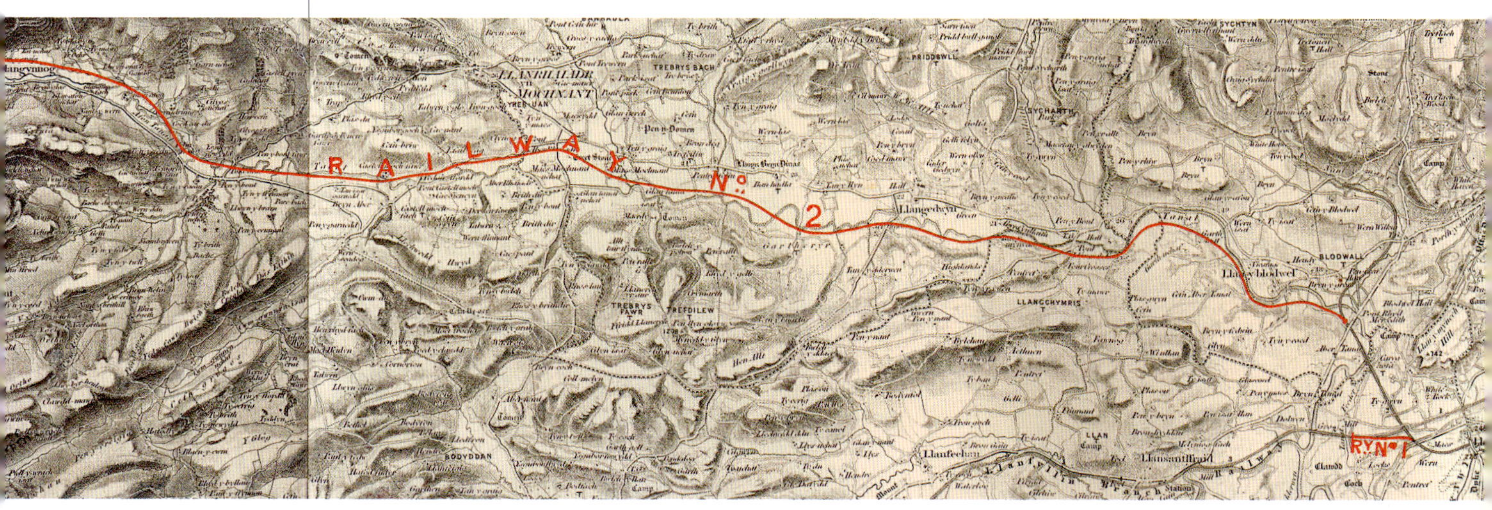

The plan for the Shropshire Railways' proposed Llangynog branch and the connection to the Llanfyllin branch that was built later by the Cambrian Railways. (Parliamentary Archives)

it as it was in the way but, said a member, 'by a providential episode' it had not, as it had found that it would cost £100, and it did not have much money (*Wellington Journal*, 24 January). The Shropshire Archaeological and Natural History Society had also discussed the pulpit at its AGM in November, and had done so in 1880 (*Eddowes's Shrewsbury Journal*, 8 December 1880/18 November 1891).

Chambers was sufficiently advanced to arrange a trip from Shrewsbury to a point half-a-mile past Kinnerley for the directors and friends on 17 February, although riding in open wagons in February would have required much fortitude on the part of the passengers. His Manning, Wardle locomotive hauled the wagons. Engineer Russell was represented by the resident engineer, Percy Wilson Symmons (1865–1958), his former pupil and assistant, who had worked on the Parliamentary and working plans.

Among the guests was Frederick J. Horniman, the tea magnate, who had previously announced his intention to subscribe for £2,000 of shares (*Eddowes's Journal*, 4 February) and who took this opportunity to say that he would also subscribe £300 towards the initial expenses for the Market Drayton undertaking; he was satisfied, he said, that he was investing in a safe concern. After lunch at the Cross Gates Inn, the party returned to Shrewsbury, not knowing that they would be the last passengers to travel on the Shropshire Railways (*Eddowes's Journal*, 25 February).

Cutbill took their complaint arising from the 1890 Bills, that the first money raised by the company after incorporation should be applied to paying the costs of obtaining the Act, to the Chancery Court, where it was heard on 18 March. The judge, however, found against them, although he did say that he thought that the contract the promoters had made with Cutbill was *ultra vires* as regards the railway company, but he would say nothing about that (*The Times*, 19 March). Cutbill decided to appeal but by the date set for the hearing had had

John Henry Whadcoat, the elder of the brothers who funded the Shropshire Railways.

second thoughts, paying the company's costs (*The Times*, 16 April).

Various stockholdings became a concern for the directors during 1891, initially when they realised that they did not hold the qualifying shareholding as specified by the 1888 Act. Green-Price and Smith had £250 each, Edmondson £500, and Taylor £400. Russell and the solicitors had to surrender stock issued to them as surety and receive the cash. During the year, the Railway & Public Companies Finance Association disposed of £18,100 of stock, including £7,100 to Chambers and £5,000 to Whadcoat family members. The London Finance Association Ltd made disposals and acquisitions.

On 17 April, the directors had been notified that Whadcoat Brothers had transferred 447 mortgage debenture bonds to John Henry Whadcoat (1851–1924) and 362 to William Edward Whadcoat (1854–1901), as security for advances of £21,000 and £15,946 4s 0d respectively. They were unnerved by this and ordered that they must be informed before any future transfers were registered. The parties to a transfer of £65,157 ordinary shares were not

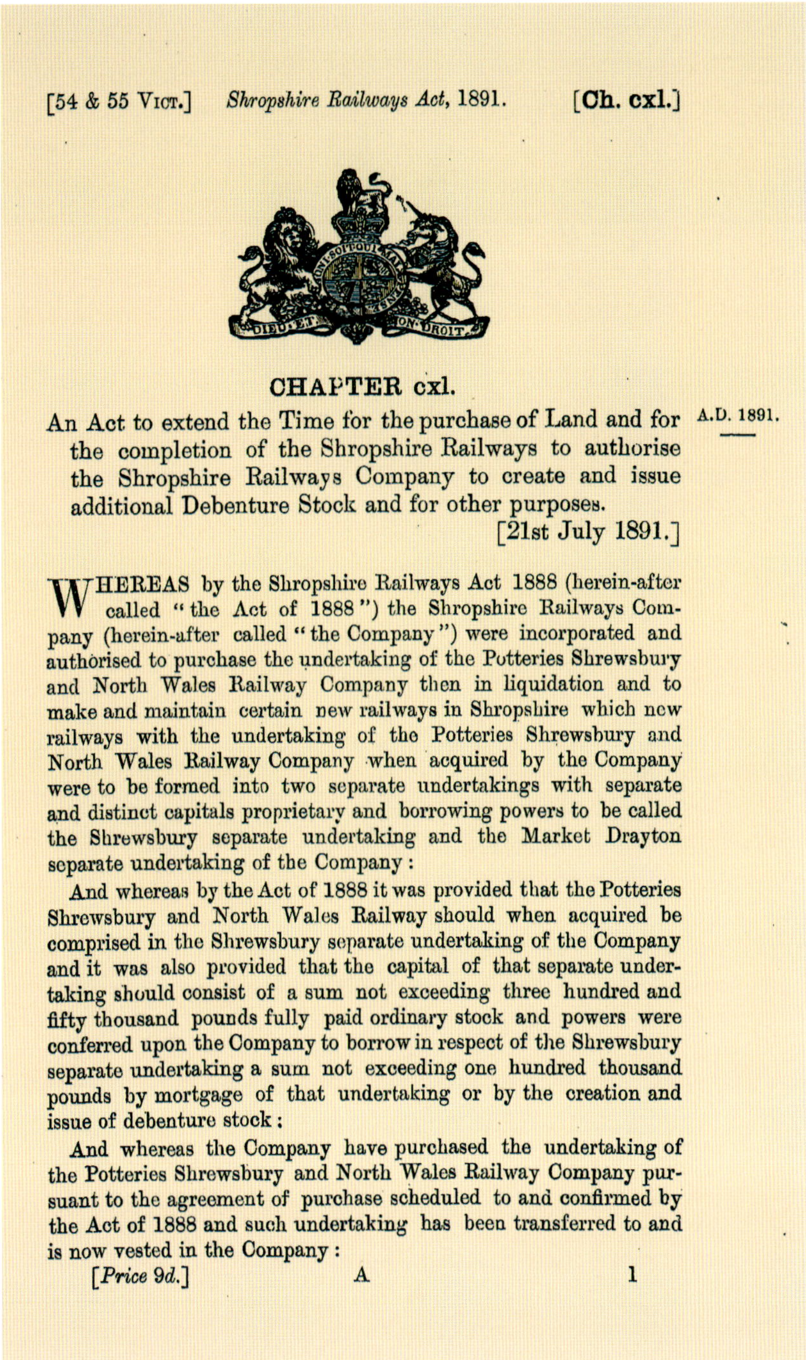

[54 & 55 VICT.] *Shropshire Railways Act*, 1891. [Ch. cxl.]

CHAPTER cxl.

An Act to extend the Time for the purchase of Land and for the completion of the Shropshire Railways to authorise the Shropshire Railways Company to create and issue additional Debenture Stock and for other purposes. A.D. 1891.

[21st July 1891.]

WHEREAS by the Shropshire Railways Act 1888 (herein-after called "the Act of 1888") the Shropshire Railways Company (herein-after called "the Company") were incorporated and authorised to purchase the undertaking of the Potteries Shrewsbury and North Wales Railway Company then in liquidation and to make and maintain certain new railways in Shropshire which new railways with the undertaking of the Potteries Shrewsbury and North Wales Railway Company when acquired by the Company were to be formed into two separate undertakings with separate and distinct capitals proprietary and borrowing powers to be called the Shrewsbury separate undertaking and the Market Drayton separate undertaking of the Company:

And whereas by the Act of 1888 it was provided that the Potteries Shrewsbury and North Wales Railway should when acquired be comprised in the Shrewsbury separate undertaking of the Company and it was also provided that the capital of that separate undertaking should consist of a sum not exceeding three hundred and fifty thousand pounds fully paid ordinary stock and powers were conferred upon the Company to borrow in respect of the Shrewsbury separate undertaking a sum not exceeding one hundred thousand pounds by mortgage of that undertaking or by the creation and issue of debenture stock:

And whereas the Company have purchased the undertaking of the Potteries Shrewsbury and North Wales Railway Company pursuant to the agreement of purchase scheduled to and confirmed by the Act of 1888 and such undertaking has been transferred to and is now vested in the Company:

[*Price 9d.*] A 1

The Shropshire Railways (Extension of Time) Act, 1891.

identified when its registration was recorded on 17 October, but the new owners were the Whadcoat brothers.

Construction stopped on 15 July 1891, when Chambers withdrew his men after Whadcoat Brothers ceased funding the railway. Russell was given permission to remove his agent, P. W. Symmons, from the site on 17 October.

The company and Chambers commenced proceedings against Whadcoat Brothers, the directors declaring that the company was in default of the contract on 16 July. They also offered to fund the £209 13s 6d debenture interest due on 1 July personally and read a circular sent to stockholders by the Railways & Public Finance Association on 13 July. The Association had the same directors as Whadcoat Brothers (*Shrewsbury Chronicle*, 6 November 1891).

The Shropshire Railways Act 1891 received the royal assent on 21 July. Rather than petitioning against the bill, Cutbill had tried to obtain an injunction to prevent it proceeding, but its application was refused as being beyond the court's remit. The Act extended the compulsory purchase powers until 7 August 1893 and the time for completion until 7 August 1896. New share capital of £75,000, £16,600 additional borrowing on the original capital, and £25,000 borrowing on the new capital were also authorised. Voting rights, omitted from the 1888 act, were defined. The 'general powers' Bill passed through the Commons and the committee stage but was withdrawn because the company had no funds for its deposit (*Wellington Journal*, 8 August 1891).

CHAPTER 5

ANOTHER RECEIVERSHIP

It cannot have been a coincidence that on 31 July 1891 W. E. Whadcoat applied to have the Shropshire Railways Company placed in receivership, arguing that he owned 362 £100 debentures and was owed £893 interest. The company had responded by pointing out that there was no income and that the debentures were really owned by Whadcoat Brothers Ltd, who had failed to provide the income to pay the interest. The judge was not persuaded (*Wellington Journal*, 1 August 1891), however, and Richard Rabbidge (1843–1921) was appointed receiver on 11 November. Several dilapidated cottages, including those at Wern Las and Kinnerley, were repaired to make them lettable and to provide Rabbidge with an income with which he could administer the company.

Receivership was arguably the least of the railway's problems for by the end of the year it was involved in no fewer than five legal actions. The company and Charles Chambers had sued Whadcoat Brothers and had been counter-sued; a Mr Webb, Chambers' clerk, and Inman had both issued writs against the company and then there was 'Whadcoat Brothers' libel action'. Cutbill had also issued a writ over the construction contract earlier in 1891 and during 1892 the London Finance Association issued a writ for unknown reasons.

The railway company had claimed that the contract with Whadcoat Brothers was null and void because it had been broken by them; Whadcoat Brothers counterclaimed for £20,000 damages, saying they had not been issued with any 'A' class debentures, presumably requiring the majority of all classes. The libel action arose from the company's half-year report published in December 1891; in it Whadcoat Brothers had been accused of manipulating the stock to secure more influence. The transfer of bonds to the Whadcoat brothers individually and the subsequent purchase of £65,157 ordinary shares by them had been done in such a way as to maximise the number of votes available to them. If they were able to get a place, or places, on the board, the directors suggested, they would be in a position to stop the suit brought against them by the company.

Simultaneously, James Inman was pursuing a refund of the 1888 Parliamentary deposit to which he had contributed, an activity that included an attempt to have the Parliamentary Deposits Act of 1892 amended. The last correspondence retained by the Board of Trade on his complaint was dated 1907.

Among all this legal activity was the death of nine-year-old Richard Beeton Jones, who had fallen from a dilapidated bridge into a stream near Melverley and was drowned on 27 September 1891. The son of a blacksmith, he had been placed in the care of an aunt, Agnes Grainger (1843–1921), whose husband

Prominent in the creation of the Shropshire Railways, Captain James Inman had been an infantryman and was the son of Grantham School's headmaster. He was buried in the town's public cemetery, his estate valued at £136,301 15s 7d, £12.3 million in 2022.

worked at the Farm Hall brickyard in Kinnerley. At 10.00pm she had taken the boy with her when she went to take her husband his supper, walking along the Breidden branch trackbed instead of along the road. It was dark, they had no light, he walked in front. She heard him shout, followed by a splash. One of the inquest witnesses said that the bridge was dangerous even in daylight. After the jury had returned a verdict of accidental death, stating that Grainger was to blame and calling for Sir R. Green-Price to be notified of the bridge's dangerous condition, the coroner called her in and reprimanded her for 'such recklessness' in taking the boy with her and declaring that it would be a reflection on her during her lifetime (*Wellington Journal*, 3 October). Presumably she had taken him with her because the alternative was to leave him on his own. Of her six children, five of them died in childhood.

The legal activity prompted one shareholder to write to a magazine calling for other investors to take action to protect their interests. His letter was reprinted in the *Shrewsbury Chronicle* on 6 November 1891. He was unhappy that the Whadcoats and Whadcoat Brothers had so many debentures, and also about new voting powers authorised by the 1891 Act. Holders of £100 stock were entitled to ten votes, with one vote for every £50 holding up to £1,000 and then one vote for every £100 over £1,000, so twenty-eight votes for £1,000 and thirty-eight for £2,000, which, he said, encouraged those with larger holdings to split them into £100 blocks to get more votes (*Shrewsbury Chronicle*, 4 December 1891), the subject of the libel action mentioned on Page 91.

In the boardroom, engineer John Russell was ordered to prepare plans for the Market Drayton line on 28 November 1891, when shares were issued to Green-Price, Smith and Taylor, fifty each, Russell, two, and several others, one each. Soon afterwards, the instruction to Russell was countermanded.

A summary of the situation was given in the directors' report published on 4 December 1891 (*Shrewsbury Chronicle*), the day before the shareholders' meeting. Russell also reported that 54% of Chambers' contract had been completed and he had a considerable amount of materials on the ground ready to use. Work to raise the level at Shrewsbury was nearly complete, and the main and loop lines had been re-sleepered throughout. Fencing was complete. Bridge work was well advanced, including replacing the timber ones with concrete and brick, with wrought iron or steel girders and timber floors. The outstanding work was mainly at stations, junctions, sidings and level crossings, and completing the 1888 Act's Railway No 1.

At the shareholders' meeting director Richard Edmondson complained that the accounts had not been signed by Rabbidge, the receiver, taking a position that suggests that he might have been the author of the letter published on 6 November, although he also said that he doubted if a better agreement than that made with Whadcoat Brothers could have been made. His attempt to have the report refused until it was signed by Rabbidge was rejected.

The shareholders succeeded in obtaining the appointment of a Committee of Consultation to look into the company's affairs. One of its members was Henry Doughty Browne, who also held shares in the London Finance Association (*Eddowes's Journal*, 9 December 1891).

In its annual report, the Association informed its members that it had received £77,491 Shropshire Railways Company fully paid stock, which cancelled £442,914 of Potteries, Shrewsbury & North Wales Railway stock (*Morning Post*, 3 February 1892).

The railway then went into limbo, the frequency of board meetings reducing considerably. Its moribund state left others in its locality feeling helpless, too. For example, when the Oswestry Highways Board wrote to Green-Price about the state of a bridge on the Nantmawr branch and its approaches, it received a reply from the Shropshire Railways saying that their letter had

Henry Doughty Browne, a Shropshire Railways shareholder who became a member of the Committee of Consultation. Also the chairman of the London, Tilbury & Southend Railway and a shareholder in the London Finance Association, it was his connection with the Stock Exchange that was remembered on his grave in Highgate Cemetery, London. His estate was valued at £144,237 19s 5d, £13,705,652 in 2022.

been forwarded to the receiver (*Oswestry Advertiser*, 16 March). Russell was instructed to inspect the branch, which remained in operation, for mineral traffic only, by the Cambrian Railways.

The lack of any report from the Committee of Consultation annoyed one debenture holder so much that he wrote three letters to the *Shrewsbury Chronicle* (12 February / 25 March / 27 May) on the subject. With his third he quoted replies that he had received from Rabbidge, who said that nothing would be settled until the outstanding litigation had been resolved and that there would be nothing for the debenture holders until the railway was opened and earning money. The letter writer had also addressed his complaints to the *Wellington Journal*, which had refused to publish them, but on 23 July that paper explained that it had done so because it thought the directors and the Committee should be given time to sort things out; now it thought that it was time something was said.

During May, the Reverend Thomas Brown Foulkes (1817–95), writing from Llanyblodwel vicarage, complained to the Board of Trade about the dangerous condition of the bridges in the area and the Highways Board observed that the fences were in poor condition, too.

Another court case was also heard during the month, when the Midland Railway Wagon Company made what appears to have been an opportunistic bid to acquire railway land at Shrewsbury, claiming that the Lands' Clauses Act of 1845 ruled that any superfluous railway land that remained unused should be sold within a specified time and if unsold would vest in the adjoining land owners, making a claim to all or part of the 5 acres adjoining its works. Despite evidence being given that the land had accommodated a turntable and sidings, the Wagon Company claimed that it had the appearance of a desert and was only used for growing potatoes. Much was made of the railway being impecunious, to which the railway's QC replied that if the land was really superfluous then an impecunious railway would have sold it when it was selling other unwanted land. After much argument, and evidence from witnesses including J. B. Cooper and J. Wade, the jury found in favour of the railway (*Wellington Journal*, 23 July 1892).

On 11 October 1892 the directors resolved to accept the Cambrian's offer to commute the toll on the sixty chains of the Nantmawr branch used by Llanfyllin branch trains provided that any agreement did not put the company under any liability regarding signalling, and did not inhibit the railway from using the branch without paying tolls to the Cambrian.

News of yet another application for Parliamentary powers came in November 1892, when the North Salop Railway bill was deposited, seeking authority to form a company that would take over the Market Drayton undertaking and for other purposes.

One of the legal cases was dealt with in November, when Whadcoat Brothers' libel action was heard. The company had

stated that Whadcoat Brothers had refused to provide money as agreed and that proceedings had been started against them as they ought to be held to the contract and they had the ability to pay. Whadcoat Brothers' position was that they were not bound to make any payments until they had agreed the schedule of prices to be paid to the contractor, a contention that was already the subject of litigation. However, the directors' QC stated that they had no intention of imputing anything dishonourable to Whadcoat Brothers and the action was stayed. No less a person than the attorney general represented the financiers (*London Evening Standard*, 23 November 1892).

For the purpose of the hearing, three of the actions involving the railway were amalgamated and dealt with over several days in December 1892 and January 1893. In the first action J. H. Whadcoat claimed that all revenue should be applied to the debenture holders; in the second the stockholders sought a ruling that the agreements with Whadcoat Brothers and the shares and debentures issued to them were *ultra vires* (beyond the powers of) the company, because it had the effect of selling the railway's stock at a discount, and restraining Whadcoat Brothers from dealing in the debentures; in the third the London Finance Association sought a ruling that the debentures were null and void. This description is much simplified (*Wellington Journal*, 10 December 1892). On 16 January the judge ruled that the agreements with Whadcoat Brothers were fair, reasonable and proper, that the *ultra vires* claim was extraordinary because railway companies had a long history of discounting the stock when better terms could not be obtained and that the action failed. The failure of the *ultra vires* claim resulted in the failure of the others (*London Evening Standard*, 16 January 1893).

The judgement enabled two supplemental agreements to be made with Whadcoat Brothers but they meant that the Whadcoats had gained control of the railway. The end for Green-Price came on 11 February, a busy day for the railway's administration.

Firstly, there were the special meetings for the shareholders of the two undertakings to approve the North Salop Railway Bill. Green-Price opened by saying that there was opposition to the Bill as it stood and that he could not recommend it but would simply submit it to the meetings, which both rejected it.

Then there was the general meeting adjourned from 5 December 1891. Here Green-Price explained that two of the Committee of Consultation members, having obtained a counsel's opinion on the railway and resigning on 8 February 1892, had initiated the stockholders' legal action against the company that had been rejected in January, which rendered any further work by the committee unnecessary.

With all the directors retiring, J. H. Whadcoat, W. G. Barcroft and W. E. Whadcoat were elected for the Shrewsbury undertaking and Green-Price, Parson Smith and Robert Ullmer (1856–1927, Whadcoat Brothers' company secretary) to the Market Drayton. Green-Price and J. H. Whadcoat spoke favourably about each other while admitting that they had not always been in agreement. It was to be Green-Price's last public participation in his creation, the scheme to revive the Potteries Railway (*Shrewsbury Chronicle*, 17 February 1893).

At the board meeting that followed, J. H. Whadcoat was elected 'permanent chairman' and was to find a new office for the company in London. That was Green-Price's last meeting. He remained a director of the Market Drayton undertaking until 13 July, when the transfer of his shares to W. E. Whadcoat was registered, the secretary reporting that he had written to Green-Price to tell him that he was no longer a director and that his successor had been appointed. Only Barcroft and Parson Smith remained from the old regime, although the latter did not attend meetings for a while.

Even with the change in control and the company still in receivership, the directors' focus remained unchanged, reopening the

The Shropshire Railways' founder, Sir Richard Dansey Green-Price, was buried in the public cemetery at Knighton, Radnorshire, now in Powys. On death, his effects were valued at £444 3s 4d, £41,745 in 2022.

Potteries Railway and building the Market Drayton line. A £2 call was made on the latter's shares in July 1893. Perhaps some part of the line was fit for traffic or nearly so, for on 22 July 1893 the chairman was authorised to 'agree terms for Mr Griffiths to convey goods and minerals on the line' but on 3 June the *Wellington Journal* had reported that on 29 May a workman had been seen lifting rails near Llanymynech, 'which does not seem to corroborate the report this line will be shortly opened for traffic'.

The explanation came in the chancery court on 18 July, when a motion to commit the contractor, Charles Chambers, for contempt of court was heard. He had removed track components to prevent the railway being used for traffic by horse power, which he had heard was the subject of negotiation and which he considered to be detrimental to his rights. Disagreeing, the judge ruled that if Chambers gave an undertaking to reinstate the track, then the motion would be stayed for four days. If it were not reinstated, then he would make an order for committal. Chambers did not want to go to gaol (*Wellington Journal*, 22 July). Nothing more was heard about Mr Griffiths or the plan to run horse-drawn trains.

The relationship with Chambers did not improve and on 22 July 1893 he was given three weeks' notice to resume work and threatened with the consequences if there were any problems arising from his activities or lack of them. A week later he was told not to use the company's name in any existing or future action. When he was seen surveying on the Nantmawr branch, a solicitor was retained to advise if he was trespassing. When Llanymynech station was found to be locked up with a notice reading 'contractors office' attached to it, the directors were more unhappy. Whatever he was doing, Chambers was not making any progress on the works. By 30 August the directors wanted to replace him but could not make contact with Russell to obtain information to enable a contractor to tender. A new engineer, who would give credit, was required.

The secretary, Edward Burgess Smith (1855–1935), received short shrift from the directors on 30 August 1893. Hearing that he had taken action against the company and

John Parson Smith was the Shrewsbury businessman who obtained the Nantmawr quarry lease in 1885 and worked closely with Sir Richard Green-Price to bring about the revival of the Potteries Railway. Buried in Shrewsbury's Longden Road cemetery, his grave is shared with other family members and marked by this large slab. His estate was valued at £72,745 16s 10d, £7 million in 2022.

had been awarded judgement in his favour because he had not been paid, they paid him £12 for his services until 30 September and sacked him with immediate effect. Robert Ullmer was appointed secretary on 6 November, his place on the board being taken by James Irvine (1833–1907), managing director of Eley Brothers Ltd, ammunition manufacturers; William Quilter, the Potteries Railway's receiver in 1866, had been a founder director of this company when it had been floated in 1874.

The legal issues did not go away and in November 1892 and 1893, Cutbill deposited two Bills to try to regain control of the Shropshire deposit. Under the terms of the 1892 Bill, the North Salop Railway would take ownership of the Market Drayton undertaking and control of the Shrewsbury undertaking, charging Shropshire Railways interest on the cost of completing it. Failing with this, the following year an abandonment Bill was promoted. The company petitioned against the Bill and on 4 May 1894 the House of Lords select committee found that 'the promoters have not made out their case, and the bill should not proceed'.

In the meantime, on 30 August 1893, a bill for costs of £29 0s 8d, was received in a case 're Berrington', the first the board knew of it. It was not mentioned again.

John Russell, the engineer, was replaced by Ridley & Moss-Blundell, engineers of the Uxbridge & Rickmansworth Railway, on 6 November 1893, 'the position of the company having been fully explained'. The claims for £3,398 for his work on the Shropshire Separate Undertaking and £42 in respect of the Market Drayton Separate Undertaking were deferred. Settlement was reached in January 1895 for a total of £4,000; possibly £1,000 of this was in cash provided by Whadcoat Brothers, the remainder was 1891 debentures.

The state of the infrastructure, being unfinished, was regularly before the directors' attention. On 11 April 1894 alone there were letters from Shropshire County Council, about road approaches and bridges, the joint railways, the bridge over the Hereford line; and the Shropshire Union Canal about the leaking aqueduct over the Nantmawr branch. In February the County Council's main roads committee had decided to raise an annual charge on railway companies to maintain roads on bridges; in the case of the 'Potteries Railway', six bridges with a road area of 9,204.642 square yards would attract a charge of £517s 6d (*Shrewsbury Chronicle*, 2 February). The £5 16s 1d bill for the aqueduct was passed to the receiver.

W. E. Whadcoat resigned from the board on 11 April 1894. Smith, present for the first time since the Whadcoat takeover, was required to read the minutes for the meetings that he had missed. J. H. Whadcoat resigned on 7 January 1895 and it may be relevant that £36,363 of 1891 debentures were registered to him the next day. He was replaced by George Bush, a director of the Devon & Somerset Railway, while Irvine was elected chairman. Surely someone was indulging in wishful thinking when they suggested that the Whadcoat brothers should be authorised to have free lifetime passes on the railway, its branches and extensions? Smith resigned on 27 February 1895 and was replaced by Edward Bertie Haselden (1856–1918), a stockbroker, shortly afterwards.

W. E. Whadcoat acquired 1891-issue debentures with a face value of £36,364 during 1895–96 and J. H. Whadcoat transferred his £41,364 holding to his wife, Emma (1858–1922); she transferred most of it back to him in 1900. Notable names among the debenture holders were Samuel Morton Peto, the contractor, with £1,000, John Plimsoll Brocklebank, the shipping magnate, a third share in £7,403; the Mid Wales Railway, £31, and the Cambrian Railways, £374. An insignificant holding of only £7 registered on 19 April 1895 is of interest because its owner, Frederick Pring Robjent, a stockbroker, became a director of the Festiniog Railway Company in 1908.

Not all investors were confident about their investment. The magazine *Truth* ran an advice column on railway stocks and on 10 May 1894 it had told 'Novice' that there was no market for the stock. It added that,

although there had been sales at 10% over par, it would be impossible to sell at par or even under, concluding 'this was a very injudicious investment on your part' and to stick to purchasing stocks of well-known lines in future.

In a move that sounds a bit suspect given that the company was in receivership, it was agreed on 19 June that the rent on a cottage at Kinnerley should be paid directly to J. H. Whadcoat 'in reduction of indebtedness by company to him'.

The Regulation of Railways Act of 1889, which, inter alia, required railways to interlock points and signals, motivated the Cambrian to improve its access to the Llanfyllin branch, making use of part of the Llanyblodwel branch to do so. Hitherto, trains had been reversed into and out of the north end of Llanymynech station; henceforth the access would be direct, from the south. On 11 April 1894 it had agreed to pay £150 annually for an easement over the acre of Shropshire land required, the *Shrewsbury Chronicle* noting the start of work on 19 October. The canal siding, which had not been used since the railway had been closed, was removed in the process.

It was while working on the cutting at Carreghofa on 18 October 1895 that Albert Morris, aged 29, was killed, with 12–15 tons of earth falling on him. Warned, his last words were 'I do not think it will come down.' The inquest jury returning a verdict of accidental death (*Wellington Journal*, 26 October), the registered cause of death was 'fracture of skull and other injuries sustained accidentally'. Morris died just over thirty years after Peter Robinson and Samuel Jones had lost their lives undertaking similar work nearby.

The connection was completed early in 1896, Colonel Horatio Arthur Yorke (1848–1930) submitting his report on what he called the Llanfyllin curve on 30 January; it became known as Wern Junction. The present method, he wrote, where branch trains were backed into the station 'along what is little more than a siding' was 'highly objectionable'. The curve was 37 chains, 50 links in length, and laid in partly worn steel 72lb rails. This material would normally be deprecated on new works, he

Linking the Shropshire Railways' Llanyblodwel branch with the Cambrian's Llanfyllin branch, this plan is signed by the latter's engineer, George Owen, and dated 1895. (National Archives)

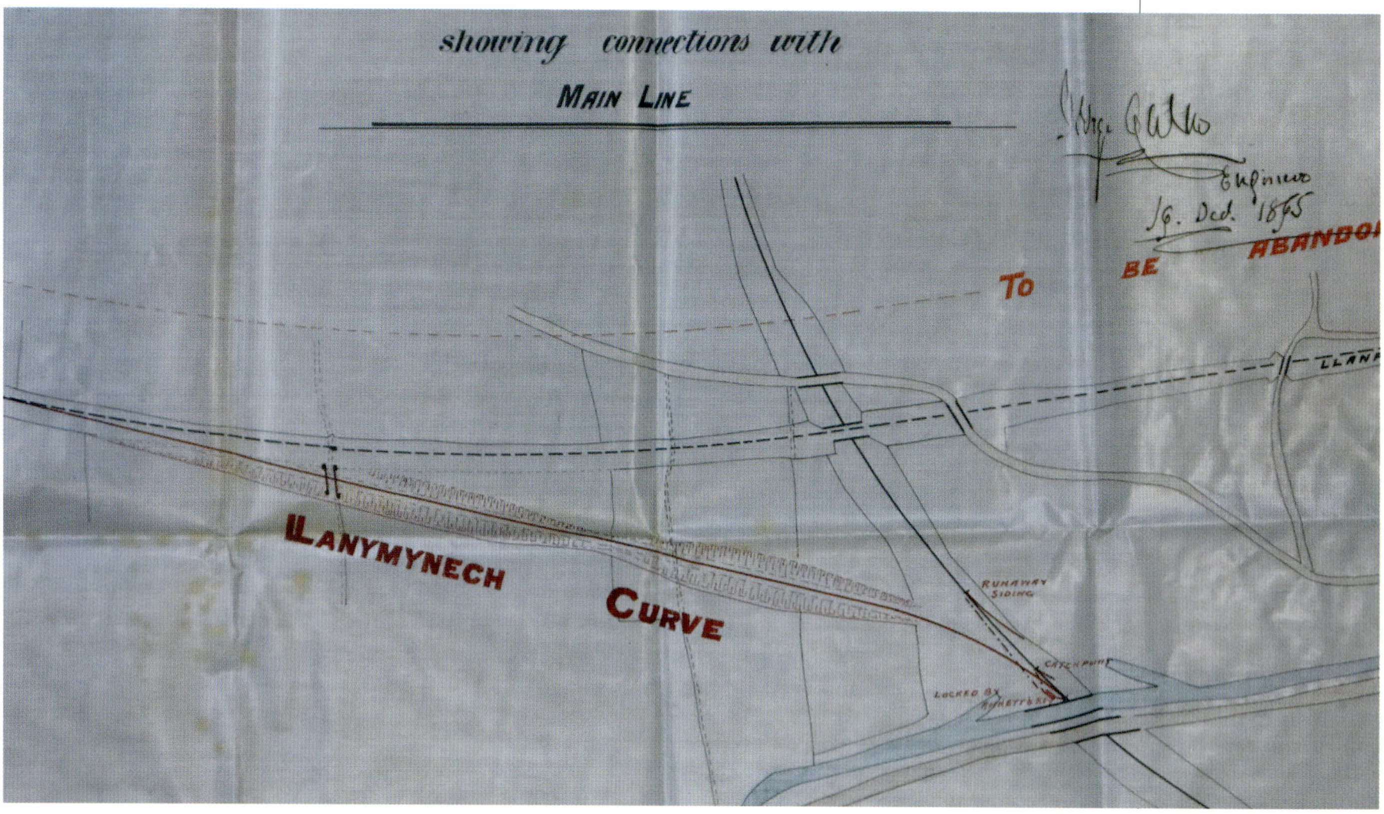

Wern Junction seen from the canal bridge. It is protected by both a gate and a trap siding on the Blodwel line. The bridge that originally carried the Llanfyllin branch across the Shropshire line has been demolished, exposing the road bridge behind. Subsequently, the junction was controlled by a signal box installed between the two lines. (F. E. Fox Davies)

Wern Junction is just beyond the bridge, the route to Llanfyllin diverging to the left. The bridge, built when R. S. France still had ambitions of running a double-track main line to Wales, remains in situ, the Shropshire Union Canal bridge beyond it supported by a prop. In 1938 the GWR built a halt on the ground on the left of the picture and named it Carreghofa. (F. E. Fox Davies)

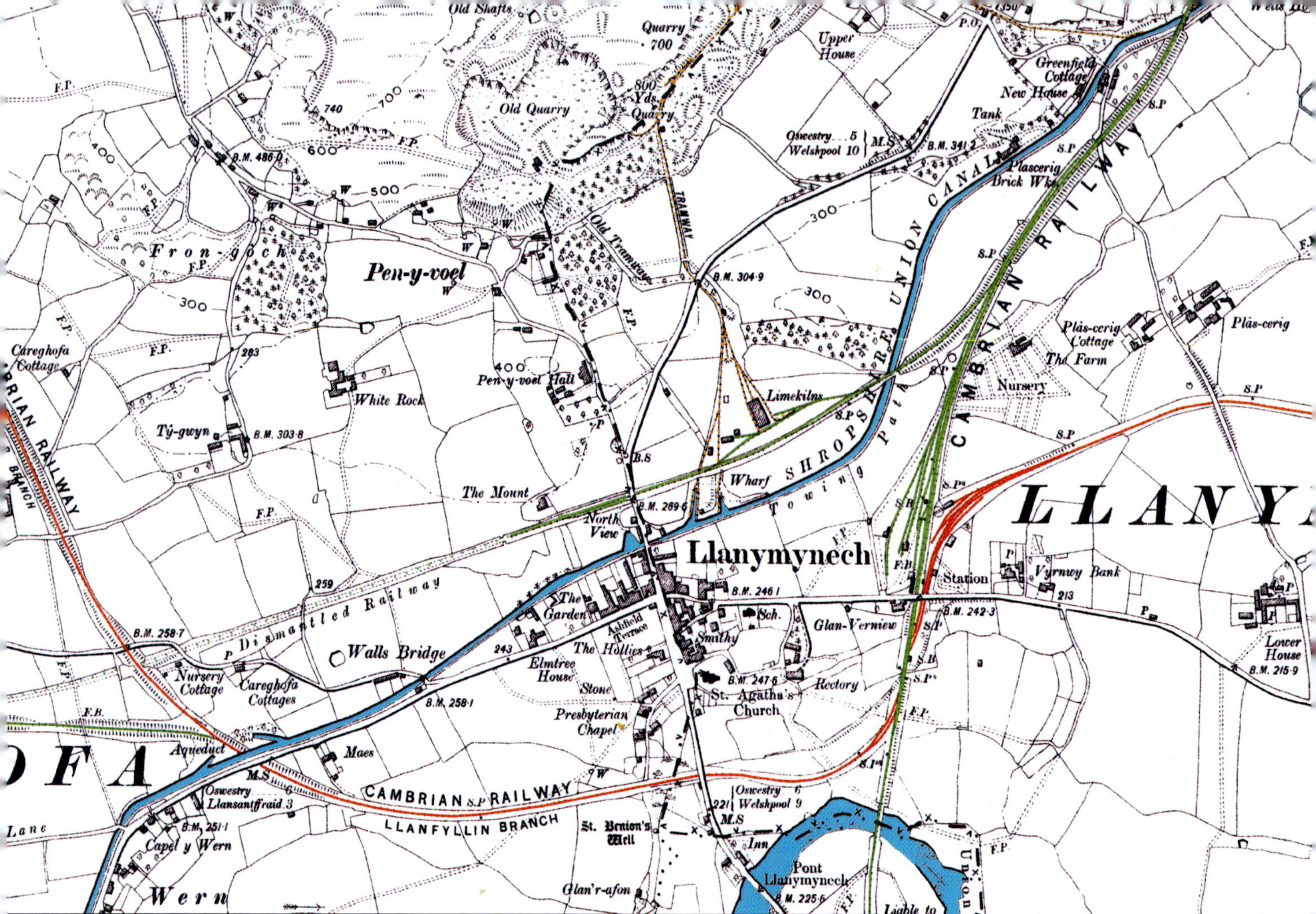

Railways and canal at Llanymynech, revised 1900, published 1902. (Ordnance Survey)

reported, but as the new arrangement was a big improvement on its predecessor, the remainder of the rail on the branch was the same and speeds were low, he thought it should be accepted as a special case without setting a precedent. The line being well sleepered and ballasted and the interlocking being satisfactory, he recommended that the Board of Trade sanction the use of the curve and associated works for passenger traffic.

The Cambrian had obtained a Board of Trade certificate authorising £8,041 capital to fund the work on 16 December 1892 but when the question arose as to whether it should also obtain a certificate issued under the Railway Construction Facilities Act, 1864, which it could do because no compulsory powers had been required, the Board agreed to powers being obtained retrospectively in one of the company's portmanteau Acts, which occurred later in 1896. Earlier, powers for the curve had been obtained in the West Shropshire Mineral Railway (New Lines) Act of 1864.

At the start of 1895 it had looked as though there was progress towards getting the railway reopened. Despite a fresh contract having been made between Whadcoat Brothers and Chambers in 1894, a provisional contract was also made with Walter Edward Clayton-Smith (1854-1927); a solicitor and, with Green-Price, a director of the Golden Valley Railway, he was not heard of again in this context. The Whadcoat brothers, acting separately, were appointed trustees to each of the parties to oversee it. Debenture holders had been asked, and most had agreed, to capitalise their interest payments until 1897. Young was urged to wind up the Potteries Railway and a new prospectus was about to be issued.

There is no obvious explanation for Young's prevarication over the liquidation; perhaps he was able to claim fees or expenses as long as it lasted. The prompt had some effect for he applied to complete the liquidation on 11 February 1895. Most of the transactions in his certified accounts were dated 1890–91, and the most recent, concerning a claim in respect of land was in 1893, so the work cannot have taxed him for some time.

The prospectus was a very different issue, however, and resulted in a great

deal of negative publicity that resulted in its withdrawal and brought an end to any ambitions for resuscitation and expansion.

The saga started with a shareholders' meeting to approve the issue of £75,000 5% perpetual preference stock and to borrow £41,600 secured on the Shrewsbury undertaking held on 7 January 1895. When the directors met to approve the prospectus on 27 February, they decided to seek

SHROPSHIRE RAILWAYS COMPANY.

Notice is Hereby Given, that an EXTRAORDINARY GENERAL MEETING of the SHROPSHIRE RAILWAYS COMPANY will be held at the Company's Offices, 3, Crown-court, Old Broad-street, London, E.C., on MONDAY, January 7th, 1895, at Twelve o'clock Noon, for the purpose of considering, and, if so determined, passing the following RESOLUTIONS:—

(1) A Resolution authorising the creation and issue of £75,000 Additional Capital, authorised by the Shropshire Railways Act, 1891, Section 8, as a Five per Cent. Preference Stock.

(2) A Resolution authorising the Directors to borrow on mortgage of the Shrewsbury Separate Undertaking any sum or sums of money not exceeding in the whole the sum of £41,600 (being the amount which the Company is authorised to borrow under Sections 12 and 13 of the said Shropshire Railways Act, 1891), and authorising the Company to raise from time to time all or any part of the said sum of £41,600 by the creation and issue of Debenture Stock at such rate of interest as the Meeting shall determine.

Dated this 22nd day of December, 1894.

R. ULLMER, Secretary.

Notice for the Shropshire Railways Company's extraordinary meeting held on 7 January 1895, published 22 December. (The Globe)

The List of Applications will open on Monday, the 25th inst., and close on or before the 30th inst.

ISSUE OF THE BALANCE OF

£100,000 5 % Perpetual First Mortgage Debenture Stock

(SHREWSBURY SEPARATE UNDERTAKING),

ISSUED UNDER THE "SHROPSHIRE RAILWAYS ACT, 1888."

The Interest of 5 per cent. per annum is payable to the Registered Proprietors Half-yearly, on the 1st January and 1st July in each year, and will commence to accrue from the date on which the Stock is fully paid up. The first payment will be made on the 1st July, 1895.

The Interest to the 1st January, 1897, is guaranteed on the amount of Stock subscribed under this Prospectus by the deposit of £6,957 10s. at the Capital and Counties Bank, Limited.

£69,575 of the above 5 per cent. Perpetual First Debenture Stock is now offered for Subscription at £100 per £100 nominal Stock.

PAYABLE AS FOLLOWS:—£5 0 0 per cent. on Application.
£20 0 0 per cent. on Allotment.
£35 0 0 per cent. on 30th April, 1895.
£40 0 0 per cent. on 30th May, 1895.

Total ... £100 0 0 for each £100 Debenture Stock.

Payment in full may be made on Allotment, or on 30th April, 1895. Interest on Stock so paid will accrue upon the full amount from date of payment.

The Shropshire Railways Company

(Incorporated by Special Act of Parliament).

AUTHORIZED CAPITAL

(SHREWSBURY SEPARATE UNDERTAKING).

£100,000 Five per cent. Perpetual First Mortgage Debenture Stock, £69,575 of which is now offered for Subscription.

£41,600 Five per cent. Perpetual Second Debenture Stock, £16,600 Issued.
£75,000 Five per cent. Preference Stock, unissued.
£350,000 Fully-paid Ordinary Stock, all issued.

Directors.

JAMES IRVINE, Esq., Brinsworth, Twickenham, *Chairman* (Director of Eley Bros., Limited).
W. GREER BARCROFT, Esq., Bryntirion, Wrexham.
GEORGE BUSH, Esq., 34, Cleveland Square, Hyde Park, W. (Director of the Devon and Somerset Railway).
EDWARD B. HASELDEN, Esq., Broadwater, Beckenham, Kent.

Bankers.

CAPITAL AND COUNTIES BANK, LIMITED, 39, Threadneedle Street, London, E.C.

Engineer.

A. S. MOSS BLUNDELL, Esq., M. Inst., C.E. (Consulting Engineer to the Government of Siam), 28, Victoria Street, Westminster, S.W.

Auditor.

RICHARD RABBIDGE, Esq., F.C.A., 32, Poultry, London, E.C.

Secretary and Offices.

MR. ROBERT ULLMER, 3, Crown Court, Old Broad Street, London, E.C.

The prospectus that brought an end to the Shropshire Railways' ambitions to revive the Potteries Railway.

advice on whether it should mention that the company was in receivership, which maybe should have acted as a warning. Advised that the receivership need not be mentioned, the prospectus was approved for publication on 16 March and issued in an abridged form in several newspapers on 23 March.

Under the heading, 'An outstanding state of affairs', the *Pall Mall Gazette* (26 March) identified the problems with the prospectus, and was outraged that it made no reference to the 1891 receivership, and aghast that Rabbidge, the receiver, was listed as the auditor. It would be madness, the paper said, for anyone to subscribe to the issue. Like a dog with a bone, it continued attacking until the prospectus was withdrawn and a promise made to return any money already subscribed.

The *Gazette* said that there was no information available about the company and no evidence that any debenture interest had been paid. The prospectus listed the debenture stock of other railways but said nothing about the value of the railway's existing stock, nor did it say anything about the debenture bonds that were to be redeemed by the 5% preference stock. It had also noticed that the Whadcoat brothers had recently resigned and asked why.

The next day, the paper was pleased to report that the *Financial Times* had picked up the story and had published an anonymous letter that said the company was in default on the first mortgage debentures issued in 1893 and that the debenture bonds to

be redeemed had probably been issued to Whadcoat Brothers.

On 28 March the paper asked why everyone involved with the prospectus had nothing to say about it. It could understand why the Whadcoat brothers could afford to be 'hippopotamus-hided' as they had an interest in it, but the others involved – the receiver, the bankers and the directors – had reputations to protect.

Meeting on 29 March, and transferring to their solicitors' office, the directors resolved to write to the *Pall Mall Gazette* and to copy the letter to *The Times*, which had made a brief comment on the affair on that day.

The *Gazette* was delighted. Its headline was 'AT LAST. RECEIVERSHIP ADMITTED. ALLOTMENT POSTPONED'. The company's letter, signed by Ullmer, was published in full. It explained that the receiver had been appointed to protect the rights of the debenture holders and to receive revenue on their behalf. He was not a liquidator, with power to wind up the company. In this case he would be discharged when payment of £881 15s interest, due on £4,820 stock out of £100,000, had been satisfied. The location of some of the owners of the £4,820 stock was unknown and the company had a claim against one of the holders for a larger amount than the interest owed.

The 1891 litigation, which ended in the company's favour, had resulted in the works being suspended and the company liable to pay debenture interest before it had any income. The funding was available to settle the interest and the line was expected to be completed and opened for traffic during the year.

Allotment of debentures had been postponed and the list would be kept open until 5 April. Any applicants who wished to withdraw could do so, Ullmer concluded.

The letter still left questions about the purpose of the issue. On 30 March *The Times* railed: 'we have no hesitation in saying that the fact [regarding the receivership] now admitted should have been stated … we are surprised that men

Charles Chambers was the contractor who started to reconstruct the Potteries railway until the funding was withdrawn. He had previously built the Golden Valley Railway in Herefordshire and the Southwold Railway in Suffolk, among others. Buried in London's Kensal Green cemetery, his effects were valued at £27,554 3s 1d, £2,646,382 in 2022.

of business should have imagined … that any other course should have been right or expedient. The fact alleged … that the receivership will end on the payment of a not very large sum has nothing to do with the case, and the assertion that a receiver and a liquidator are not identical in function is equally irrelevant. The directors ought to have foreseen that the actual position … was certain to be discovered very speedily, and that the discovery could not fail to impress intending investors unfavourably. Possibly they may have been technically correct in their idea that the fact referred to need not be disclosed. Their lawyer, it appears, advised them in this sense; but even supposing their view of the strict letter of the law can be defended, the board would have been wiser … if they had openly stated the real position of the company. Lawyers are good servants, but bad masters …'

The writer, 'a well-informed source', of a letter signed simply A. on 2 April, also in *The Times*, made it worse, if such were possible, by remarking: 'I should have thought it would have been even more interesting to know what the receiver receives' and summarised the railway's history. His final remark, on the railway's partial reconstruction and abandonment, concluding as it did 'Whether the contractor was paid I cannot say', leads the writer to speculate that Chambers was the culprit. If that was not enough,

the company's banker, the Capital & Counties Bank, then declared (*Pall Mall Gazette*, 4 April) that it had not known that the company was in receivership and had instructed the company to inform the applicants of the situation in order that they could withdraw.

On 5 April the directors decided that no allotment of debentures should take place and that any money received would be refunded, *The Times* to be informed accordingly. In publishing his letter on 6 April, the paper commented: 'We are glad to receive the following letter … the course announced being the only proper one in the circumstances.'

But the final nail had been driven in the railway's coffin by the *Pall Mall Gazette* the day before. Even with the information revealed and confirmed, it would still not recommend the debentures as the company's actions had shown it to be untrustworthy. And if anyone really wanted to invest in the Shropshire Railways there was no need to buy debentures at par when there were hundreds on the market that could be had for around 25% discount, but they could still not be recommended.

On 6 April, the *Pall Mall Gazette* positively gloated, with the headline 'Shropshire Railways work complete' and starting its report 'It is over.' It was, it said, a happy ending.

Meanwhile, in Shropshire, the *Wellington Journal* (30 March 1895) had been looking forward to the railway being reopened. A correspondent had obtained a copy of a report made Arthur Spence Moss-Blundell (1853–1950), one of the engineering partners appointed in 1893, compiled after inspecting the line earlier in the month. Apart from sections totalling 3 miles, the track was in good order and could be made fit for traffic in a few months. The stations required little work. Except for two near Shrewsbury and three near Llanymynech, the bridges were substantial and ready for traffic. The other five bridges could be made ready in three months. The railway could be completed in nine months he concluded.

Just how the directors, a group of competent, experienced businessmen, got themselves into a position where they issued a prospectus that brought ignominy on the company and hastened its downfall is open to speculation. As is the reason for the Whadcoat brothers withdrawing from a company in which they had invested so much. As it was, the directors abandoned the undertaking to its own devices. Irvine, Bush and Haselden submitted their resignations before the year's end, but technically they remained in office, because there was no one in office to accept them.

The receiver continued to administer the moribund company and railway. From 1897, the railway's entry in the Board of Trade returns was marked: 'There are neither directors nor officers to make the return.'

In Shropshire, however, the railway was not forgotten. When the Light Railways Act became law in 1896, Kinnerley Parish Council received a letter suggesting that it should do something to get it reopened as a light railway. The council passed the idea on to the county council (*Wellington Journal*, 8 August). On 5 September Montford Parish Council agreed that every effort should be made to have the railway reopened and passed copies of its resolution on to local landowners (*Wellington Journal*, 12 September). The county council discussed the notion the following year (*Shrewsbury Chronicle*, 12 February 1897) but nothing came of these efforts and it was several years before the railway was reopened as a light railway.

Abandoned once again, it was not long before the railway's road and bridges required attention, or before its movable property brought someone before the courts. Oswestry Rural District Council took unilateral action over a section of road (*Montgomery County Times*, 25 April 1896), Atcham Rural District Council passed a complaint about a road overbridge near Melverley to the receiver (*Shrewsbury Chronicle*, 15 January 1897) and Henry Wardle was fined £1 and costs for stealing four boards that he said he

had found on the road (*Wellington Journal*, 28 November 1896).

Another accident occurred on 23 June 1899, when John Jones, aged 60, a labourer, fell through a bridge in Shrewsbury and was found unconscious. Taken to hospital in the LNWR's Coleham loco shed ambulance, he was well enough to be discharged after several days. He had been walking along the trackbed at night (*Wellington Journal*, 24 June 1899).

The directors next met on 6 June 1900, the impetus being the need to approve an agreement made by Rabbidge for the Cambrian to lease the Llanyblodwel branch for ninety-nine years, which had been signed on 1 May 1900. The Cambrian guaranteed a minimum annual payment of £550 and also agreed to pay £5 annually for an easement to make a connection with the Llanyblodwel branch and its Llanfyllin line, and a £150 annual rental for the use of the part of the Llanyblodwel branch by Llanfyllin trains. Irvine, Barcroft and Bush attended the meeting as directors. The resignations were accepted and then Irvine and Bush were re-elected. J. H. and W. E. Whadcoat were also elected, the former in place of Haselden. J. H. Whadcoat was elected chairman and proposed as receiver and manager subject to Rabbidge resigning. On Whadcoat's proposal, it was agreed to exchange debenture bonds for debenture certificates, for the benefit of the Whadcoat brothers of course, although bonds to the value of £16,775 were not converted until 7 January 1907.

J. H. Whadcoat chaired the stockholders' meeting held on 7 July to confirm the agreement, explaining that the Potteries Railway's liquidator had given the Cambrian Railways authority to use the Llanyblodwel branch as a mineral line in 1885 and that in 1894 Shropshire Railways had given the Cambrian running powers over part of the branch and use of a plot of land on which the Llanfyllin branch junction was made on payment of £150 a year. Since then, the Cambrian had been paying £300 a year. The new agreement was the outcome of the railway's

Richard Rabbidge was the receiver described as the auditor in the Shropshire Railways' ill-fated prospectus. Buried in Teddington cemetery in 1921, his £48,871 estate would be worth £4,712,152 in 2022.

opposition to the Tanat Valley light railway order application. Over the seven years to the end of 1899, the receipts had been £2,112 14s 6d, £716 11s 4d had been paid into court and there was a balance of £298 14s 10d. Irvine added that the payment would cover expenses and help keep the line in repair.

One of the shareholders objected to the ninety-nine-year commitment, although he had been told that it did not prevent the railway from running its own trains, none of the £550 would benefit the shareholders and they might as well stay as they were (*Wellington Journal*, 14 July).

An editorial on the subject in the same issue concluded that the railway was 'doomed to prolonged if not perpetual paralysis, and its shareholders to the chronic sickness of hope deferred'.

At around this time the Nantmawr quarry lease was taken on by the Lilleshall Company Ltd; a contract was made between the company and the Cambrian on 14 November 1899. Under Lilleshall's control the stone was taken to its iron and steel works at Oakengates, Shropshire, via Llanymynech and Oswestry, hardly the

most direct of routes. Some of it was burned into lime in kilns located close to the incline foot. Close to the quarry a terrace called Lilleshall Cottages stands as testimony to the period of that company's operation.

Still frustrated by the continued lack of activity, the debenture holder who had written three letters to the *Shrewsbury Chronicle* in 1891 decided to enlist the support of the *Pall Mall Gazette* (11 April 1901). In his letter, he said that he had concluded that very few of the debentures were in the hands of the public and that most of them were held by the contractors, who had probably found some way unknown to him of realising their security. He made this claim because in 1891 he had appealed for other investors to join with him in taking action to protect their interests but had received no response. He was mistaken to point the finger at the contractor as the debentures were surely held by the financiers, Whadcoat Brothers, and their associates.

Passing through Shrewsbury in 1902, T. R. Perkins (Bibliography) stopped to explore the railway. At Shrewsbury he found a gate placed across the track at the end of the platform, and mounds of earth placed by Chambers to raise the level covering the incline trackbed for half of its length. Beyond the gate, girders from the original bridge over the River Rea lay in the water, while part of its brick replacement had been pushed into the river. Some lengths of rail had been levered off their sleepers with chairs attached, but the remainder was still in place. The junction signal box, its signals and the engine shed had gone. The site of Red Hill station was marked by the overturned ground frame.

At Llanymynech he found the station in a state of ruination, books and fittings lying on the floor, and the Cambrian using its tracks as sidings. The engine shed was derelict and the turntable so overgrown as to be almost invisible. All the level crossing gates having disintegrated, they had been replaced by hurdles and bundles of brushwood. At Kinnerley he saw the only wagon left on the railway. The signal box and water tank were both in a state of dereliction, the bay platform was completely overgrown and a haystack had been built under the road bridge.

Books, waybills, and other matter had been abandoned at Nesscliff, the crossing house and station building derelict. At Shrawardine the platforms were disintegrating, and the buildings gone. The nearby river bridge was passable with care,

Abandoned track crossing a bridge on the Potteries Junction section. Seeing the condition of it, it is no wonder that trespassing pedestrians sometimes came to grief. (F. E. Fox Davies)

Llanymynech station in dereliction, the Cambrian using the tracks to stable wagons. (F. E. Fox Davies)

with holes in the decking giving views of the river below. The building remained at Ford & Crossgates, where several notices were posted on the walls, one of them an LNWR timetable dated 1880. Finally, the platform at Hanwood was derelict and a signal so far out of vertical that he expected it to fall at any time.

On the Breidden branch the fences had vanished and the track was completely hidden by undergrowth. Another haystack had been erected at Melverley, but on the track in this instance. The river bridge had collapsed soon after the line had closed, leaving only a few posts driven into the riverbed to mark its position.

Perkins made a separate excursion to Criggion, reaching it on foot from Middleton on the Welshpool line, finding the crossing gates still standing and the crossing keeper's house used as a post office. The track here was so heavily overgrown that he was unable to visit Llandrinio and Crew Green.

H. G. Archer (Bibliography) seems to have visited the line during 1903 and found one place where an embankment

Llanymynech locomotive water tank. (F. E. Fox Davies)

had collapsed, leaving the rails suspended across the gap.

The possibility that Shropshire Railways might have a future was only hinted at when the directors met again on 22 November 1906: 'Correspondence between the chairman and the managing

Kinnerley looking towards Llanymynech. (F. E. Fox Davies)

Ford & Crossgates station in a state of dereliction. (F. E. Fox Davies)

director of the Kent & East Sussex Railway was discussed,' the directors agreeing to offer the rails, chairs and other ironwork for sale by tender, noting that the receiver had been running the railway at a small profit, accumulating £3,471 18s since 1891.

The Kent & East Sussex Railway's managing director was none other than Holman Fred Stephens (1868–1931), an engineer based in Tonbridge, Kent, who was achieving a measure of notoriety for his interest in the management and construction of light railways. He had studied engineering at University College, London, and mechanical engineering as a pupil at the Metropolitan Railway's Neasden works. In 1896 he had been appointed a second lieutenant in the 1st Sussex Royal Engineers (Volunteers), raising 600 men for service in the Boer War. He was promoted to captain before transferring to the 2nd Cinque Ports Division in the Royal Garrison Artillery in the same rank in 1905.

The meeting had been triggered, somewhat belatedly, by W. E. Whadcoat's death on 21 January 1901. He was replaced by James Moorman (1862–1918), who had married Whadcoat's widow in 1902 and moved into his Tufnell Park house.

How Moorman came into his money is not known; his father was a steam engine driver. He was living on his own means in 1901 and 1911 but died with assets of only £272 1s. As he cannot be found in earlier census returns, he might have been abroad. He was buried in Brookwood Cemetery. His widow, formerly Emma Whadcoat, had assets valued at £5,556 16s 7d (£249,379 in 2022) when she died in 1922, aged 64.

J. H. Whadcoat visited the railway on 20 December 1906, finding that some of its property was 'in occupation by various parties without the payment of rent'. At Shrewsbury, the Midland Railway Wagon Co. was using a siding and had buried a rail stack under several tons of cinders, and at Llanymynech he also found that it was quite obvious that the Cambrian had been making use of a siding; the secretary was to try to agree rental terms with both parties. Before long both claims were placed

In common with engineer J. H. Tolmé and Shropshire Railways shareholder H. D. Browne, William Edward Whadcoat, one of the Shropshire financiers, was also buried in London's Highgate Cemetery. His estate was valued at £139,750 3s 5d, £13,567,970 in 2022. His widow was buried with him, notwithstanding that she had married James Moorman in 1902.

with the solicitors – after more than ten years of inaction it took no time at all for the directors to enmesh the railway with the law. Travelling between Hanwood and Llanymynech by trolley, he had found that the stations were in course of demolition, including one that was being let when he last visited, probably at least ten years previously.

Meeting Stephens in Shrewsbury, Whadcoat decided that the rails should not be sold after Stephens had said that he expected to be able to make an offer to take over the railway and to work it as a light railway.

Discussing the matter on 17 January 1907, the directors resolved to ask Stephens to make an offer and that interest on the cost of reconstruction should form a first charge on new receipts or traffic. Agreeing to further expenditure, even if not theirs, seems rather foolhardy for a company so seriously in debt. On the same occasion, Joseph Henderson (1852–1911) was elected to the board to replace the recently deceased James Irvine.

Colonel H. F. Stephens. He revived the Potteries Railway and enabled it to exist for nearly another fifty years. (P. A. Harding Collection)

Maintaining contact with the directors, on 22 March Stephens said that he estimated that it would cost £32,000 to complete and equip the main line for traffic. At a later date a further £8,000 was added in respect of the Breidden branch, known as the Criggion branch in light railway days. On 15 April he asked for 'certain options to induce him to obtain powers'. Ullmer, still secretary, replied on 9 May: '… I am authorised … to give you the option to purchase at par, by completing and opening the main line … providing the rolling stock, working capital and other matters as per your estimate, £32,000 4½% stock if and when the same is authorised to be issued, such stock to rank in priority to the existing stock etc. of the company. The security for the interest on such stock to be the net traffic receipts of the main line when completed and opened, but exclusive of the existing revenue receipts which will continue to belong to the existing debenture holders.

'The company will do all in its power to assist your application for the Light Railway Order and in the issue to you of the £32,000 stock when authorised.

'Providing you make the application in due form during this month and without delay proceed with the same, this option will remain in force for six months after the granting of the Light Railway Order or up to the date of its rejection by the Commissioners.

'In any event it is understood no charge or claim is to be made on this company for costs or expenses or services of any description.'

By this means the company would retain ownership in the unlikely event that Stephens' proposed operation struck the proverbial pot of gold while apparently funding the reconstruction using the money raised from the issue of a new class of debentures. In practice, the debentures would be issued, not for cash but in exchange for work carried out, following the precedents set by Chambers and France. At the same time the debenture interest would be secured on the net revenue of the railway operation, something that would be beyond the directors' control.

THE SHROPSHIRE & MONTGOMERYSHIRE LIGHT RAILWAY

The first approach to the Board of Trade concerning the operation of the Shropshire Railways as a light railway had been made on 3 December 1906. H. F. Stephens wrote that he had 'had a proposal to reopen the line as a light railway'. He was informed that either the Shropshire Railways company, if it still existed, could apply for an order or 'a new body of promoters' could make an application for 'an order authorising the construction of a new railway over the same route and the compulsory acquisition of the land on which the derelict line was laid'.

The Board had actually missed the point that Stephens tried to make in his handwritten letter. His next was typewritten: 'If the railway was reconstructed, could it be reopened following an inspection, i.e. using the original powers but meeting the

A map showing the railway's place in the network produced by the Light Railway Company.

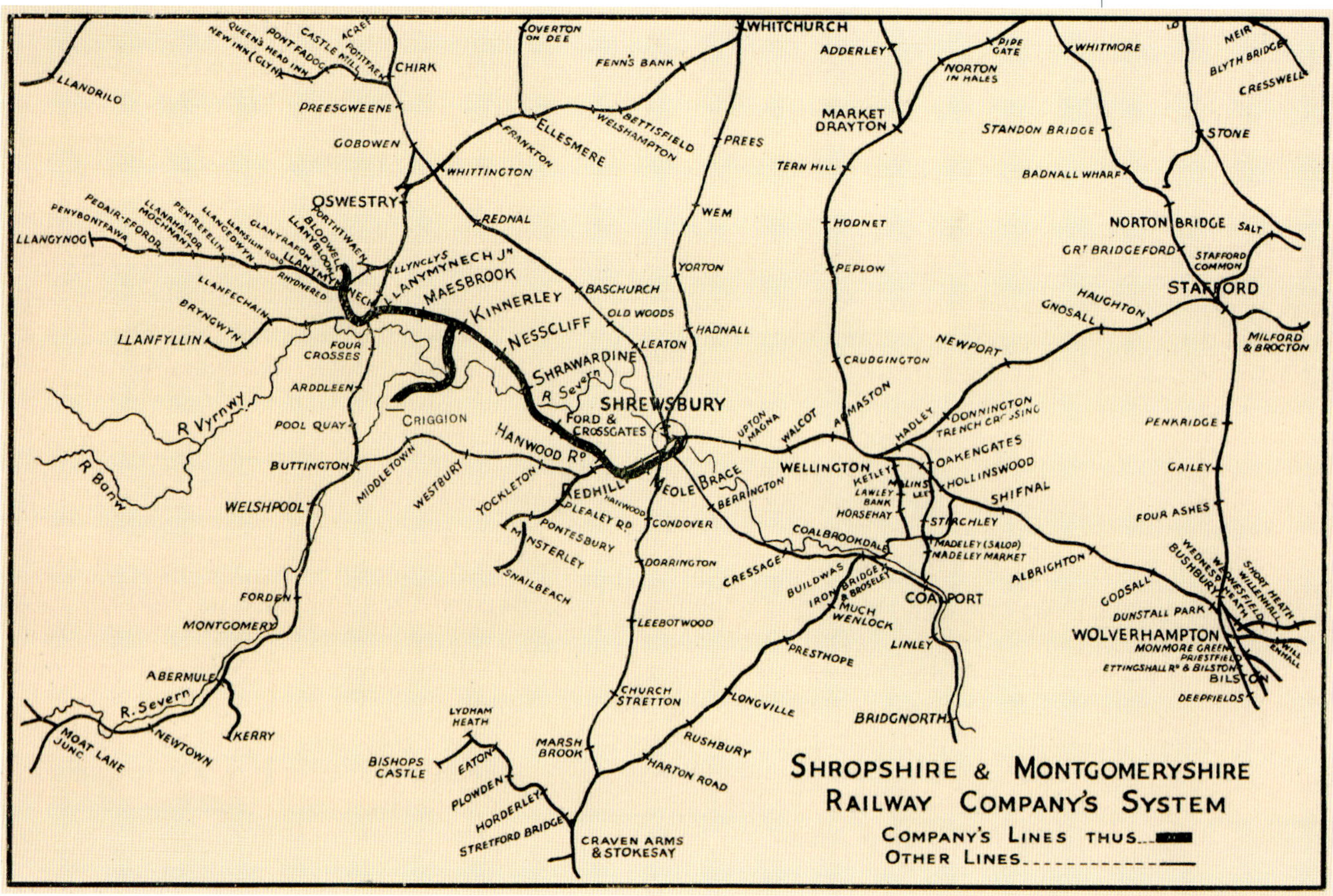

The inspection trolley at Hanwood Road during the dereliction era. Sitting at the front is Richard Reeves, who had been a Potteries Railway guard. The bridge's stonework was built by France, while the brickwork, some of which is deteriorating, was carried out by Chambers. (F. E. Fox Davies)

requirements of a light railway?' The file containing the correspondence is annotated: 'Mr Stephens is still rather vague and does not say for whom he is acting.' The suggestion that he be sent a copy of F. H. Rich's 1880 report was rejected, the Board replying that it had no information concerning the current state of the line on which to base an opinion, but would expect to receive detailed proposals that could be referred to the railway inspecting officers.

It should probably be no surprise that when the Light Railways Bill had been in Parliament in 1896 some minds had turned to the abandoned Potteries Railway, as mentioned on Page 102.

Exactly what prompted Stephens to take an interest ten years later is unknown. An intermittent stream of items in the railway press might well have played a part in raising the moribund railway's profile and thus bringing it to his attention but it was three years since T. R. Perkins' in-depth article had been published in *Railway Magazine*. It is equally possible that Stephens and J. H. Whadcoat might have met in Kent, for in 1908 Whadcoat moved to the Manor House at Bodiam, a locality served by the Kent & East Sussex Railway that Stephens ran.

Had the 1888 powers been deemed valid the promoters might also have expected to have a claim on the Act's deposit in respect of the Shrewsbury separate undertaking. A similar situation arose with the revival of the Welsh Highland Railway, where the then Department of Transport said that the 1922 Light Railway Order did not permit the railway's reconstruction and a High Court judge ruled that construction powers could only be used once.

Following further consultations with the Board of Trade, on 21 May 1907 Stephens published a notice of intention to apply for a Light Railway Order in the *London Gazette*.

At this stage Stephens appeared to be working without the benefit of legal advice, in that his advertisement did not adopt the usual form for such notices, it was not published in local newspapers, and he

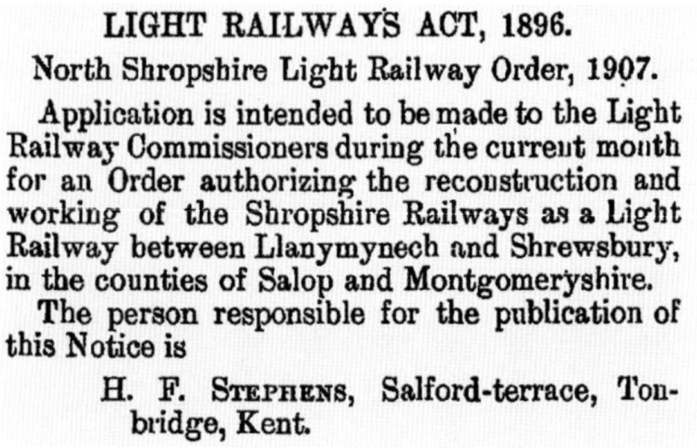

LIGHT RAILWAYS ACT, 1896.

North Shropshire Light Railway Order, 1907.

Application is intended to be made to the Light Railway Commissioners during the current month for an Order authorizing the reconstruction and working of the Shropshire Railways as a Light Railway between Llanymynech and Shrewsbury, in the counties of Salop and Montgomeryshire.

The person responsible for the publication of this Notice is

H. F. STEPHENS, Salford-terrace, Tonbridge, Kent.

The advertisement for what became the Shropshire & Montgomeryshire Light Railway Order. (*London Gazette*, 21 May 1907)

did not produce plans and sections or a book of reference showing land ownership and occupation for deposit with the local authorities affected.

The draft order named Stephens, the Earl of Bradford (1845–1915, the fourth Earl), William Rigby (1850–1929) and J. H. Whadcoat as the first directors. Rigby was a contractor who had worked with Stephens on the Sheppey Light Railway (*Sheerness Times Guardian*, 23 February 1901) and in 1911 they were to build a three-mile branch of the East Kent Light Railway together (*Evening Mail*, 6 November 1911).

News of the reopening proposal prompted a contributor to the *Cambrian News* (14 June) to recall his memories of the Potteries Railway, on which he claimed he had been a regular traveller. One advantage of it, he wrote, was that the trains would stop anywhere to pick up or set down passengers but on one occasion the timber station building caught fire and could not be saved because there was no water. Its only drawback, he concluded, was that there was no population in the locality to speak of.

The promoters wrote to the local authorities, seeking their support for the Order and in particular for the clause that would empower them to make advances, although the railway's supporters tended to say that there was no intention of asking for financial assistance from them and it was merely a gesture whereby their support would be demonstrated. Atcham Rural District Council saw no reason to dissent providing its interests were not interfered with (*Shrewsbury Chronicle*, 14 June), while Oswestry Rural District Council deferred making a decision until it had more information (*Wellington Journal*, 22 June). Bicton, Forden and Nesscliff Parish Councils, which would not have powers to invest, all approved of the order being made (*Shrewsbury Chronicle*, 14/28 June/*Wellington Journal*, 22 June).

On 1 July, Oswestry councillors overrode their chairman's preference and voted to support (*Wellington Journal*, 6 July). He had claimed that if they supported it then they debarred themselves from being represented at the public inquiry. Among the members, there was a feeling that if the railway reopened it would be a benefit to them as a road-maintaining authority, as some of the roads in the area would be designated main roads and maintained by the county council. The council had nothing to lose by supporting the order, asserted the *Shrewsbury Chronicle*'s (5 July) editorial.

An analysis of the application at the Board of Trade dated 24 June drew attention to its weaknesses, saying: 'This is an application of a very exceptional nature… [It] is made by Mr Stephens, the engineer, and Mr Rigby, of whom we know nothing. As it is proposed to … impose on [the Shropshire Railways] new liabilities … it would seem that the Shropshire company or the receiver on its behalf should have concurred in the application.

The 4th Earl of Bradford, George Cecil Orlando Bridgeman, was actively involved in promoting the Light Railway Order for the Shropshire & Montgomeryshire Light Railway, withdrawing from the company once it had been made.

The Shropshire company has not done so, but on the other hand they have sent in objections to some of the proposals and have asked for protection in some other respects. We have not heard from the receiver, nor is there anything to show that he has had notice of this application. … There are no drawings except a 1in Ordnance map, and there is no information as to the present state of the works and equipment. It is therefore impossible to criticise the estimate.

'The proposal is that the money should be raised by the Shropshire company … It seems to me that if the Shropshire company can raise the money, the interposition of a new company will only give rise to endless disputes between the two companies. There is no provision that the Shropshire company shall have any control over the expenditure of the money either on the capital or revenue account. To get over this initial difficulty the Shropshire company ask for the power to appoint a certain number of directors. This may mean entire control or no control at all. Already the Shropshire company object to the present provision out of revenue for depreciation and reserve, and there is nothing in the order as to the ownership of the works and equipment paid for out of the money raised by the Shropshire company …' Of course, as noted, the Shropshire Company was not going to raise any money itself.

The public inquiry held in Shrewsbury on 9 July was reported extensively in the local press. During the proceedings, Stephens said that as a contractor with experience in light railways, Rigby was a good person to have among the promoters as it was in his interests to get the work done as cheaply as possible.

The Abbey station was derelict and the junction with the Shrewsbury–Wellington line had been removed. The bridge over the Severn Valley line required reinstatement. Red Hill station would be reinstated. Hanwood was ruinous. Rails (75lb double-head, iron, he thought) were still in place, but some chairs had been removed. All the sleepers and keys needed replacing. Except for two near Llanymynech, all the bridges were substantial – they had been rebuilt by Chambers, of course. The Potteries Railway had earned an average of £5 10s per mile per week, not bad for a light railway, he thought; the implication was that the revived railway should be able to match that, but it was clear that there was no proper business plan as would be understood in the twenty-first century.

The population of the area served by the railway was 10,500. The largest community was Meole Brace, on the outskirts of Shrewsbury, with 1,845 residents, who would not generate much fare income even if they all travelled to Shrewsbury every day. Kinnerley, the site of the largest intermediate station, had 1,072 and Llanymynech, where the residents were as likely to want to go to Oswestry or Welshpool via the Cambrian as to Shrewsbury, only had 529.

The main line would cost £32,000 to reinstate, to which £8,000 should be added to restore the Breidden branch. Rigby had tendered £17,480 to undertake the restoration. One of the Commissioners noted that the rolling stock budget was only £5,000, at less than £300 a mile, not much scope for carrying much traffic, he thought, to which Stephens replied that they would get by with three locos, and a few carriages would carry a lot of people.

Notices had been served on the county councils. Shropshire had not replied but he understood that it was not hostile. Montgomeryshire had sent a notice dissenting but there had been no other response. The LNWR and GWR had not objected, and the Cambrian had asked for the same protections given in the 1888 Act.

Stephens said that the method of raising capital, securing it on the Shropshire Company's debenture stock, was unusual but the money would be 'unraisable' without it.

Asked about the possibility of running trains into the general station, he said that it was the right thing to do but it was a question of £sd and would be expensive to achieve. There would be a junction, but only for goods traffic.

In the absence of its chairman, J. H. Whadcoat, injured in a motor accident, the Shropshire Company's solicitor said he had a basis of agreement made with Stephens to submit but threatened to go to Parliament if they did not get what they wanted.

A Shropshire county councillor, Thomas Ward Green (1863–1950) of Maesbrook, who spoke in favour of the railway being reopened, also corresponded with Stephens about it, the correspondence surviving. He invested £100 in the Shropshire Railways' prior charge debentures and became a director of the Light Railway company in 1932.

The inquiry chairman complimented Stephens, 'You have put the matter before us in a very able way, as you always do; but it is a novel application.' In closing the inquiry he said they, the Commissioners, were anxious to see the railway reopened and it would be of public benefit but they would reserve their decision until they had been able to discuss the application back in London (*Shrewsbury Chronicle*, 12 July 1907).

Reading a report on the inquiry, *Wellington Journal* correspondent *Moel y Golfa* (20 July) suggested that the reconstructed Red Hill station be renamed Hookagate or Hookagate and Annscroft to reflect the names of habitations with 200–300 inhabitants close to the station site.

On 28 August a three-year-old child was another victim of the derelict bridges, Thomas Henry Douglas falling from one of them near the wagon works and his wounds being treated at Salop infirmary. The *Wellington Journal* (31 August) offered no explanation for an infant being on the railway trackbed. One of eight children, Thomas became a bus conductor and died in 1985.

Before the Board of Trade would agree to the insertion of a clause authorising the local authorities to support the railway financially in the Light Railway Order, it required their consent. Two of them, Shrewsbury Town Council and Oswestry Rural District Council, gave their approval in September, a councillor at the latter saying that while 'there was not the slightest possibility of their advancing the promoters any money, it would be a shame to stop other people from doing it if they wished' (*Wellington Journal*, 14 September 1907). The following June, Shrewsbury agreed to obtain powers to advance up to £500 (*Staffordshire Sentinel*, 20 June).

When Shropshire Railways' shareholders met to approve the Light Railway Order application on 7 January 1908, Stephens explained that while the cost of working a main line ranged from 2s 8d to 4s 6d per train mile, he was working light railways at costs ranging from 10d to 1s 2d per train mile. It was not an aristocratic service, he said, as goods and passengers ran together, but it was better than walking.

Among the six shareholders present was the contractor Charles Chambers, who wanted to know how the various debenture

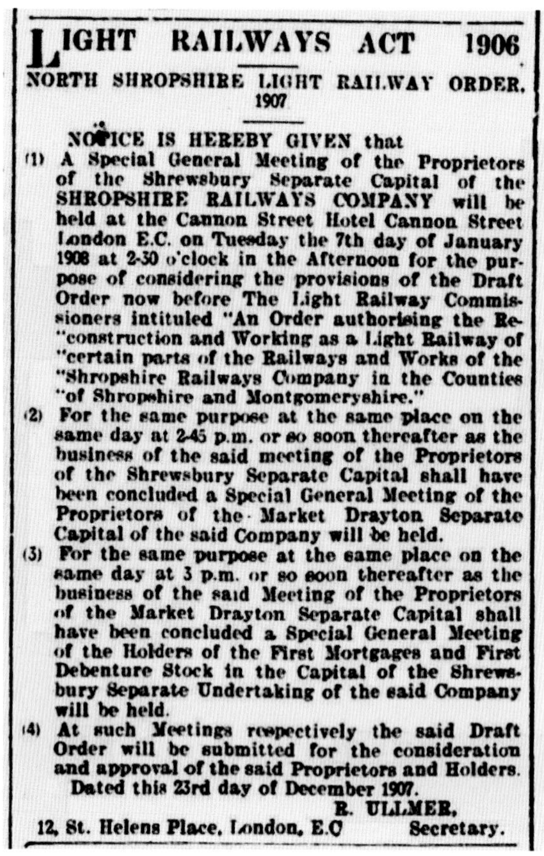

LIGHT RAILWAYS ACT 1906

NORTH SHROPSHIRE LIGHT RAILWAY ORDER, 1907

NOTICE IS HEREBY GIVEN that

(1) A Special General Meeting of the Proprietors of the Shrewsbury Separate Capital of the SHROPSHIRE RAILWAYS COMPANY will be held at the Cannon Street Hotel Cannon Street London E.C. on Tuesday the 7th day of January 1908 at 2-30 o'clock in the Afternoon for the purpose of considering the provisions of the Draft Order now before The Light Railway Commissioners intituled "An Order authorising the Re-"construction and Working as a Light Railway of "certain parts of the Railways and Works of the "Shropshire Railways Company in the Counties "of Shropshire and Montgomeryshire."

(2) For the same purpose at the same place on the same day at 2-45 p.m. or so soon thereafter as the business of the said meeting of the Proprietors of the Shrewsbury Separate Capital shall have been concluded a Special General Meeting of the Proprietors of the Market Drayton Separate Capital of the said Company will be held.

(3) For the same purpose at the same place on the same day at 3 p.m. or so soon thereafter as the business of the said Meeting of the Proprietors of the Market Drayton Separate Capital shall have been concluded a Special General Meeting of the Holders of the First Mortgages and First Debenture Stock in the Capital of the Shrewsbury Separate Undertaking of the said Company will be held.

(4) At such Meetings respectively the said Draft Order will be submitted for the consideration and approval of the said Proprietors and Holders.

Dated this 23rd day of December 1907.

R. ULLMER, Secretary.

12, St. Helens Place, London, E.C

The notice calling a meeting of Shropshire Railways' shareholders to approve the Light Railway Order application. (*Shrewsbury Chronicle*, 27 December 1907)

issues ranked for payment of dividend and interest. Unhappy after learning that his own holding was ranked after the £32,000 reconstruction capital, the £2,000 working capital and the £80,000 debenture bonds, he declared that 'the line will never produce anything for the debenture stockholders' (*Wellington Journal*, 11 January).

Talk of the railway being reopened was behind an opinion piece published in the *Wellington Journal* on 1 February. As well as commenting on the historical and legal situation, it described the state of some of the features. Apart from some half-obliterated letters on the station canopy, it was hard to detect any sign of railway activity at the Abbey station, the writer said. At the country end there were some rusty broken rails and neglected signal posts. Sleepers disintegrated into dust when trodden on. Parts of the track were obscured by 'thick bushes and sturdy saplings'. At Red Hill and Hanwood the station buildings had gone and signal posts were rotting. The bridge over the Cruckton Road had been fenced off to protect the illicit track walkers from falling through it. The timber had gone from the Shrawardine river bridge, but he thought the ironwork looked sound. Not far from Criggion a timber building had been erected on the track near a road crossing. At an unspecified location the ground had been washed away, leaving the track suspended in the air.

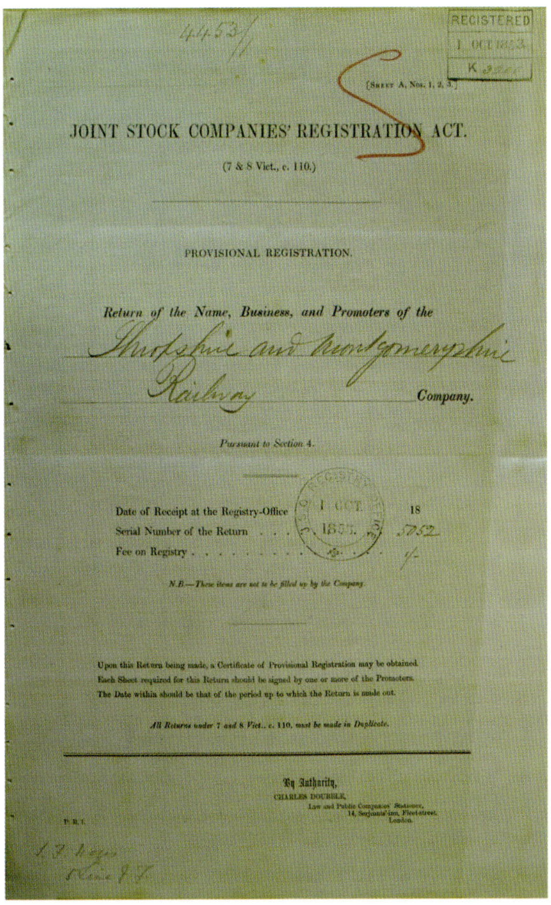

4453/1

REGISTERED 1 OCT 1853 K

[Sheet A, Nos. 1, 2, 3.]

JOINT STOCK COMPANIES' REGISTRATION ACT.

(7 & 8 Vict., c. 110.)

PROVISIONAL REGISTRATION.

Return of the Name, Business, and Promoters of the

Shropshire and Montgomeryshire Railway **Company.**

Pursuant to Section 4.

Date of Receipt at the Registry-Office 1 OCT 1853 18

Serial Number of the Return . . . 5752

Fee on Registry 1/-

N.B.—These items are not to be filled up by the Company.

Upon this Return being made, a Certificate of Provisional Registration may be obtained. Each Sheet required for this Return should be signed by one or more of the Promoters. The Date within should be that of the period up to which the Return is made out.

All Returns under 7 and 8 Vict., c. 110, must be made in Duplicate.

By Authority,
CHARLES DOUBBLE,
Law and Public Companies' Stationer,
14, Serjeants'-inn, Fleet-street,
London.

Return made by the first Shropshire & Montgomeryshire Railway in 1853. (National Archives)

The possibility of confusion with the North Staffordshire Railway when either railway was referred to by its initials prompted Stephens to write to the Board of Trade on 13 May 1908, asking if the name of his railway could be changed to the Shropshire & Montgomeryshire Light Railway. He added that as the Montgomeryshire County Council had taken powers to subscribe to the proposed company, 'the change will appeal to local sentiment'.

This was not the first time the Shropshire & Montgomeryshire Railway name had been used, for in 1853 it had been given to a proposed railway between Shrewsbury and Welshpool. The initiative for it seems to have been a fear of missing out in Shrewsbury, worried that the Montgomeryshire Railway, which had had a Bill deposited for a railway between Oswestry and Newtown in 1852, would take all the Welsh traffic that had previously been routed via the Shropshire centre. No Bill was deposited, although a company was registered at the joint stock companies registry on 1 October 1853, its purpose being 'the construction of a railway from Shrewsbury …. via the valley of the River Rea to Newtown … and from Caer Flos … through Welshpool to Oswestry …'

Its secretary had been R. S. France (*Shrewsbury Chronicle*, 28 October 1853) and in 1855 he had said that the scheme was 'frustrated through circumstances totally unforeseen' (*Shrewsbury Chronicle*, 7 September). As the Shrewsbury & Welshpool Railway, with France as its contractor, it was opened in 1862. The

Montgomeryshire Railway became the Oswestry & Newtown Railway and a constituent of the Cambrian Railways.

Although the major companies did not object to the Light Railway Order application, they did require clauses for their protection and some delay in processing it was caused by the GWR's intransigence over connections with the Hereford and Wellington lines. The objection was protectionist, insofar as it claimed that the Hereford line's junction's existence would prevent the diversion of traffic to the Cambrian at Llanymynech. Stephens, on the other hand, complained that as its cost was an unknown quantity, he should have some flexibility over its installation.

The need to get court approval for the clauses and schedules that affected the Shropshire Railways also caused delays, despite the debenture holders having approved the order as early as 7 January 1908. Eventually, the order was sealed on 11 February 1909 and was signed by the president of the Board of Trade, Winston S. Churchill. Containing seventy-four clauses and three schedules, it was quite wide-ranging in scope.

The Shropshire & Montgomeryshire Light Railway Company was incorporated and was to have five directors, three elected by the shareholders and two nominated by the Shropshire Railways. Named in the order, the first directors were Stephens, Rigby and the Earl of Bradford.

The railways authorised were the line between Llanymynech and Shrewsbury, the Breidden branch, and the junctions with the Wellington and Hereford lines. As defined in the 1888 Act, the Wellington line junction was to be opened with the remainder of the railway, but this was not a requirement if the Hereford line junction was made. The Llanyblodwel branch was excluded from the railways authorised and the Cambrian's rights over it were protected. Except for the Breidden branch, the works were to be started within twelve months of making the order and completed within eighteen months. The Breidden branch was

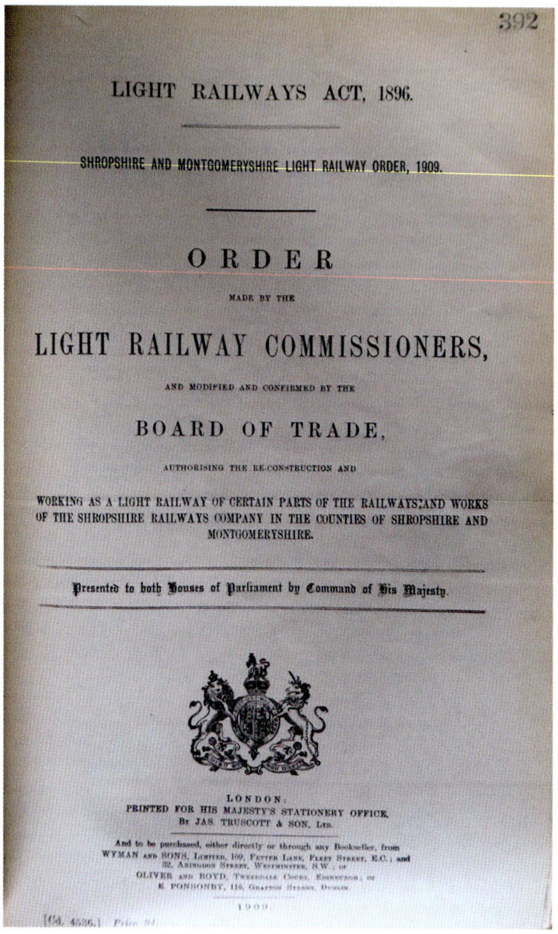

392

LIGHT RAILWAYS ACT, 1896.

SHROPSHIRE AND MONTGOMERYSHIRE LIGHT RAILWAY ORDER, 1909.

ORDER

MADE BY THE

LIGHT RAILWAY COMMISSIONERS,

AND MODIFIED AND CONFIRMED BY THE

BOARD OF TRADE,

AUTHORISING THE RE-CONSTRUCTION AND

WORKING AS A LIGHT RAILWAY OF CERTAIN PARTS OF THE RAILWAYS AND WORKS OF THE SHROPSHIRE RAILWAYS COMPANY IN THE COUNTIES OF SHROPSHIRE AND MONTGOMERYSHIRE.

Presented to both Houses of Parliament by Command of His Majesty.

LONDON:
PRINTED FOR HIS MAJESTY'S STATIONERY OFFICE,
BY JAS. TRUSCOTT & SON, LTD.

And to be purchased, either directly or through any Bookseller, from
WYMAN AND SONS, LIMITED, 109, FETTER LANE, FLEET STREET, E.C.; and
32, ABINGDON STREET, WESTMINSTER, S.W.; or
OLIVER AND BOYD, TWEEDDALE COURT, EDINBURGH; or
E. PONSONBY, 116, GRAFTON STREET, DUBLIN.

1909.

[Cd. 4586.] Price 9d.

The Shropshire & Montgomeryshire Light Railway Order, 1909.

to be completed within eighteen months of consent for its reconstruction being given by Shropshire Railways, providing that was within two years of the remainder of the railway being reopened.

As agreed previously, Shropshire Railways could issue up to £40,000 in 'prior charge debenture stock' on request of the light railway providing that half of the £2,000 capital had been issued. Holders of the debenture stock were entitled to vote at meetings of both Shropshire Railways and the Light Railway.

The local authorities, Shropshire and Montgomeryshire County Councils, Shrewsbury Town Council and Oswestry, Forden and Atcham Rural District Councils were permitted to invest up to £5,750 between them.

A legal agreement made between the promoters and Shropshire Railways to define the relationship between the two companies was incorporated in the order

The Bradford family mausoleum at Weston-under-Lizard. The third Earl, who supported the Potteries Railway and the Shropshire Railways, was interred in its vault, although his successors in title have preferred to be buried in the adjoining cemetery.

as a schedule. *Inter alia*, it required the light railway to be equipped with not less than £5,000 of 'proper engines' and rolling stock. After the payment of working expenses, the net revenue was to be directed first to the debenture interest, then to ordinary dividends (a maximum of 5% was specified), and then to reserves and renewals 'a sum not exceeding what may be under the circumstances reasonable'. Any balance was to be transferred to Shropshire Railways.

While the application was being processed, there were several issues that had required the Shropshire Railways' directors' attention. In January 1908 a writ was served on the Midland Railway Wagon Co., claiming £1,000 damages and an injunction over the misuse of the company's property; judgement was awarded to the company in March 1910, when £750 damages and £50 for privileges was paid to the receiver. On 12 November 1908 the directors had declared that it could not 'entertain any applications for shooting rights over the line' after the submission of two applications for this purpose to the receiver. Following a meeting between Barcroft and Whadcoat on 4 November 1908, the company applied for a court order that any moneys held in court or by the receiver should be paid to the bondholders.

The first meeting of the light railway directors was held on 26 February 1909. Bradford, Rigby and Stephens were present, with the first acting as chairman and the last as secretary. After dealing with administrative matters, Bradford resigned as a director and was replaced by William Arthur Wardley (1860–1926), a barrister who had been a solicitor practising in Tonbridge, Kent. The meeting closed with Rigby proposing a vote of thanks to Bradford for his assistance in promoting the order. A qualifying shareholding (£50) was registered to the directors on 26 March.

Having obtained their order, the promoters were faced with a shortfall of £12,000 on the capital account. At a meeting chaired by the 4th Earl of Powis (1862–1952) held in Shrewsbury on

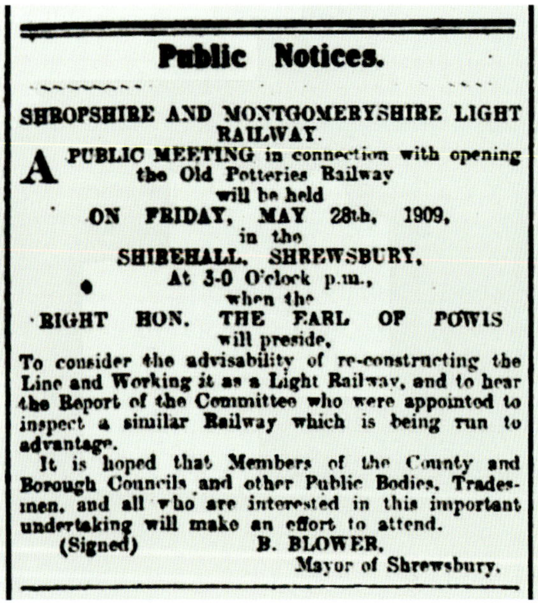

Public Notices.

SHROPSHIRE AND MONTGOMERYSHIRE LIGHT RAILWAY.

A PUBLIC MEETING in connection with opening the Old Potteries Railway will be held ON FRIDAY, MAY 28th, 1909, in the SHIREHALL, SHREWSBURY, At 3-0 O'clock p.m., when the RIGHT HON. THE EARL OF POWIS will preside,

To consider the advisability of re-constructing the Line and Working it as a Light Railway, and to hear the Report of the Committee who were appointed to inspect a similar Railway which is being run to advantage.

It is hoped that Members of the County and Borough Councils and other Public Bodies, Tradesmen, and all who are interested in this important undertaking will make an effort to attend.

(Signed) B. BLOWER,
Mayor of Shrewsbury.

Far left: Notice for a public meeting in Shrewsbury to discuss the light railway proposal on 28 May 1909. (*Shrewsbury Chronicle*, 21 May 1909)

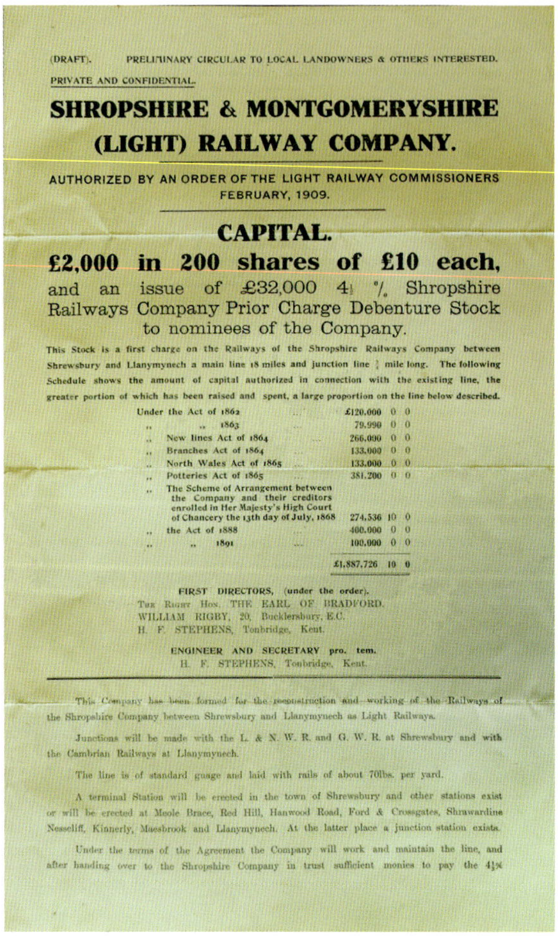

(DRAFT). PRELIMINARY CIRCULAR TO LOCAL LANDOWNERS & OTHERS INTERESTED.

PRIVATE AND CONFIDENTIAL.

SHROPSHIRE & MONTGOMERYSHIRE (LIGHT) RAILWAY COMPANY.

AUTHORIZED BY AN ORDER OF THE LIGHT RAILWAY COMMISSIONERS FEBRUARY, 1909.

CAPITAL.

£2,000 in 200 shares of £10 each,

and an issue of £32,000 4½ % Shropshire Railways Company Prior Charge Debenture Stock to nominees of the Company.

This Stock is a first charge on the Railways of the Shropshire Railways Company between Shrewsbury and Llanymynech a main line 18 miles and junction line ¼ mile long. The following Schedule shows the amount of capital authorized in connection with the existing line, the greater portion of which has been raised and spent, a large proportion on the line below described.

	£	s	d
Under the Act of 1862 ...	£120,000	0	0
" " 1863 ...	79,990	0	0
" New lines Act of 1864 ...	266,000	0	0
" Branches Act of 1864 ...	133,000	0	0
" North Wales Act of 1865 ...	133,000	0	0
" Potteries Act of 1865 ...	381,200	0	0
" The Scheme of Arrangement between the Company and their creditors enrolled in Her Majesty's High Court of Chancery the 13th day of July, 1868	274,536	10	0
" the Act of 1888 ...	400,000	0	0
" " 1891 ...	100,000	0	0
	£1,887,726	10	0

FIRST DIRECTORS, (under the order).
THE RIGHT HON. THE EARL OF BRADFORD.
WILLIAM RIGBY, 20, Bucklersbury, E.C.
H. F. STEPHENS, Tonbridge, Kent.

ENGINEER AND SECRETARY pro. tem.
H. F. STEPHENS, Tonbridge, Kent.

This Company has been formed for the reconstruction and working of the Railways of the Shropshire Company between Shrewsbury and Llanymynech as Light Railways.

Junctions will be made with the L. & N. W. R. and G. W. R. at Shrewsbury and with the Cambrian Railways at Llanymynech.

The line is of standard guage and laid with rails of about 70lbs. per yard.

A terminal Station will be erected in the town of Shrewsbury and other stations exist or will be erected at Meole Brace, Red Hill, Hanwood Road, Ford & Crossgates, Shrawardine Nesscliff, Kinnerly, Maesbrook and Llanymynech. At the latter place a junction station exists.

Under the terms of the Agreement the Company will work and maintain the line, and after handing over to the Shropshire Company in trust sufficient monies to pay the 4½%

Draft prospectus for £2,000 share capital in the Light Railway Company and £32,000 of 4½% Shropshire Railways prior charge debenture stock.

13 March, the audience had been told that £2,000 had already been subscribed and it was hoped to obtain support from the local authorities (*Shrewsbury Chronicle*, 19 March). A committee was appointed with the remit of visiting an established light railway, Stephens' Kent & East Sussex, and as a result of its report the Earls of Bradford and Powis agreed to subscribe £1,000 each and the shortfall had been reduced to £8,500 (*Wellington Journal*, 17 April). One of the committee members was the Mayor of Shrewsbury, Benjamin Blower (1849–21), who had been a passenger on the Snowdon Mountain Railway's fateful first train on 6 April 1896, when the locomotive ran away.

Some details of the committee's report were given at another Shrewsbury meeting on 28 May. Credit was given to Lord Bradford who, it was said, had enthusiastically supported the notion of reviving the railway since the Light Railways Act had been passed in 1896.

A number of comparisons were made between the railways, as shown in the table, which tended to show that the proposed light railway was a better prospect than the established one. The district served by the Kent & East Sussex was purely agricultural, it had very little mineral traffic, it served no large towns and was not a prosperous area. It also had to pay a £221 annual charge to run into Robertsbridge station, whereas the Shropshire line had its own terminal

	Kent & East Sussex Light Railway	Shropshire & Montgomeryshire Light Railway
Length	16 miles	17 miles
Fixed charge	£19,000 4% debentures £16,000 5% Lloyds Bank loan	£32,000 4½%
Annual charge	£760 + £800 = £1,560	£1,400
Dividend (1908)	1½% (£731)	

stations. Coal and water cost 25% more in the south than in Shropshire, too.

The £32,000 proposed capital comprised: reconstruction, £17,430; rolling stock, equipment, &c, £5,770; junction with main line (at Meole Brace), £500; fees, light railway order and legal, £2,250; fees, financial, £3,000. The last amount would be reduced if they could raise more money locally, and not require the services of financiers.

The Earl of Powis said that while he had regarded earlier schemes to revive the railway with suspicion, he had concluded that this one was satisfactory, it was not a 'wildcat' scheme and he thought that the offer of a modest 4½% interest would encourage investors rather than deter them. When £10,000 of local investment had been subscribed, he would act as a local trustee to protect their interests (*Shrewsbury Chronicle*, 4 June).

On 24 July Shropshire County Council voted to subscribe £2,000 to the railway (*Wellington Journal*, 31 July). Shrewsbury Town Council followed with £500 on 13 September. On that occasion, one of the councillors suggested that if the former Potteries Junction line remained unused the council should ask for first refusal on it and transform the land into a recreation ground. He also asked that the council should formalise the situation whereby residents of the Cherry Orchard area walked along the railway to get to their work at Coleham sheds (*Wellington Journal*, 18 September). Neither proposal was adopted but some sixty years later the Potteries Junction land was transformed into a road.

One way of resolving any intra-company conflict, as feared by the Board of Trade in 1907, would be for one company to control the other. In a way this had been achieved on 15 July 1909, when the transfer of 254 Shropshire mortgage debenture bonds, £9,875 first debenture stock, £5,000 second debenture stock and £39,029 11s ordinary stock as well as £963 ordinary stock from Whadcoat to Stephens was registered. It was noted that the 'secretary called attention … that the transfers … comprised the entire holding … of Mr J. H. Whadcoat'. Stephens was appointed a director in place of Whadcoat. As he had already been elected managing director at a general meeting on 26 March he was now in control of both companies.

When the Shropshire directors met next, on 22 July, in Stephens' absence, they demonstrated a measure of independence by electing Henderson as chairman and deferring the nomination of directors to the board until the reconstruction contract had been approved.

The complicated, and potentially expensive, arrangements over the joint line junctions proved a sticking point with Stephens despite his grudging acceptance of them. For this and other reasons an application for an amendment Light Railway Order was submitted in May 1909. The order was not referred to at all in the minutes, although it was submitted to and approved by the Shropshire directors. The Board of Trade processed the application by correspondence and there was no public inquiry.

The company wished to obtain approval to substitute a new junction at Meole Brace for either or both of those intended to connect with the Wellington or Hereford lines, to pay debenture interest out of capital during construction, to enhance its trespass provisions, and to increase line speed from 25mph to 30mph.

The GWR and LNWR objected to the junction proposals, claiming that they were in breach of the rules because no plans or book of reference had been deposited. The order, made on 19 July 1910, contained three main clauses.

The Meole Brace junction was approved, the offence of trespass would be committed provided warning notices were displayed at the station and public road crossing nearest to the location where an alleged trespasser was found, and up to £1,500 interest was allowed to be paid out of capital during construction, instead of the £2,500 requested. The request to increase line speed was refused.

Creating a junction at Meole Brace would save money by reducing the amount

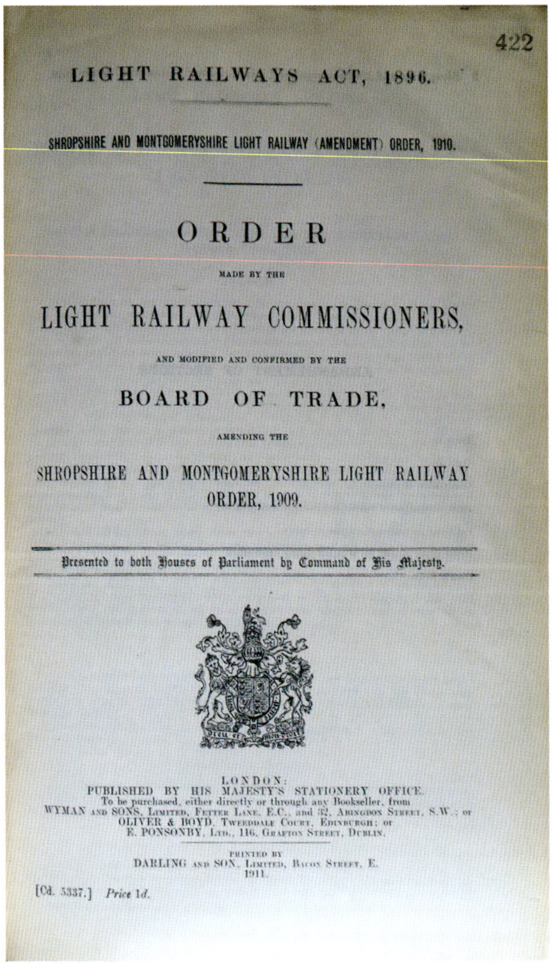

422

LIGHT RAILWAYS ACT, 1896.

SHROPSHIRE AND MONTGOMERYSHIRE LIGHT RAILWAY (AMENDMENT) ORDER, 1910.

ORDER

MADE BY THE

LIGHT RAILWAY COMMISSIONERS,

AND MODIFIED AND CONFIRMED BY THE

BOARD OF TRADE,

AMENDING THE

SHROPSHIRE AND MONTGOMERYSHIRE LIGHT RAILWAY ORDER, 1909.

Presented to both Houses of Parliament by Command of His Majesty.

LONDON:
PUBLISHED BY HIS MAJESTY'S STATIONERY OFFICE.
To be purchased, either directly or through any Bookseller, from
WYMAN AND SONS, LIMITED, FETTER LANE, E.C., and 32, ABINGDON STREET, S.W.; or
OLIVER & BOYD, TWEEDDALE COURT, EDINBURGH; or
E. PONSONBY, LTD., 116, GRAFTON STREET, DUBLIN.

PRINTED BY
DARLING AND SON, LIMITED, BACON STREET, E.
1911.

[Cd. 5337.] *Price 1d.*

The 1910 amendment Order.

of track and associated signalling to be installed and maintained. Concerning trespassing, Stephens was concerned that as the railway had become an unofficial footpath while it had been closed it would be difficult to break people of the habit of using it when services were resumed.

Earlier, Shropshire Railways' complaint against the Midland Wagon Company over incursions, including dumping 2,000 tons of ash, on the company's property at Shrewsbury, had been heard in October 1909. The Wagon Company claimed that as the land had been disused since 1880 it had gained possessory title to it and had erected sheds on some of it. A settlement was reached that included the company agreeing to pay rent for the sheds, and £750 damages, £50 for various easements, and costs (*Wellington Journal*, 18/30 October).

Despite support from the Earl of Powis, Montgomeryshire County Council refused to make an advance to the railway. His Lordship replied to a councillor's claim that the light railway would not be of much benefit to the county by saying that it had supported the Mawddwy Railway scheme for a 3% return and no promise of repayment,

The Meole Brace exchange sidings on 3 September 1937. To be doubly sure that there could be no unauthorised movements through the gate, a crash bar was also locked in place across the track. (R. K. Cope)

whereas the light railway offer was 4½% and repayment in forty years (*Cambrian News*, 24 December 1909). An editorial in the *Liverpool Daily Post* (25 December) observed that the council's support for the Welshpool & Llanfair and Tanat Valley Light Railways had been poor investments and only the prospect of reduced road maintenance costs had persuaded it to support the Mawddwy Railway.

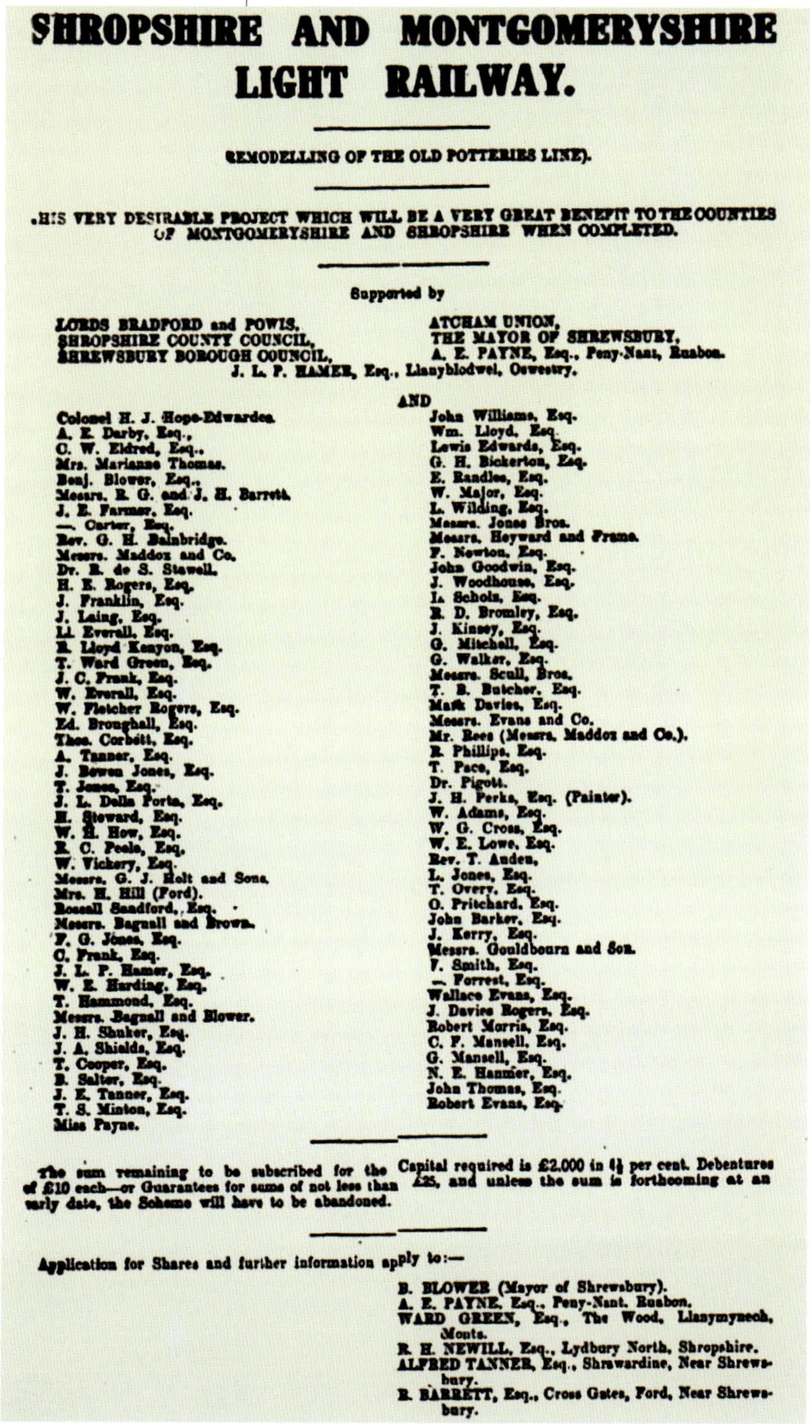

SHROPSHIRE AND MONTGOMERYSHIRE LIGHT RAILWAY.

(REMODELLING OF THE OLD POTTERIES LINE).

THIS VERY DESIRABLE PROJECT WHICH WILL BE A VERY GREAT BENEFIT TO THE COUNTIES OF MONTGOMERYSHIRE AND SHROPSHIRE WHEN COMPLETED.

Supported by

LORDS BRADFORD and POWIS,
SHROPSHIRE COUNTY COUNCIL,
SHREWSBURY BOROUGH COUNCIL,
ATCHAM UNION,
THE MAYOR OF SHREWSBURY,
A. E. PAYNE, Esq., Peny-Nant, Ruabon.
J. L. P. HAMER, Esq., Llanyblodwel, Oswestry.

AND

Colonel H. J. Hope-Edwardes.
A. E. Darby, Esq.,
C. W. Eldred, Esq.,
Mrs. Marianne Thomas.
Benj. Blower, Esq.,
Messrs. R. G. and J. H. Barrett.
J. E. Farmer, Esq.
—. Carter, Esq.
Rev. G. H. Bainbridge.
Messrs. Maddox and Co.
Dr. R. de S. Stawell.
H. E. Rogers, Esq.
J. Franklin, Esq.
J. Laing, Esq.
Ll. Everall, Esq.
R. Lloyd Kenyon, Esq.
T. Ward Green, Esq.
J. C. Frank, Esq.
W. Everall, Esq.
W. Fletcher Rogers, Esq.
Ed. Broughall, Esq.
Thos. Corbett, Esq.
A. Tanner, Esq.
J. Bowen Jones, Esq.
T. Jones, Esq.
J. L. Della Porta, Esq.
H. Steward, Esq.
W. H. How, Esq.
R. C. Peele, Esq.
W. Vickery, Esq.
Messrs. G. J. Holt and Sons.
Mrs. H. Hill (Ford).
Rossall Sandford, Esq.
Messrs. Bagnall and Brown.
F. G. Jones, Esq.
C. Frank, Esq.
J. L. P. Hamer, Esq.
W. E. Harding, Esq.
T. Hammond, Esq.
Messrs. Bagnall and Blower.
J. H. Shuker, Esq.
J. A. Shields, Esq.
T. Cooper, Esq.
B. Salter, Esq.
J. E. Tanner, Esq.
T. S. Minton, Esq.
Miss Payne.

John Williams, Esq.
Wm. Lloyd, Esq.
Lewis Edwards, Esq.
G. H. Bickerton, Esq.
E. Randles, Esq.
W. Major, Esq.
L. Wilding, Esq.
Messrs. Jones Bros.
Messrs. Heyward and Frame.
F. Newton, Esq.
John Goodwin, Esq.
J. Woodhouse, Esq.
L. Scholz, Esq.
R. D. Bromley, Esq.
J. Kinsey, Esq.
G. Mitchell, Esq.
G. Walker, Esq.
Messrs. Scull, Bros.
T. B. Butcher, Esq.
Mark Davies, Esq.
Messrs. Evans and Co.
Mr. Rees (Messrs. Maddox and Co.).
R. Phillips, Esq.
T. Pace, Esq.
Dr. Pigott.
J. H. Perks, Esq. (Painter).
W. Adams, Esq.
W. G. Cross, Esq.
W. E. Lowe, Esq.
Rev. T. Auden,
L. Jones, Esq.
T. Overy, Esq.
O. Pritchard, Esq.
John Barker, Esq.
J. Kerry, Esq.
Messrs. Gouldbourn and Son.
F. Smith, Esq.
—. Forrest, Esq.
Wallace Evans, Esq.
J. Davies Rogers, Esq.
Robert Morris, Esq.
C. F. Mansell, Esq.
G. Mansell, Esq.
N. E. Hanmer, Esq.
John Thomas, Esq.
Robert Evans, Esq.

The sum remaining to be subscribed for the Capital required is £2,000 in 4½ per cent. Debentures of £10 each—or Guarantees for sums of not less than £25, and unless the sum is forthcoming at an early date, the Scheme will have to be abandoned.

Application for Shares and further information apply to:—

B. BLOWER (Mayor of Shrewsbury).
A. E. PAYNE, Esq., Peny-Nant, Ruabon.
WARD GREEN, Esq., The Wood, Llanymynech, Monts.
R. H. NEWILL, Esq., Lydbury North, Shropshire.
ALFRED TANNER, Esq., Shrawardine, Near Shrewsbury.
R. BARRETT, Esq., Cross Gates, Ford, Near Shrewsbury.

The hard sell for the last £2,000 4½% Shropshire Railways prior charge debenture stock to be raised took the form of this advertisement listing all the committed subscribers, which would surely be a breach of modern data protection rules. (*Shrewsbury Chronicle*, 15 April 1910)

In January 1910, the company issued a prospectus for £14,000 Shropshire prior charge debenture stock to 'local landowners and others interested', claiming that local authorities had already applied for £3,000 of stock. On 13 January Stephens made an application to the Board of Trade for a twelve-month extension to the time permitted by the 1909 order because 'we have not yet been able to raise all the necessary capital'; a six-month extension was granted.

Stephens informed the Shropshire directors on 21 March that subscriptions for £1,000 ordinary Light Railway stock had been received, permitting, in compliance with the Light Railway Order, the release of the prior charge debenture stock.

The draft contract for the 'construction and equipment of the line for £30,000 of prior charge debenture stock of the Shropshire company' was submitted to the Light Railway directors on 10 May and approved. The contractors were Stephens and Francis Claughton Mathews (1842–1923), a solicitor who had acted on Shropshire Railways' matters for Whadcoat Brothers since 1893; he had also been the London, Tilbury & Southend Railway's solicitor since 1882 and a director of that company since 1908 (*Railway News*, 24 October 1908). No explanation has been found for Rigby not taking the contract.

On 10 May the railway's £1,000 share capital also became fully subscribed, for following acceptance of the contract Stephens was allocated forty-three ordinary shares and Mathews forty. It appears that Stephens had been extremely careful with his choice of words when the Shropshire directors had met on 21 March.

The contract was sealed on 22 August when the receiver gave the Light Railway company formal permission to take possession of the railway. Stephens' formal declaration that he was involved in the

contract had been made to the directors on 15 November. Most likely the work was actually carried out by direct labour under Stephens' direction.

In June, Oswestry Rural District Council had agreed to subscribe £250 in the Light Railway. Objectors to the proposal because the reopened railway 'would hurt Oswestry' included the chairman but the supporters won the vote. One of the councillors pointed out that with the railway abandoned, it earned nothing in rates; reopened it could earn up to £90 a year (*Shrewsbury Chronicle*, 17 June). The following week the same paper said that the funding shortfall then stood at £700, and reminded readers that no money would be handed over to the promoters until the railway had passed a Board of Trade inspection. It also acknowledged the contribution made by the Mayor, Benjamin Blower, who had 'secured support to the extent of £3,300'.

Reading about the £700 shortfall, an out of work joiner signing himself 'Wood-butcher' wrote to the *Shrewsbury Chronicle* (1 July) to say that he would subscribe £40, 'a large portion of my savings', if one of the 'influential subscribers' would give him work until construction started, when he would hope to find work building waiting rooms and signal boxes. His appeal went unheeded.

The Shropshire Railways' cash held by the receiver, Rabbidge, and the court had been released by an order made on 29 June 1910. After reserving £1,500 for costs, the remainder was distributed to debenture holders, who were entitled to interest up to the date the receiver was appointed, 11 November 1891, and the debenture bondholders. When the costs of the order had been assessed and paid out of the £1,500, the balance was also to be paid to the bondholders.

The Board of Trade was clearly unimpressed when Stephens requested a further extension of time on 21 July, writing 'although ready to commence work we are unable to obtain sleepers'. In giving approval for a further six months the file was annotated 'the reason given … is hardly convincing'.

Reconstruction probably started on 1 September, the same day the directors met. The *Shrewsbury Chronicle's* 2 September issue said that it had started. Clearance was started at Shrawardine and headed towards the Severn (*Shrewsbury Chronicle*, 9 September). By October, fifty men were employed, and track had been re-sleepered between Llanymynech and Maesbrook, so the sleeper supply issue had been resolved, and a loco had travelled as far as Kinnerley on the old track. The resident engineer was William Henry Austen (1878–1956),

Benjamin Blower, the Shrewsbury mayor whose enthusiasm for the railway's revival ensured its success, had his trading premises in the town's Castle Street. The majority of the site is now occupied by Shropshire's county archives but this magnificent stone gateway survives.

The 0-6-0ST used during the railway's reconstruction arriving at Shrewsbury by rail. (H. Miller)

Labourers jacking up rail preparatory to re-sleepering the track. (F. E. Fox Davies)

Stephens' assistant (*Shrewsbury Chronicle*, 14 October).

Work in the Shrewsbury area is evidenced by the report of labourer Edward Price (aged 28) falling through one of the bridges and into the brook, hurting his head on 13 November 1910, a Sunday, his injuries sufficient for him to be detained at the Salop Infirmary (*Shrewsbury Chronicle*, 18 November). Presumably Sunday working was intended to progress the work and advance the railway's reopening. In 1939 Price was living in the Poor Law Institution at Market Drayton; his death has not been identified.

At the directors' meeting on 2 September 1910, Stephens had reported that Shropshire Railways had given him authority to allocate stock, something that was not recorded in the Shropshire's comprehensive minutes. Nevertheless, the directors resolved to allocate £5,380 prior charge debentures to those persons listed in the allotment register. Stephens' salary as managing director was set at £100 per annum and as engineer and locomotive superintendent at £200 for five years from the opening of the line. Stephens and Mathews guaranteed a £4,000 loan from the Capital & Counties Bank in Shrewsbury on the same date. It was repaid from the proceeds of the prior charge debenture stock when the line opened.

The company had access to £7,940 by 15 November 1910, insufficient to finance a contract estimated at £17,480. Another £1,000 borrowed from the bank was guaranteed by the Earl of Powis in January 1912, an equivalent amount of debenture stock being reserved for him as surety. The Earl of Bradford also guaranteed a bank loan and was the registered holder of £1,000 prior charge debentures.

Stephens' efforts to encourage support by the local authorities were rewarded with £4,750 being subscribed: £2,000 by Shropshire; £750 Montgomeryshire; £500 each Shrewsbury Town and Atcham Rural District; £250 each Oswestry and Forden Rural Districts, in total £1,000 less than

W. H. Austen, H. F. Stephens' assistant who ran the railway after his death.

the maximum allowed for by the Light Railway Order.

A total of £20,904 was subscribed by the end of 1913; nearly 100 subscribers were local residents contributing amounts up to £100. Local enterprises that supported the railway included the Buildings Material Supply Stores Ltd £78, Ceiriog Granite Co. £50, and Phillips Stores Ltd £10. The company's auditor, Sir William Barclay Peat (1852–1936), invested £1,110 initially but subsequently disposed of £270; he was a member of the Barclay banking family and his firm became a part of KPMG, today's international professional services company.

Back on 12 December 1910, with work under way, Stephens had informed the Shropshire directors that he had inspected the Breidden branch and was convinced that if it was reconstructed it would make enough profit to pay the interest on 4½% prior charge debentures. They consented to the work being carried out, approved a draft contract and authorised the creation of £8,000 prior charge debentures, Stephens not voting on these decisions. Afterwards his offer to pay not more than three guineas for a new seal press was accepted. Whether the offer was linked to the decision is not known.

Legal agreements were the sole topic of a directors' meeting held on 10 February 1911. Contracts with the LNWR and the GWR 're Meole Brace junction' and W. H. Smith & Son for bookstall and advertising privileges were sealed and approval was given to seal operating agreements with the LNWR, GWR and Cambrian Railways, and an agreement to purchase a locomotive from the LNWR.

This was to be one of only two references to locomotives contained in the minutes during the Stephens era and it was to be twenty years before an LNWR locomotive was purchased; perhaps the minute-taker meant the London & South Western Railway (LSWR). Stephens cast his net far and wide in his search for locomotives for his railways and the six locomotives with which the railway was equipped in 1911 came from very disparate sources, ranging in size from the diminutive 2-2-2WT *Gazelle*, which weighed only 6 tons, to an ex-LSWR 0-6-0 and two chunky 0-6-2Ts supplied new by Hawthorn, Leslie & Company and allegedly designed by Stephens himself. In age, the six machines ranged from fifty-eight years for an ex-St Helens Railway 0-4-2T bought from a colliery, to the new Hawthorn, Leslies. There is perhaps more to the story of these new locomotives than meets the eye, for on 5 March 1912 the manufacturer invested £1,725 in the prior charge debentures, although they could represent the final payment for the locomotives.

Invariably described as an 'inspection locomotive', the tiny *Gazelle* was unlikely to have been used during the reconstruction as claimed elsewhere, but it found a home on the Criggion branch after being rebuilt as an 0-4-2T. In 1912–13 the back of its cab was also fitted with a small enclosure that was sometimes occupied by passengers, a facility that did not always meet with approval, Robert Brock (1842–1925), the vicar of Criggion, complaining to the Board of Trade about it on 23 November 1912. In 1916 a double-deck horse tramcar was obtained from London County Council and adapted to increase its passenger capacity.

All the railway's hauled stock was second-hand. Passenger stock initially was

Thisbe, one of the two Hawthorn, Leslie 0-6-2Ts built for the railway in 1911 but which were probably too heavy for the track. Both were sold to the War Department in 1914.

The diminutive *Gazelle* as received in Shropshire. (John Scott Morgan Collection)

Gazelle when first converted to an 0-4-2T with its lightweight carriage converted from a London double-deck horse tram. A roof mounted over the passenger area was accessed from the back, the facility not appreciated by all who had to use it. (A. M. Davies Collection)

Gazelle arriving at Kinnerley from Criggion in 1926. Behind the train is a rake of wagons loaded with stone, also from Criggion, and on the left is the start of a line of disused equipment that the railway became known for. Some of the tramcar's surplus top-deck seats were placed on station platforms for passenger use. (H. C. Casserley)

four ex-Midland Railway bogie carriages, followed shortly afterwards by six former LSWR four-wheeled carriages obtained from the Plymouth, Devonport & South Western Junction Railway. These were classified in the returns as five composites and five of 'uniform' class.

The Midland Railway supplied two passenger brake vans in 1911, too. Goods stock comprised sixteen 8-ton open wagons, ten covered wagons, four cattle trucks, three timber trucks, and a brake van. Service stock comprised a travelling crane plus two match trucks,

Two ex-Midland Railway bogie carriages obtained in 1911. (A. M. Davies Collection)

for loading/unloading heavy items at stations without a fixed crane, not a breakdown crane as sometimes claimed, and a stores van.

Rather than make use of the limited facilities established at the terminals by the Potteries Railway, the railway centralised operations at Kinnerley, building an engine shed equipped with a workshop capable of undertaking running repairs and erecting a locomotive water tank in the junction between the main line to Llanymynech and the Breidden branch. As the site became filled with disused locomotives and rolling

Two ex-London & South Western Railway four-wheeled carriages obtained from the Plymouth, Devonport & South Western Junction Railway and a Midland Railway four-wheeled brake van. (A. M. Davies Collection)

Kinnerley locomotive shed before there was so much clutter; the workshop is in the lean-to extension. (A. M. Davies Collection)

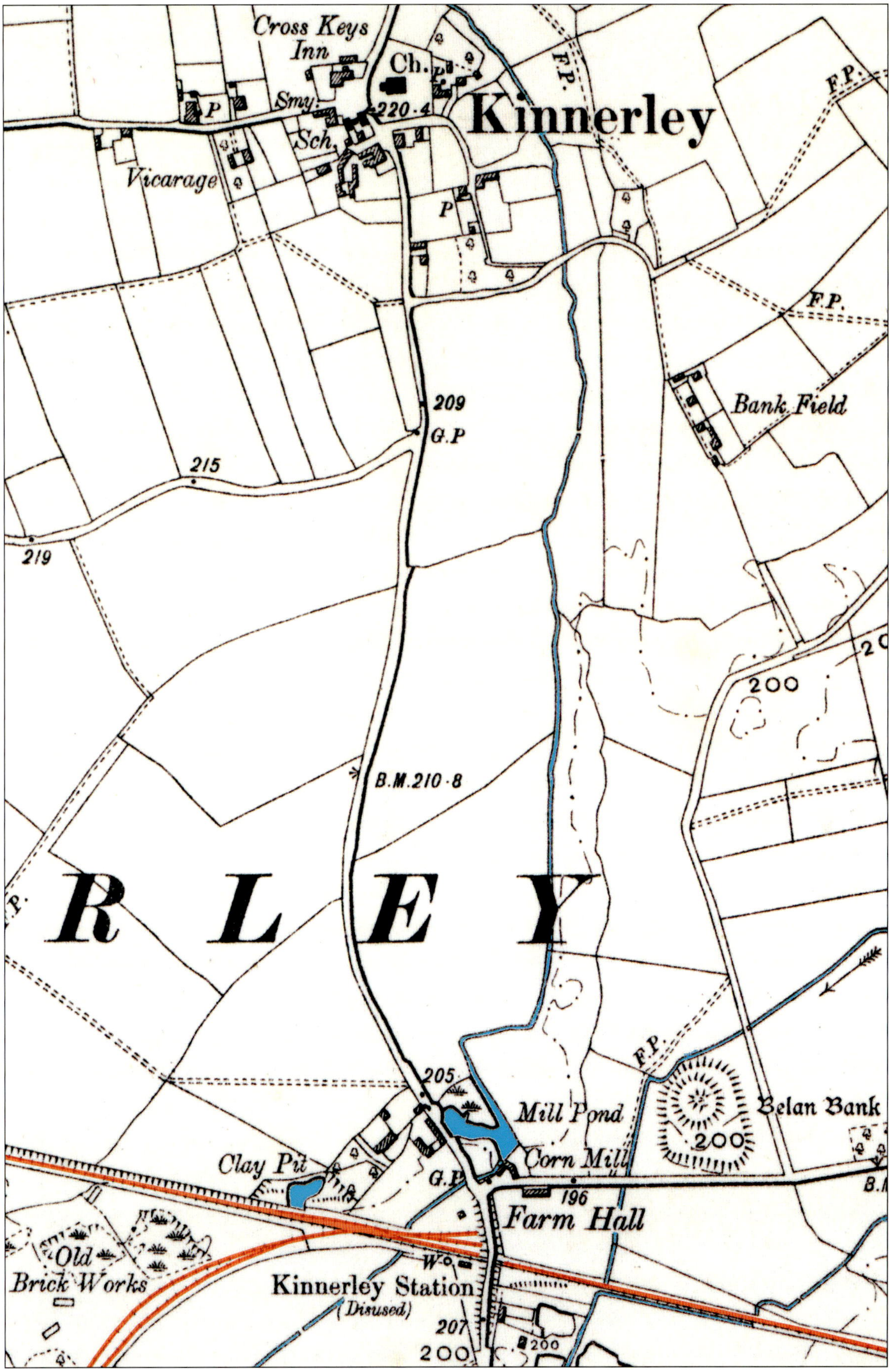

A section of a 6in Ordnance Survey map showing the relationship between Kinnerley station and the village that it served.

stock over the years, it became a Mecca for enthusiasts.

The Board of Trade's Colonel Edward Druitt (1860–1922) inspected the railway and submitted his report on 7 April 1911. He said the steepest gradient was 1 in 47, approaching the Abbey station; the sharpest curve, at Llanymynech, had a radius of ten chains; the country through which the railway ran was generally flat; embankments and cuttings were 'of moderate dimensions', the greatest being about 35ft in each case. The original 24ft-long wrought iron rails were 70lb per yard. All the sleepers were new; in some places at stations half-round sleepers were used, 'as the full supply of rectangular ones could not be obtained'.

There were stations at Shrewsbury, Red Hill, Hanwood, Ford & Cross Gates, Shrawardine, Nesscliff, Kinnerley, Maesbrook and Llanymynech, with a halt at Meole Brace. Ford & Cross Gates and Kinnerley were passing places. The terminals and the passing places each had two platforms. All stations had name boards and telephones but only Shrewsbury had conveniences, for both sexes.

Shrewsbury had an eight-lever ground frame with two levers spare. Ford & Cross Gates had a seven-lever frame, with one spare lever, interlocked with a two-lever frame at the western end. Kinnerley had a thirteen-lever frame with one spare lever; at its western end a single lever worked a siding facing up trains. At Llanymynech there was a five-lever frame and, at the eastern end, two sidings facing down trains worked by separate single levers. All the other stations had a siding worked by a single lever. Except at Shrewsbury, all points and frames were locked by the train staff, a key on the staff or an Annett's key. Meole Brace was a staff section for following trains with a two-lever ground frame on the platform working a home signal in each direction.

An interior view of the workshop. (A. M. Davies Collection)

The contractor's 0-6-0ST on the bridge at Shrawardine in 1910, probably on the occasion of the deflection tests mentioned in the text. Two fishermen on the left-hand bank look rather suspiciously at the photographer. (F. E. Fox Davies)

There were twenty-five underbridges, four with segmental brick arches on masonry abutments and twenty-one with wrought-iron plate girders with masonry or brick piers and abutments. One bridge had seven spans, two had four and one two. The widest span was about 48ft and seven of the largest spans were bridged by girders, cross-girders and rail bearers. All the wrought iron on the bridges was in very good condition, as were their piers and abutments.

The viaduct across the Severn was 320ft long and 35ft above the average water level. It had six spans, two of 60ft, two of 43ft and two of 40ft; it consisted of wrought-iron plate girders with wrought-iron cross girders 6ft apart. The 60ft spans were carried on piers formed of cast iron cylinders filled with concrete. The weight of the girders was carried on the concrete; some of the cylinders had cracked and had wrought-iron strengthening bands placed around them. The cracks appeared to be old, opined Druitt, probably due to the expansion of the concrete, and he thought additional strengthening bands would be desirable. There was no sign of settlement of any of these piers, which were 5ft in diameter for a distance of 10ft above the ordinary water level and 4ft diameter above that.

Deflection tests on the bridge were carried out with the heaviest loco available, an 0-6-0T weighing 30 tons and 26ft long. Two of the bridges gave Druitt cause for concern. Identified only as Nos 8 and 13, he said that they had spans of 20ft 3in and 22ft 7in and girders of an open trough section. They were the only bridges that had not had their timber decks renewed – he thought that the timber should be lifted in order to examine the troughs, although he recognised that this would be difficult because the longitudinal rail bearers, hence the track, would have to be removed too. One of the bearers of bridge No 13 had moved a quarter of an inch under load and was possibly not properly seated on its abutment, he thought.

There were twelve crossing the railway, nine on public roads, the rest on occupation roads. Four had brick abutments, cast-iron girders and jack arches. Six had masonry abutments and segmental brick arches. One, a cattle crossing, had rolled wrought-iron joists and timber decking. There was one timber footbridge. All were in good condition.

The line was to be worked on train staff and ticket combined with the absolute block telephone; signals normally passed by block instruments were passed by telephone.

A temporary speed limit of 10mph was placed on the viaduct until check rails had been installed and on bridge No 13 until its loose girder had been secured. At some of the bridges, Nos 39, 40 and 44 were instanced, sleepers required securing to the longitudinal timbers. At Shrewsbury a frame was to be erected around the ground frame to prevent its users from falling down the embankment behind it while working it.

With these relatively minor requirements, Druitt recommended the approval of the railway for passenger use. In the circumstances this report was quite a good result, certainly an improvement on France's effort in 1866. It is unfortunate that there is no sign of the contract to say just what work was carried out. While the work undertaken by Chambers in 1895 must have made things easier, some of that would have needed revisiting if the complaints made about it by the local authorities were anything to go by. A newspaper report of unknown origin stated that surplus materials from double-track structures were taken down for reuse elsewhere on the railway.

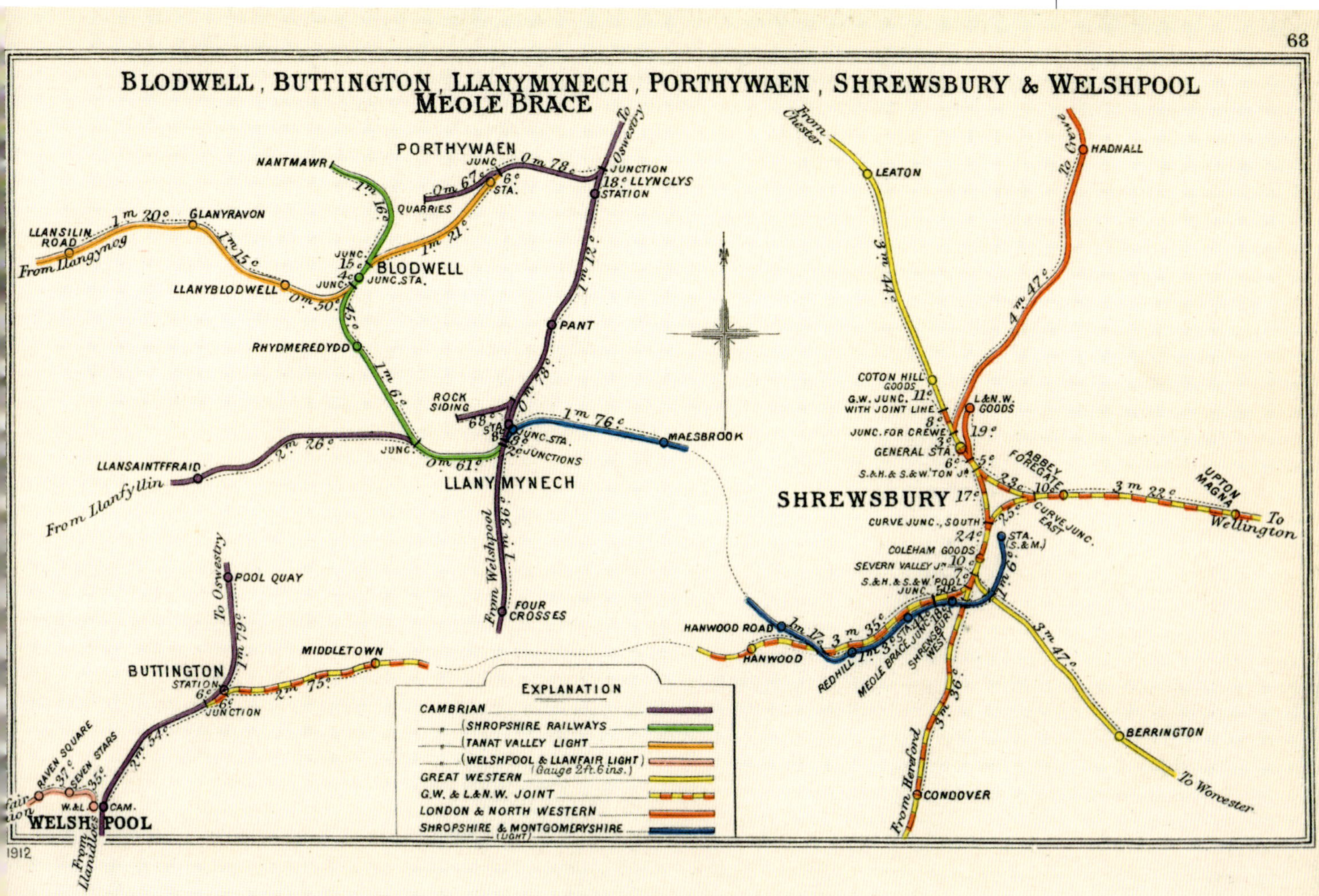

The 1912 junction diagram showing the railway's connections at Shrewsbury and Llanymynech. (Railway Clearing House)

CHAPTER 7

TRAINS RUNNING AGAIN

The official opening was performed by the mayor of Shrewsbury, Major Charles R. B. Wingfield, on Maundy Thursday, 13 April 1911. Some 200 members of the locality's great and good were invited to travel on the first train to Llanymynech. The mayor climbed on to the roof of a carriage at the Abbey station and toasted the railway from the town's ceremonial loving cup. The train stopped at Ford & Cross Gates station for a group photograph and again at Kinnerley, 'the engineering headquarters', for an inspection of the 'engine sheds, fitting shops and stores' before proceeding to Llanymynech, where they arrived to the sound of detonators being exploded by the train.

Right: The scene at Shrewsbury on the opening day, 13 April 1911, the mayor C. R. B. Wingfield standing on the carriage roof to address the crowd.

Below: Some of the crowd after the inaugural train had arrived at Llanymynech.

There, the guests had thirty minutes for sandwiches supplied by Shrewsbury's deputy mayor, Benjamin Blower. The loving cup had travelled on the train and was passed among the guests. Amongst these was Richard Reeves, aged 82, the guard of the Potteries Railway's last train, wearing his old uniform. He had been employed by the receiver as caretaker of the line and in 1894 had carried out repairs to railway property at Wern Las and Kinnerley.

At Llanymynech, Parish Council, chairman John Kemble (1847–1911) welcomed the revival of the railway but complained that there had been insufficient notice to arrange a proper celebration; he was a caterer and confectioner by trade. One report noted that the junction at Meole Brace was under construction, while another said that because of its absence the Cambrian at Llanymynech had benefited from the transport of materials for the reconstruction.

A report in *The Locomotive* (15 May 1911) commented on rail chairs dated 1865 and said that 36,000 new sleepers had been laid and the signals at Llanymynech, Kinnerley, Ford & Cross Gates and Shrewsbury had been supplied by Tyer & Co. Intermediate stations were equipped, it said, with diamond-shaped stop signals for use by passengers – the lack of comment on this feature suggests that they were not present when Druitt had made his inspection.

No 3 Hesperus with a short train in the 1930s. Built by Beyer, Peacock for the London & South Western Railway in 1875, it had been one of a class of eight locomotives used on the Ilfracombe branch. Their light axle load making them suitable for light railways, Stephens bought six of them, three of them coming to Shropshire. No 3 was scrapped in 1941.

The public opening took place on Good Friday, 14 April. By 1.30pm a large crowd had gathered at Abbey station and formed a long queue at the booking office to travel on the first train at 1.45pm. Some 250 people travelled, it was reported, with the most popular destinations being Red Hill and Llanymynech.

The initial timetable had three return workings each day described as mixed,

Ford & Crossgates station. Intending passengers turned the diamond signal through 90 degrees to stop a train. (F. E. Fox Davies)

The public entrance to the Abbey station, 4 October 1937. (R. K. Cope)

The view from the station throat, wagons stabled against the gate to the Wagon Company yard, and the turntable, 3 October 1937. (R. K. Cope)

A goods train in the platform at Kinnerley. Through the bridge, which looks as though it has been painted recently, a stone train can be seen heading towards Shrewsbury.

Llanymynech when the paint was still fresh in the Light Railway era, the board on the right promoting the route as the shortest to Shrewsbury. Two or three trains a day could hardly be called frequent though. In the background the Potteries Railway's shed has been demolished. (John Keylock Collection)

which could be worked with a single train, with running times ranged from fifty-six to seventy-six minutes. As the first train did not arrive at Shrewsbury until 9.39am there was obviously no intention of encouraging commuting, while a Saturday evening excursion to Shrewsbury allowed only twenty-five minutes in the county town. On Sundays, when there were two return workings, trains did not start until after morning church services had been concluded. The options seemed to have been to provide four hours in Llanymynech or six hours twenty-five minutes in Shrewsbury, or a mere ten minutes there if returning on the first train back.

As much as the directors might have wished the railway to settle into a steady routine, that was not to be, for on Saturday 15 April the loco, but not the tender, and three of the five carriages that formed the 6pm departure from Llanymynech derailed near Red Hill. The locomotive was 0-6-0 No 3 *Hesperus*, running tender first. With assistance from an LNWR breakdown gang the line was cleared in less than twenty-four hours. On the holiday Monday, 500 passengers were carried.

The 1911 timetable.

		a.m.	a.m.	p.m.	Saturdays only. p.m.	Sundays. p.m.	p.m.
Llanymynech Jun dep	..	8 36	1125	5 39	8 0	1230	6 45
Maesbrook........ ,,	..	8 42	1133	5 45	8 6	1238	6 52
Kinnerley Jun.... ,,	..	8 50	1141	5 53	8 14	1245	7 1
Nesscliff.......... ,,	..	8 56	1149	6 1	8 22	1253	7 11
Shrawardine...... ,,	..	s	1157	6 6	8 30	1 1	7 20
Ford & Crossgates ,,	..	9 10	12 3	6 12	8 36	1 9	7 26
Cruckton.......... ,,	..	—	—	—	—	—	—
Hanwood Road... ,,	..	9 19	1211	6 22	8 44	1 16	7 3[illegible]
Redhill............ ,,	..	s	1214	6 25	s	s	s
Meole Brace...... ,,	..	s	1217	s	8 50	1 22	7 4[illegible]
Shrewsbury West ,,	..	—	—	—	—	—	—
Shrewsbury.......arr.	..	9 39	1241	6 39	9 5	1 35	7 5[illegible]

	a.m.	a.m.	a.m.	a.m.	Saturdays only. p.m.	p.m.	Sundays. p.m.	p.m.
Shrewsbury....... dep		9 48	1 26	6 45	9 30		1 45	8 0
Shrewsbury West. ,,		—	—	—	—		—	—
Meole Brace...... ,,		s	1 34	6 54	9 40		1 52	8 6
Redhill.......... ,,		s	1 40	6 59	9 46		1 57	8 11
Hanwood Road.. ,,		10 1	1 47	7 6	9 52		2 1	8 15
Cruckton......... ,,		—	—	—	—		—	—
Ford & Crossgates ,,		1012	1 58	7 15	10 1		2 10	8 24
Shrawardine...... ,,		s	2 4	7 21	s		2 15	8 29
Nesscliff.......... ,,		1025	2 10	7 27	10 14		2 20	8 34
Kinnerley Junc.. ,,	7 38	1030	2 19	7 31	10 20	1210	2 27	8 40
Maesbrook........ ,,	7 45	s	2 27	7 35	10a27	1215	2 30	8a45
Llanymynech Jun arr.	7 50	1047	2 35	7 41	10a35	1222	2 37	8a52

a—Stops to set down only from Shrewsbury.

s—Stops to pick up or set down by signal at station, or on informing guard on joining train.

A more serious incident, although not involving passengers, occurred on 19 June, when Thomas Howle, aged 59, was killed falling from a trolley between Kinnerley and Melverley. He was making an inspection when the trolley tilted, tipping him off and running over him (*Hartlepool Northern Daily Mail*, 20 June). His death certificate recorded that he sustained a broken neck. Neither of these incidents appear to have been reported to the Board of Trade.

An investment holding company called the Severn Syndicate Ltd, which shared its address with Mathews' office, had acquired control of the Shropshire Railways from 28 April 1911. Four substantial holdings, including Stephens' and possibly that of the late W. E. Whadcoat, were transferred, totalling 538 mortgage bonds, £26,775 first debenture stock, £9,600 1891 debenture stock and £97,590 ordinary stock. A further £1,000 of first debenture stock was acquired on 5 December 1912.

The Syndicate's function was to supply Mathews and Stephens with the funds needed, in addition to those raised by subscription, for the railway's reconstruction. It is reasonable to assume that Mathews and Stephens were a part of it, but it is not known if anyone else was involved or why they chose to conceal their financial links to the companies. Neither is it known if the Syndicate was just a shell for Stephens' and Mathews' own money, or if money was obtained from a third party or parties. On 28 April 1911 it had been recorded as holding £26,775 of prior charge debentures, and a further £1,500 by 30 June 1913. At 4½%, the Syndicate would receive £1,272 per annum from the Light Railway; perhaps that was the reason for the anonymity. Stephens and Mathews made themselves personally liable to pay the interest due.

Work on reconstructing the Breidden branch was reported to be in progress when the main line was reopened, although the contract was not sealed until

28 November 1911. On 31 December 1911 the company agreed with the Pyx Granite Company, new lessees at Criggion, that the branch would be rebuilt in return for the quarry company committing to transport its stone by rail and subscribing £1,000 of prior charge debenture stock.

Goods traffic on the branch commenced from 20 February 1912 (*Staffordshire Sentinel*, 21 February 1912). Another, unknown, newspaper reported that a further £1,500 was required to bring the line up to passenger standards and local residents were expected to make up the shortfall. Whether it was really fit, even for goods traffic, must be open to question for when Colonel E. Druitt made his inspection on 22 May he found serious deficiencies and it was certainly not fit for passenger services. (Shades of Rich's experience in 1870.)

After his second inspection Druitt, on 20 June 1912, was able to recommend that the branch be approved for use by

The scene of the 15 April derailment at Red Hill. It appears that by the time the photograph was taken the locomotive had been re-railed and that work was concentrating on the carriages.

Melverley bridge during its reconstruction preparatory for reopening the Breidden branch. (F. E. Fox Davies/ John Scott Morgan Collection)

Melverley bridge restored for traffic. (F. E. Fox Davies)

passenger trains. He had found, however, that the ballast still required breaking up, another repeat from Rich's 1870 inspection. Like the rest of the line, the branch was to be worked by train staff and ticket and absolute block telephone, Criggion station having been provided with a telephone, trap points and a down home and starting signal to accommodate this.

The river bridge between Melverley and Crew Green was described in detail. There were eight spans, three of which, between 12ft and 15ft 10in, consisted of timber baulks supported on timber piles or trestles. One span, 14ft 4in, consisted of a wrought-iron plate girder under each rail. The other four spans varied between 27ft 10in and 40ft 2in and consisted of wrought-iron girders with cross girders 6ft apart and timber longitudinals. These spans were supported on timber piers composed of piles, the piers carrying the bridge across the river comprising eight piles each driven about 30ft into the riverbed and braced together.

He explained that they had shown no sign of sinking and had ample holding power for the weight supported on them. The girders had sufficient theoretical strength for engines and rolling stock not exceeding 10 tons. He had tested the bridge with two engines coupled together and found the deflections not excessive. No guard or check rails had been provided and until they were the speed over the bridge was limited to 10mph.

According to the *Birmingham Daily Gazette* on 1 June, the branch had been opened 'this week'. The paper also said that a delay in opening had been caused by reconstruction of a bridge that had been washed away by floods.

Stephens had transferred some of his Light Railway ordinary stock to four of his Tonbridge employees on 5 January 1912. Alfred Willard, Albert Osborne and W. H. Austen had ten shares each and George Henry Willard had eight. Stephens retained ten shares for himself.

By February 1912 a number of management positions had been filled. John Lloyd White (1848–1927), previously an LNWR district inspector at Shrewsbury, was passenger and goods superintendent.

Traffic off the railway was subject of comment under two headings during 1874. Existing traffic, shareholders were told, had been affected by strikes closing iron furnaces for a 'considerable period' in Staffordshire; 150 furnaces had been 'blown out' (*Birmingham Daily Post*, 20 August). Future prospects were improved by the Railway Commissioners' decision to support the railway's application to the LNWR for a through rate to Widnes for Breidden stone, mentioning it in their first annual report. When the LNWR heard that the Commissioners were minded to support the railway, it backed down and conceded the rate (*Railway News*, 19 September). The applications, to the LNWR in the first place, and then to the Commissioners, must have been Judd's work.

The year 1875 started with the railway's finances being mentioned in two court appearances. Poor fencing at Meole Brace had resulted in the death of three cattle on 18 November and farmer John James claimed £36 for the animals plus £1 for the cost of burying them and £3 for loss of sale. John Clift, the foreman ganger, said the fence was good and locomotive superintendent Edward Tandy claimed that £25 of damage had been done to the loco involved. After James and his witnesses had given evidence about the fences and his barrister had urged that the want of funds on the company's part was no indemnity, the judge awarded £37 without costs (*Eddowes's Journal*, 25 November / 20 January 1875). The farmer knew the fences were bad but still left the cattle in the adjoining field.

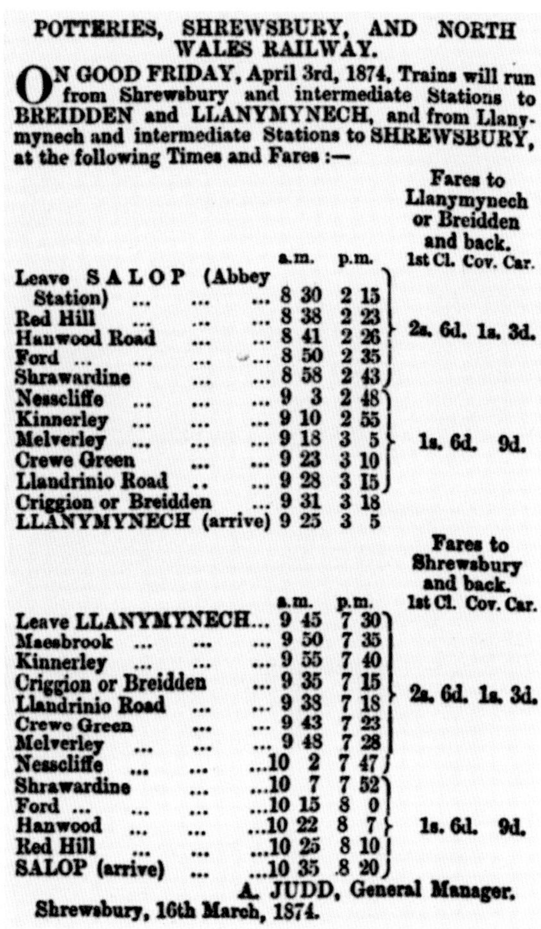

POTTERIES, SHREWSBURY, AND NORTH WALES RAILWAY.

ON GOOD FRIDAY, April 3rd, 1874, Trains will run from Shrewsbury and intermediate Stations to BREIDDEN and LLANYMYNECH, and from Llanymynech and intermediate Stations to SHREWSBURY, at the following Times and Fares :—

	a.m.	p.m.	Fares to Llanymynech or Breidden and back. 1st Cl.	Cov. Car.
Leave SALOP (Abbey Station)	8 30	2 15		
Red Hill	8 38	2 23		
Hanwood Road	8 41	2 26	2s. 6d.	1s. 3d.
Ford	8 50	2 35		
Shrawardine	8 58	2 43		
Nesscliffe	9 3	2 48		
Kinnerley	9 10	2 55		
Melverley	9 18	3 5	1s. 6d.	9d.
Crewe Green	9 23	3 10		
Llandrinio Road	9 28	3 15		
Criggion or Breidden ...	9 31	3 18		
LLANYMYNECH (arrive)	9 25	3 5		

	a.m.	p.m.	Fares to Shrewsbury and back. 1st Cl.	Cov. Car.
Leave LLANYMYNECH...	9 45	7 30		
Maesbrook	9 50	7 35		
Kinnerley	9 55	7 40		
Criggion or Breidden ...	9 35	7 15		
Llandrinio Road	9 38	7 18	2s. 6d.	1s. 3d.
Crewe Green	9 43	7 23		
Melverley	9 48	7 28		
Nesscliffe	10 2	7 47		
Shrawardine	10 7	7 52		
Ford	10 15	8 0		
Hanwood	10 22	8 7	1s. 6d.	9d.
Red Hill	10 25	8 10		
SALOP (arrive)	10 35	8 20		

A. JUDD, General Manager.
Shrewsbury, 16th March, 1874.

Advertisement for Good Friday excursions in 1874, *Eddowes's Shrewsbury Journal*, 1 April. There were several similar published over the years.

Later in January, Tandy appeared instead of Judd in another case of failing to abide by the rules in respect of cattle van cleanliness, saying they 'exercised great care ever since they were fined before … the company was not a rich company, and everybody seemed bent on making it poorer'. Finding the case proved, the magistrates inflicted a fine of £5 and 10s 10d costs (*Eddowes's Journal*, 3 February). Given that livestock traffic was only a small part of its business, £72 7s 6d in the first half of 1875 (*London Evening Standard*, 11 August 1875), it was surely taking up a disproportionate amount of management time and expense.

A loss of £742 had been incurred during the second half of 1874, leaving a debit balance of £3,680 and arrears of debenture interest standing at £155,822 (*Manchester Evening News*, 24 February).

Not only was the railway in a dire financial situation, it was having to tolerate public complaints being made about the quality of its ride, its timekeeping and its staff, prompting a vicar to leap to its defence with a letter, saying that as a regular user he had not found it any worse than on other railways. On 2 June *Eddowes's Journal's* editor supported him, saying it was not the fault of the staff that the railway was unfinished or that it did not pay 5% dividend, and that even as it was it was a great public convenience.

But the railway was not being maintained as it should have been, which

Dealing with a fire at Kinnerley in the days before the widespread availability of telephones, motor vehicles and petrol engine pumps would not have been an easy matter. Therefore a works fire brigade was established, manned by railway personnel and using this horse-drawn Merryweather appliance. There are no reports of it ever having been used in anger and it went for scrap in 1941.

John Stockdill (1849–1937), previously in charge of the goods rates department of the London & South Western Railway, became responsible for rates and fares. Archibald James Matthew (1882–1966), previously in the South Eastern & Chatham Railway's accounts department, was audit accountant, and Samuel John Wensley Knott (1874–1956) had been appointed accountant.

White, born in Aylesbury, Buckinghamshire, lived in Shrewsbury in a fifteen room house, sharing it with his wife, four children and two servants, apparently well rewarded by his railway career but his estate was valued at a mere £164 14s 4d in 1927. Matthew became secretary of the Sudan Government Railway.

After the opening there were a number of changes among the directors, some of them very short-lived. W. A. Wardley resigned from 27 February 1912, being replaced by Alfred Malby (1850–1919), recently retired as the London & South Western Railway's chief goods manager. However, he had resigned before the next board meeting, on 30 July, and was replaced by Lewis Daniel Price (1848–1931), who had been an LNWR district traffic superintendent. He submitted his resignation on 10 November and was replaced by Ronald Edward Elphinstone Hall (1872–1947), an insurance company secretary. He had resigned by 22 June 1915, to be replaced by Arthur Purdy Tabraham (1864–1925), a stockbroker. F. C. Mathews had been elected a Shropshire Railways director on 5 December 1912.

The railway was not so coy about its shooting rights as the Shropshire Railways had been, on 30 July 1912 registering an agreement to let them to Colonel H. P. Hall for £4 10s per quarter.

In another attempt to add to the railway's revenue-earning activities, the directors agreed, on 19 November 1913, to apply to the Postmaster General to become a party to the 1891 'single post letter by railway' agreement whereby the railway could carry letters on payment of a fee. The railway produced its own stamps for the service.

A series of linked property transactions was conducted in 1912–13 that appeared to be 'revenue neutral'. On 19 December 1912 the directors sealed a contract for the rental of four cottages at Kinnerley from the Shropshire Railways for £30 per annum, then on 26 June 1913 they agreed to rent them to the Severn Syndicate, also for £30 per annum. Possibly Stephens and Mathews wanted holiday homes or, more likely, had entered the 'rent-to-let' market.

At the general meeting on 30 July 1912 a 5% dividend was declared on ordinary shares covering the period from the opening until 31 December 1911. At 5%, £50 on £1,000 issued capital, the company was able, apart from the four war years, to pay a dividend until 1929. The shares were fully paid up by 20 April 1914. A total of 42,003 passengers had been carried during the year (*Liverpool Daily Post*, 22 July).

After seven years as managing director, Stephens' position received board attention on 9 February 1916. As he had not accepted the salary voted to him as managing director and engineer in 1910 it was resolved to appoint him as manager at £200 per annum as from 4 January 1916 'pending current crisis'. A year later he was awarded a further £25. Because of the war, shareholder approval was delayed, resulting in a settlement in January 1918 whereby he was awarded £200 for 1914 followed by a £25 annual increase, rising to £300 from 1918.

On the railway, an injury to a porter guard, Ernest Nathanial Fardoe (1895–1969), which occurred on 8 July 1913, was properly reported. He had been using a coupling pole to attach a wagon to a moving loco at Kinnerley when he slipped and caught his left hand between the buffers, causing a slight injury. Although the incident was attributed to his inexperience, the railway was required to issue instructions that coupling poles were not to be used until the buffers had touched.

A Hudswell, Clarke 0-6-0ST *Walton Park* was transferred to the railway from the Weston, Clevedon & Portishead Railway for a brief period in 1913 but it was moved on to the East Kent Light Railway within a few weeks. On 19 November 1913, six wagons were hire-purchased from the Wagon Finance Corporation on payment of £147 10s 6d over three years, with an option to purchase. As this acquisition was not reflected in the returns, perhaps six old wagons were withdrawn or sold, or maybe the new ones were overlooked. The LSWR agreed to the hire purchase of a locomotive in August 1916; the cost was £701, also payable over three years.

The construction contract was not finalised until 4 August 1916, when Stephens, as engineer, certified that the work had been completed. A summary of the construction accounts included in the minutes show that the Earl of Powis and the Earl of Bradford (the 4th presumably, who had died in 1915) had loaned £1,000 each, an R. Sandford £100, and T. W. Green £50. Stephens and Mathews had therefore been paid £23,054 in cash on the £38,000 contract, leaving a balance of £14,946 outstanding. Prior charge debentures were issued to Stephens and Mathews for this amount, subject to them not attracting interest until the net revenue of the company was sufficient to pay it.

On 22 September, Mathews objected to the open-ended nature of this

E. N. Fardoe at Nesscliff & Pentre on 27 September 1958. Born in Kinnerley, he had joined the railway as an assistant gamekeeper, and was a guard by the time he was called up for military service in 1915, serving with the Royal Engineers. His older brother, Arthur (1886–1959), also worked for the railway, as a platelayer. (A. M. Davies)

Hudswell, Clarke 0-6-0ST *Walton Park*, which spent a few weeks in Shropshire in 1913, at Shepherdswell on the East Kent Light Railway on 7 July 1922.

commitment; it was limited to two years on 17 November. The joint holding was split in 1919, with Stephens taking two thirds and Mathews the remainder. The reader may wish to speculate whether the railway had had the benefit of £23,054 or £38,000 of work. No details were given about any arrangements for repaying the loans, although interest was paid on them.

Stephens and Mathews received another payout in May 1918, when they accepted £956 16s 11d in settlement of any claims against the company for non-compliance with the contract by the company. The amount comprised: wages, materials, coal, etc. supplied between 1911 and 1914, £895 4s 9d; the engine acquired from the LSWR in November 1914, £550; legal charges in June 1915, £39 8s 8d, a total of £1,484 13s 5d. The company had already made payments for wages, materials and cash advances totalling £527 16s 6d. Quite why Stephens and Mathews had been subsidising the railway after it had opened, if that is what happened, is not clear. It may be relevant that the loans increased from £500 in 1914 to £2,660 in 1915. On 14 April 1920, Stephens reported that '£310 had been credited to the contractors for the loss incurred by delay in payment of the balance on the Criggion branch'.

From the moment the Light Railway Order application was made it must have been clear to Stephens that the established railway companies would give nothing to the railway that they did not have to, and that they would do everything possible to contain it. The order gave it running powers to Oswestry subject to the Cambrian's agreement. The Cambrian did not agree so the company went to the high court for a ruling, with a judgement in the Cambrian's favour being made on 24 January 1913. The Light Railway depended on the Light Railway Order's section No 4, which incorporated section No 65 of the 1888 Act, which gave the running powers, while the Cambrian relied on the Order's section No 28, which said any powers had to be by agreement.

The judgement was overturned by the appeal court in October, ruling that section 28 was not intended to remove powers conferred elsewhere in the order (*Liverpool Daily Post*, 28 October). It might be argued that the Cambrian had given its agreement in 1888.

Stephens must also have had his eye on the Nantmawr traffic right from the start, knowing that it would transform the railway's business. The Cambrian's ninety-nine-year Nantmawr branch lease was no deterrent to him trying to find a way in. On 5 December 1912, the Shropshire Railways had given the Cambrian six months' notice, as required, that it intended to resume running over the branch with the intention that it would delegate its powers to the Light Railway. Nothing came of this move and on 30 December 1916 the Cambrian made a new agreement with the Lilleshall company that was to be used as a weapon to prevent the Light Railway from getting the Nantmawr traffic when Stephens tried again after the war. The companies made a new agreement regarding rates in 1917.

In common with most other railway companies, the railway was taken under government control from 5 August 1914, a situation that appeared to have little effect on the day-to-day operation apart from reducing the already minimal maintenance; only the financial returns were reported while hostilities continued. During the war wages were increased by decree, bringing them in line with those paid by the main-line companies.

This was intended to restrict unnecessary travel and to enable the main-line companies to send locomotives and rolling stock overseas, but had the effect of encouraging railway users to seek alternative forms of transport, to the railways' detriment. The first post-war report, made for 1919, reveals that 2,280 prisoners of war had been carried during the year, an average of six per day on a six-day week basis. Financially, the government guaranteed net profits to 1913 levels.

Stephens, who had been continuing his activities as a volunteer officer in the Royal Engineers alongside his railway career, had been awarded the Territorial Decoration in 1913 and raised and commanded 2,4000 and 200 officers for the European war in 1914. These activities saw him promoted to the substantive rank of major and granted the honorary rank of lieutenant colonel on 4 January 1916, which rank was made substantive on 27 August 1921. From 3 February 1923 he was transferred from the Sussex (Fortress) Engineers to the Cinque Ports (Fortress) Engineers with the pay and allowances of a captain. On 20 September 1924 he would resign his commission with permission to 'wear the prescribed uniform'. Henceforth, he was known by his former rank.

During the war, an accident with potentially fatal consequences had occurred on 19 July 1915, when the 2.30pm ex-Shrewsbury, a mixed train hauled by Hawthorn, Leslie 0-6-2T No 6 *Thisbe,* derailed on Shrawardine bridge. The train consisted of two passenger carriages, a tar tank and a guard's van, the twenty passengers escaping without injury. William Onions (1844–1952), a local farmer, was early on the scene and climbed under the train to extract the

The 4th Earl of Bradford was buried with members of his family in the small cemetery at Weston-under-Lizard, Staffordshire, his personal estate valued at £572,928 4s 2d, £46,704,463 in 2022. He had been enthusiastic for the revival of the Potteries Railway.

Abbey station and its environs as revised in 1925 and published in 1929. The turntable was apparently still connected, though it may not have been in regular use. (Ordnance Survey)

walkway planks from between the rails, placing them on the cross beams to make a safe path for the passengers to regain *terra firma*.

As well as the disturbance to the passenger accommodation, the tar tank split a seam and leaked its contents over the river bank and a quantity of empty milk churns fell out of the brake van and were last seen floating down the river.

The locomotive was said to have broken a pony truck spring but a photograph shows one of the longitudinal timber beams that carried the track was broken in a manner that suggests to the author that it might not have been as sound as it should have been.

W. H. Austen, the engineer, told the *Liverpool Echo* (20 July) that the bridge was inspected weekly, was in perfect order and the accident's cause was a mystery, and that someone must have put something on the line.

Despite nationwide reporting and illustrated reports appearing in local newspapers, the incident was another one not reported to the Board of Trade. It might explain the early disposal of the 1911-built Hawthorn, Leslie locomotives in 1916, as they had a heavier axle loading than the tender locomotives.

They were replaced by two more ex-LSWR 0-6-0s that took the same numbers and names; a 1916 purchase has already been mentioned. There is a conflict here with recorded data, insofar as the first 0-6-0 is supposed to have been obtained in 1914. This was the subject of a hire purchase agreement between the LSWR and the Kent & East Sussex Railway that sanctioned its use on the railway dated 19 November 1914. Capital expenditure and receipts reported in the returns do not correlate to these acquisitions and disposals.

No 6 as derailed at Shrawardine on 19 July 1915. Farmer William Onions removed some of the walkway planks from under the train to make a temporary path to allow passengers to escape. (A. M. Davies Collection)

One fine day at Ford & Crossgates in 1930, *Pyramus*'s driver checks his stead for warm or overheating bearings. The loco had been bought in 1914, the second of the London & South Western Railway 0-6-0s to run on the railway, and was scrapped in 1932, its boiler being passed to No 6 *Thisbe*. (B. B. Edmonds)

CHAPTER 8

THE INTER-WAR YEARS

It was during the inter-war years that the Shropshire & Montgomeryshire Light Railway gained its reputation among enthusiasts for its quirky appearance and use of vintage locomotives and rolling stock. Although the war had ended in 1918, the railway remained under government control until 15 August 1921.

Full reporting to the Board of Trade had been resumed in 1919, when the railway had 'lost' two open and one covered wagon and acquired three more carriages, four-wheelers from the North Staffordshire Railway. A passenger brake was, at least nominally, exchanged for a horsebox at the same time. A Great Eastern Railway four-wheeled brake-third was obtained from the Kent & East Sussex Railway before 1920 and a brake van from the North London Railway in 1921; the former was used as a breakdown van.

The ambition to extend to Market Drayton and escape the clutches of the GWR and the LNWR, first attempted by the Potteries Junction Railway in the 1860s and then by the Shropshire Railways in the 1890s, had not gone away, but the third attempt was to be no more successful than the first two.

Shareholders had been told that steps were to be taken to carry out the Market Drayton undertaking in the directors' report published in 1914 (*Chester Chronicle*, 16 May) but the war had prevented any action from being taken until a notice of intention to apply for the Shropshire (Light) Railways Light Railway Order was published on 26 November 1918 (*London*

The ex-Great Eastern Railway brake-third ready for use as a breakdown van. (John Scott Morgan Collection)

Gazette, 29 November). The Order was intended to incorporate the Shrewsbury & Market Drayton Light Railway and authorise it to build a connection with the Shropshire line and terminating with the North Staffordshire Railway's Market Drayton branch close to the point where it crossed the Shropshire Union Canal, just under 22 miles in all. With Stephens' £199,095 estimate, the £230,000 capital required would have comprised £10,000 ordinary stock and £220,000 Shropshire Railways 5% prior charge debentures. The order was promoted by the Severn Syndicate, Charles Myles Mathews (1879–1928) and Stephens. Mathews, a solicitor, was a nephew of F. C. Mathews.

As might be expected, the application met with concerted opposition from the Cambrian, GWR and LNWR, particularly objecting to clauses authorising the local authorities to invest, pointing out that as they paid rates it was unfair for the authorities to use the money to invest in a competitor. It is a wonder that they had not used the same argument against the railway in 1909. After a six-hour public inquiry held in Shrewsbury on 19 March 1919, the application was rejected. In their annual report the Light Railway Commissioners said that the application made the case for better facilities 'in the district traversed', but that it failed because the basis of the financial proposals and the route required reconsideration. This information was not passed to Stephens in the letter informing him of the rejection.

Although the main-line railway companies had defeated the Market Drayton proposal, Stephens was still not deterred from fighting over the Nantmawr traffic. He resumed his campaign in 1920, while a light railway transfer order to allow the Cambrian to take over the Tanat Valley Light Railway was being processed, when he asked for running powers to Nantmawr, a mixed train between Blodwel Junction and Llanymynech and a through carriage from Llanymynech, originating at Oswestry, to Shrewsbury.

None of these requests succeeded, but he must have thought that he was making progress on 27 November when he persuaded the Lilleshall company to commit to a six-day trial despatch via the Light Railway. This never happened either, because none of the other companies wanted it to happen.

The Cambrian's Lilleshall agreement required the railway companies that were not party to it to approve any traffic, so Stephens was just given the run-around. When the LNWR agreed to accept the traffic at Meole Brace the GWR would not. The Cambrian required the wagons to be weighed before they could be accepted, but the Nantmawr weighbridge had been condemned. Lilleshall thought the Cambrian was going to replace it, which it would but not if the Light Railway was working the traffic. Samuel Williamson, the Cambrian's general manager, had some of his replies to Stephens' letters vetted by the company's solicitor to protect himself. Stephens' frustration comes through in his letters, particularly those to Williamson, and extracts, all from 1920, are worthy of quotation:

- 'I want to see you personally … The Nantmawr agreement seems so complicated that one almost wishes it could be declared obsolete and a new agreement entered into on a somewhat different basis. I am sure we shall never have any comfort as it is now.' (10 September)
- 'We do not get very far with our negotiations, it seems to be a question of putting it off, month after month, in the hope of some catastrophe happening, which will render further negotiations useless. No doubt this is good diplomacy, but it is not practical politics.' (9 November)
- 'I find we wrote to you on [four dates], you acknowledged same on the 7 ultimo, stating you would be writing to me shortly after a meeting of your directors … Is there any chance of a board meeting within the next few months on your line? I know the difficulties you labour under, but

A busy day for stone traffic at Kinnerley.

if you could let me have a reply …' (17 November)

- 'Hope you have a merry Christmas, and that your conscience will be clear and that the ghost of the starving S&M Company will not haunt your troubled Christmas sleep.' (21 December)

Stephens persevered into 1921, on 22 April arranging for the Shropshire Railway's receiver, now Ian Macdonald Henderson (1877–1957), to give the Cambrian the requisite six months' notice of intention to use the Llanyblodwel branch. A similar notice had been served in 1912, manager Williamson noted. In August the Cambrian went so far as to set the rates for passing traffic through Llanymynech station, and then declared that it would charge for a minimum of 6 miles and £300 per annum, the 6 miles being quickly reduced to four because it exceeded the Cambrian's maximum permitted rate. The correspondence carried on for some time, but Stephens withdrew from it, leaving it to Mathews. The Cambrian file was closed with the railway Grouping in 1923. No GWR equivalent has come to light.

The railway Grouping in 1923 could have seen the railway, and the rest of Stephens' empire, absorbed into the large regional companies. Stephens, however, fought a strong campaign to prevent this happening and got the minor railways excluded. As a precursor to the 1921 Railways Act, in 1920 the Ministry of Transport had set up a Light Railways (Investigation) Committee to inform its light railways policy.

The Committee circulated light railways, and a few that were not, with a questionnaire to obtain information, the railway's being returned in November 1920 and including the following: motor bus competition had been started since fares had been increased (by ministerial decree, by 50% from 1 January 1917); maximum gradient – 1 in 50; minimum radius, running line 10 chains, sidings 6 chains; maximum axle load 9 tons; maximum booked speed 20mph, maximum authorised speed 25mph, maximum speed safely possible, 45mph (wishful thinking on Stephens' part?); fencing was quick-set hedges with post and wire in gaps; bonus mileage of 2 miles was (still) charged for crossing either of the river bridges; stations, other than junctions, seven; halts, eight; intermediate sidings, one; points locked by key on train staff; 5-ton travelling crane available for use at all

The 50cwt crane at Shrewsbury, made in R. S. France's Abbey Works.

stations, 50cwt fixed crane at Shrewsbury, road weighbridges at all stations, rail weighbridge at Kinnerley, cattle pens at principal stations; larger stations had a capacity for twenty to forty wagons, small stations, eight to ten wagons; Kinnerley workshop carried out all repairs except wheel turning, done by main-line companies; automatic vacuum brake used on passenger trains, hand brake on goods trains; tender locomotives were not turned; the maximum load hauled by locomotives, 300 tons; acetylene gas lighting and steam heating in carriages; cost of construction – £40,442, rolling stock – £1,720; works and plant – £572.

On its organisation Stephens noted: 'For practical purposes, this line is grouped, and has been grouped for many years, with the Kent & East Sussex, the Weston, Clevedon & Portishead, East Kent Railway, Chichester & Selsey, Rye & Camber, etc. A local clerk-in-charge is employed who supervises details locally, all secretarial, accountants, audit department and rate fixing work is farmed out privately, for a small payment per annum.' He also made it clear that he was very unhappy with the 50% fare increase imposed in 1917 without consultation.

Although the railway retained its independence at the Grouping, the Llanyblodwel/Nantmawr branch was absorbed into the GWR (*Western Mail*, 13 May 1921), which closed it between Blodwel Junction and Wern Junction in 1925, routing the stone traffic via the Tanat Valley Railway and Porthywaen

To make its mark as an independent entity, the railway published a range of publicity material, including a small guidebook. To encourage holidaymakers, five 'camping huts' were set up on the banks of the Severn near Crew Green station and staying there cost 7s per week each.

As a symbol of modernity, an attempt to reduce costs, and perhaps to increase traffic, a three-car passenger railmotor, using Ford engines and with a seating capacity of 120, was acquired from Edmonds of Thetford in 1923. The annual reports show expenditure totalling £1,263 under this heading in 1923–24. *The Locomotive* (14 July) said that it had consumed just 1.75 gallons of petrol

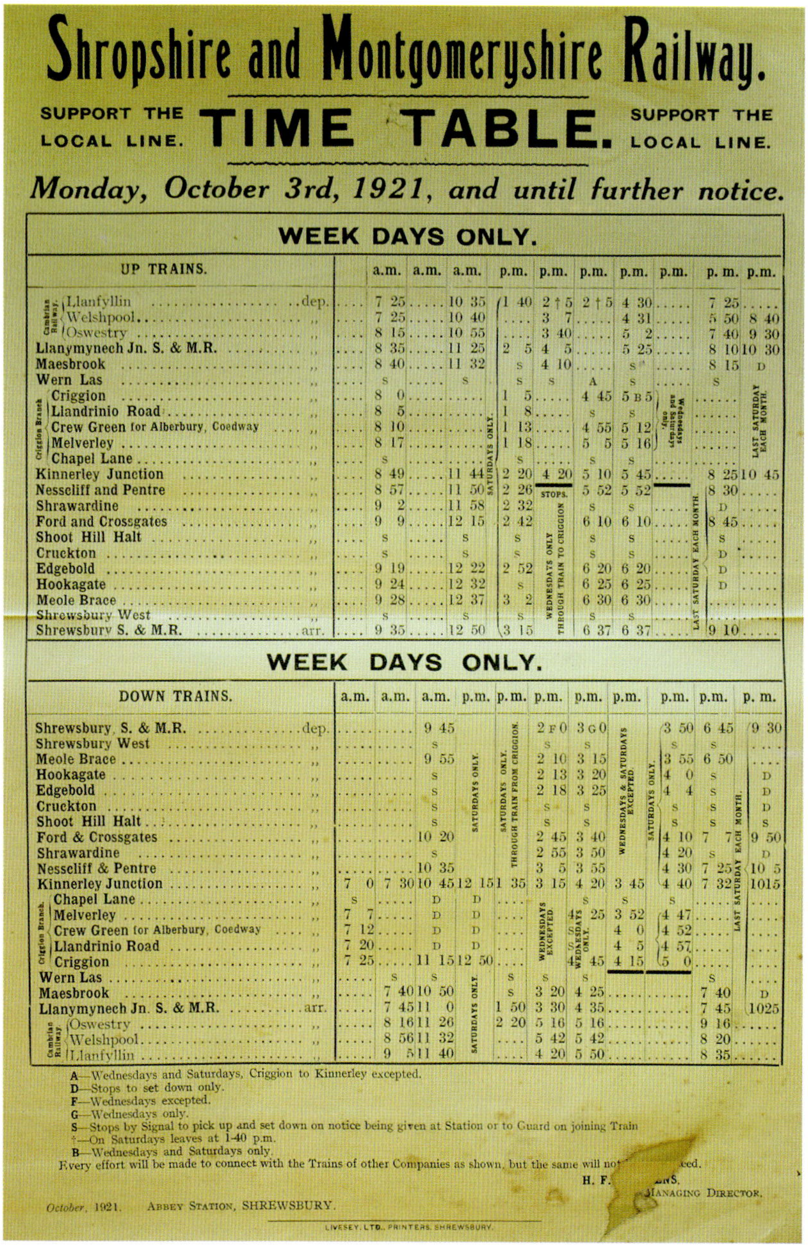

Shropshire and Montgomeryshire Railway.

SUPPORT THE LOCAL LINE. **TIME TABLE.** SUPPORT THE LOCAL LINE.

Monday, October 3rd, 1921, and until further notice.

WEEK DAYS ONLY.

UP TRAINS.	a.m.	a.m.	a.m.	p.m.	p.m.	p.m.	p.m.	p.m.	p.m.	p.m.
Cambrian Railway. Llanfyllin ..dep.	7 25		10 35	1 40	2 † 5	2 † 5	4 30		7 25	
Welshpool ,,	7 25		10 40		3 7		4 31		5 50	8 40
Oswestry ,,	8 15		10 55		3 40		5 2		7 40	9 30
Llanymynech Jn. S. & M.R. ,,	8 35		11 25	2 5	4 5		5 25		8 10	10 30
Maesbrook ,,	8 40		11 32	s	4 10		s		8 15	D
Wern Las ,,	s		s	s	s	A	s		s	
Criggion Branch. Criggion ,,	8 0			1 5		4 45	5 B 5			
Llandrinio Road ,,	8 5			1 8		s	s			
Crew Green for Alberbury, Coedway ,,	8 10			1 13		4 55	5 12			
Melverley ,,	8 17			1 18		5 5	5 16			
Chapel Lane ,,	s			s		s	s			
Kinnerley Junction ,,	8 49		11 44	2 20	4 20	5 10	5 45		8 25	10 45
Nesscliff and Pentre ,,	8 57		11 50	2 26	STOPS.	5 52	5 52		8 30	
Shrawardine ,,	9 2		11 58	2 32		s	s		D	
Ford and Crossgates ,,	9 9		12 15	2 42		6 10	6 10		8 45	
Shoot Hill Halt ,,	s		s	s		s	s		s	
Cruckton ,,	s		s	s		s	s		D	
Edgebold ,,	9 19		12 22	2 52		6 20	6 20		D	
Hookagate ,,	9 24		12 32	s		6 25	6 25		D	
Meole Brace ,,	9 28		12 37	3 2		6 30	6 30			
Shrewsbury West ,,	s		s	s		s	s			
Shrewsbury S. & M.R. arr.	9 35		12 50	3 15		6 37	6 37		9 10	
				SATURDAYS ONLY.	WEDNESDAYS ONLY THROUGH TRAIN TO CRIGGION			Wednesdays and Saturdays only.	LAST SATURDAY EACH MONTH.	LAST SATURDAY EACH MONTH.

WEEK DAYS ONLY.

DOWN TRAINS.	a.m.	a.m.	a.m.	p.m.	p.m.	p.m.	p.m.	p.m.	p.m.	p.m.	p. m.
Shrewsbury, S. & M.R. ..dep.			9 45			2 F 0	3 G 0		3 50	6 45	9 30
Shrewsbury West ,,			s			s	s		s	s	
Meole Brace ,,			9 55			2 10	3 15		3 55	6 50	
Hookagate ,,			s			2 13	3 20		4 0	s	D
Edgebold ,,			s			2 18	3 25		4 4	s	D
Cruckton ,,			s			s	s		s	s	D
Shoot Hill Halt ,,			s			s	s		s	s	s
Ford & Crossgates ,,			10 20			2 45	3 40		4 10	7 7	9 50
Shrawardine ,,			s			2 55	3 50		4 20	s	D
Nesscliff & Pentre ,,			10 35			3 5	3 55		4 30	7 25	10 5
Kinnerley Junction ,,	7 0	7 30	10 45	12 15	1 35	3 15	4 20	3 45	4 40	7 32	1015
Criggion Branch. Chapel Lane ,,	s		D	D			s	s	s		
Melverley ,,	7 7		D	D			4 25	3 52	4 47		
Crew Green for Alberbury, Coedway ,,	7 12		D	D			S	4 0	4 52		
Llandrinio Road ,,	7 20		D	D			S	4 5	4 57		
Criggion ,,	7 25		11 15	12 50			4 45	4 15	5 0		
Wern Las ,,		s	s		s	s	s			s	
Maesbrook ,,		7 40	10 50		s	3 20	4 25			7 40	D
Llanymynech Jn. S. & M.R. arr.		7 45	11 0		1 50	3 30	4 35			7 45	1025
Cambrian Railway. Oswestry ,,		8 16	11 26		2 20	5 16	5 16			9 16	
Welshpool ,,		8 56	11 32			5 42	5 42			8 20	
Llanfyllin ,,		9 5	11 40			4 20	5 50			8 35	
				SATURDAYS ONLY.	SATURDAYS ONLY. THROUGH TRAIN FROM CRIGGION.	WEDNESDAYS EXCEPTED	WEDNESDAYS ONLY.	WEDNESDAYS & SATURDAYS EXCEPTED	SATURDAYS ONLY.		LAST SATURDAY EACH MONTH.

A—Wednesdays and Saturdays, Criggion to Kinnerley excepted.
D—Stops to set down only.
F—Wednesdays excepted.
G—Wednesdays only.
S—Stops by Signal to pick up and set down on notice being given at Station or to Guard on joining Train
†—On Saturdays leaves at 1-40 p.m.
B—Wednesdays and Saturdays only.
Every effort will be made to connect with the Trains of other Companies as shown, but the same will not [illegible]eed.

H. F. [illegible]ENS,
Managing Director.

October, 1921. Abbey Station, Shrewsbury.

Livesey, Ltd., Printers, Shrewsbury.

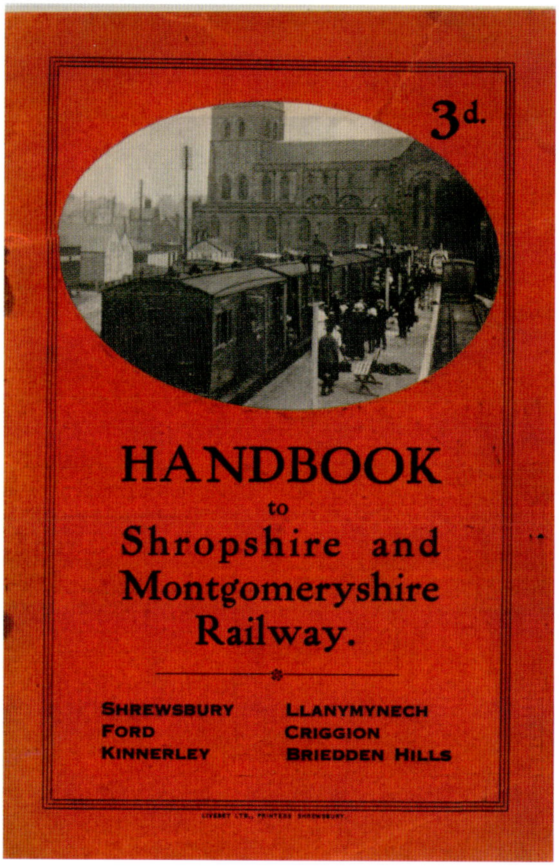

making the 23-mile journey with a full load. In 1923, 9,109 miles were operated, a figure that doubled in 1925. Photographs show that the unit usually ran in a two-car formation.

On the locomotive front, three ex-London, Brighton & South Coast Railway 'A1'class 0-6-0Ts, known as 'Terriers', were acquired in 1921 and 1923. The Manning, Wardle 0-6-0T *Morous* was sent on hire to the West

Above left: Timetable for the winter of 1921–22. (National Archives)

Above right: Published after the first railmotor had entered service in 1923, this handbook was at least partially funded by advertisements. Printing the cover on a different coloured paper with a cutout to reveal a photograph must have made it seem very modern.

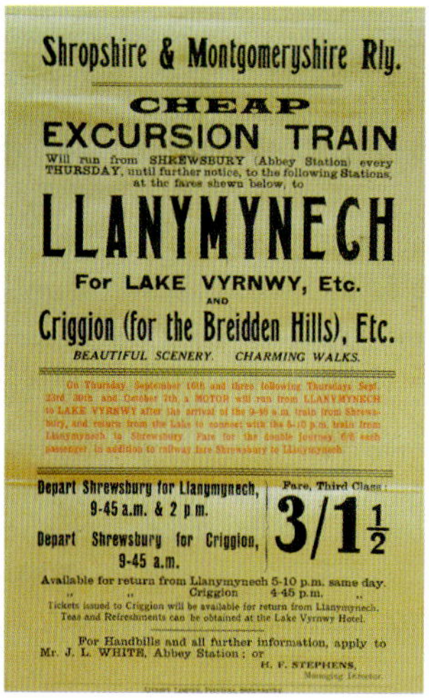

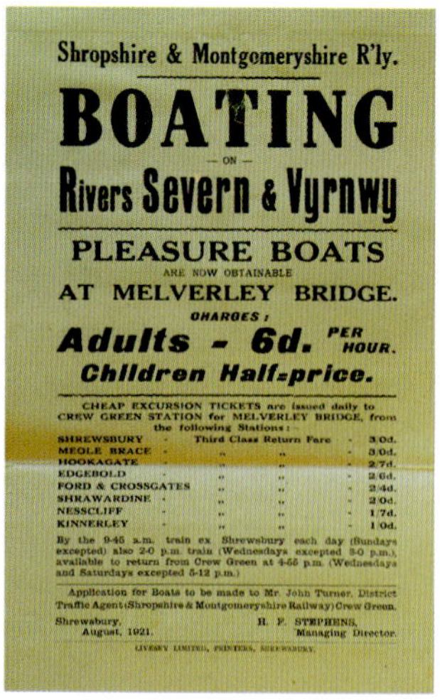

Right: Promotional material for 1922. (National Archives)

Above left: The manufacturer's photograph of the three-car Ford railmotor. Judging by the lack of photographs it rarely ran in this form and was probably underpowered on the gradient out of Abbey station.

Above right: A more typical view of the Ford set, at Ford & Crossgates in the summer of 1930, clearly a quiet day for traffic. (B. B. Edmonds)

Sussex Railway, otherwise known as the Selsey Tramway, in 1924.

There were several changes among the directors during the 1920s. On 22 February 1923, W. G. Barcroft, who had been involved with the railway since 1888, resigned from the Shropshire Railways and was replaced by Jeremiah MacVeagh (1870–1932), an Irish MP who was also a director of the East Kent and the Devon & Cornwall railways. Light Railway director A. P. Tabraham died on 7 February 1925 and was replaced by Sidney Albert Parnwell (1880–1945), a chartered surveyor. MacVeagh became the Shropshire Railways' nominated director on 21 May 1929, replacing Parnwell.

William Rigby, Stephens' associate and Light Railway chairman from 1909, retired in 1929. James Ramsey (1868–1943) took his

The three 'Terriers' at Kinnerley, from the left, *Daphne*, *Hecate* and *Dido*.

place and Stephens became chairman. From 1920 the directors met only once a year, on the same day as the annual meeting. Shropshire Railways directors also met infrequently. Robert Ullmer, the Shropshire Railways' secretary and sometime director, died on 5 February 1927; he had been associated with the railway since 1890. He was replaced by Francis Launcelot Beard (1849–1929), an accountant, and when he died Robert Edwin Boyce (1891-1963) was appointed acting secretary.

On the railway another tragedy had occurred on 26 May 1921, when Alfred Harold Glyde (aged 25) fell off his engine at Kinnerley while shunting and died of his injuries in the Royal Salop Infirmary a few hours later. He was one of several young men recruited in Kent by Stephens to work in Shropshire. The Kinnerley stationmaster, Herbert George Funnell (1900-73), who had found Glyde, was another.

The company had enough cash to spare to invest £2,250 in Consols, Government debt, in 1922, an amount that was increased to £3,993 in 1924. Some of this money must have been the £2,443 compensation received from the government during 1923. The Consols were used as security for a £1,500 loan in 1924 and were sold at a loss of £220 in 1925.

The most distinguished vehicle used on the railway was obtained in 1926, a four-wheeled saloon built in 1848 for the London & South Western Railway royal train. Also obtained from the Plymouth, Devonport & South Western Junction Railway via the Kent & East Sussex Railway, it retained its original plush sofas and carpet.

Six 10-ton open wagons were added to stock in 1928 and six 8-ton wagons were disposed of in 1931; the War Office failed to distinguish between the two types when it conducted its survey in 1940. The arrival of a Wolseley-Siddeley railmotor and rail-mounted Ford lorry from the West Sussex Railway in 1928 failed to make an appearance in any of the company's surviving records; the railmotor may not have entered service, and the lorry, which is known to have run with one of the Ford railmotors, was out of use by the early 1930s.

The Ceiriog Granite Company, lessee of the Criggion quarries from 1925, had obtained a vertical boiler, four-wheel shunting locomotive from Shrewsbury

No 8236, one of the LNWR 0-6-0s, with the royal saloon in its train, at Llanymynech. The saloon was Number 1A in the railway's fleet. No 8236 had been bought in August 1932; it was the only one of the three to retain its smokebox number plate. (John Keylock collection)

Planning a journey in the royal saloon. (John Scott Morgan Collection)

The Ford lorry coupled with one of the rail motors would have made for economy in operation, albeit the lorry was probably underpowered. The ensemble was seen at Llanymynech. (J. A. Hignett)

Above: Ceiriog Granite Company's Sentinel with a good load at Kinnerley.

Right: One of Sentinel's experimental locomotives on test at Shrewsbury in 1955. (John Scott Morgan Collection)

builder Sentinel Waggon Works Ltd in 1927. The railway had provided a test facility for some of Sentinel's new locomotives in 1925–26. The Criggion locomotive remained in use until 1959, and with its relatively low weight and speed of 5mph, it had been the only locomotive to work on the Criggion branch for several years. It was scrapped in 1962.

Fresh traffic was on offer when the directors met on 2 July 1930. The British Quarrying Company had taken over the Criggion quarries and had obtained a contract to supply stone for the Liverpool–Manchester arterial road. The company had said that it required the stone to be routed to the GWR at Llanymynech. The railway replied that the choice of routing was its prerogative; it would make more if the traffic was routed via Meole Brace.

The Criggion branch rail was in poor condition and Austen was authorised to purchase 14 tons of second-hand rail from the Southern Railway, to sell the scrap for £3 per ton, and to employ Sunday labour, at overtime rates, to lay it. Installing the 'new' rail was delayed because overtime payments were in arrears and the gangers refused to undertake the Sunday working. Relaying was completed by early October.

At the same time attempts were made to sell two of the 'derelict' engines. George Cohen offered £70 for 'the *Severn*' and Thomas Ward, £134 for Beyer, Peacock 0-6-0 No 5, both delivered to Shrewsbury. As the GWR and LMSR refused to accept these locomotives on their own wheels and their value as scrap was deemed to be too low, on 9 October the directors decided that they should be dismantled as the opportunity presented and their components sold for scrap when the market improved. It also decided that No 8 should be equipped with No 7's boiler and overhauled while No 7 and No 8's boiler should be scrapped. The wheels and axles of No 7 were sold to the Kent & East Sussex Railway at £3 per ton in part liquidation of the company's (unspecified) debt to the KESR.

Severn at Kinnerley, awaiting its date with dismantling and the scrap man.

With most of the railway's locomotive fleet out of use, approaches were made to the LMSR for ex-LNWR 0-6-0 coal engines. Two were offered, for £420 and £390, in 1930–31 but were deemed unacceptable. In March 1931 No 8182 was offered for £380 standing at Sutton Oak and purchased; it was reported as working satisfactorily in May. No 8236 cost £375 when purchased on 21 June 1932. No 8108 appears to have been purchased in 1930 but the transaction

Pyramus in happier days.

Above: A grainy photograph of No 8182 at Llanymynech. The second of the ex-LNWR 0-6-0s, the locomotive had been built in 1879 and bought in June 1931.

Right: The old order changeth. An 'Ilfracombe goods' alongside one of the 'new' ex-LNWR 0-6-0s at Kinnerley shed. Indicative of Stephens' demise, the additions to stock were not named and retained their LMS numbers until 8108 was renumbered after its rebuilding.

was not recorded; it might have been one of those rejected earlier. None of these purchases were recorded as capital expenditure.

Of the old fleet, Nos 2, 5, 6, 7 and 8 were ordered to be broken for scrap in July 1931. Nos 5 and 7 had been broken up by November, when work was proceeding on Nos 2 and 8. By 17 October 1933, the boilers from Nos 2, 6, 7 and 8 had been sold to G. R. Jackson Ltd, Wednesbury, for £100. Another old loco, the Manning, Wardle

Seen here at Kinnerley, *Morous* was hired to the West Sussex Railway in 1924 and sold in 1932.

0-6-0T No 4 *Morous*, on hire to the West Sussex Railway since 1924, was sold to that railway for £50 in 1932.

The directors also 'expressed their deep regret at the continued illness of Colonel Stephens'. A problem had arisen because he held one of the keys to the company seal and share transfers could not be registered without it. On 26 February 1931 he told them that he was incapacitated by the loss of use of his right hand; he had had a stroke, probably not the first. His absence prompted some concern over administrative procedures when he said that he had authorised his office manager, James Arthur Iggulden (1899–1979), to sign cheques for him. It was also the practice of the Tonbridge office to hold pre-signed cheques to issue when required. Iggulden's signing authority was withdrawn on 25 March 1931 and the cheques were transferred to the London office, where they were signed by two directors.
On 9 January 1931, Austen had been appointed acting traffic and locomotive superintendent and engineer, backdated to 1 January.

Ramsey, acting as chairman in Stephens' absence, reported on 9 October 1930 that he had visited the Tonbridge office and found that the company was £15,000 in debt, the major creditors being the LMSR, the GWR and the bank.

He need not have gone to Tonbridge to find this out, as the information was contained in the annual reports and was not a new phenomenon; taking the so-called temporary loans and the other unpaid bills into account the company had owed at least £10,000 for more than ten years. Even in 1913, the first year for which the full accounts are available, the company did not have enough resources to pay its bills. The major asset on the balance sheet was always undepreciated capital expenditure (made from revenue), a false figure insofar as the assets had been bought earlier, could not be realised and had since deteriorated in value. This lack of allowance for depreciation was a weakness of all railway company accounts as it maintained assets at their original value regardless of their current worth.

The inability of the company to pay its way was undoubtedly aggravated by the prior charge debenture interest, which fluctuated at around £1,000 annually. A sign that the situation was deteriorating had occurred in April 1927 when Stephens advanced £539 17s 1d to enable a payment to be made to the LMSR on the traffic account. He subsequently guaranteed a bank loan of £2,500 'to be drawn upon when required'. From 1927, Stephens did not take his salary, although in 1930 the reduction was offset by a salary increase to clerical staff recommended by the auditor.

Although Stephens apparently had a lackadaisical attitude towards financial matters it is difficult to understand why his co-directors, experienced professional men, could take no action about the company's dire financial position until he was absent. Liquidating the debt became their main concern, with priority given to paying the overtime and ensuring continuity of supplies. It may be ironic that although the main-line companies did all they could to hinder the railway, they did not, apart from the incident cited earlier, pursue it for the moneys owing to them. With Ramsey in the chair the board met more often, and the minutes contained considerably more operational information.

Colonel H. F. Stephens, engineer and railway manager, died on 23 October 1931 and was buried with his parents in London's West Brompton cemetery. His name is recorded on the left-hand side of the plinth. His estate was valued at £30,197 14s 2d, £1,559,080 in 2022.

Stephens died on 23 October 1931. Paying tribute to him on 4 November, Ramsey said that he was 'a man with a striking personality and a very warm heart and that this was best exemplified in his unbounded hospitality', concluding that 'not only had they lost their principal colleague but a much-valued personal friend'. The company owed his estate £1,125 for arrears of salary and £373 for loans and advances made by him.

The Criggion stone traffic gave the directors cause for optimism. Traffic averaged fifty wagonloads per day, all sent via Meole Brace; the £4,483 earned from this source in September 1930 was typical. Walking passes issued to the quarrymen permitted them to use Melverley bridge when the local roads were flooded. Sugar beet had become another source of freight traffic since 1927, although it was seasonal and was affected by the weather; some 2,000 tons was carried annually until 1931. The following year, 1932, this traffic was poor, only 1,108 tons being carried because of the weather, but after a two-year respite the trend was down, falling to 525 tons in 1938.

Over the following three years the level of indebtedness was reduced to fluctuate at around £10,000. The company managed to maintain a good relationship with its bank while slowly reducing its borrowings. By 9 July 1931 the board noted 'very few pressing applications for payment now being received'. It did not make such good progress with the £1,100 it owed the Inland Revenue, however, paying a mere £40 per month when the Revenue wanted more.

A programme of track improvements was put in place on the main line. The Southern Railway became the railway's source of 'serviceable' double-head rail; 17½ tons bought from Chilworth in 1931

Above: The Lord Warden Hotel in Dover, where Stephens was living at the time of his death. (F. Hartmann)

Left: A GWR pannier tank waiting to take a train of loaded stone wagons from the exchange sidings at Meole Brace. (John Scott Morgan Collection)

cost £3 5s per ton plus £1 2s 8d per ton transported to Meole Brace, while 10 tons came from Paddock Wood in 1932. The Midland Bank (?) was the supplier of around 5,000 Brazilian hardwood sleepers that could be paid for as used; inevitably some were not paid for. In May 1931, 2,000 oak rail chair keys were purchased for £4 15s. Additional permanent way gangers were employed with the main line then patrolled and maintained by three gangs instead of two.

Passenger numbers continued to decline and an experiment of issuing return tickets

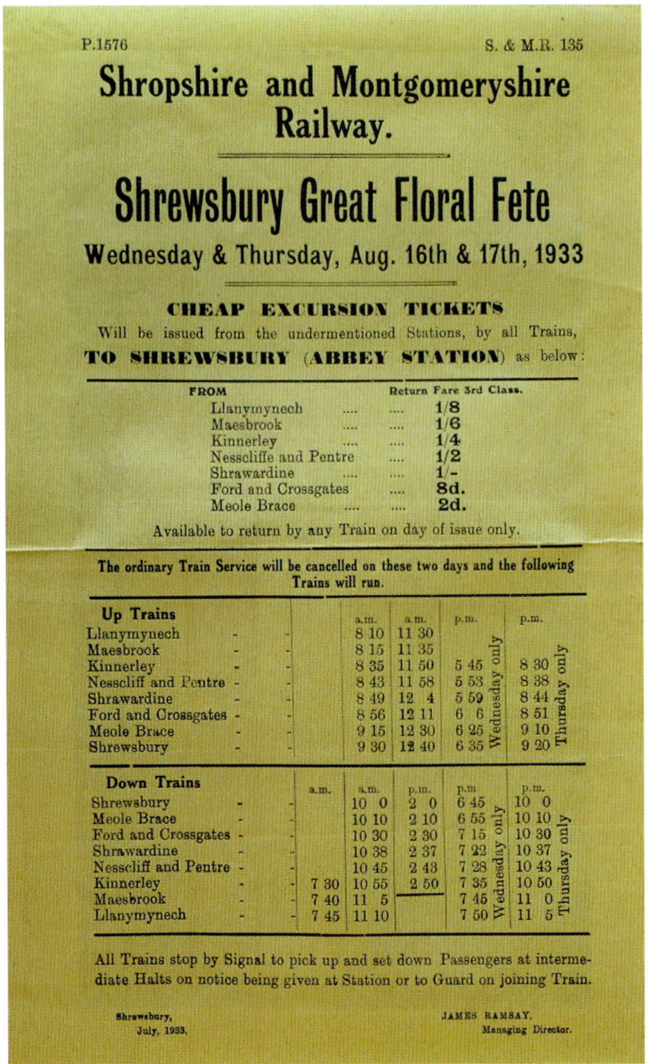

P.1576 S. & M.R. 135

Shropshire and Montgomeryshire Railway.

Shrewsbury Great Floral Fete

Wednesday & Thursday, Aug. 16th & 17th, 1933

CHEAP EXCURSION TICKETS

Will be issued from the undermentioned Stations, by all Trains,
TO SHREWSBURY (ABBEY STATION) as below:

FROM	Return Fare 3rd Class.
Llanymynech	1/8
Maesbrook	1/6
Kinnerley	1/4
Nesscliffe and Pentre	1/2
Shrawardine	1/-
Ford and Crossgates	8d.
Meole Brace	2d.

Available to return by any Train on day of issue only.

The ordinary Train Service will be cancelled on these two days and the following Trains will run.

Up Trains		a.m.	a.m.	p.m. Wednesday only	p.m. Thursday only
Llanymynech		8 10	11 30		
Maesbrook		8 15	11 35		
Kinnerley		8 35	11 50	5 45	8 30
Nesscliff and Pentre		8 43	11 58	5 53	8 38
Shrawardine		8 49	12 4	5 59	8 44
Ford and Crossgates		8 56	12 11	6 6	8 51
Meole Brace		9 15	12 30	6 25	9 10
Shrewsbury		9 30	12 40	6 35	9 20

Down Trains	a.m.	a.m.	p.m.	p.m Wednesday only	p.m. Thursday only
Shrewsbury		10 0	2 0	6 45	10 0
Meole Brace		10 10	2 10	6 55	10 10
Ford and Crossgates		10 30	2 30	7 15	10 30
Shrawardine		10 38	2 37	7 22	10 37
Nesscliff and Pentre		10 45	2 43	7 28	10 43
Kinnerley	7 30	10 55	2 50	7 35	10 50
Maesbrook	7 40	11 5		7 45	11 0
Llanymynech	7 45	11 10		7 50	11 5

All Trains stop by Signal to pick up and set down Passengers at intermediate Halts on notice being given at Station or to Guard on joining Train.

Shrewsbury, July, 1933. JAMES RAMSAY, Managing Director.

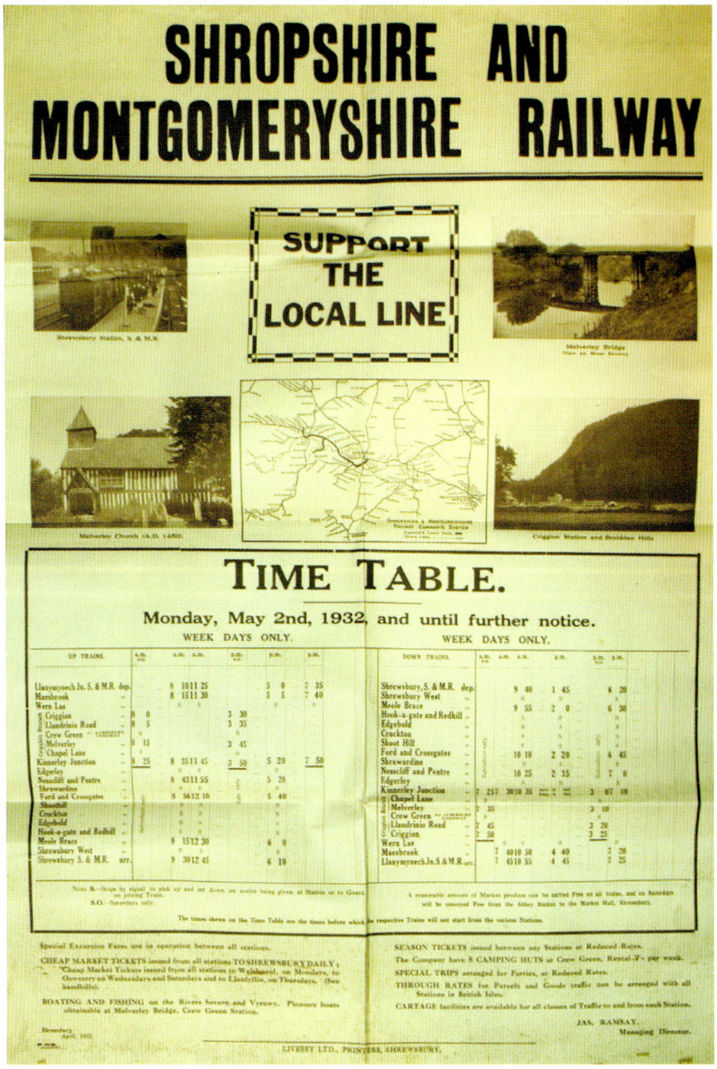

Above left: Promotional material issued with chairman James Ramsey's name. Named the Shrewsbury Flower Show, the event continues to make a major contribution to horticultural life in the town and claims to be the longest-running flower show in the country.

Above right: A timetable poster for 1932. Also signed by Ramsey, the slogan 'Support the local line' had been inherited from Stephens, who had used it on several of his railways.

for the single fare was tried in August 1931. As there was no report back to the board it probably did not have the desired result. Another source of passenger revenue came to an end on 30 April 1931. Criggion quarry had agreed to pay a flat £1 7s per week for a workmen's train in February 1918, to run as required; the facility had not been used for some time and the quarry gave notice that it would end the payments.

Savings on the stone traffic were expected after Austen tried one of the coal engines on the improved Melverley bridge and reported that there was no undue deflection on it or stress on the track. Regular use was started on 13 July 1931, despite the bridge not being reported as completed until November 1932. Railmotor petrol consumption had increased by 25% to 50 gallons per week despite reduced mileage earlier in 1931. The directors decided to dispense with the railmotors for the summer service in 1932; their driver, Samuel Nevitt, had resigned on health grounds in April.

Changes in station facilities were sometimes required to keep up with

A scene at Melverley on 6 October 1931. The identity of the customer who collected stone from the station is not known. (John Scott Morgan Collection)

changing traffic trends. The Criggion refreshment room was moved to Nesscliff to be used as a store in 1931 and the following year a building used as a clubroom at Kinnerley was moved to Shrewsbury for use as a warehouse. Another change in trends saw a second-hand motorcycle that cost £10 being bought for the canvasser, F. Jones, in May 1931; he was required to maintain it and to take out third-party insurance.

Several changes in personnel took place after Stephens' death. T. W. Green was elected director in his stead on 22 February 1932 and Austen's acting position was made substantive. MacVeagh died in Dublin on 17 April 1932 and was replaced by John Pike (1868–1946). On 24 May 1932 Austen and Iggulden were appointed Shropshire Railways directors, with Austen becoming that company's representative on the Light Railway board.

A meeting with Stephens' beneficiaries, Austen, Iggulden, and the Willard brothers, who were also his executors, took place on 29 April 1932. They agreed to accept 50% of the salary due, subject to review at the end of the year, but if the railway's fortune made a significant turn for the better, they wanted all of it. In the event they got none of it.

Government restrictions on road-building expenditure in the autumn of 1932 affected the Criggion traffic and caused the directors to seek economies. Several employees were sacked or put on part-time and the locomotive crew's wages were reduced, a process that was kept under review and which continued into 1933. The midday train was cancelled from 3 October 1932 and from 6 February 1933 the 'afternoon double trip … suspended to the public, but that railcars, or a steam train, would be run … according to the requirements of the traffic'.

A saving of £100 per annum was expected from transferring the telephone and tablet apparatus maintenance contract from the North Wales Power Company to the LMSR. Although the railmotor service had been ordered to be withdrawn after 30 April 1932, they still ran nearly 8,000 miles during the year, half the mileage of 1931, and in 1933 they ran 5,146 miles. It is not altogether clear why railmotor use declined, and it does not seem to be completely because of the reduction in passengers. They had run 36,000 miles in 1928, their best year.

It had been the company's practice to transfer £125 per month to a special account to pay the prior charge debenture interest. Arising from the reduction in traffic, the board ordered the allocation to be suspended from 1 November 1932. This was the first threat to the interest since the railway had opened; the ordinary dividend had not been paid since 1931. It was decided to ask the holders of more than £100 if they would agree to accept a share of the company's net revenue, even if that meant receiving less than the interest to which they were entitled.

On 1 March 1933 it was reported that Iggulden and the Willard brothers had given, and then withdrawn, their assents to the scheme. The Severn Syndicate Ltd, of which Iggulden was a director, also dissented; between them they held £14,371 of the debentures. They applied for the interest that had been due on 1 January 1933 and on being informed that no funds were available, the Syndicate and the Willard brothers petitioned for the appointment of a receiver and manager, recommending Iggulden for the appointment. The directors resolved to resist the petition but agreed that if an appointment was to be made they would recommend Ramsey. The petition was withdrawn the day before a hearing set for 7 February.

The Syndicate assented to the scheme of arrangement on 28 March, however, but later in the year it requested the issue of £279 3s in debentures to represent the interest owing. The company replied that in view of the personal guarantee given to the Syndicate by Stephens and Mathews the Syndicate should pursue the issue with their respective executors; Mathews had died in 1923. When the interest moratorium expired in 1937 the holders agreed to a five-year extension.

The 5th Earl of Bradford was only briefly involved with the railway. Buried close to the family mausoleum at Weston-under-Lizard, his personal estate was £306,569 4s 10d, £587,234 in 2022.

Aspects of the infrastructure, both on and off the railway, were an issue in May 1933. At Llanymynech, Henry Pooley & Son informed the company that the weights and measures inspector had condemned the weighbridge because it was old and obsolete, while at Shrewsbury the corporation had asked for a £50 contribution towards repairs to Rocke Street, where the railway was a frontager; it crossed the road by a bridge close to the former Potteries Junction. The weighbridge was scrapped and the ground made good and the corporation was informed that the railway could not afford the £50. On 29 October 1937 a shed at Llanymynech was destroyed by fire, the company receiving a £250 settlement from its insurance company.

The finances were obviously tighter than usual, because in October 1933 the bank threatened to withdraw the £500 overdraft facility on the general revenue account unless it was guaranteed; the directors agreed to act as guarantors. The Earl of Bradford (1873–1957, the 5th) renewed his guarantee of a £1,000 bank loan for five years from June 1935. The directors had not taken their fees since 1932.

The following month, passenger traffic had declined so much that the service was suspended from 6 November in the interest of economy. Passengers carried in 1933 were just over a third of the 9,142 conveyed in 1932. Goods train revenue was only £5,001, compared with £9,772 the year before, and train operation made a loss (£816) for the first time. A journalist visiting in 1934 was told that at the end there had only been two regular passengers (*Express & Star*, 30 October).

Despite the passenger service being withdrawn, bank holiday specials continued to be run, and over the next

A rare colour photograph, albeit with degraded colour, of *Gazelle* and its tramcar carriage. (R. G. Jarvis)

five years 1,716 passengers were carried and the coaching stock ran 963 miles. In 1934–35 the railmotors ran 4,940 miles before making their swansong of 204 miles in 1936. In the absence of the passenger train the locality was served by a 30cwt Chevrolet bus 'but the accommodation afforded is not very luxurious' it was said. Lacking covered accommodation for them, the carriages were stored in the open at Kinnerley and Shrewsbury.

Sadly, the opening of the Anglo-American Oil Company's oil and spirit depot adjoining the Shrewsbury terminus in June 1934 did little to help the company despite generating 2,538 tons of traffic by the end of the year. By 1937 this figure had reached 5,157 tons.

Another serious incident had occurred on 23 September 1930, when the railmotors sustained considerable damage when derailed after dark. An internal inquiry concluded with the driver being sacked; no explanation was recorded but perhaps he had been drinking. During the year £75 was spent on motor repairs, undoubtedly a

The Birmingham Locomotive Club's 23 April 1939 excursion train posed for photographs at Llanymynech.

In 1937 No 8108, the first acquired of the LNWR 0-6-0s, was taken into the workshop and rebuilt, re-emerging as No 2 in May 1939, looking as good as it had done when built in 1874. Its boiler had been retubed and a new smokebox fitted. No doubt had the war not intervened the other two would have received similar attention. When the government took over No 2 became 8108 again. All three were withdrawn in 1946 and scrapped at Swindon in 1950. (R. G. Jarvis)

portion of it due to the accident that, once again, was not reported. On 12 February 1936 another incident was reported in *The Times*, a goods train running into five horses belonging to Harry Davies of Melverley Hall at Chapel Lane crossing on the Breidden branch. Two were killed outright and a third was put down later.

After several years out of use, and looking increasingly derelict, *Gazelle* was overhauled at Kinnerley and returned to service in 1937. The tramcar body having rotted beyond repair, the Wolseley-Siddeley railmotor body was mounted on the tramcar chassis for *Gazelle* to pull, the ensemble being used for inspections and special parties. The Birmingham Locomotive Club was one such party, organising probably the first enthusiast tours of the railway, on 23 and 30 April 1939. Following *Gazelle* in the works was ex-LNWR 0-6-0 No 8108, returning to service as No 2 during 1939.

A link with the past was broken in 1937 when the land formerly occupied by the Potteries Junction's line to Potteries Junction, some 9 acres, was sold to Shrewsbury Corporation.

On the outbreak of war in 1939 the company received a letter dated 1 September informing it that under the defence of the realm, defence regulations 1939, the railway was now under government control. It was the last of eleven in a list of railways affected. The only other light railways were the East Kent Light Railway and the Kent & East Sussex Light Railway, two other lines once run by Stephens, and probably selected because of their strategic significance.

By the end of 1939 the company owed £16,439, offset by less than £2,000 of realisable current assets. The remainder on the so-called credit side of the balance sheet was £9,756 of capital expenditure paid from revenue and £4,929 of accumulated losses. Of the five locomotives owned by the railway, only one, No 2, the former No 8108, was in use. It really was in a pretty poor state.

CHAPTER 9

THE WAR OFFICE RAILWAY

The Second World War gave the railway a new lease of life, but not immediately. Until January 1941 things carried on much as they had done before. The winter of 1939–40 was, however, extremely severe and played a cruel trick on the railway. On 27 January 1940 the Melverley river bridge was damaged by ice, with six piles and their bracings being washed away, 'rendering the bridge unsafe for traffic'. Crew Green, Llandrinio Road and Criggion were isolated from the railway, as were sixty-four stone wagons. A report was sent to the Ministry of Transport and the Railway Executive.

Five months later the company was told the terms by which the government would take over the railway. The average net revenue of 1935, 1936 and 1937 would be guaranteed but as the railway had made a loss it would receive just £1. Maintenance, including renewals, would be allowed on the basis of the average expenditure of those three years, £900. No provision would be made for paying the prior charge debenture interest. Clearly, being under government control was not going to be of much benefit to the company or its shareholders.

Chairman James Ramsay was deputed to press for special consideration in respect of arrears of maintenance and the repair of the Melverley bridge. He met the GWR's general manager, Sir James Milne (1843–1958), representing the Railway Executive, on 28 May 1940. The following day the directors agreed to tell Milne that the main traffic, from Criggion, could be handled via Llanymynech and the section between Kinnerley and Meole Brace could be closed, with the track recovered for reuse or sold. They would accept this provided the Executive agreed to repair the line between Criggion and Llanymynech, and between Meole Brace and Shrewsbury, and the British Quarrying Company would guarantee a minimum tonnage for a period of years. If the proposals were acceptable, the letter concluded, 'some mutually advantageous arrangement could probably be made for the provision of locomotive power on the two severed portions of the railway'.

Milne replied on 3 June that the proposals were acceptable and that British Quarrying was willing to contribute £500, a third of the estimate, towards the bridge repair and to guarantee 30,000 tons per annum for three years. However, the quarry company had second thoughts about the guarantee and the matter was left to await developments.

Later in the year, 29 October 1940 is the earliest date in the file, the War Office decided that the railway could be used under military control, to serve a new ammunition depot to replace existing facilities at Wem and Nantwich and capable of accommodating 50,000 tons of ammunition, requiring fifty ammunition sheds not less than 200 yards apart.

A reconnaissance was made on 4–5 November. One of the WO personnel involved was Major Dennis McMullen (1902–73) who achieved the rank of colonel and became the Chief Inspecting Officer of Railways; he inspected the Talyllyn and Festiniog railways in the 1950s.

The reconnaissance established that the line between Kinnerley and Shrawardine would be suitable for an ordnance depot as it was fairly level and not subject to flooding. The locomotives were adjudged to be incapable of heavy work and would need to be replaced by 'engines which have had a recent railway workshop overhaul'.

Locomotives at Hookagate waiting to be scrapped, 6 February 1949. The line-up includes two of the ex-LNWR 0-6-0s and the tender of the third.

Goods stock was generally in poor condition; the travelling crane required a new jib, the open wagons required new floors and bodies, the cattle wagons were in poor condition and one of two brake vans was under repair. The coaching stock was 'in a very bad state of repair' and while some carriages could be cleaned up for military use they would require new roofing canvas. In the Kinnerley workshop a Cochrane boiler provided steam for a horizontal stationary engine and two Worthington pumps. A 10in screw cutting lathe was in fair order, the 1½in vertical drill was in poor order and inaccurate, an old planing machine was of little use, and the steam hammer was not in order. There was also a grindstone and a 3ft forge with belt-driven bellows. Approximately 25% of the sleepers required replacement. The War Office team's London bias was betrayed, incidentally, by reference to 'Abbey Road' station.

After the reconnaissance, it was recommended that the War Department should take over the railway, except the Breidden branch, and that existing civil traffic be continued. An area between Shrawardine and Nesscliff was identified for the ammunition depot. It was proposed that military traffic be routed via Shrewsbury (Meole Brace), with Llanymynech used in emergency. The Shrawardine river bridge formed a good target, it was noted, and 'must be considered vulnerable'. As building materials could be arriving within two months, the first phase of construction would involve increasing siding capacity at Meole Brace and Red Hill and the lengthening of some loops.

Government officials met Ramsey, John Pike, and W. H. Austen on 15 November 1940, when it was agreed that the War Office could enter the property for the purpose of renewing and/or strengthening track and bridges. When the track was sufficiently improved the Ministry of Transport would relinquish control to the War Office.

As there was no scope for expansion at Meole Brace the War Office proposed developing an exchange facility at Red Hill, Hookagate, the site of Red Hill Junction, which the LNWR and GWR had prevented from being brought into use in 1866. When the plans were discussed with the GWR on 9 December, that railway's assistant superintendent said that while the situation was not ideal the difficulties were not insurmountable. His attempt to divert the War Office to a site near the GWR at Honeybourne, Worcestershire, that had been inspected previously, was ignored.

Shoot Hill level crossing on 1 April 1947, showing the water tank, level crossing barriers and a weather-worn sign reminding drivers to comply with rule No 103. (John Scott Morgan Collection)

Discovering that its powers did not permit the operation of a revenue-earning civilian service if the railway was requisitioned, the War Office decided that it would be better to take over the railway by agreement with the company. The railway would provide all facilities and labour for handling civilian traffic and War Office personnel would operate the trains. In exchange for the line being refurbished and for retaining the civilian traffic revenue, no rent would be paid. On termination of the agreement the War Office undertook to return the assets in 'as good a condition (ordinary wear and tear excepted) as existed at the time taken over', a full inventory being taken. Pending completion of a formal contract, an indemnity was given to the company on 6 January 1941.

While these hectic negotiations were in process the increased demand for stone for runway building ensured that some effort was made to secure the reconstruction of the Melverley bridge. On 8 May the GWR undertook to put the branch and bridge into a condition that would take the LNWR coal engines.

The contractor, Sir Alfred McAlpine, offered two 0-6-0STs at Ellesmere Port and some four-way bottom-emptying wagons to the War Office in March 1941, but the correspondence did not note the outcome. The ex-LNWR locomotives were sent to Crewe one at a time to be repaired and by 22 March one had been returned and the second had been despatched.

Visiting, Austen saw that uncreosoted sleepers were being used and when he complained, he was informed that it was not policy to use creosoted sleepers on emergency work. Putting his complaint in writing on 9 April 1941, he said that the works were not temporary and that creosote would add little to the cost but add ten years to the sleepers' use. He was then informed that creosoted sleepers were not available and that as the work was nearly complete it was too late to do anything about it. As part of the War Office accommodation work the track between Nesscliff and just outside Kinnerley was doubled. Locomotive water tanks were installed at Ford & Crossgates, Shoot Hill and Shrawardine and the high-level tank at Kinnerley was replaced.

The War Office, in the guise of No 1 Railway Group, Royal Engineers, formally took over the railway on 1 June 1941 and Lieutenant William Proctor (1916–47) was appointed operating officer. Employees not required by the company transferred to military control (Appendix 18). There was

Kinnerley on 21 September 1958. The Nissen hut housed the Drewry railcars. (H. C. Casserley)

actually no change in their position, for the company continued to pay their wages and was reimbursed by the War Office. A similar arrangement applied to the supply of locomotive coal. The employees' families were allowed to retain their privilege of travelling in the goods train's brake van without charge, a facility that took eight letters to confirm (Appendix 19).

With the Melverley bridge repaired, the Breidden branch was available for traffic from 27 October. The War Department agreed to work it for 17s per hour, except on Sundays when the charge would be £1 per hour; the rates were increased to 18s 3d and 21s 6d from 1 January 1942. The £2,000 bridge repair fund created in 1931 was closed in 1943 and the money applied to other purposes.

The locomotive fleet was soon found to be inadequate. Ex-GWR 0-6-0 No 2552, WD No 200, arrived at Kinnerley from the Longmoor Military Railway on 12 December and, after some minor repairs, entered service on 18 December. On 15 December the War Office was

Kinnerley with several GWR 0-6-0 'Dean goods' on shed in August 1947.

informed that 'arrangements had been made to send two additional GWR 0-6-0 tender engines and one additional diesel'. A second ex-GWR 0-6-0, No 2442, had actually arrived on 15 December and entered service the next day. A Drewry and three Barclay 0-4-0DMs were supplied new in 1941; whether the locomotive referred to in the letter was one of those is not known. Over the years a variety of locomotives were put into service on the railway.

Thirteen bogie carriages were obtained for passenger services, eight from the London, Tilbury & Southend Railway, four from the GWR and one from the LMS, some of them on loan. Even with more basic longitudinal seating to suit their

Above: Great Eastern Railway R24 0-6-0T No 388 (LNER J69 No 3387) at Kinnerley as WD No 70084 in 1945. It was one of two locomotives of this class to spend time on the railway. (John Scott Morgan Collection)

Left: Seen at Kinnerley, No 1872 *Ashford* was an ex-Great Eastern Railway 0-6-0T that stayed on the railway for seven years from 1942. Behind it is 70096, formerly GWR No 2425. (John Scott Morgan Collection)

Below left: An ex-London, Tilbury & Southend Railway composite carriage looking neglected at Kinnerley on 21 June 1947; it has two windows missing. There were three carriages like this. (H. C. Casserley/John Scott Morgan Collection)

Below right: Five more modern carriages also came from the London, Tilbury & Southend Railway, becoming the last passenger stock to operate on the line. They looked very modern compared with anything used previously. The seating used by London commuters was removed and replaced by simple longitudinal slatted benches.

Two ex-Great Eastern Railway vans formed the military breakdown train, seen on 21 June 1947. Other vans used by the War Department had originated on the Great North of Scotland, the Lancashire & Yorkshire and the Midland railways. (H. C. Casserley/ John Scott Morgan Collection)

new use, they were probably the most comfortable vehicles ever used on the railway.

Twenty LNWR camping carriages were put to use as accommodation at Kinnerley but they appear to have gone by the time camera-wielding enthusiasts started visiting as they don't seem to have been photographed.

Goods wagons, vans and brake vans were also obtained from main-line railways and incoming traffic brought vehicles from far and wide, including four-wheeled vans from French railways, Nord, Paris–Orleans and PLM.

Ramsey and GWR representatives met at the War Office on 23 December 1941. Ramsey complained that claims for pilferage from the goods train had increased, citing timber, tea and cigarettes as targets and asked for wagons to be brought onto the railway from Meole Brace as quickly as possible. A few months later there were complaints that the railway's own mishandling of goods in transit was the cause of damage and pilfering.

Ramsey also said that he had been surprised to learn that War Office engineers had placed a 9-ton axle limit on the Melverley bridge in view of the GWR's undertaking of 28 May. The War Office supported Ramsey's understanding of the undertaking, but the GWR denied that it had never been the intention to strengthen the bridge to carry anything heavier than the quarry's Sentinel locomotive. The arrangement whereby the quarry locomotive propelled the wagons to the Kinnerley side of the bridge for collection continued.

While the War Office concentrated on making the railway fit for use, parts of its estate received unwanted attention. Kinnerley locomotive shed was being repaired in January 1941 when a heavy snowstorm demolished part of it. Repairs, initially hindered by continuing cold weather and the blackout, took some time. When Shrawardine station house was gutted by fire on 1 November 1941, the directors noted that 'the question of reconstruction was in hand'; no explanation was offered for the cause of the fire. The house is still standing and occupied.

At a meeting held between the director of works, the contractor and others on 30 January 1941, Sir Alfred McAlpine, the man not the partnership, complained about the constraints of working on a site with no road access and the shortage of locomotive power. He could use eight locomotives but had to make do with four, he said, but it was pointed out that his staff had only ever asked for four locomotives. The director said that locomotives were difficult to get hold of; he had two small locomotives, one called *Yeovil* (Hudswell, Clarke 0-6-0ST 1529 of 1924) which needed repairs, its wheel flanges were too sharp, and a contractors' locomotive called *Victory* (Neilson 0-4-0ST 420 of 1859), which had broken stays. *Yeovil* was in use by 12 February 1942, by which date there were eleven operational locomotives on the railway, four of them under repair, including two of the new diesels. McAlpine regularly complained about a shortage of locomotives, but his staff seemed happy with what was available.

A memo dated 1 April 1942 reviewed the situation, there now being thirteen locomotives on the railway, including one that was hired. Five were out of action; two were being repaired locally, one was to be sent to Stafford, *Yeovil* would have to be sent away, and a diesel locomotive was awaiting spares. Of the working locomotives, four were working for McAlpine, three at Shrawardine and one at Kinnerley. Ford depot was being worked by the train loco. To strengthen the fleet, a new diesel locomotive was en route from Kilmarnock and No 47, another diesel, was due from Branston within a week; a GWR steam locomotive would be available to be sent to Long Marston when 'the new Hunslet' was run in; two contractors' locomotives had been offered by the Ministry of Works and Buildings, which would probably be accepted, even if not entirely suitable. At Shrawardine, 800 tons of materials were being handled a day, but McAlpine needed 1,200 tons a day to maintain the agreed rate of progress.

The Hookagate exchange sidings had been brought into use by 29 January 1942. Already a considerable amount of traffic had been received for both railway and depot construction (see table). The first ammunition had been received (346 wagons), and despatched (seventy-three wagons), by the Royal Army Ordnance Corps during the first three weeks of February 1942.

Record of loaded wagons received and despatched (for use in war diary)

January–December 1941			
	Railway construction company	Contractors	Public
Received	5,928	5,798	2,389
Despatched	57	54	520
January 1942			
Received	465	1,102	203
Despatched	3	3	82

Military and reconstruction traffic also contributed to a considerable increase in civilian traffic in 1941: 122,525 tons compared with 20,984 tons in 1940. In 1942, however, the traffic fell back to 49,150 tons.

The original depot at Nesscliff was followed by others at Kinnerley, Argoed, Maesbrook, Shrawardine, in two parts, and Ford. Eventually there were 206 rail-served depots and a camp station, at Shrawardine. The railway was operated in accordance with the military

The War Department's plan of the railway and the depots, from the 1956 Working Instructions.

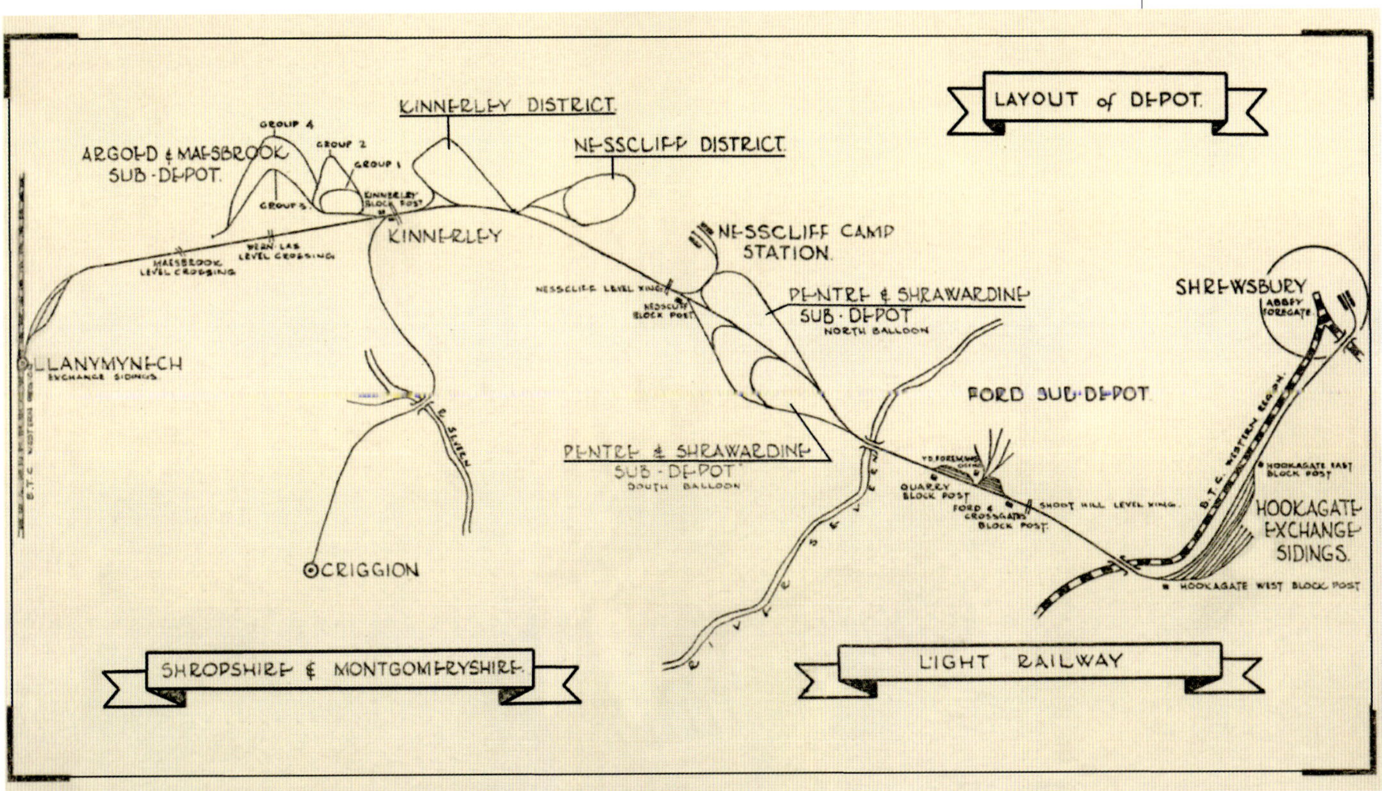

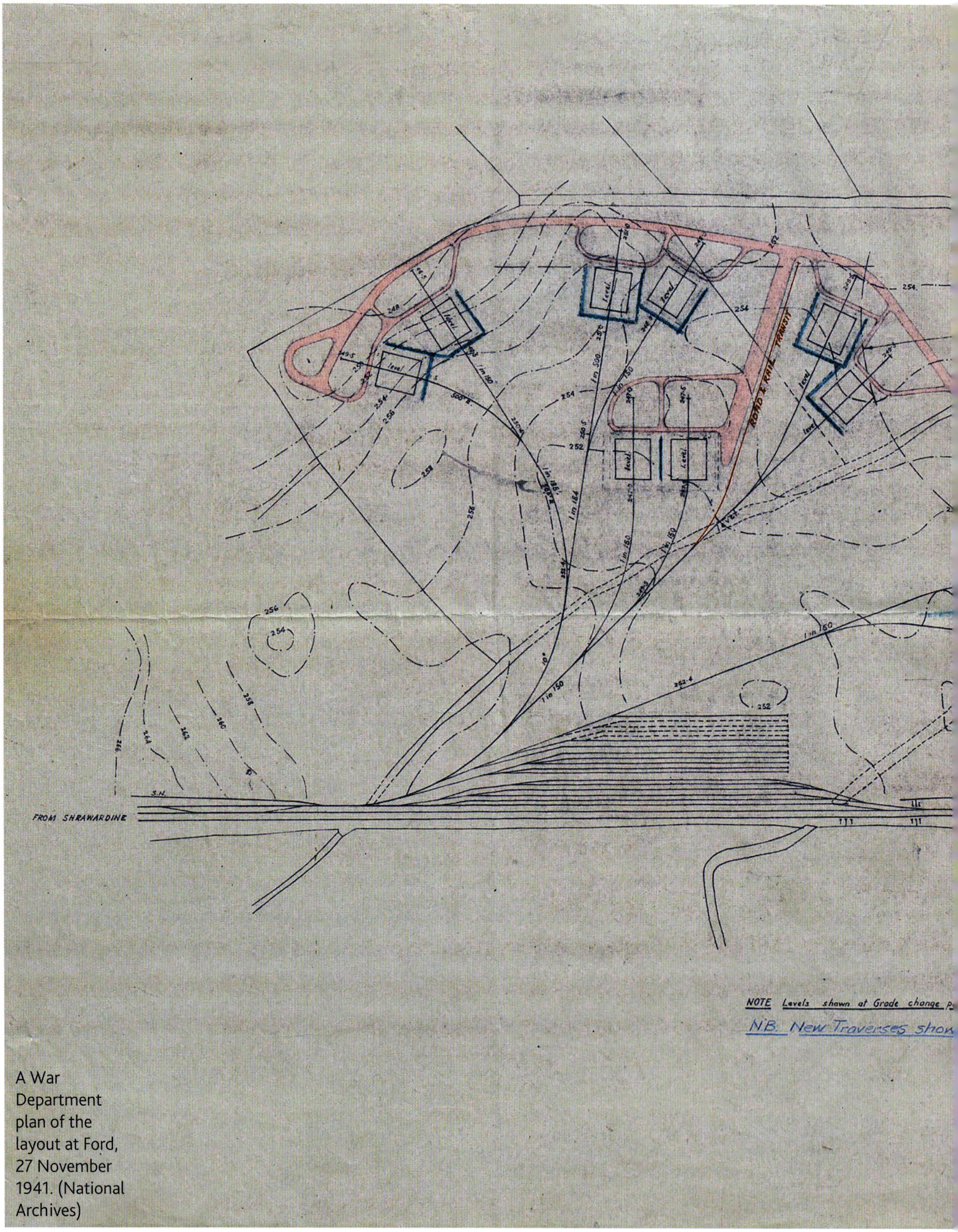

A War Department plan of the layout at Ford, 27 November 1941. (National Archives)

FORD.
N
A
B
C
D
E
7½ M.P.
FORD & CROSSGATES STATION
TO SHREWSBURY
TO SHREWSBURY
CROSSGATES.
FROM WELSHPOOL
S & M. FORD AREA
SCALE 1/2500
SECRET
WAR OFFICE
Tn. 4
Plan No. 5234/11
NEG: No 565

Seen in the 1950s, this is the halt built by the army to serve workers at Ford depot. (John Scott Morgan Collection)

A public passenger train passing Meole Brace during the military control era. (P. W. Whitehouse)

railways rule book, published in 1938, as modified by local instructions. The lines between Kinnerley and Llanymynech and Hookagate and Shrewsbury were worked with a one-engine-in-steam key. Kinnerley to Nesscliff east was worked by electric token, the remainder of the line by telephone and ticket. Transfer of traffic to and from the Criggion branch required the Kinnerley–Llanymynech one-engine-in-steam key. Access to sidings at Nesscliff, Pentre, Shrawardine and Meole Brace was by Annett's key. Block posts were established at Hookagate, east and west, Ford & Crossgates, Quarry, Nesscliff and Kinnerley. The maximum line speed was 25mph and the axle loading was 16 tons.

In addition to trains run for the contractor, the daily goods and the ammunition workings, the line was approved for the operation of workmen's trains from 1 January 1942. For the benefit of workers at Ford depot an additional platform was installed on the Shrawardine side of Ford & Crossgates station.

A light railway goods train crossing the Severn at Shrawardine during the war. (John Scott Morgan Collection)

Ramsey died on 5 February 1943, having served twelve years as chairman and managing director. Pike became chairman and Austen was appointed managing director. The latter's salary was agreed as: managing director £150, fees £50, expenses £125, as well as traffic and locomotive superintendent and engineer £100, as existing, in total £425. On 8 September 1943, Cornelius James Selway (1875–1948), CVO, CBE, MInstT, took Ramsey's place on the board; he was a career railwayman, awarded the CBE in 1918, when he was the Great Northern Railway's Superintendent of the Line, and the CVO in 1941, when he had recently retired as the passenger manager of the LNER's southern area passenger department (*London Gazette*, 4 June 1918/1 January 1941). His obituary in the *Derby Daily Telegraph* (28 December 1948) credited him with introducing half-day excursions with very cheap fares.

During 1942 the company received a complaint about the locomotive shed being cluttered with its unused 'assets'. The unwanted vehicles raised £798 when sold for scrap during 1943.

The background to an order made under the Emergency Powers (Defence) Regulations relaxing the train speed when engines were running tender first is not known. The 1909 Light Railway Order ruled that engines running tender first were limited to 15mph but an Order relaxing this rule was signed on 5 July 1943.

The operation of the main line by the War Office left the Breidden branch under the control of the Ministry of War Transport. The 1940 agreement was reviewed by the Ministry and new conditions imposed, effective from 1 January 1942, but it was November 1943 before the directors considered and accepted them. As a result, the railway became caught between two branches of government over the interpretation of the agreement with regard to responsibility for maintenance of certain station buildings. On 7 March 1944 the company informed the War Office that it was passing the correspondence on to the Ministry in order that the departments could sort it out themselves.

Some buildings on the main line had not been taken over by the War Office, yet if the £900 maintenance budget could only be applied to the Criggion branch the buildings on the main line could not be maintained. Agreement for a more flexible interpretation of the rules allowed the directors to record

Melverley bridge as rebuilt, 21 May 1953. (P. J. Garland/ John Scott Morgan Collection)

that urgent repairs were being carried out to Ford station yard in March 1945.

The £7,597 4s 5d cost for repairing the Melverley bridge and the Criggion branch had been notified to the directors in time for consideration at their 7 March 1944 meeting. A figure of £1,177 would be taken from the unexpended maintenance balance and the Minister of Transport had authorised a special charge be made to the company's net revenue account of the residue. Austen reported that more work was required on the bridge in May 1945.

The railway's ecclesiastical monument, the refectory pulpit, once a part of the adjacent Abbey, had been scheduled as an ancient monument in 1934. Arrangements to transfer control of it to Shrewsbury Corporation were completed on 27 September 1944, after nearly eighty years in railway ownership.

With the end of the war, in October 1945 the War Department asked the company if it could consider taking over the operation and maintenance of the railway and the Department's sidings on their behalf, to reduce the numbers of War Department personnel. The directors agreed to take on the operation, subject to conditions and civilian labour being available; a meeting was to take place at the War Office, but nothing more was said of the proposal.

When the directors met on 27 February 1946, John Pike was ill so Selway acted as chairman. Green tendered his resignation and John Pattinson Thomas MIEE, MInstT (1879–1974) was appointed in his stead. In 1938 he had retired as general manager (railways) of the London Passenger Transport Board. After Pike died on 2 March 1946, Selway said that his death was a matter of personal regret,

The Birmingham Locomotive Club excursion, mentioned on Page 186, on the bridge in 1955.

he 'was a man of great conscientiousness and integrity and the company has suffered a heavy loss'. Iggulden was appointed the Shropshire Railways' nominee director on 4 February 1946 and Ralph George Davidson FSAA, ACIS, MInstT (1881–1954) was appointed a director on 8 May 1946. Iggulden's nomination seems not to have been notified to the company for he was never recorded as a director of it, although he was, however, recorded as attending the last board meeting in 1948. Davidson was an accountant with the Southern Railway.

The Kinnerley station agent, H. G. Funnell, who had been unwell since 28 November 1945, was thought to be unlikely to recover sufficiently to resume his duties. He had been on full pay, £5 3s 6d, until 5 March, when he was put on half pay. On 8 May 1946 the directors resolved to give him one month's notice to retire and to make him a 'compassionate' gift of £25. He recovered sufficiently well, however, to be employed to 'look after' Kinnerley shed and was rostered to light up the loco for the Stephenson Locomotive Society's farewell tour on 20 March 1960. He died in 1973, aged 73.

Compulsory trades union membership by company employees was sought by the National Union of Railwaymen, writing on 2 August 1946. The matter was considered on 1 October, when the directors noted that a similar application had been made to the main-line companies and decided to await developments.

Austen reported, also on 1 October, that the War Department had produced plans for the repair or renewal of nine bridges on the main line, including those over the Severn at Shrawardine and over the Hereford railway line. The Shrawardine bridge was replaced by a new structure located between the piers of the original in 1947. The old one was demolished in 1954.

With the election of a new government in 1945 the nationalisation of railways was put in hand, which led to another, brief, chapter in the railway's history and to the demise of the Shropshire Railways and the Shropshire & Montgomeryshire Light Railway Companies.

Shrewsbury Abbey and the refectory pulpit, the public entrance to the coal yard on the right. Coal merchant William Toye (1854–1932) was a public figure in the town, member of the council, mayor in 1920–21 and magistrate (*Kington Times*, 13 February 1932). Unmarried, among the bequests from his £42,892 16s 7d (£2,364,896) estate he left £50, his Rolls-Royce, and its accessories, and several properties to his chauffeur, and £200 plus four houses in St George's Terrace, Shrewsbury, to his housekeeper.

In 1947–48 eight locos were broken up at Hookagate. The one on the right had had a bracket mounted on its smokebox to enable it to be equipped with air brakes.

No 70091 (GWR No 2433) at Hookagate on 21 June 1947. To the left is the Light Railway's ex-LNWR 0-6-0 No 8182. (H. C. Casserley/ John Scott Morgan Collection)

Seen at Hookagate on a later date, 70196 was another locomotive that was once equipped with air brakes. (John Scott Morgan Collection)

The renewed Shrawardine river bridge seen from a distance.

CHAPTER 10

NATIONALISATION, THE FINALE, AND CLOSURE

The Light Railway company was notified by letter dated 28 November 1946 that it was included in the list of companies that would vest in the British Transport Commission on 1 January 1948. The Shropshire Railways Company was also included in the list. The directors met for the last time on 3 March 1948 when, among their normal business, they noted that the company had been absorbed into the Railway Executive, Western Region, and that the transfer of functions was well in hand. There was no need, they decided, to call an annual general meeting.

The penultimate item they had dealt with was the renewal of two bridges on the Breidden branch, at Melverley and near Kinnerley. The Ministry of Supply having decided that Criggion stone was of strategic importance, the Ministry of Transport agreed to make a loan of the £10,512 10s contract price at 2¾% interest to the company for their renewal. They had agreed to the arrangement on the basis that the liability for the loan would be transferred to the British Transport Commission on vesting day. The Severn catchment board had offered £6,000 and the British Quarrying Company £1,000 towards the bridges, which eventually cost £23,300. The contract with E. A. Farr Ltd of Westbury, Wiltshire, was signed on 27 November 1947.

On this note the Shropshire & Montgomeryshire Light Railway became a part of the national network, albeit remaining under War Office control. The irony was that during the last ten years of its independent

Kinnerley, 20 March 1960.

existence the government had benefited by £37,091 from its operation because of the control agreement. The company lost £3,511 over the same period (Appendix 20). Of course, the government paid for the refurbishment and new bridges, but the ammunition traffic was calculated to be worth nearly £2 million over six years, so if the railway had cost the government anything it was not very much (Appendix 21).

To complete the nationalisation process the British Transport Commission submitted its valuation of the Light Railway company's, and Shropshire Railways', securities to the Transport Arbitration Tribunal. No one contested the Commission's assertions and the Tribunal accepted the assessment. The Shropshire Railways' debenture bonds, issued to the Whadcoat brothers in 1890, were valued at 50% of their original capital worth, calculated on the cost of buying out the Breidden branch income, which went to the bondholders, over thirty years. The prior charge debentures were valued at 5% because the company's directors argued that with the ammunition depots the railway would be much busier post-war and the holders had expectations that it would produce a net revenue in excess of that previously achieved. The Commission pointed out that no interest had been paid since 1931 and thought that the prospect of receiving more was remote.

The first and second Shropshire debentures and the ordinary stock were described as being 'virtually worthless' and awarded a nominal ¼% compensation. The Light Railway shares attracted the same valuation, effectively valuing the company at a mere £2 10s. If R. S. France had concentrated on quarrying instead of trying to build a railway empire, he and a lot of other people would have been much better off. Similarly, a lot of money would have been saved if R. D. Green-Price had found something else to keep him occupied.

After eighty-two years and nearly £2 million of capital expenditure, the entire enterprise had a cash value of less than £30,000. The Severn Syndicate was the biggest beneficiary, holding all of the bonds, £28,275 of the first debentures, £9,600 of the second, £6,520 of the prior charge, and £97,590 of the ordinary stock. Between them, Iggulden, Austen, the Willard brothers and Mathews' executrix had £15,870 of the prior charge debentures. Austen and Iggulden had small holdings of the ordinary stock.

The compensation was paid in the form of British Transport Commission 3% stock redeemable between 1978 and 1988 and issued on 18 May 1948. In 1949, the directors were paid £50 between them for their expenses incurred in the company's dissolution.

As managing director, and the receiver and manager of the Kent Light & East Sussex Railway and general manager and engineer of the East Kent Railway, Austen was given six months' notice to retire on 30 June 1949 with an ex-gratia payment of £400 (£11,208 in 2022); he had completed forty years of railway service. His light railway salary had been £525; the KESR had paid him £500, and the EKR £650 as well.

Shropshire Railways – valuation of securities

Title of old security	Capital amount	Value per £100	Amount of BTC 3% stock at par
5% debenture bonds	£53,800	£50	£26,900
5% first debenture stock	£46,175	5s	£115 8s 9d
5% second debenture stock	£16,600	5s	£41 10s
4½% prior charge debenture stock	£36,870	£5	£1,843 10s
Ordinary stock	£345,860 13s 1d	5s	£864 13s

Captain William Proctor, the first commander of the War Department railway, was buried in Shrewsbury's General Cemetery. Because he had died within the designated period, which expired on 31 December 1947, his burial was marked by a Commonwealth War Graves Commission memorial. He had gone into the army from a career in traffic control with the LNER so was clearly suited to running a railway.

Reginald Frank Bowmaker (1871-1954), the part-time accountant, was given three months' notice. On 20 December 1949 an assistant secretary of the Board of Trade certified that there was no reason for the continued existence of the Shropshire & Montgomeryshire Light Railway Company.

With the company no longer existing there was no reason for the Severn Syndicate to exist either. On 31 January 1950 Iggulden published a notice in the *London Gazette* to say that the company had agreed to be wound up voluntarily and to appoint Stanley Gordon Hillyer (1884–1965) as liquidator. The final meeting was held on 25 September (*London Gazette*, 8 August).

On the railway, Lieutenant Proctor had relinquished his commission on account of disability on 13 March 1946 and was granted the honorary rank of captain (*London Gazette*, 12 March). He was replaced by Major Charles Henry Calder (1894–1960) in 1947. Proctor died in the Royal Salop Infirmary with two abscesses on his brain on 20 November. Calder remained in post until he died, of natural causes, at his desk at Kinnerley on 3 May 1960; with the railway closed he was preparing to take up a posting at the RE's Hounslow headquarters (*Birmingham Daily Post*, 4 May). He was buried in London's Brompton cemetery.

With the military now totally responsible for the railway's operation, most services served the depots between Kinnerley and Hookagate, with a daily train, except Sundays, to Shrewsbury for civilian traffic. There was little traffic for Llanymynech,

A Western Region train arrives at Llanymynech, the Light Railway tracks behind becoming overgrown. In 1950 one of the tracks was leased for wagons to be dismantled.

where in 1950 a loop line was let to the North Wales Wagon Co. Ltd to use for breaking up old wagons. There are no surviving records of the traffic carried during this period but the file dealing with the closure reveals that 2,258 tons of freight was carried in 1958.

From 1947 the life-expired ex-main-line locomotives were replaced by modern War Department 'Austerity' 0-6-0STs, twenty-one of them being allocated for various periods by 1960. The three ex-LNWR coal engines were sent to Swindon for scrapping in 1950 and the travelling crane followed them in 1953.

A fleet of four Baguley railcars, seating sixteen, and trailers was introduced in 1950. They joined a fleet of smaller Wickham vehicles, eight or twelve, the records are unclear, that had been put into service during the war.

The Royal Engineers took a fancy to *Gazelle*, and in 1950 arranged with the British Transport Commission for it to be

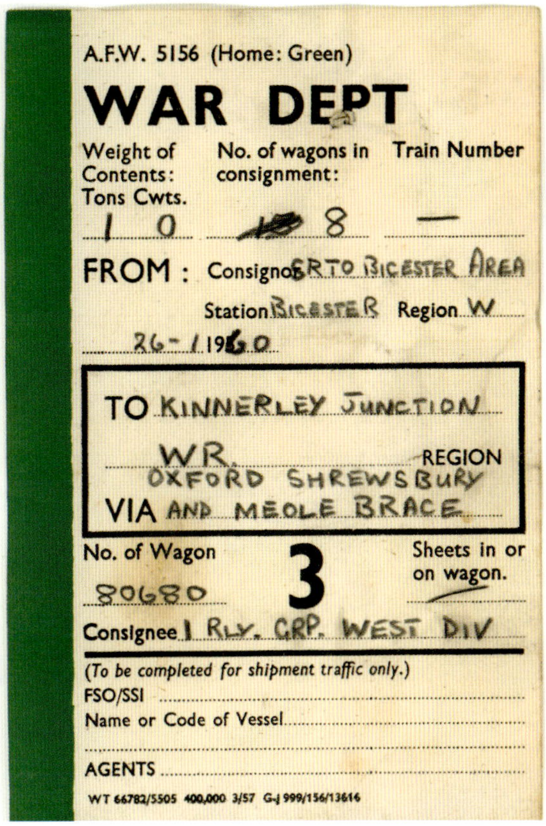

A.F.W. 5156 (Home: Green)

WAR DEPT

Weight of Contents: Tons Cwts. 1 0 | No. of wagons in consignment: 8 | Train Number —

FROM: Consignor SRTO Bicester Area

Station Bicester Region W

26-1-1960

TO KINNERLEY JUNCTION

WR REGION

VIA OXFORD SHREWSBURY AND MEOLE BRACE

No. of Wagon 80680 | 3 | Sheets in or on wagon.

Consignee 1 RLY. GRP. WEST DIV

(To be completed for shipment traffic only.)

FSO/SSI

Name or Code of Vessel

AGENTS

WT 66782/5505 400,000 3/57 G-J 999/156/13616

A wagon label for goods despatched from Bicester to Kinnerley on 26 January 1960.

The new order, 'Austerity' 0-6-0ST No 141, built by Hunslet in 1944 .

Top: 'Austerities' Nos 193 and 188 on shed at Kinnerley during an enthusiast visit. (Hugh Ballantyne)

Above left: No 125 waits to leave Shrewsbury on 10 October 1959.

Above right: The mobile crane at Kinnerley on 25 April 1954. (F. W. Shuttleworth)

Left: A Wickham railcar, left, and a pair of Baguley railcars at Kinnerley in 1955.

Above: Railcar No 9105 at Ford during an enthusiast visit on 12 October 1957. (M. N. Bland)

Left: *Gazelle* at the Longmoor Military Railway. After subsequent spells of display at the National Railway Museum, York, and the National Army Museum, Beverley, in 1997 *Gazelle* was transferred to the Colonel Stephens Railway Museum at Tenterden, where it is a significant attraction.

loaned to them and put it on display at the Longmoor Military Railway.

Two level crossings of minor roads on the military branch line that had served the Central Ammunition Depot at Kinnerley since 1941 were given formal recognition in the Retention of Railway Across Highways (Shropshire) (No 1) Order, which was made on 26 November 1951.

During the 1950s the railway was quite welcoming to enthusiasts, a letter seeking permission to ride on the goods train being met with a permit to show the train crews. In return, the visitors were expected to visit

Above: No 189 with a railtour at Nesscliff & Pentre on 22 May 1955. (Brian Hilton)

Right: An enthusiast tour at Criggion with a pair of Baguley railcars and the British Quarrying Company's Sentinel on 21 September 1958.

Major Calder in his Kinnerley office for a chat. After one group asked for permission to walk from Kinnerley to Llanymynech, they were given the services of a railcar and driver for an impromptu rail tour to the Melverley bridge and then to Llanymynech. The Birmingham Locomotive Club reprised its 1939 visit in June 1955 and the Stephenson Locomotive Society made two visits in 1958.

The No 1 Railway Group, Royal Engineers, had issued a new book of working instructions effective from 1 January 1956. The railway was to be operated in accordance with the instructions and those laid down in the Military Railway Rule Book of 1938, and amendments, it declared. The main line was defined as the light railway from the buffer stop at Abbey

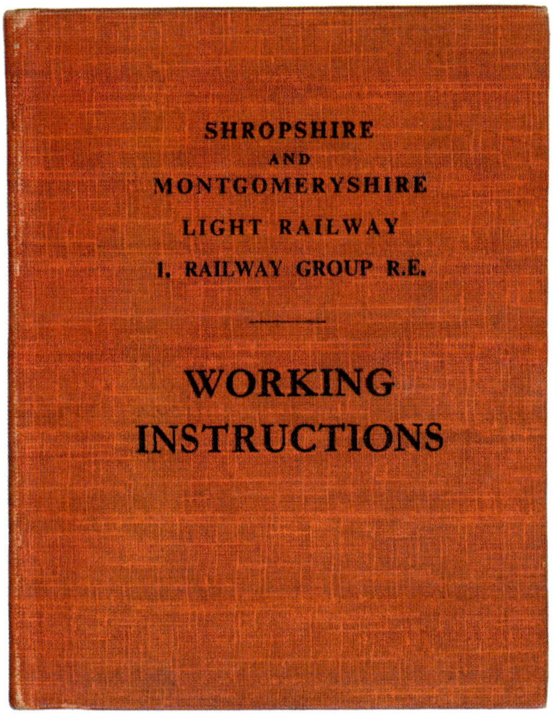

BRITISH TRANSPORT COMMISSION
BRITISH RAILWAYS
(WESTERN REGION)

PUBLIC NOTICE

The British Transport Commission hereby give Notice that, on and from Monday, 29th February, 1960, freight and parcels facilities will be withdrawn from Meole Brace, Ford and Crossgates, Shrawardine, Nesscliff and Pentre, Kinnerley and Maesbrook Stations on the line known as the Shropshire and Montgomeryshire Light Railway.

The existing arrangements for the collection and delivery of parcels, goods "smalls", and freight traffic in full truck loads requiring this facility will be maintained.

Alternative facilities for the handing in and/or collection by the public of parcels traffic and for dealing with other freight traffic in full truck loads, including coal and coke, will be available as indicated below :-

Present Station	Alternative
Meole Brace	Shrewsbury
Ford and Crossgates	Westbury (Salop)
Shrawardine	Shrewsbury
Nesscliff and Pentre	Baschurch
Kinnerley	Llanymynech (WR)
Maesbrook	Llanymynech (WR)

Any further information can be obtained on application to :-

Mr. O. VELTOM,
District Traffic Superintendent
SHREWSBURY
Tel: Shrewsbury 3614 Extn. 77

or

Goods Agent,
SHREWSBURY
Tel: Shrewsbury 3614
Extn. 57

Station Master,
WESTBURY (SALOP)
Tel: Halfway House 345

Station Master,
LLANYMYNECH
Tel: Llanymynech 203

Station Master,
BASCHURCH
Tel: Baschurch 216

Paddington Station, W.2
January, 1960

J. R. HAMMOND
General Manager

Far left: The 1956 Working Instructions.

Left: The 1960 closure notice as displayed at Kinnerley. (A. M. Davies)

station to the 'Limit of W. D. Maintenance' boards adjacent to the connection with British Railways at Llanymynech. The Criggion branch, beyond a board painted 'Limit of W.D. Operating and Maintenance' situated at the south end of the loco roads at Kinnerley, was excluded.

Decisions made by the War Department in 1957 not to retain the sub-depot at Ford and to close the Central Armaments Depot at Nesscliff by 1960 brought with them the axiomatic conclusion that the railway should be closed and handed back to civilian control. The 1951 Order that retained level crossings near Kinnerley was revoked by the Retention of Railway Across Highways (Shropshire) (No 1) Order, 1951 (Revocation) Order on 26 August 1960.

The British Transport Commission soon decided that the railway had no future and calculated that it would save £5,818

Shunting rail at Hookagate welded rail depot in 1961.

Plan of the chord linking the Abbey station with the Severn Valley line for the benefit of the oil traffic.

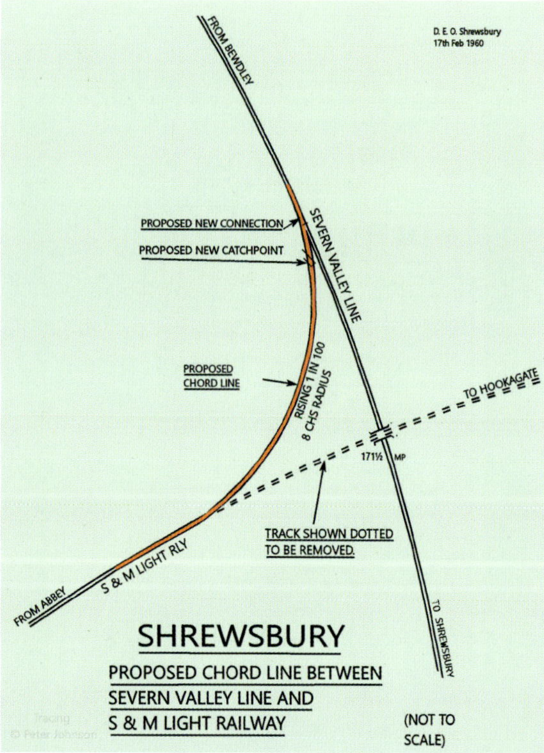

annually by not operating it. A formal closure application was submitted to the Transport Users Consultative Committee in July 1959. Because the War Office's 11,000v power supply was conveniently routed via Hookagate, British Railways decided that the site was suitable for the establishment of a rail-welding depot, and took it over on 1 January 1959. Ford depot was closed on 1 September.

The first stages in the dismemberment and dismantling of the railway came on 4 January 1960, with the closure of the Breidden branch, the last of the stone trains having run during December. On 26 February 1960 the main line was broken at Hookagate and west of Shrewsbury station, the former in connection with the welding depot construction, the latter to facilitate the construction of a spur to the Severn Valley line. Completed on 11 March, the spur made it possible for the Esso oil depot alongside the station to continue in operation. Although the remainder of the railway was closed with effect from 29 February, an excursion over the railway, from Hookagate to Llanymynech and back to Kinnerley, was run for the Stephenson Locomotive Society on 20 March.

Much of the correspondence between the War Department and the British Transport Commission concerning the railway had been conducted by Major Alan N. Stacey MBE (1908–83) of the Royal Engineers and John L. Bullock of the Commission's

The Abbey site after the military had left.

Above: The Abbey station site seen from the Abbey tower in the 1980s. The platform and station buildings are at the lower left of the photograph. (Mike Shaw)

Left: The farewell tour stopped for photographs on Shrawardine bridge. (Hugh Ballantyne)

commercial office. On 26 February 1960, the latter wrote to Stacey: 'The Shropshire & Montgomeryshire Light Railway has been fighting a valiant but losing battle for many years, and although the scars of the early occupation were partly healed by the present occupiers, this last engagement was decisive and it is sad to think that its demise will be without medals,' which pretty much sums up the railway's history since the 1860s.

Recovered military materials were worked via Llanymynech over the next few weeks and the railway was formally released to the Commission on 30 April 1960, leaving just a few administrative chores to complete. The War Department and the Commission worked their way through the 1941 inventory to account for anything that was missing or improved. A permanent way trolley valued at £600 was missing, the replacement of the original 70lb double-head rail with 75lb flat bottom rail was assessed to be a £500 per mile improvement, and in the stores were found identifiable parts from locomotives long since scrapped or disposed of, namely *Severn*, *Pyramus* and *Morous*. On 25 November 1964 the War Department received a cheque from British Railways, London Midland Region, for £7,550 in respect of the recovery of sidings and signalling at Llanymynech. There must have been other unfiled transactions.

Segments of the Potteries Railway survived the closure of the main line. Blodwel Junction, which had been closed to passengers on 15 January 1951, was closed to freight on 6 January 1964, and the southern end of the Llanyblodwel branch closed with the Llanfyllin branch on 18 January 1965. The railway was left to nature, with a few vehicle bodies deemed to be not worth scrapping left on site.

Stone traffic to Nantmawr continued after services to Llangedwyn ended on 6 January 1964, the track being cut back to Blodwel Junction, the layout there being simplified to eliminate the need for a signalman but requiring the use of gravity to effect the reversal.

An accident near Nantmawr on 1 February 1967 involved the unintended use of gravity and resulted in the Cefn Lane level crossing gates being demolished. At Nantmawr seven loaded hopper wagons and a brake van had been placed on the single line while the steam locomotive fetched two more loaded wagons and added them to the train preparatory for propelling

A steam crane being used to lift rails from Nesscliff depot in 1960. (A. M. Davies)

After the Tanat Valley Light Railway was closed, the former Potteries Railway's Nantmawr Tramway was broken on the eastern side of the Llanyblodwel road bridge, 9 September 2006.

Ford & Crossgates station abandoned, 3 August 1966. (Tim Edmonds)

Derelict body of the Wolseley-Siddeley railmotor at Kinnerley on 17 August 1966. (Tim Edmonds)

Derelict carriage body, also at Kinnerley on 17 August 1966. (Tim Edmonds)

the ensemble to Blodwel Junction, where the reversing move would place it in the right order for the remainder of its journey. However, the guard forgot to couple the extra wagons and released his brake, causing the seven wagons and van to run away, demolishing the gates. The train crew had no authority to make the propelling move, which was brought to the attention of all concerned and 'strong disciplinary action' was taken with the guard 'with a view to avoiding a similar future incident'.

On 11 May 1967 the London Midland Region's general manager gave the line a few more years' use when he told the divisional manager at Stoke-on-Trent that the civil engineer could obtain 37,000 tons of stone a year from the Chirk Castle Lime & Stone Company, Nantmawr's then operator, for use in the Shrewsbury area, but if the line, which was marginally profitable, was closed his costs would be increased, turn-round times would be longer and more wagons would be required.

The stone traffic lasted until 21 October 1971, the last train over the line said to be a general manager's special at around that time (*Branch Line News*, No 285). In 1975 the Branch Line Society reported that the track remained in use for the removal of twenty wagon loads of stone a week from Llanddu quarry, the track beyond, to Nantmawr, being overgrown and having rotten sleepers; the report was apparently based on observations made during an otherwise unreported brake van tour of the line (*Branch Line News*, Nos 281, 284, 285).

No doubt the construction of a run-round loop to eliminate the gravity movement in 1985 was a delayed reaction to the introduction of 1975's Health & Safety at Work Act. It was, of course, an enhancement of the facilities on the Tanat Valley Light Railway. The Llanddu traffic ended in 1989.

The operators of Criggion quarry, the British Quarrying Company, had leased Nantmawr from 1974 and closed it in 1977. The incline had been taken out of use in the

The Nantmawr branch looking downhill towards Cefn Lane crossing on 9 September 2006.

A lorry loaded with stone heading down the Nantmawr incline.

1950s and the track covered in stone and a thin layer of tarmac to enable use by lorries. Rails can still be seen where the surface has broken. The quarry, now leased by Hanson Aggregates, a subsidiary of Heidelberg Aggregates, is used for leisure activities but in 2006 Hanson said that while it had planning consent to resume quarrying, the quarry was dormant under the terms of the Environment Act 1995. Criggion, also

Maesbrook station with barriers on the level crossing.

The Abbey station interior when it was being restored in 2011. Most likely the paintwork dates from the 1860s.

leased by Hanson, is still in production, its output transported by road.

Elsewhere, because road traffic over the open crossings at Pentre and Shoothill had been so heavy during the war, they had been upgraded with barriers. Noticing that the barriers had been removed, Shropshire County Council changed the road signs and invoiced the War Department £32 0s 10d for doing so.

From 1963 until 1975 Welsh Highland Light Railway (1964) Ltd had had a base at Kinnerley on which it stored various locomotives until it secured its site in Porthmadog. The Hookagate rail welding depot was closed in 1986.

At Shrewsbury, the public goods service was withdrawn on 7 October 1968, the oil depot closed on 15 July 1988 and the track lifted in 1990 when the site became a car park. After a campaign to prevent their demolition, the station buildings have been leased by the Shrewsbury Railway Heritage Trust since 2004 and a small museum established there. A road that uses part of the rail formation is named Old Potts Way and a section of the A5112 on Bage Way occupies a part of the Potteries Junction Railway.

Despite the closure of the ammunition depots, the Ministry of Defence still has a presence in several locations in the area, around Nesscliff, Pentre and Shrawardine in particular. At Pentre the trackbed has been made into an access road. Aerial photographs accessible on the internet reveal the classic ammunition store dispersal pattern near Kinnerley.

The Nantmawr stub of the Potteries Railway, and a tiny part of the Tanat Valley Light Railway at Porthywaen, remained in the ownership of British Rail and its successors until 2004, when it was purchased by the Oswestry-based Cambrian Railways Society.

In 2005 it was taken over by the newly formed Tanat Valley Light Railway Company, a charity registered with the objective of preserving the railways and industrial heritage of the area, which

The overbridge on the B4398 near Maesbrook, one of R. S. France's double-track structures with a new parapet by Charles Chambers, 9 September 2006.

Shrawardine bridge site looking westwards, 31 July 2007.

is developing the site of the former Nantmawr sidings as a visitor centre.

For those armed with a good map there are still traces of the old railway to be found, notably some of R. S. French's bridges, although only the abutments of his largest structure, the Shrawardine river bridge, survive. The northernmost abutment, accessed by a section of trackbed that is now a public footpath, serves as a viewing platform, complete with a thoughtfully provided fence. At Melverley, the river bridge was adapted to take road traffic in 1962; residents had been calling for the river to be bridged for more than fifty years (*Shrewsbury Journal*, 15 September 1899), and the distinctive brick-built, multi-arched bridge at the station was demolished soon after the railway was closed. The site of the Llanymynech exchange sidings have been incorporated into a housing development with a road appropriately named Heritage Way. In parts, the trackbed has been ploughed out of existence, in others a corridor of overgrown scrub and unkempt trees delineate it.

The end of the line at Nantmawr sidings in 2006.

Shrewsbury Abbey station as restored, 3 August 2014.

Melverley bridge adapted for road transport, 7 October 2007. In the distance Rodney's column surmounts the Breidden.

APPENDICES

APPENDIX 1

ACTS OF PARLIAMENT

Date	Name	Purpose	Capital	Borrowing
1862	West Shropshire Mineral Railway	Llanymynech–Westbury	£90,000	£30,000
1863	West Shropshire Mineral Railway	Deviation to terminate at Red Hill instead of Westbury	£60,000	£20,000
1864	West Shropshire Mineral Railway (New Lines)	Llanymynech–Llangynog and branches, including one to Shropshire Union Canal	£200,000	£66,000
1864	Shrewsbury & North Wales Railway	Name change, branches from Kinnerley to Nesscliff and Breidden	£100,000	£33,000
1865	Shrewsbury & North Wales Railway	Deviations, preference shares, any shares can be divided into half shares to be called preferred half shares and deferred half shares	£100,000	£33,000
1865	Shrewsbury & Potteries Junction Railway	Market Drayton–Red Hill plus three branches connecting to the Shrewsbury & Hereford and Severn Valley railways at Shrewsbury	£400,000	£133,300
1866	Shrewsbury & North Wales Railway (Deviations &c.)	Further deviations	£80,000	£26,000
1866	Shrewsbury & Potteries Junction Railway (Deviations)	Further deviations and three short branches, any shares can be divided into half shares to be called preferred half shares and deferred half shares	£80,000	£26,000
1866	Potteries, Shrewsbury & North Wales Railway	Dissolution of Shrewsbury & North Wales and Shrewsbury & Potteries Junction and undertakings united into one undertaking		
1874	Potteries, Shrewsbury & North Wales Railway	Extensions to Treflach and Trefonen	£50,000	£16,500
1888	Shropshire Railways	Transfer of undertaking, Market Drayton–Shrewsbury	£650,000	£250,000
1891	Shropshire Railways	Extension of time	£75,000	£16,600

APPENDIX 2

LOCOMOTIVES AND ROLLING STOCK

France's locomotives were the same type as Manning, Wardle's 0-6-0ST *Maidstone*. Many were built for contractors.

R. S. France

Manning, Wardle (140 of 1864) 0-6-0ST *Alyn*	To Mawddwy Railway contract
Manning, Wardle (151 of 1865) 0-6-0T *Powis*	To Potteries, Shrewsbury & North Wales Railway
Manning, Wardle (167 of 1865) 0-6-0T *Sir Watkin*	To Potteries, Shrewsbury & North Wales Railway
Manning, Wardle (168 of 1865) 0-6-0T *Viscount*	To Potteries, Shrewsbury & North Wales Railway

Potteries, Shrewsbury & North Wales Railway

Manning, Wardle (151 of 1865) 0-6-0T *Powis*	From France 1866, sold for £210, 24 August 1888
Manning, Wardle (167 of 1865) 0-6-0T *Sir Watkin*	From France 1866, sold *c.*1873
Manning, Wardle (168 of 1865) 0-6-0T *Bradford*	From France 1866, formerly *Viscount*, sold for £305, 24 August 1888
Bury, Curtis & Kennedy (1847) 0-4-2	LNWR No 1859, acquired 1872, scrapped by 1875
T. W. Worsdell (1863) 0-4-2T *Tanat*	Sold for £85, 24 August 1888
Yorkshire Engine Co. (185 of 1872) 2-4-0T *Hope*	New, hired from the London Finance Association and Brown, Shipley & Co., advertised for sale November 1881, sold for £200, 24 August 1888, to East & West Junction Railway, later to Cannock & Rugeley Colliery Company, Staffordshire

Hawthorns Co. (1865) 0-4-0WT *Breidden*	New, to Walker Brothers (Wigan) Ltd, 1873
Hughes (1864) 0-4-0ST *Nantmawr*	To Walker Brothers (Wigan) Ltd, 1873

There were four other locomotives, three disposed of in 1866 and one in 1872. Two of the three locomotives sold to unknown purchasers in 1888 remained at Shrewsbury until *c.*1890.

Charles Chambers

Manning, Wardle (1037 of 1887) 0-4-0ST *Wye*	Delivered to Chambers when working on Golden Valley Railway contract, left unused at Shrewsbury for 2½ years after the Shropshire Railways work stopped in 1891, then to Redheugh Colliery, Gateshead.

Shropshire & Montgomeryshire Light Railway

1	Dodman (1893) 0-4-2WT *Gazelle*	Acquired from Thomas Ward & Co., then rebuilt from 2-2-2WT by Bagnall in 1911. After a period out of use from early 1930s, returned to service in 1937. Taken over by the War Department in 1941 and by British Railways in 1948. Transferred to the WD on loan, 1950. National Railway Museum 1975–81, Ministry of Defence, Leconfield 1981–3, Museum of Army Transport 1983–97, Colonel Stephens Museum 1997 to date.
2	Bury, Curtis & Kennedy (1853) 0-4-2ST *Hecate*	New to St Helens Railway, sold by LNWR to Griff Colliery, Nuneaton, *c.*1870, named *Crewe*. Acquired 1911, renamed *Severn* in 1916 and scrapped April 1937, probably out of use since 1932.
3	Beyer, Peacock (1517 of 1875) 0-6-0 *Hesperus*	London & South Western Railway No 0324, acquired 1911 following overhaul at Eastleigh Works; livery dark green with light green lining. Allegedly reboilered in 1928. In 1937–38 only worked on Mondays, 'when the stone traffic is light', 'a grand old engine'. Laid aside when seen by War Office personnel in October 1940. Taken over by the War Department in 1941, probably scrapped October 1941.
4	Manning, Wardle (178 of 1866) 0-6-0ST *Morous*	Stratford & Midland Junction Railway No 1, acquired 1910, hired to the West Sussex Railway (Selsey Tramway), 1924, sold to WSR for £50 in 1932.
5	Hawthorn, Leslie (2878 of 1911) 0-6-2T *Pyramus*	New to Light Railway, to War Department, Woolmer Military Instruction Railway, *c.*1916.
6	Hawthorn, Leslie (2879 of 1911) 0-6-2T *Thisbe*	New to Light Railway, to War Department, Woolmer Military Instruction Railway, *c.*1916.
	Hudswell, Clarke 0-6-0ST *Walton Park* (2459 of 1881)	Weston, Clevedon & Portishead Light Railway No 4, acquired 1913 but sent to East Kent Light Railway, 28 April 1913; not numbered.
5 (2)	Beyer, Peacock 0-6-0 *Pyramus* (1428 of 1874)	London & South Western Railway No 0300, acquired 1914, said to have been withdrawn in 1928 but photographed in service in 1930, scrapped 1931, boiler fitted to No 6 (2).
6 (2)	Beyer, Peacock (1209 of 1873) 0-6-0 *Thisbe*	London & South Western Railway No 0283, acquired 1916, cost £745. Out of service 1935, sold for scrap 1937, £136.

7	London, Brighton & South Coast Railway (Brighton 1880) 0-6-0T *Hecate*	London, Brighton & South Coast Railway No 681 *Beulah*, acquired from the Admiralty at Invergordon, 1921, reported to be still in LBSCR livery in 1923. Withdrawn 1930, scrapped 1931, parts reused in other locomotives.
8	London, Brighton & South Coast Railway (Brighton 1878) 0-6-0T *Dido*	London, Brighton & South Coast Railway No 638 *Millwall*, acquired from War Stores Disposals Board, 1923, withdrawn 1930, scrapped 1934, parts reused in other locomotives.
9	London, Brighton & South Coast Railway (Brighton 1880) 0-6-0T *Daphne*	London, Brighton & South Coast Railway No 683 *Earlswood*, acquired from War Stores Disposals Board, 1923, apparently withdrawn 1931 but reported in an unidentified railway magazine to be still in service in 1933, to Southern Railway, Eastleigh, for spares.
8108	London & North Western Railway (Crewe 1869 of 1874) 0-6-0	London, Midland & Scottish Railway No 8108, acquired 1930, seen 'in store' in May 1937, retubed 1938. Overhauled at Crewe in 1941. Taken into British Railways stock in 1948. Withdrawn by 1948, scrapped at Swindon 1950.
8182	London & North Western Railway (Crewe 2333 of 1879) 0-6-0	London, Midland & Scottish Railway No 8182, acquired 1931, taken into British Railways stock in 1948. Withdrawn by 1948, scrapped at Swindon 1950.
8236	London & North Western Railway (Crewe 2459 of 1881) 0-6-0	London, Midland & Scottish Railway No 8236, purchased 21 June 1932, taken into British Railways stock in 1948. Withdrawn by 1948, scrapped at Swindon 1950.

A Hunslet 0-6-0T was used during the railway's reconstruction. Sources on its origins vary, either Manning, Wardle (654/1877), which it looks like, or Hunslet (7/1866). It was scrapped during the war.

War Department

In addition to the five locomotives taken over, some fifty steam locomotives and seven four-wheeled diesel locomotives were allocated to the railway for various periods between 1941 and 1960. Predominant initially were nine GWR Dean 0-6-0s; four of them were fitted with pannier tanks to increase their water capacity. Twenty-one WD 'Austerity' 0-6-0Ts were used after 1946, the replacement of Shrawardine bridge permitting the use of heavier locomotives. Three USA-built Porter 0-6-0STs were transferred during 1944 but were scrapped the following year. Thirteen or seventeen Wickham and Baguley petrol trolleys were also used from around 1950.

Railmotors

- Three-car passenger set built by Edmonds of Thetford with Ford engines in 1923. The centre car was taken out of use shortly after the set entered service and was transferred to the West Sussex Railway in 1931. The power cars were out of use from 1937 and sold for scrap 1943.
- A single railmotor built by Wolseley-Siddeley for the WSR in 1923, acquired *c.*1928, may not have been used, certainly out of use by 1934.
- A Ford lorry with rail wheels was also obtained from the WSR with the Wolseley railmotor. It sometimes worked with one of the Edmonds railmotors, *c.*1928 until 1930s.

APPENDIX 3

POTTERIES, SHREWSBURY & NORTH WALES RAILWAY AND THE SHROPSHIRE RAILWAYS – CAPITAL

	Capital authorised			Capital created or sanctioned		
	Stocks and shares £	Loans £	Total £	Stocks and shares £	Loans £	Total £
1862 Act	90,000	30,000	120,000	90,000	30,000	120,000
1863 Act	60,000	19,990	79,990	60,000	19,990	79,990
1864 New lines Act	200,000	66,000	266,000	200,000	66,000	266,000
1864 Branches Act	100,000	33,000	133,000	100,000	33,000	133,000
1865 North Wales Act	100,000	33,000	133,000	100,000	33,000	133,000
1865 Potteries Act	400,000	133,000	533,000	248,200	133,000	381,200
B Debentures					314,990	
A Debentures		70,000	70,000		70,000	70,000
1868 Scheme of arrangement between the company and creditors at the Chancery Court – issued in settlement of debt. (Debentures classified B)	60,000	19,800	79,800	60,000	19,800	79,800
C Debentures		135,000	135,000		135,000	135,000
1874 Act	50,000	16,600	66,600			
1888 Act			400,000			400,000
1891 Act	75,000	25,000	100,000		16,600	100,000
	908,200	581,390	1,963,600	858,200	556,390	1,897,000

APPENDIX 4

POTTERIES, SHREWSBURY & NORTH WALES RAILWAY – STATEMENT OF RECEIPTS, ETC. 1866–80

	Length of line open	Passenger traffic £	Goods traffic £	Mineral traffic £	Misc £	Total £	Working expenditure £	Net receipts £	Proportion per cent of expenditure to total receipts
1866	30	759	32	285		1,076	1,175	-99	109
1867	30		74	198		272			
1869	18	2,005	444	1,621	109	4,179	4,806	-627	116
1870	20	2,030	603	3,684	338	6,655	6,907	-252	104
1871	25	2,303	635	5,194	406	8,538	8,053	485	94
1872	28	2,246	762	5,681	512	9,201	8,182	1,019	89
1873	28	2,275	955	6,494	684	10,408	10,375	33	100
1874	28	2,453	1,016	4,161	920	8,550	10,765	-2,215	126
1875	28	2,422	1,222	6,966	461	11,071	13,552	-2,481	122
1876	28	2,240	1,008	3,179	412	6,839	9,106	-2,267	133
1877	28	2,282	741	1,560	427	5,010	6,182	-1,172	123
1878	28	2,369	958	1,612	528	5,467	6,740	-1,273	123
1879	28	2,277	875	1,490	340	4,982	5,851	-869	117
1880	28								

Appendix 5

POTTERIES, SHREWSBURY & NORTH WALES RAILWAY – REVENUE ACCOUNT 1874–75 – EXTRACTS FOR HALF YEAR ENDING 30 JUNE

	1874	1875
Special and miscellaneous receipts		
	£ s d	**£ s d**
Cloakroom	2 14 11	2 3 1
Rents	37 1 6	20 15 6
Weighbridge	4 11 3	3 3 4
Wagon hire	74 11 3	
Sale of old stores	187 15 7	73 2 4
Timber loading	91 9 9	54 13 4
Hay		17 13 8
Demurrage and mileage	67 8 9	
	465 13 0	171 11 3

	1874	1875
Maintenance of way and works		
	£ s d	**£ s d**
Wages	614 3 2	675 5 4
Materials	331 15 7	490 18 5
Repairs and renewals	374 10 3	
	1,320 9 0	1,166 3 9

	1874	1875
Locomotive power		
	£ s d	**£ s d**
Wages	237 1 5	331 0 3

	1874	1875
Locomotive power		
	£ s d	**£ s d**
Coal and coke	887 18 3	769 17 10
Water	39 19 7	27 9 5
	1,221 16 6	1,212 8 0
Repairs and renewals	350 5 8	456 12 4
Hire	96 9 0	319 13 9
	1,668 2 2	1,988 14 1

	1874	1875
Repairs of carriages and wagons		
	£ s d	**£ s d**
Wages	260 3 8	224 3 0
Materials and stores	194 7 7	440 17 5
Hire	206 10 2	269 6 11
	667 1 5	934 7 4
Received for mileage and demurrage		7 11 3
	667 1 5	926 16 1

	1874	1875
Traffic expenses		
	£ s d	**£ s d**
Salaries and wages	559 15 9	613 10 1
Fuel, lighting, water and general stores	45 5 1	30 13 6
Printing, stationery and tickets	75 0 3	89 15 7
Horse provender, etc.	20 5 4	25 11 6
Joint station expenses	90 5 8	78 16 6
Miscellaneous expenses	27 4 6	34 17 0
Working tramway at Nantmawr	273 5 9	318 3 10
Clothing		19 19 0
	1,091 2 4	1,211 7 0

	1874	1875
General charges		
	£ s d	**£ s d**
Directors	175 0 0	150 0 0
Auditors	20 0 0	20 0 0
Salaries of secretary, general manager, accountant and clerks	612 12 2	496 19 6

	1874	1875
General charges		
	£ s d	**£ s d**
Office expenses, London and Shrewsbury	74 1 6	56 17 5
Advertising	7 4 6	
Railway Clearing House expenses	29 8 4	38 9 1
Travelling expenses	24 19 6	21 5 0
Fire insurance	5 9 6	5 9 6
	948 15 10	5 9 6
	1874	1875

General balance sheet 1875			
	£ s d		**£ s d**
Unpaid debenture interest	168,055 3 8	Capital account balance	648 5 5
Debts due to other companies	168 14 9	Net revenue account balance	4,600 10 2
Sundry outstanding accounts	4,714 15 1	Interest due on debenture stock	168,055 3 8
Temporary loans	2,30 13 6	Cash at bankers – current account	953 14 0
		General stores – stock on hand	417 17 7
		Traffic accounts due to company	319 0 5
		Debts due by other companies	13 0 0
		Amount due from Railway Clearing House	83 6 1
		Sundry operating accounts	147 16 2
	175,238 13 6		175,238 13 6

APPENDIX 6

POTTERIES, SHREWSBURY & NORTH WALES RAILWAY – TRAFFIC AND RECEIPTS 1866–79

	1866	1867	1868	1869	1870	1871	1872	1873	1874	1875	1876
Passengers	18,654			56,043	68,517	68,532	68,259	73,295	77,631	74,697	67,124
Merchandise	294	602		1,153	2,119	2,692	3,878	4,742	4,791	4,919	3,387
Coal	1,050	842									
Minerals	4,823	2,623		15,465	47,096	85,130	88,813	95,977	61,474	121,393	51,332
	6,167	4,067		16,618	49,215	87,822	92,691	100,719	66,265	126,312	54,719
Expenditure	£1,175	£272		£4,806	£6,907	£8,053	£8,182	£10,375	£10,765	£13,552	£9,106
Receipts	£1,076	£272		£4,179	£6,655	£8,538	£9,201	£10,408	£8,550	£11,071	£6,839
Net receipts	-£99			-£627	-£252	£485	£1,019	-£33	-£2,215	-£2,481	-£2,267

	1877	1878	1879
Passengers	73,294	75,497	73,601
Merchandise	1,934	5,195	4,249
Coal			
Minerals	16,767	22,202	23,837
	18,701	27,397	28,086
Expenditure	£6,182	£6,740	£5,851
Receipts	£5,010	£5,467	£4,982
Net receipts	-£1,172	-£1,273	-£869

Appendix 7

POTTERIES, SHREWSBURY & NORTH WALES RAILWAY – EMPLOYEES

Clerk
William Hughes (1854–1928) – 1863-9

Drivers
Samuel Davies – 1871, sued for pay
Thomas Hollis (1827–75) – killed at Shrewsbury, born Haversham, Bucks
James Morgan – 1879
Samuel Povey (1827–90) – 1869
Reece – 1870

Firemen
Richard Ebrey – 1870, resident Llanymynech
Richard Edwards – 1869
John Ison – 1875

Gangers
Thomas Howle (1852–1911) – killed between Farm Hall and Melverley, born Shrewsbury
Mason – 1870

Guards
James Biddle (born 1833) – 1866–70, became publican and emigrated to Canada after 1901
Richard Dodgson (1838–67) – killed at Nantmawr
Edwin Harrison – 1879
Frederick Perks – 1866
Richard Reeves (1830-1913) - guard of the last train in 1880 and railway caretaker during the period of abandonment

Stationmasters
John Birch – Nesscliff, 1870
James Davies – Shrawardine, 1870
Hatton – Abbey station, 1871, formerly at Oswestry
George Horner – Ford, 1870, Abbey station, 1875
J. Williams – Kinnerley, 1869
William Williams – Llanymynech/ Maesbrook, 1877

- Names extracted from newspaper reports.

APPENDIX 8

SHROPSHIRE RAILWAYS – ESTIMATE OF EXPENSES, 1888 ACT

Railway No 1	**3f 4½ch**	**Double**
Gauge	**4ft 8½in**	**£ s d**
Embankments, including roads – 6,000cu yd		3,500 0 0
Retaining walls		3,600 0 0
Culverts and drains		1,000 0 0
Permanent way, including fencing: cost per mile: 3f 4½ch @ £4,100		1,768 2 6
Permanent way for sidings and cost of junctions		4,000
Stations		8,000
Contingencies at 10%		2,186 17 6
Total for construction of railway No 1		24,055 0 0
Land and buildings 4a 0r 0p		
Total cost of construction and of acquisition of land and buildings		24,055 0 0

Railway No 2	**2f 2½ch**	**Double**
Gauge	**4ft 8½in**	**£ s d**
Embankments, including roads – 4,000cu yd		2,300 0 0
Accommodation bridges and works		125 0 0
Culverts and drains		570 0 0
Permanent way, including fencing: cost per mile: 2f 2½ch @ £4,100		1,153 2 6
Permanent way for sidings and cost of junctions		1,000
Contingencies at 10%		518 10 10
Total for construction of railway No 1		5,700 0 0
Land and buildings 2a 1r 0p		500 0 0
Total cost of construction and of acquisition of land and buildings		6,200 0 0

Railway No 3				13 miles	Double
Gauge				**4ft 8½in**	
Construction of line	**cu yd**	**Price/yd**	**£ s d**		**£ s d**
Earthworks					
Cuttings – soft soil	420,000	1s 2d	24,500 0 0		
Roads	1,100	1s 6d	82 10 0		
Total	421,100		24,582 10 0		24,582 10 0
Embankments, including roads – 400,000cu yd					
Bridges – public roads – 14					9,200 0 0
Accommodation bridges and works					7,800 0 0
Retaining walls					3,600 0 0
Viaducts					11,250 0 0
Culverts and drains including river bridge					3,300 0 0
Metalling of roads					1,130 0 0
Permanent way, including fencing: cost per mile: 13 miles @ £4,100					53,300 0 0
Permanent way for sidings and cost of junctions					8,000
Stations					6,000
Contingencies at 10%					12,456 10 0
Total for construction of railway No 3					137,019 0 0
Land and buildings 123a 0r 0p					18,450
Total cost of construction and of acquisition of land and buildings					155,469 0 0

Railway No 4				7 miles 2½ch	Double
Gauge				**4ft 8 ½in**	
Construction of line	**cu yd**	**Price/yd**	**£ s d**		**£ s d**
Earthworks					
Cuttings soft soil	330,000	1s 2d	19,250 0 0		
Roads	1,400	1s 6d	105 0 0		
Total	331,400		19,355 0 0		19,355 0 0
Embankments, including roads – 231,000cu yd					
Bridges – public roads – 12					7,600 0 0
Accommodation bridges and works					1,050 0 0
Culverts and drains					2,800 0 0
Metalling of roads					660 0 0

Railway No 4				7 miles 2½ch	Double
Permanent way, including fencing: cost per mile: 7 miles 2½ch @ £4,100					28,828 2 6
Permanent way for sidings and cost of junctions					5,000
Stations					4,000
Contingencies at 10%					6,929 17 6
Total for construction of railway No 4					76,223 0 0
Land and buildings 70a 0r 0p					7,000 0 0
Total cost of construction and of acquisition of land and buildings					83,223 0 0

The derelict engine shed at Llanymynech in 1902. (F. E. Fox-Davies)

SHROPSHIRE RAILWAYS – FINANCE REQUIREMENT 1889

Cash for works	£54,200 0s 0d
Costs of 1881 act and liquidation expenses	£5,514 8s 5d
Costs of 1888 act	£2,401 7s 2d
Land claims	£3,721 9s 9d
Cash per order	£2,031 15s 4d
Law and engineering expenses	£4,000 0s 0d
Establishment charges	£1,000 0s 0d
Interest on construction	£5,000 0s 0d
	£77,869 0s 8d

An abandoned wagon at Kinnerley in 1902. (F. E. Fox-Davies)

APPENDIX 10

SHROPSHIRE RAILWAYS – ESTIMATE OF EXPENSES, 1891 ACT

Railway No 1				4f 3ch	Single
Gauge				**4ft 8½in**	
Construction of line	**cu yd**	**Price/yd**	**£ s d**		**£ s d**
Earthworks					
Cuttings – soft soil	27,000	1s 2d	1,575 0 0		
Total			1,575 0 0		1,575 0 0
Accommodation bridges and works					250 0 0
Culverts and drains					100 0 0
Permanent way, including fencing: cost per mile: 4f 3ch @ £2,300					1,236 5 0
Permanent way for sidings and cost of junctions					1,200
Contingencies at 10%					436 15 0
Total for construction of railway No 1					4,798 0 0
Land and buildings 4a 0r 0p					800 0 0
Total cost of construction and of acquisition of land and buildings					5,598 0 0

APPENDIX 11

NORTH SHROPSHIRE LIGHT RAILWAY – ESTIMATE OF EXPENSES

	£
Re-sleepering and relaying	7,800
Repairs and renewals to 40 bridges	1,250
Fencing	500
Repairs and renewals to all stations	3,950
Signalling and locking	900
Telephone	250
Allow for reconstructing Criggion branch	8,050
Equipment, rolling stock, engine shed and tools	6,100
Miscellaneous expenses	2,250
Light Railway Order, law, etc.	750
Contingencies, say	2,450
Working capital	2,250
Financial fees, discounts, etc.	3,500
	£40,000

Estimate of expenses for reconstructing the branch to Criggion

Length of line 5 miles 10 chains	£
Fencing, gates, and repairs to level crossings	1,841 5 0
Re-sleepering and relaying permanent way	3,309 9 7
Renewing Severn bridge and repairing one overbridge	1,289 5 5
Fencing	500 0 0
Repairs and renewals to three stations	1,260 0 0
Signalling and locking	250 0 0
Telephone	100 0 0
Total	8,050 0 0

Appendix 12

SHROPSHIRE LIGHT RAILWAYS – ESTIMATE OF EXPENSES

Preliminary Expenses					£10 0s 0d
Line No 1				**2f 2½ch**	
Gauge				**4ft 8½in**	
Construction of line	**cu yd**	**Price/yd**	**£ s d**	**£ s d**	
Earthworks					
Cuttings – rock soft soil	1,088	2s	108 16 0		
Total	1,088		108 16 0	108 16 0	
Embankments, including roads – 8,176cu yd					
Bridges – public roads – none					
Accommodation bridges and works				50 0 0	
Viaducts					
Culverts and drains				1,650 0 0	
Metalling of roads and level crossings					
Gatekeepers' houses at level crossings					
Permanent way, including fencing: cost per mile: 2fg 2½ch @ £2,870				807 3 9	
Permanent way for sidings and cost of junctions				1,000 0 0	
Stations and buildings					
Plant, including signalling and telegraphic apparatus				120 0 0	
Contingencies at 10%				373 0 3	
Total for construction of line No 1				4,109 0 0	
Land and buildings to be acquired for Line No 1 2a 2r 0p				375 0 0	
Total cost of construction and of acquisition of land and buildings					4,484 0 0
Rolling stock					120 0 0

General charges					20 0 0
Interest on capital during construction					807 0 0
Sundries					40 0 0
Total amount to be charged to capital					5,481 0 0
Preliminary Expenses					£490 0 0
Line No 2				21 m 7f	
Gauge				4ft 8 ½in	
Construction of line	cu yd	Price/yd	£ s d	£ s d	
Earthworks					
Cuttings – rock	45,000	3s 6d	7,875 0 0		
soft soil	209,500	2s 0d	20,950 0 0		
Total	255,930		29,003 15 0	29,003 15 0	
Embankments, including roads – 184,940cu yd					
Bridges – public roads – one				700 0 0	
Accommodation bridges and works				2,500 0 0	
Viaduct over River Severn				7,000 0 0	
Culverts and drains				6,500 0 0	
Metalling of roads and level crossings				625 0 0	
Gatekeepers' houses at level crossings					
Permanent way, including fencing: cost per mile: 21m 7fg @ £2,870				62,781 5 0	
Permanent way for sidings and cost of junctions				6,000 0 0	
Stations and buildings				5,000 0 0	
Plant, including signalling and telegraphic apparatus				5,880 0 0	
Contingencies at 10%				12,599 0 0	
Total for construction of line No 2				138,589 0 0	
Land and buildings to be acquired for Line No 2 176a 0r 0p				17,600 0 0	
Total cost of construction and of acquisition of land and buildings					156,189 0 0
Rolling stock					5,880 0 0
General charges					980 0 0
Interest on capital during construction					28,115 0 0
Sundries					1,960 0 0
Total amount to be charged to capital					193,614 0 0

APPENDIX 13

SHROPSHIRE & MONTGOMERYSHIRE LIGHT RAILWAY – TRAFFIC AND RECEIPTS 1913–38

	1911	1912	1913	1914	1915	1916	1917	1918	1919	1920	1921	1922
Passenger traffic			64,976						68,156	74,702	67,166	52,289
Merchandise			5,841						5,514	4,299	2,014	1,992
Minerals			16,979						44,131	53,813	41,423	58,030
Coal			4,402						13		45	9
Tonnage			27,222						49,658	58,112	43,482	60,031
Livestock			8,556						3,965	3,371	3,721	2,087
Gross receipts			£4,768	£5,219	£6,998	£8,987	£11,438	£16,814	£16,737	£21,245	£23,426	£15,384
Expenditure			£3,649	£4,525	£6,110	£8,031	£10,374	£15,863	£14,078	£19,907	£21,760	£14,138
Net receipts			£944	£694	£888	£956	£1,064	£951	£2,659	£1,337	£1,666	£1,246

	1923	1924	1925	1926	1927	1928	1929	1930	1931	1932	1933
Passenger traffic	49,730	45,571	38,182	27,821	22,102	19,719	16,555	13,637	11,352	9,116	3,248
Merchandise	2,305	2,685	1,824	1,607	1,083	1,040	1,345	694	641	845	692
Minerals	51,933	60,696	63,095	46,015	57,225	57,644	63,838	99,030	143,253	79,611	29,958
Coal	30	16		14	19	17	112			7	26
Tonnage	54,268	63,397	64,919	47,636	58,327	58,701	65,295	99,724	143,894	80,463	30,676
Livestock	2,938	6,235	4,731	4,086	3,197	999	1,720	1,605	959	579	523
Gross receipts	£15,074	£13,461	£13,471	£9,992	£11,252	£10,276	£10,416	£13,244	£16,499	£10,349	£5,334
Expenditure	£13,443	£12,146	£12,279	£10,340	£9,942	£8,783	£9,009	£11,679	£14,839	£10,060	£6,150
Net receipts	£1,631	£1,315	£1,192	-£348	£1,310	£1,493	£1,407	£1,565	£1,660	£289	-£816

	1934	1935	1936	1937	1938
Passenger traffic	604	474	212	164	262
Merchandise	520	1,085	983	991	984
Minerals	22,855	41,853	23,969	20,533	16,931
Coal	74		19		
Tonnage	23,449	42,938	24,971	21,524	17,915
Livestock	129	297	269	32	66
Gross receipts	£4,401	£6,288	£5,329	£4,950	£4,134
Expenditure	£5,510	£6,173	£6,064	£6,361	£5,712
Net receipts	-£1,109	£95	-£735	-£1,411	-£1,578

A busy scene at Kinnerley on 5 August 1935. The LSWR royal saloon is attached to the rear of the Llanymynech train while the railcar set is loading for Criggion. Notice the rail trolley on the platform. (H. F. Wheeller/John Scott Morgan Collection)

APPENDIX 14

SHROPSHIRE & MONTGOMERYSHIRE LIGHT RAILWAY – TRAFFIC HANDLED 1938–40

	1938			1939			1940 (7 months)		
Station	**Inwards tons**	**Outwards tons**	**Total**	**Inwards tons**	**Outwards tons**	**Total**	**Inwards tons**	**Outwards tons**	**Total**
Abbey	13,782	92	13,874	15,580	68	15,648	7,360	53	7,413
Meole Brace	71	4	75	15		15	20		20
Hookagate	57	28	85	104	5	109	43	2	45
Edgebold	23		23	141		141	63		63
Cruckton	15		15	11		11		8	8
Ford & Crossgates	1,121	437	1,558	1,248	378	1,626	815	357	1,172
Shrawardine	62	13	75	59	616	675	74	311	385
Nesscliff	629	9	638	849	10	859	451	13	464
Kinnerley	1,473	17	1,490	1,383	11	1,394	729	4	733
Maesbrook	345	6	351	346	2	348	255	5	260
Llanymynech	567	3	570	440	1	441	116	1	117
Criggion	929	13,785	14,714	549	10,005	10,554	18	360	378
Crew Green	78		78	17		17	20		20
Llandrinio Road	1		1		1	1			
Melverley	2	3	5	8		8	20		20
	19,155	14,397	33,552	20,750	11,097	31,847	9,992	1,106	11,098
Average daily tonnage			92			88			53

APPENDIX 15

SHROPSHIRE & MONTGOMERYSHIRE LIGHT RAILWAY – WAR OFFICE SURVEY OF FACILITIES 1940

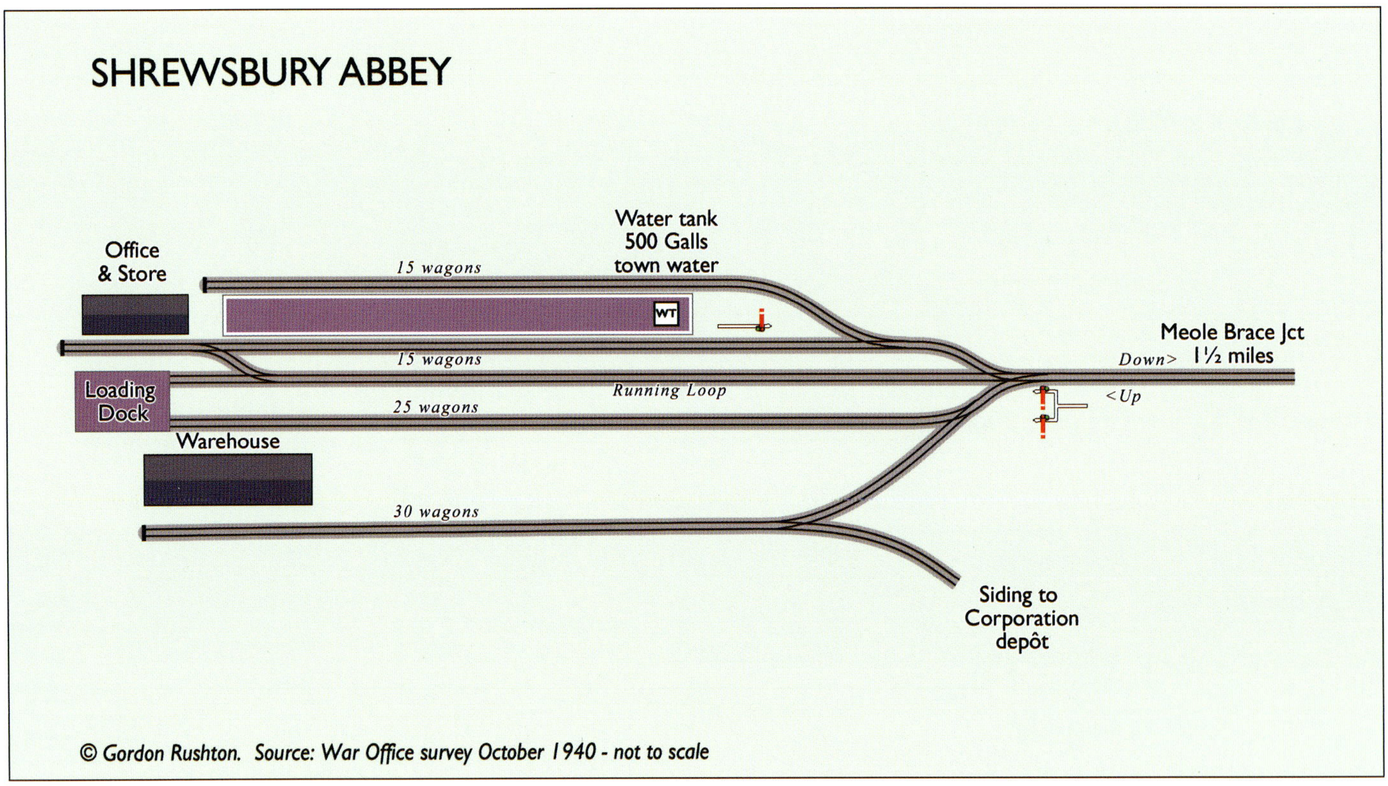

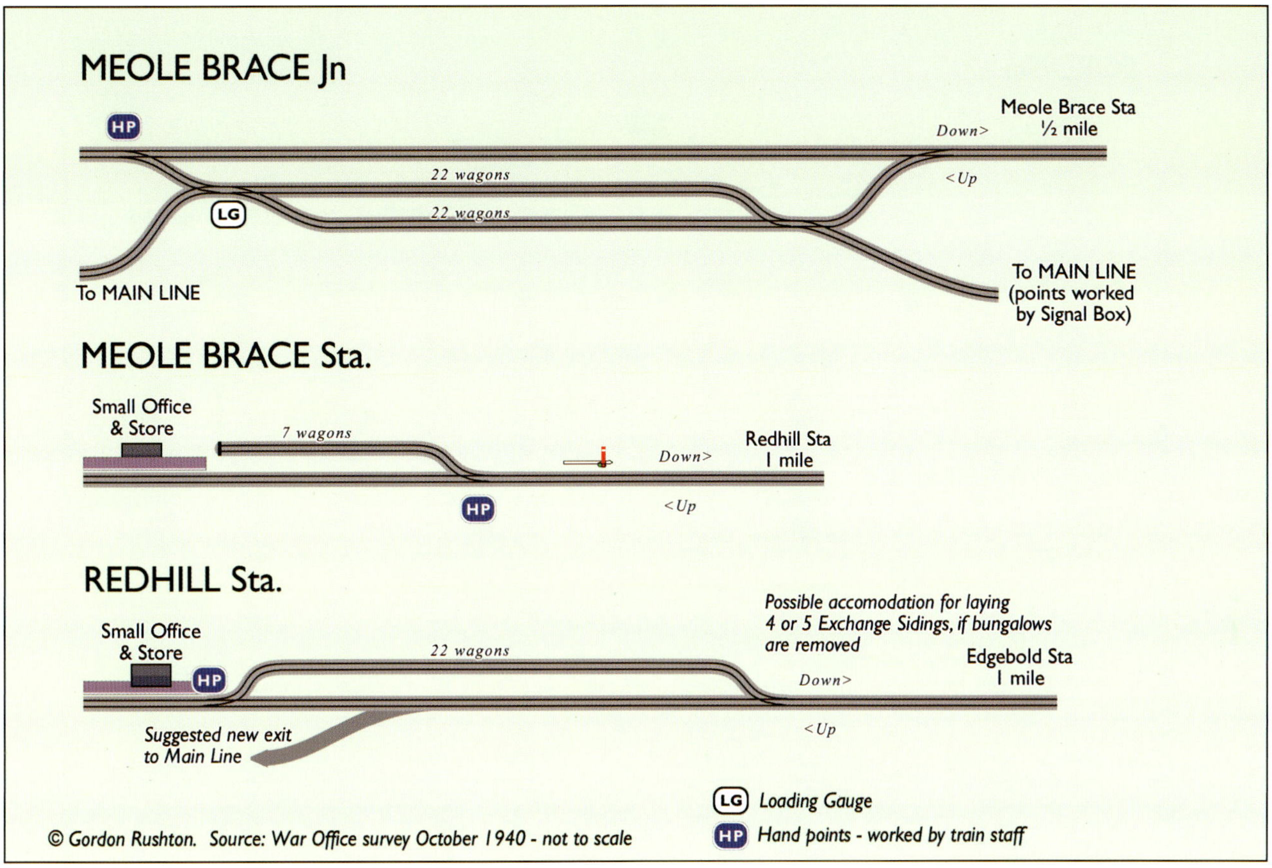
MEOLE BRACE Jn
HP
Meole Brace Sta
½ mile
Down>
<Up
22 wagons
22 wagons
LG
To MAIN LINE
To MAIN LINE
(points worked
by Signal Box)
MEOLE BRACE Sta.
Small Office
& Store
7 wagons
Down>
Redhill Sta
1 mile
HP
<Up
REDHILL Sta.
Small Office
& Store
HP
22 wagons
Possible accomodation for laying
4 or 5 Exchange Sidings, if bungalows
are removed
Down>
Edgebold Sta
1 mile
<Up
Suggested new exit
to Main Line
LG Loading Gauge
HP Hand points - worked by train staff
© Gordon Rushton. Source: War Office survey October 1940 - not to scale

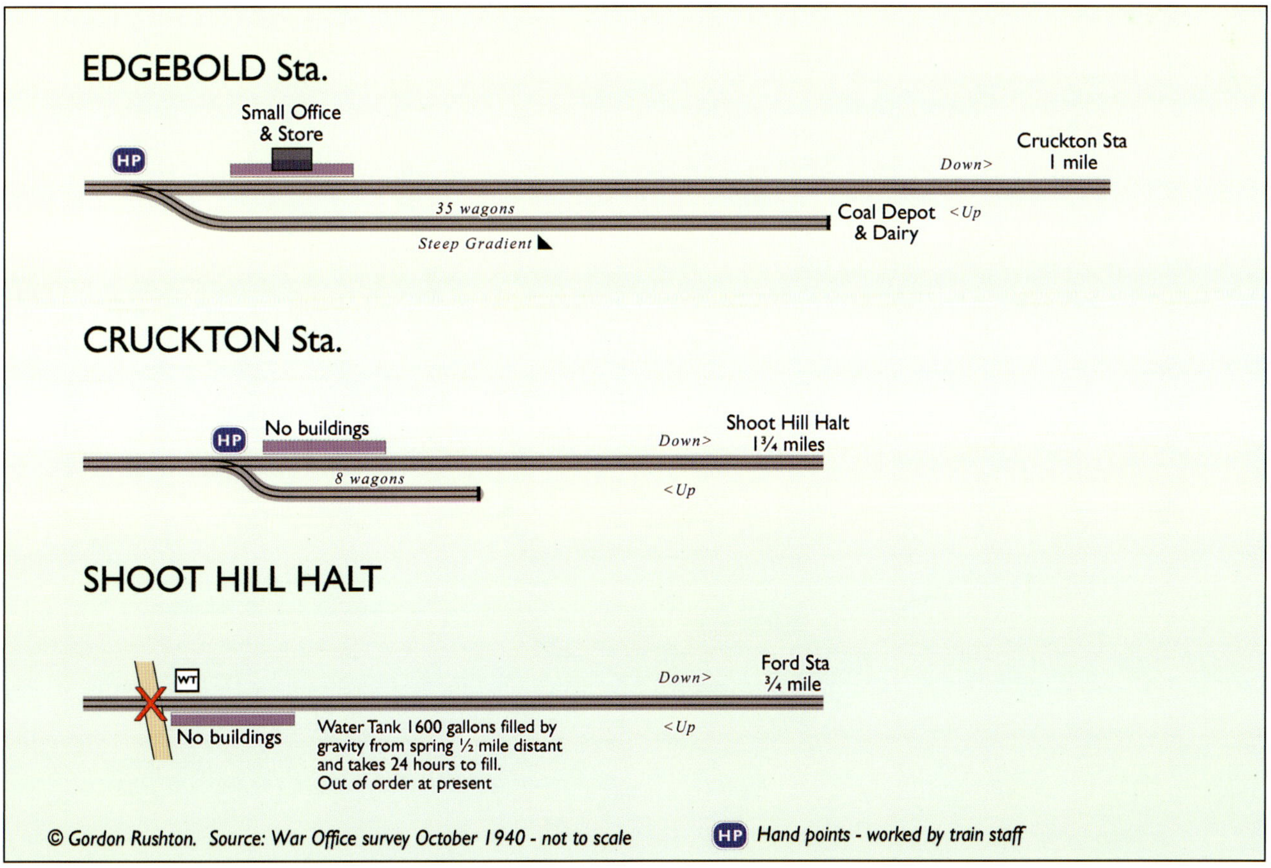
EDGEBOLD Sta.
Small Office
& Store
HP
Down>
Cruckton Sta
1 mile
35 wagons
Coal Depot
& Dairy
<Up
Steep Gradient
CRUCKTON Sta.
HP
No buildings
Down>
Shoot Hill Halt
1¾ miles
8 wagons
<Up
SHOOT HILL HALT
WT
Down>
Ford Sta
¾ mile
<Up
No buildings
Water Tank 1600 gallons filled by
gravity from spring ½ mile distant
and takes 24 hours to fill.
Out of order at present
© Gordon Rushton. Source: War Office survey October 1940 - not to scale
HP Hand points - worked by train staff

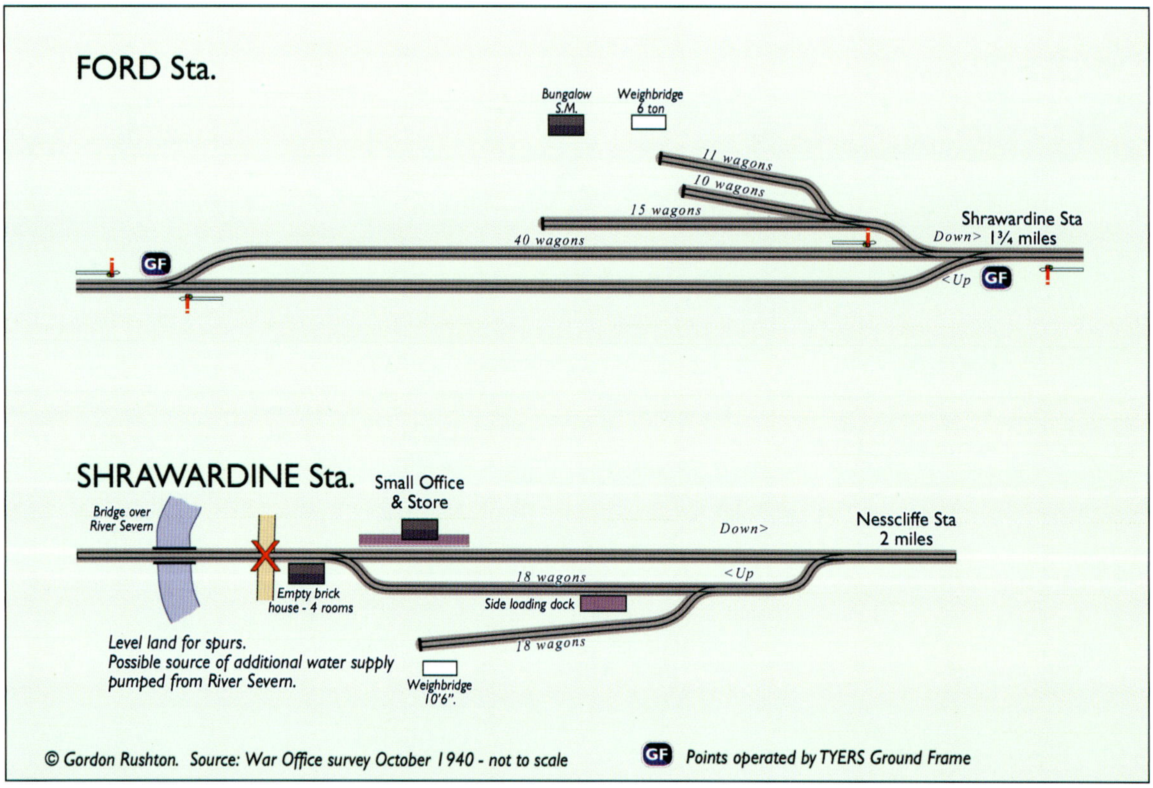
FORD Sta.
Bungalow S.M.
Weighbridge 6 ton
11 wagons
10 wagons
15 wagons
40 wagons
Shrawardine Sta
Down> 1¾ miles
<Up
GF
SHRAWARDINE Sta.
Small Office & Store
Bridge over River Severn
Down>
Nesscliffe Sta 2 miles
<Up
18 wagons
Empty brick house - 4 rooms
Side loading dock
18 wagons
Level land for spurs.
Possible source of additional water supply pumped from River Severn.
Weighbridge 10'6".
© Gordon Rushton. Source: War Office survey October 1940 - not to scale
GF Points operated by TYERS Ground Frame

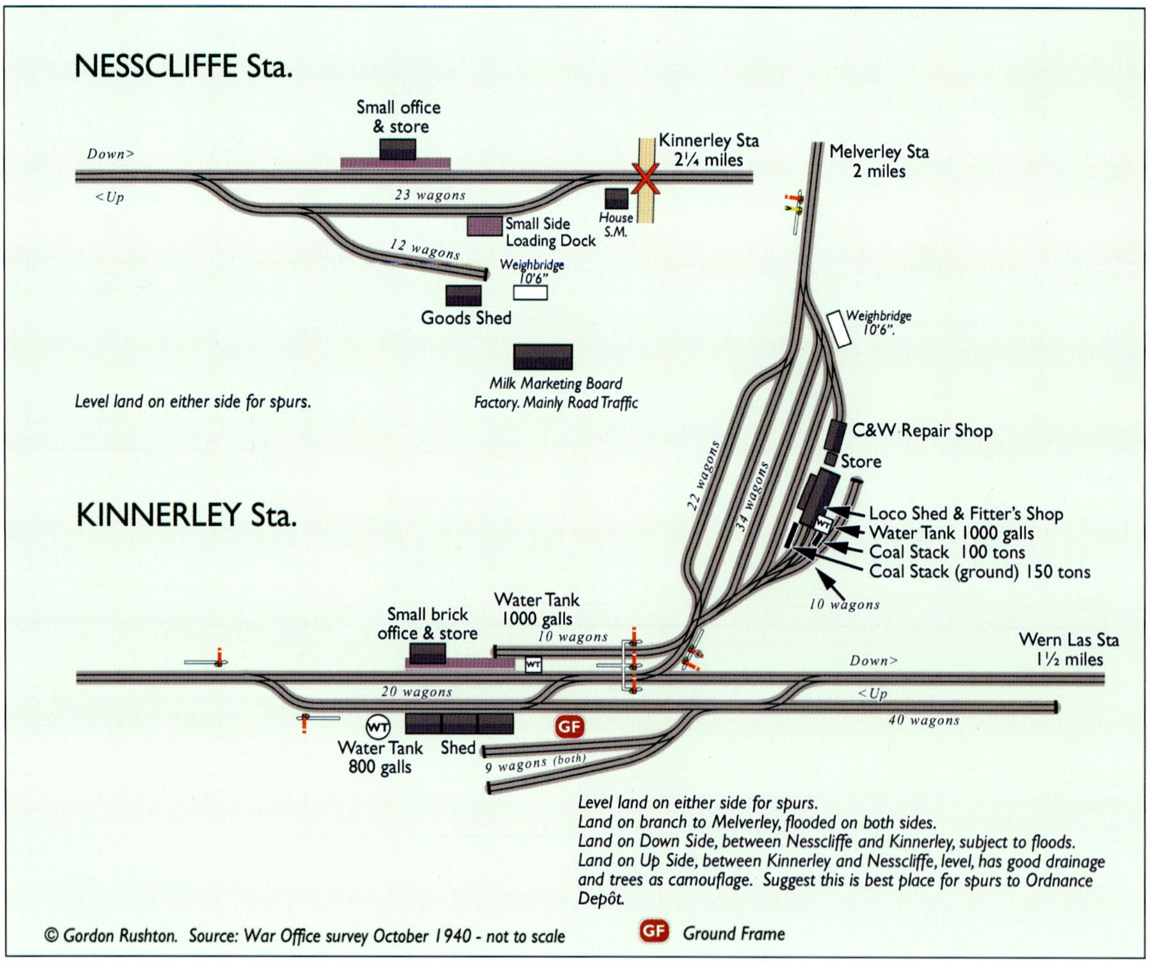
NESSCLIFFE Sta.
Small office & store
Down>
<Up
Kinnerley Sta 2¼ miles
Melverley Sta 2 miles
23 wagons
House S.M.
Small Side Loading Dock
12 wagons
Weighbridge 10'6"
Goods Shed
Weighbridge 10'6".
Milk Marketing Board Factory. Mainly Road Traffic
Level land on either side for spurs.
C&W Repair Shop
Store
22 wagons
34 wagons
KINNERLEY Sta.
Loco Shed & Fitter's Shop
Water Tank 1000 galls
Coal Stack 100 tons
Coal Stack (ground) 150 tons
10 wagons
Water Tank 1000 galls
Small brick office & store
10 wagons
Wern Las Sta 1½ miles
Down>
20 wagons
<Up
40 wagons
Water Tank 800 galls
Shed
GF
9 wagons (both)
Level land on either side for spurs.
Land on branch to Melverley, flooded on both sides.
Land on Down Side, between Nesscliffe and Kinnerley, subject to floods.
Land on Up Side, between Kinnerley and Nesscliffe, level, has good drainage and trees as camouflage. Suggest this is best place for spurs to Ordnance Depôt.
© Gordon Rushton. Source: War Office survey October 1940 - not to scale
GF Ground Frame

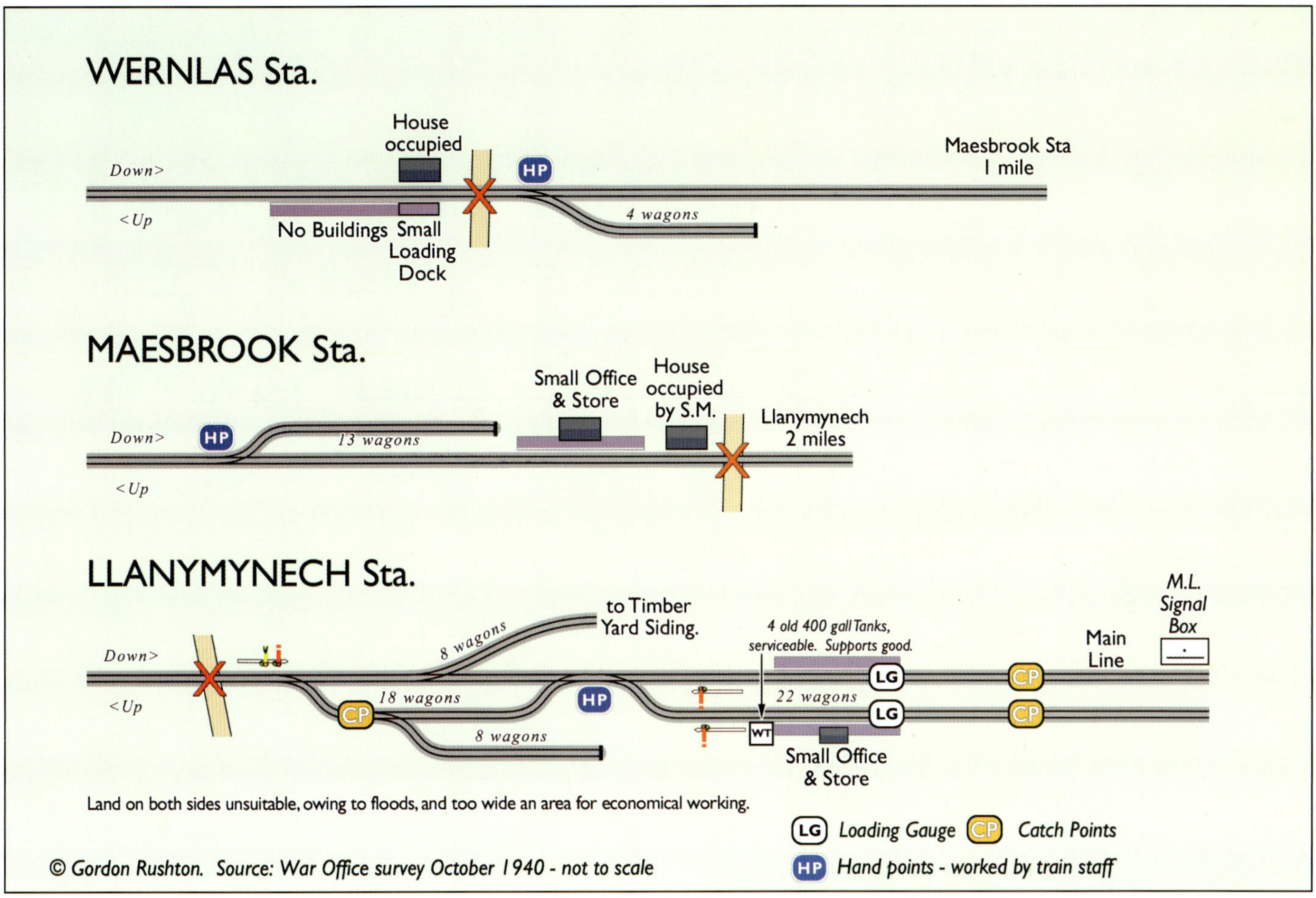

Thomas Ward Green was an enthusiast for the Light Railway and was appointed a director in 1932. He is buried in Maesbrook Methodist Chapel, where he had laid one of the foundation stones in 1899.

APPENDIX 16

SHROPSHIRE & MONTGOMERYSHIRE LIGHT RAILWAY – APPROXIMATE MILEAGE AND METHOD OF WORKING 1940

Stations	Approx mileage between stations	Block working
Abbey		Staff and ticket
Meole Brace Junction	1½	
Meole Brace	½	Staff and ticket
Hookagate (Red Hill)	1	
Edgebold	1	
Cruckton	1	
Shoothill Halt	1¾	
Ford & Crossgates	¾	Tyers Electric Tablet No 7
Shrawardine	1¾	
Nesscliff	2	
Kinnerley	2¼	Staff and ticket
Wernlas Halt	1½	
Maesbrook	1	
Llanymynech	2	
	18	

Notes: Omnibus telephones at Shrewsbury, Meole Brace, Edgebold, Ford & Crossgates, Shrawardine, Nesscliff, Kinnerley, Maesbrook and Llanymynech; block circuit between Ford & Crossgates and Kinnerley; Post Office telephone at Kinnerley.

APPENDIX 17

SHROPSHIRE & MONTGOMERYSHIRE LIGHT RAILWAY – ROLLING STOCK SURVEY BY WAR OFFICE PERSONNEL, OCTOBER 1940

Goods Stock

Quantity	Type	Comment
1	5 ton hand travelling train	New jib required
14	Open wagons, low sided, 8 tons	Bodies in poor condition, wheels and frames in fair order
9	Covered goods wagons	Wheels and frames in fair order, bodies developing defects, now being used as stores vans
7	Cattle wagons	In poor condition, now being used as stores vans
6	Bolster wagons	In fair order
2	Brake vans	One in use, the other under repair
1	Stores van	In poor condition

The stock generally is in poor condition but could be made serviceable within the depot.

Coaching stock

Quantity	Type	Comment
2	4-wheel	Ex-North Staffordshire Railway
4	4-wheel	Ex-Midland Railway
3	8-wheel	Ex-Caledonian Railway

The coaching stock is in a very bad state of repair. Some of the coaches could be cleaned up for military use on the line but would require new roofing canvas. Subject to the roofs being repaired and interiors removed, other coaches could be used in the depot for temporary offices.

Appendix 18

SHROPSHIRE & MONTGOMERYSHIRE LIGHT RAILWAY – EMPLOYEES SUBJECT TO TRANSFER TO WAR DEPARTMENT, JANUARY 1941

Permanent Way Department					
		Date of birth	Date joined company	Wage (weekly)	Residence
Crump, F. G.	Ganger	30 April 1895	28 March 1918	£2 14s	3 Sefton Villas, New Road, Meole Brace
Williams, W. A.	Ganger	19 September 1877	10 October 1910	£2 16s	Shoothill Crossing Cottage, Ford
Mansell, H. W.	Ganger	25 February 1882	January 1916	£2 14s	The Cobs, Wern Las
Frost, E.	Underman	13 June 1909	22 March 1928	£2 8s	3 Drawell, Shrewsbury
Williams, E.	Underman	14 March 1877	11 July 1913	£2 8s	2 New Street, Ford
Lewis, E.	Underman	28 November 1872	1 October 1918	£2 8s	Ash Tree Cottage, Pant
Richards, G.	Underman	30 March 1896	4 September 1939	£ 8s	Holly Tree Cottage, Knockin Heath
Mansell, E.	Underman	21 December 1909	15 April 1931	£2 8s	2 Station Houses, Kinnerley
Locomotive Department					
King, F.	Driver	20 July 1882	20 September 1912	£4 3s	4 Bungalow, Kinnerley
Mansell, J.	Fireman	28 December 1921	14 December 1938	£2 8s 6d	Wern Las Cottage, Maesbrook

Shop and artisan staff					
		Date of birth	Date joined company	Wage (weekly)	Residence
Owen, C.	Fitter	23 September 1880	September 1911	£3 16s	Bankfields, Kinnerley
Beeston, G.	Assistant fitter	22 August 1910	11 March 1926	£2 17s	Greystones, Llanymynech
Jones, A. M.	Carpenter	29 March 1880	2 June 1919	£3 7s	3 Station Houses, Kinnerley
Traffic Department					
Jones, W.	Guard	8 June 1905	5 October 1929	£2 17s	Lineside Bungalow, Kinnerley

A passenger train at Hookagate in 1946. (Michael Whitehouse Collection)

APPENDIX 19

SHROPSHIRE & MONTGOMERYSHIRE LIGHT RAILWAY – PASSES ISSUED TO EMPLOYEES, JULY 1941

Station agent	A. Jones and wife
Clerk/canvasser	G. H. Gibbs and wife
Station agent	H. G. Funnell junior and wife
Station agent	H. G. Funnell senior and wife
Station agent	E. N. Fardoe and wife
Porter/agent	W. Davies and wife
Fitter	C. Owen and wife
Driver	F. King and wife
Carpenter	A. M. Jones and wife
Assistant Fitter	G. H. Beeston (between Kinnerley and Llanymynech)
Mrs W. Jones (wife of guard Jones)	(between Kinnerley and Shrewsbury)

Seen on 14 October 1960, Cruckton platform returns to nature.

APPENDIX 20

SHROPSHIRE & MONTGOMERYSHIRE LIGHT RAILWAY – TONNAGE AND RECEIPTS 1939–47

	1939	1940	1941	1942	1943	1944	1945	1946	1947
Goods	3,381	11,437	38,730	15,723	14,477	12,966	11,754	10,896	9,532
Coal and coke	1,882	6,853	7,647	6,789	6,211	5,687	5,397	4,953	4,387
Other minerals	16,472	2,694	76,148	26,638	19,764	28,306	26,750	25,887	26,991
Stone traffic									
To Kinnerley (for construction)				12,985	10,210	13,398	179		
Off Light Railway destinations	12,128			1,624	6,261	9,534	22,717	21,304	
Petrol	5,879	4,812	4,069	3,052	1,213	672	259	187	
Sugar beet									
Wagons	58	330	158	181	183	218	226	370	392
Tonnage	468	2,753	1,343	1,434	1,499	1,933	1,854	3,384	3,611
Receipts	£4,168	£1,480	£4,307	£10,406	£11,015	£13,410	£20,914	£20,088	
Expenditure	£5,793	£5,953	£5,034	£5,569	£6,112	£6,582	£7,461	£7,298	
Net receipts	-£1,625	-£4,473	-£727	£4,837	£4,903	£6,828	£13,453	£12,790	

WAR DEPARTMENT – TONNAGE AND RECEIPTS, 1939–47

	Forwarded (tons)	Receipts	Received (tons)	Receipts
1942	71,323	£128,380	137,893	£248,206
1943	216,881	£390,385	133,105	£239,588
1944	119,739	£204,739	175,854	£316,536
1945	52,719	£114,694	93,611	£164,498
1946	24,535	£46,456	14,028	£26,652
1947	15,289	£29,059	16,312	£30,993
Total	500,486	£913,713	570,803	£1,026,473

A cattle wagon awaits its appointment with the scrap merchant at Hookagate on 23 August 1954.

BIBLIOGRAPHY

Archer, H. G.; '*A Derelict Railway*'; The Car Magazine, April 1904

Baughan, Peter; *A Regional History of the Railways of Great Britain Vol 11 North and Mid Wales*; David & Charles, 1980, 2nd Edition 1991

Bridges, Alan J. (Editor); *Industrial Locomotives of Cheshire, Shropshire & Herefordshire*; Industrial Railway Society, 1977

Carpenter, Roger; *The Criggion Branch of the Shropshire & Montgomeryshire Light Railway*; Wild Swan Publications, 1990

Carpenter, Roger; 'The colliers of the S&M'; *British Railway Journal*, No 18

Carpenter, Roger; 'The S&M Ford Railcar'; *British Railway Journal*, No 63

Carpenter, R. S.; 'Abbey Station of the Shropshire & Montgomeryshire Railway'; *British Railway Journal, No 23*

Garrett, Stephen & Scott Morgan, John; *Colonel Stephens Railmotors*; Irwell Press, 1995

Hutchins, John M.; Sentinel Locomotives on the Shropshire & Montgomeryshire Light Railway; *Industrial Railway Record*, No 202, September 2010

Janes, Brian; 'The "Potteries" Railway and how it failed'; *Journal of the Railway & Canal Historical Society*, Nos 195/6, 2006

Lambert, A. P. & Woods. J.C.; *Continent, Coalfield and Conservation – the biographical history of the British army austerity 0-6-0 saddle tank*; Industrial Railway Society, 1991

Lake Vyrnwy and the Vyrnwy water supply of Liverpool Corporation; *The Engineer*, 15 July 1892

Lawton, Paul, & Robinson, Neil; *The Shropshire & Montgomeryshire Railway – Memories of a Lost Line*; Second Chapter Books, 2021

Mitchell, Vic & Smith, Keith; *Branch Line to Shrewsbury – The Shropshire & Montgomeryshire*; Middleton Press, 1991

Mowat, Charles Loch; *The Golden Valley Railway*; University of Wales Press, 1964

Peaty, Ian; *Moving Mountains by Rail – a history of quarry railways*; Tempus Publishing, 2006

Perkins, T. R.; 'A Derelict British Railway'; *The Railway Magazine*, May/June, 1903

Perkins, T. R.; *The Shropshire & Montgomeryshire Railway*; The Railway Magazine, September 1911

Rhodes, Neil; *Trains on the Border – the Railways of Llanymynech and Pant*; Neil Rhodes Books, 2012

Shaw, Philip & Mitchell, Vic (Compilers); *Colonel Stephens – insights into the man and his empire*; Middleton Press, 2005

Handbook to Shropshire & Montgomeryshire Railway; Shropshire & Montgomeryshire Light Railway Co, no date, *c.*1920

Shropshire & Montgomeryshire Light Railway Working Instructions; 1 Railway Group, Royal Engineers, 1956

Swift, P. H.; 'The LSWR Ilfracombe Goods 0-6-0s'; *British Railway Journal*, No 22

Taylor, James; 'Limited liability on trial: the commercial crisis of 1866 and its aftermath'; Paper presented to Economic History Society Conference, 2003

Tonks, Eric S.; *The Shropshire & Montgomeryshire Railway*; Author, 1949; 2nd edition, Industrial Railway Society, 1972

Turner, Keith & Susan; *The Shropshire & Montgomeryshire Light Railway*; David & Charles, 1982

INDEX